TECHNOLOGICAL
FORECASTING
FOR
INDUSTRY
AND
GOVERNMENT

Contributions by

Robert U. Ayres

John R. Bird

James R. Bright

F. H. Buttner

Marvin J. Cetron

E. S. Cheaney

Halvor T. Darracott

A. L. Floyd

S. C. Gilfillan

T. J. Gordon

Olaf Helmer

Frank J. Husic

Raymond S. Isenson

Erich Jantsch

Ralph C. Lenz, Jr.

Harold A. Linstone

Joseph P. Martino

Peter S. Miller

Thomas I. Monahan

Charles M. Mottley

Harper Q. North

Frederick S. Pardee

Robert H. Rea

Theodore J. Rubin

A. W. Schmidt

D. F. Smith

Lincoln R. Thiesmeyer

Howard A. Wells

Manuscript Assistant

Melvin R. Copen
Associate Professor,
College of Business Administration
University of Houston

TECHNOLOGICAL FORECASTING FOR INDUSTRY AND GOVERNMENT

Methods and Applications

Editor

JAMES R. BRIGHT

Professor, Graduate School of Business Administration
Harvard University

Prentice-Hall, Inc., Englewood Cliffs, New Jersey

PRENTICE-HALL INTERNATIONAL, London
PRENTICE-HALL OF AUSTRALIA, PTY. LTD., Sydney
PRENTICE-HALL OF CANADA, LTD., Toronto
PRENTICE-HALL OF INDIA PRIVATE LTD., New Delhi
PRENTICE-HALL OF JAPAN, INC., Tokyo

Library of Congress Catalog Card No.: 68-24784

Printed in the United States of America

Current printing (last digit):
10   9   8   7   6   5   4   3   2   1

PREFACE

Business and government long ago learned the value of anticipating the character, intensity, and timing of environmental forces and changes. Forecasts of industrial production, markets, agricultural production, sociological change, government spending, political attitudes, and the weather are regarded as essential to help institutions meet their futures. The wisdom of studying the things that shape the future is proven, even though everyone realizes that predictions about them will lack perfection. Now one of the most powerful forces in our environment—and at times by far the most important for many firms and even for nations—is technology.

Since technology plays such a major role, and its influence on business, government, and society seems to be growing, should we not be attempting to determine its directions and growth by systematic analysis and study?

Yet, strangely, not one businessman out of a thousand attempts to *forecast* technology. Although hundreds of economists have proven the great value of economic forecasting for industrial and government planning, and for management guidance, one can name scarcely a dozen technological forecasters in all of industry. Why should technology be slighted, particularly when the classical economic philosophers, ranging from Adam Smith and Karl Marx to Joseph Schumpeter and Sumner Slichter, have emphasized that technology is a major force in economic activity? Perhaps it is because the average economist, with his liberal arts education, is naturally reluctant to study the internal structure of technological progress. He has never had a course in the nature of technological evolution, for there was none when he attended college; and there are scarcely any being given today. Furthermore, until roughly 1940, activity to advance technology did not absorb enormous amounts of the national effort as it now does. The results of new technical concepts formerly required fifteen to thirty years to acquire economic impact. The economist gradually adjusted his economic forecasts as the new technologies slowly diffused through society.

Classical economics, even today, teaches that technology is a monolithic, exogenous factor, even though the economic impacts are more serious and the speed of adoption and the rate of diffusion are accelerating. There have been only a handful of major economic studies directed at the nature of technological-economic growth. One truly great attempt was developed by Professor Arthur Cole, who launched the Center for Entrepreneurial Studies at Harvard in the 1940's. After ten years and several fine studies that examined the translation of science into economic enterprise,[1] the funds ran out and the efforts ceased. In recent years, the National Science Foundation and a number of government agencies, notably NASA, have encouraged much more research on the translation of science and technology into economic reality. Since about 1960 a number of economists, such as Schmookler,[2] Mansfield,[3] and Enos,[4] have published noteworthy studies on various aspects of technology and economic progress, which constitute the beginnings of contemporary economic work in this field. They go more deeply into the nature of technological progress in specific industries and activities. More such studies are on the way. Unfortunately, basic economic courses still teach the student virtually nothing about the nature of tech-

[1] W. R. MacLaurin, *Invention and Innovation in the Radio Industry*, (New York: The Macmillan Co., 1949).

Harold Passer, *The Electrical Manufacturers, 1875–1900*, (Cambridge, Mass.: Harvard University Press, 1953).

Arthur A. Bright, *The Development of the Electric Lamp Industry*, (New York: The Macmillan Co., 1949).

[2] Jacob Schmookler, *Invention and Economic Growth*, (Cambridge, Mass.: Harvard University Press, 1966).

[3] Edwin Mansfield, *Industrial Research and Technological Innovation*, (New York: W. W. Norton & Co., 1968). See his *Economics of Technological Change*, (New York: W. W. Norton & Co., 1967) for a more popular treatment of his research findings.

[4] J. L. Enos, *Petroleum Progress and Profits: A History of Process Innovation*, (Cambridge, Mass.: The M.I.T. Press, 1962).

nological progress and its interaction with economics. Perhaps, in view of the already enormously complex field of economics and the current proliferation of data and mathematical concepts relating to it, the economist can be forgiven. But for the businessman and government administrator, technology is such a critical element in economic decisions that it dare not be neglected. By way of illustration, one need only ask:

Will atomic energy be competitive with coal?

Is the electric automobile going to be technically effective?

Will plastics match the performance of die castings or cold-rolled steel?

Does aluminum progress threaten steel?

Will the SST become a reality?

Can paper be made practical as a clothing material?

What is happening to irradiation for food preservation?

When will each of these technological advances be introduced?

When will they be widely adopted?

Questions like these make it sharply apparent that technological progress is bound to have dramatic implications for individual firms and industries, as well as for government agencies concerned with the economic health of peoples and regions. Business opportunity and threat in technology are increasingly evident. Systematic technological forecasting is, therefore, especially important to the work of those economists serving business.

In a recent, comprehensive survey entitled "How Business Economists Forecast," [5] twenty-nine of the nation's foremost practitioners describe their procedures. The concept of forecasting technology is mentioned several times but is discussed only very briefly, by one economist. His procedure (in forecasting for fuels and energy) is to start with several sets of technological assumptions and then have these "carefully reviewed by technical men to determine whether the economic and industrial forecasts will lead them to change evaluations of technological probabilities." He advises: "Forecasts must take into account probable technical breakthroughs." But what "a breakthrough," is, how it should be identified, anticipated and then "taken into account," is not explained. The lack of methodology for projecting technological progress is even more troublesome in view of the author's own keen perception of the U.S. energy outlook: "Although this (total) energy outlook appears to be in a reasonably stable situation on the surface, in reality it is almost revolutionary because of the technical developments which will be introducing nuclear power on a large scale . . ."

Is it not mandatory, then, that the economist add a technological forecasting input to his economic analysis?

Another author, using the steel industry as an example of "industrial

---

[5] W. F. Butler and R. A. Kavesh, *How Business Economists Forecast*, (Englewood Cliffs, N. J.: Prentice-Hall, Inc., 1966).

forecasting," states: "In essence the forecasting process consists of the attempt to draw future implications of the existing state of affairs. To do this effectively, it is obviously first necessary to have a thorough understanding of the phenomena that is being analyzed." One can only applaud this sound conclusion; but then one wonders why the economist and his management settle for less. For the reader is told that one of the two general assumptions that underlie all forecasts of industrial activity is: "That stable engineering relationships exist among the various sectors of the economy." Is this a reasonable assumption for many industries today? Surely it is proving untrue in the struggle between fuels and energy conversion systems, between transportation systems for people and freight, and between entertainment systems such as TV and movies, as well as within this author's own steel industry. In the past ten years steel has lost significant market sectors to reinforced concrete, to composite cans made of fibreboard-aluminum, and to aluminum parts in automobiles. Simultaneously, the open-hearth furnace has been displaced by the basic oxygen converter, the computer-controlled rolling mill has appeared, and blast furnace operation has been revolutionized. The need for systematic methods of technological anticipation should be evident to all.

Economists, it seems, are not blind to the relevance of technology to economic forecasting; they simply have no tools for dealing with it. Only two approaches are widely used: (1) to hold technology constant or (2) to ask a technologist for his opinion. The "hold technology constant" approach is acceptable for the short-run economic forecast of one to three years, perhaps, because radical shifts in technology take time to diffuse widely. However, it is a dangerous approach because it leads management to ignore those technological activities that may take five to fifteen years to materialize, yet which *must be recognized well in advance so that the firm can lay the groundwork to meet them.*

"Ask the technologist" is a very logical approach. But it assumes either that the technologist has a valid predictive technique or that his opinion will be adequate. Engineers and applied scientists have long used bits of technological time series to forecast trends and needs, and as aids to product development planning. They sometimes use such series to suggest design goals, such as the weight to horsepower rating of an engine or the cost per unit of energy of an energy production system. But the technologist keeps this forecasting work pretty much to himself. In general, technologists do not rush off to offer this data to economists, nor do economists tend to seek out technologists and ask for this kind of forecasting help.

However, top management does tend to use the technologist for long-range planning programs in the same way as the economist does: he asks his opinion. Frequently the manager compounds the problem by asking the technologist for an opinion on the *economic potential* of a new technology. How reliable is the opinion of the technological expert? While the answer obviously must vary with the individual, the technology, and the occasion, the vast majority of technical people have no logical rationale for making technological predictions. Prediction is not a topic taught in any technical discipline, and thus the technologist can only offer opinions based on his knowledge, experience, and belief, on intimations from others in the field, etc.; (unless he happens to be one of the few who has constructed a forecasting methodology).

Scientists, engineers, and inventors of unquestioned capability have a long history of prediction errors. For instance, the great Steinmetz advised General Electric's management that transmission systems of over 60,000 volts were impractical; but Sprague went ahead and did it, and General Electric lost their lead in power transmission for some ten years. In 1926 Canada's Professor Bickerton said that "shooting at the moon" was "basically impossible"; [6] and throughout the 1930's and 1940's many other scientists agreed. One of the major inventors of the computer stated in the early 1950's that six large computers could do all the computation needed by U.S. business firms. In December, 1945, Dr. Vannevar Bush, who had done such a superb job as head of the Office of Scientific Research and Development during the war and was a major contributor to the forerunner of the computer, and who guided the U.S. radar and proximity fuse development efforts so well, advised the Joint Chiefs of Staff that a 3,000-mile, high-angle rocket, armed with an atomic warhead, was impossible for "a very long time" and "should be left out of our thinking." [7] This prediction, if accepted, could have been very costly to the United States. Notice that it was made by a most thoughtful, capable scientist, educator, and administrator, who had a splendid record of technical accomplishment which earned him the nation's gratitude. Other great technologists of our times have had equal difficulties with prediction, as the following indicates.

What about collections of experts who are paid to think long and hard about technical prospects in the consulting firms? We have no evidence on their batting average, which undoubtedly includes many correct evaluations; but we also can find examples of some horrendous errors. For instance, about 1958–59 IBM was advised by one of our most prestigious and competent consulting firms that there was no significant market for the automatic office copier machine that had been developed by Haloid (new Xerox) Corporation. About that time, Haloid itself retained two other outstanding consulting firms and both reported dim prospects for xerographic office copiers.

[6] Arthur C. Clarke, *Profiles of The Future,* (New York: Harper & Row, Publishers, Inc.).

[7] Clarke, *op. cit.*

Committees convened by government agencies should embody the best technical competence in the nation. An outstanding example of value technical prediction was the report of the Army Air Force Scientific Advisory Group in December, 1945. General H. H. Arnold had convened this committee in late 1944 under the direction of Dr. Theodore Von Karman, reputed to be one of the technical geniuses of our age and later the first recipient of the nation's Science Medal. The report proved to be extremely valuable and farsighted. Yet in the last section, Dr. Von Karman himself makes this prediction:

> It appears to me that the application of atomic energy to transportation will probably precede the application to power generation for stationary purposes. In the latter case the cost is the governing factor; in transportation, it is the cost and weight of the fuel to be carried. In high-speed aerial transportation the importance of weight transcends the importance of cost. Hence it may be concluded that the extremely expensive atomic agent . . . will be used for propulsion. . . .[8]

The record of errors on the technological future seems endless, as the reader can assure himself by spending a day in the library. Yet, the foregoing comments must not be read as an implication that technical expert opinion is always wrong; it certainly is not. Nor do I suggest that it is more often wrong than right. It simply is inadequate for today's society.

These remarks do not imply for a moment that the nontechnical man (including the business school professor) can do a better job. There is no evidence or logic to suggest that being *less expert* in technology makes one more effective as a forecaster. The pattern revealed by technical expert opinion is cited merely to suggest some lessons:

1. Technologists of great accomplishment are not always good technological forecasters.
2. Technologists may be absolutely right on the technology, but very wrong on its economic impact on growth.
3. Predictions by anyone or any group of technical-economic experts must be carefully examined to determine the character and completeness of the technical and economic assumptions. Past erroneous predictions seem to have been wrong largely because of oversights in the technical assumptions, or because of influences in the nontechnical environment.
4. Opinions alone are not a satisfactory way to anticipate the technological future. There ought to be a better way.

[8] Theodore Von Karman, *Where We Stand,* a section of the Report of the Army Air Force Scientific Advisory Group, December, 1945. p. 36.

Admittedly, technological forecasting is in its infancy as a discipline. It stands where economic forecasting stood, perhaps, fifty years ago. Nor do we know very much about integrating such forecasts into the planning and operations of organizations. Yet the roots of systematic methodology are here; and many technologists, managers, and economists now are eager to see the field developed. They seek something better than the old procedure of hunch, "expert opinion," or after the fact reaction. The purpose of this book is to present these forecasting methods and their application to the needs of industry and government—to sum up the state of the art. It is intended as a starting point for a discipline needed in the decades ahead.

Technological forecasting means, to most of our authors, systems of logical analysis that lead to common quantitative conclusions (or a limited range of possibilities) about technological attributes and parameters, as well as technical-economic attributes. Such forecasts differ from opinion in that *they rest upon an explicit set of quantitative relationships and stated assumptions; and they are produced by a logic that yields relatively consistent results.*

One reason that so much confusion exists about technology is because anticipations about scientific findings, engineering developments, technological diffusion, economic results, and social impacts are loosely and thoughtlessly intermingled. Much criticism has been leveled at "technological forecasts" that were not "forecasts," but only prophecies, and that were not "technical," but were directed at economic success. The reader should first clarify for himself these levels of causality to which a forecast may be addressed:

Level 1. That certain *knowledge of nature* or level of scientific understanding will be acquired. . . .

Level 2. That it will be possible to *demonstrate a new technical capability* (on a laboratory basis). . . .

Level 3. That the new technical capability will be *applied to a full scale prototype* (field trial). . . .

Level 4. That the new technology will be put to first *operational use* (commercial introduction). . . .

Level 5. That the new technology will be *widely adopted* (as measured by such things as number of units in use, output of the new technology, dollars of sales generated, or any of these measures relative to competitive technology).

Level 6. That certain *social (and economic) consequences* will follow the use of the new technology.

Level 7. That future economic, political, social and technical conditions will *require the creation* of certain new technical capability.

It is obvious immediately that these are very different kinds of things to predict; and those who criticize technological forecasting should define their targets carefully. A few observations on these contents can be helpful.

This book does not deal with Level 1 because I was unable to find any forecasting technique in the area of scientific research, despite rumors of such techniques. (I invite readers to advise me of any developments that they may come across.)

The technologist is most capable of forecasting on Levels 2, 3, and 4; but he gets into serious trouble by deliberately or unconsciously translating his technical predictions onto Level 5—economic growth. Managers and officials aid and abet this type of error by encouraging or expecting the technologist to tell them "how important" the new technology will become. This forecast involves a complex technical, economic, political, and social interaction, about which we know very little. In this book, only the Delphi technique deals with this level. And I confess that I do not regard it as strictly meeting our forecasting definition, but it is the best thing we have at the moment.

While this is the level of the economist's work, it should be clear that the economist is an effective forecaster only if technology is stable. He needs technological input to improve his forecasts.

We omit Level 6 predictions as falling outside the main thrust of this volume, and being the area of sociology. It is clear, however, that the sociologists must pay more attention to these other levels of causality, or they will be building upon very shaky speculations.

A number of approaches to Level 7 forecasting are offered in this book. This is possibly the newest and most difficult forecasting concept.

The shortcomings there are in technological forecasting should be carefully related to these forecasting levels. The need for interdisciplinary approaches is obvious.

Recent Activity

Since the late 1940's, technological forecasting has been developing as a discipline and planning tool, largely within U.S. military departments, a few aerospace firms, and specialized consulting firms (see the chapter by Bird and Darracott, p. 385). Here and there an imaginative industrialist has used such forecasts. Research and development managers frequently have used time-series trends of technical parameters to suggest design goals and possibilities. In 1965 the President charged the National Commission on Automation and Technological Change to examine, among other things, the use of technological forecasting and its potentials for the federal government. The Commission concluded that technological forecasting was "little used";

they never did respond to the truly significant assignment: How might the federal government use technological forecasting? Somehow they ignored the work of the Army and Air Force, whose technological forecasting had, for about twenty years, shown some of the important things that could be done through technological predictions. And for many years sociologists, such as Ogburn and his followers, had shown how useful technological forecasts could be for social and economic planning.

In 1965, the twenty-two-nation Organization for Economic Cooperation and Development (Paris) assigned Dr. Erich Jantsch to study technological forecasting throughout the world. In *Technological Forecasting in Perspective* (O.E.C.D., Paris, 1966) Jantsch reported his findings after surveying some 400 references in the literature and making 250 visits to thirteen countries. This one-man study identified elements of some 100 technological forecasting and planning activities. Dr. Jantsch found that there was keen interest in, and recognition of the need for, technological forecasting throughout the world, and the U.S. military was clearly the leader in the formal recognition of technological forecasting as an aid to management planning. His resulting viewpoint is expressed in his chapter (page 426).

The Origin of This Book

Since 1959, the Harvard Business School has encouraged my efforts to develop a course to teach future managers something about technology as a major element in the business environment. Hopefully, it would give students some skill in dealing with the growing number of business situations in which technological uncertainty is a substantial part of the problem. This course quickly ran into the need for business appraisals of technological proposals. It was only a step to technological planning and thence to technological forecasting. In 1961 my students began their first exercises in the anticipation and prediction of technological progress and its business implications. We turned to the work of that early student of the technological future, Dr. S. C. Gilfillan, a sociologist and an innovator well ahead of his times,[9] and to the work of Ralph C. Lenz, Jr., U.S. Air Force, the author of the only survey of technological forecasting methodologies.[10] Our textbook exercises in technological forecasting led to attempts to find other practitioners and approaches.[11] As our files and contacts grew, and as a

[9] S. C. Gilfillan, *The Sociology of Invention*, (Chicago, Ill.: Follett Publishing Co., 1935). See also his other writings identified in Chapter 1.

[10] R. C. Lenz, Technological Forecasting, Report No. ASD-TDR-62-414. U.S. Air Force: Washington, D. C., 1962.

[11] James R. Bright, *Research, Development and Technological Innovation*, (Homewood, Ill.: Richard D. Irwin, 1964). See pp. 756–763 for exercises.

result of discussions with many executives in a variety of industries, I gradually built up an acquaintance with the leading practitioners.

In 1966, Marvin Cetron, who was heading the Navy's study of technological forecasting methods, invited me to attend a meeting at which representatives of eight government agencies met to review their activities, needs, and approaches to technological forecasting and planning. I was impressed with their efforts and believed their concepts and experiences should be made available to industry. I asked Erich Jantsch and others who had surveyed the technological forecasting field to advise me of outstanding industrial practitioners.

It was becoming increasingly apparent that industry, government agencies, business educators, and perhaps economists, would benefit from a summation of the state of the art of technological forecasting. Facilities at the Harvard Business School were booked for many months—a delay I did not want to accept—so I decided to conduct a conference through the Industrial Management Center, a private industrial education activity which I had founded fourteen years ago. In May, 1967, some twenty speakers and about 125 delegates from five countries met at the Lake Placid Club in New York, for the First Annual Technology and Management Conference: *Technological Forecasting for Industry.* This book is based on the revised papers and audience contributions of that occasion. Other practitioners since identified have been invited to contribute chapters with the goal of rounding out our knowledge in the field. Unhappily, at least two other invited contributors were unable to meet the publishing deadline. However, this volume is a reasonably complete summation of the state of the art of technological forecasting in the United States in 1967.

The Arrangement of This Volume

The book is divided into five sections, although some of the contributions clearly overlap.

Lessons from the Past, Part I, includes a historic and a recent attempt to learn something about technological forecasting from history. Part II, *Techniques of Forecasting Technology,* includes explanations of major approaches to technological prediction. Part III, *Intergrating Technological and Environmental Forecasting,* describes methods of projection based, in general, on the thesis that technological predictions can only be made through an interaction with other environmental predictions. Part IV, *Applying Technological Forecasting,* shows how forecasting can be employed to serve various organizational functions and purposes. Part V, *Organizing the Technological Forecasting Effort,* explains how a major government agency, a major corporation, and the corporations of the future may organize their technological forecasting effort.

The reader should appreciate that the chapters offer different ideas on forecasting technique, and a number of interesting positions. These are more evident, perhaps, to those of us who were present at the conference and heard them reinforced in private conversations.

There are, broadly speaking, three groups interested in technological forecasting methodology. One comprises business economists, institutional and corporate planners, and managers who are becoming increasingly concerned about technology as a part of the business environment and are eager to find tools that will give some insight on where and how fast technology is moving. They are concerned with technological opportunity and threat as well as its economic significance to industry. To most of them, technological forecasting is a new and exciting idea.

The second group represents the government agencies and, in particular, the military. This group has dealt so long and so intensively with research and development planning on a very large scale that the idea of planning for and anticipating technological change is not new; but they seek better methodology. They have developed a special language (which many industrialists deplore as jargon). They seem to live in a world of resources, goals, and sets of values that are almost incomprehensible and often seem unrealistic to the industrialist. There is a strong flavor of "What world do we want . . . Let's create it," in their attitude.

The third group is the technologists. Here one finds two attitudes: the first is a belief that better methods of forecasting would facilitate R&D planning; the other is surprise, dismay, and even a little bit of annoyance at all the furor over technological forecasting. Some of them believe that they have been doing this for years—and some of them have. Occasionally, one hears downright antagonism to the notion of technological forecasting because "you can't predict breakthroughs" (although none of our authors claim this as a goal). I surmise that this attitude is a kind of emotional reaction to the "social planner" and journalistic writings, which make such extreme or naive claims about technological impact and the technological future.

However, most technologists seem to reach one common conclusion: there has been a lack of communication. Possibly one of the best results of the conference and of this volume will be to bring about better modes of communication among the technologist, the sociologist, the economist, and management. This is clearly the theme of the chapter by Dr. North of TRW, Inc. (page 412).

Another group interested in technological progress has been omitted from this volume by design. These are the social planners, such as the

Committee For The Year 2000, the "Futurists," and others whose position is largely that of seeking technological progress for social purposes. They have been omitted because they have not (to my knowledge) explored and developed technological forecasting methodology. Rather, they have considered social forecasting based upon technological prophecy and speculation. Except for Gilfillan, Ogburn, Hartshorn, and Ridenour, few sociologists have attempted to deal with technological prediction based on a system of data analysis or logic.

Here I must stress a most curious and important possibility. The striking phenomenon of technology today is that, for the first time in history, governments are beginning to organize technology to serve social purposes other than war. Just as military planners have been defining technological needs which the nation has then mobilized to supply, government planners are about to do the same for social needs such as urban renewal, mass transportation, education, medical care, air and water pollution, and other social shortcomings.

If I may be permitted a prophecy in this book about forecasting, the next decade will see a wave of conferences about the future, with great stress on marshaling technology to serve social ends. The theme will be that we do not need to passively accept any future; we can go far toward creating the one that we want. Social planners and government agency policy makers will lead such voices for the future, and governments will listen—at least to some extent. Government programs then will arise from the speculations, needs, and demands that are revealed by conferences, speeches and books on these themes. It follows that *such voices ultimately will prove to have been forecasts of technological progress.* The industrialist should participate *now*—or at least listen very carefully.

An interesting argument appears over technological forecasting vs. technological planning. Our original conference plan was to stay strictly with forecasting methods; but readers will find one group of contributors insisting that forecasting can be considered only as part of a planning effort. They see the forecast as a statement of what is possible, not as one of what will occur. From this statement of possibilities managers and planners are supposed to choose their technological goals. Another group holds that technological forecasting methodology can be developed and examined independently of technological planning. At this stage of our knowledge, they argue, we should concentrate on identifying and developing sound methodology; and the use of such methodologies in technological planning is another subject.

The industrialist and the civil government official may be surprised and a little frustrated with the heavy emphasis on military applications. This is because I was unable to find new technological *forecasting* concepts by industry, and deliberately avoided technological *planning*, about which industry has already said a great deal in many conferences. (See the bibliographies throughout the book and in the Appendices.)

In studying these chapters, the reader will find some redundancy, and he should realize that in many instances authors are describing only slightly different ways of looking at the same thing. *Normative forecasting*, for example, is about the same thing as a *technological program* to some; while others would argue that this depends on how the program goals were established.

ACKNOWLEDGMENTS

I am, of course, deeply indebted to all our authors for their contributions, both at the conference and in this book. Each one of them has added to my knowledge, and given me the benefit of their time and experience.

Dr. Gilfillan, that grand old scholar, has amassed such a wealth of historical data on social attributes of invention that his writings are extremely provocative and useful to the teacher of management. I am personally and professionally in his debt for questions raised and managerial viewpoints inferred from his works.

Ralph Lenz, a pioneer in the field, has generously assisted me to develop teaching materials on technological forecasting. His own insights on factors influencing technological progress have been very valuable to me.

Colonel Ray Isenson, U.S. Army, has provided me with useful viewpoints on technological forecasting from his years of Army Research office experience and his Project Hindsight study.

Marvin Cetron, U.S. Navy, was a spendid help to the conference. His enthusiasm, wide range of contacts, and extremely broad knowledge of the literature have helped us all to become more knowledgeable in the field. I have deeply appreciated his suggestions on the conference program and his evaluations of forecasting concepts. Mr. Cetron himself wishes to acknowledge the guidance of Professor Nikos G. Photias, Associate Dean and Director of the Doctoral Program of American University, and his assistance on bibliographic work.

Dr. Erich Jantsch of O.E.C.D. has been my overseas resource. I was impressed by the astonishing breadth and depth of his study *Technological Forecasting in Perspective* (Paris: O.E.C.D., 1967). It is a remarkable job, particularly considering that it was done by one man in approximately one year. Dr. Jantsch has given me the benefit of his knowledge and his international contacts in planning our conference. No one was better qualified to write our closing chapter.

There is much detail and tedious work in staging such a conference. I thank Professors Ronald Jablonski of the University of Michigan and Melvin Copen of the University of Houston for their reliable and imaginative assistance during the conference. A special debt is due to Professor Copen, who has labored with me for many hours in preparing this manuscript. His quick perception, discriminating judgment, and enthusiasm were extremely valuable. Whatever shortcomings there are in the editing of this book lie at my door.

There is another group to whom I am indebted—a group too large to list, since they comprised the more than 125 delegates at the conference. Their reactions, pro and con, and the friendly assistance they have given me subsequently have been heart-warming and occasionally disturbing, but always helpful. I have appreciated their suggestions in planning new teaching materials and our next conference program.

If any reader feels he has experiences, data or concepts that will further our understanding of technological forecasting, he is hereby heartily urged to contact me. This book is only a first step in the field, and I shall welcome any assistance in advancing the science and art of technological forecasting.

JAMES R. BRIGHT

CONTENTS

PART THREE

**INTEGRATING
TECHNOLOGICAL
AND
ENVIRONMENTAL
FORECASTING**

PART FOUR

**APPLYING
TECHNOLOGICAL
FORECASTING**

TECHNOLOGICAL
FORECASTING
FOR
INDUSTRY
AND
GOVERNMENT

LESSONS FROM THE PAST

PART ONE

In assessing the state of the art of any field, historical review is a most useful first step. Therefore, the first chapter in a book on technological forecasting most properly belongs to Dr. S. C. Gilfillan, who has studied technological prediction for more than half a century and has developed statistics on the materialization of inventions. The reader will quickly recognize that early attempts at technological prediction are not rigorous enough to be characterized as technological forecasting today, since they are largely prophecies resting on opinion rather than systematic logic. Nevertheless, these speculative glimmerings of possibilities could have been valuable to leaders of all types of institutions in suggesting the kinds of changes they would have to make when and if the technology emerged. Somewhat obscured by the imperfection of the data, but extremely provocative, are timing patterns that today's industrialists should consider. Perhaps the most vital concept of all is Gilfillan's doctrine of equivalent invention. If known and applied thoughtfully, it would often change the product development policies of firms and even nations.

Philosophically, this history of predictions gives one a feeling for the grand sweep of technical progress. It dramatizes the fantastic acceleration in man's ability to master his physical environment and it suggests the beginnings of the ability and effort to mold it to his desires. It confirms that technological forecasting is itself an invention in the development stage.

The second chapter draws on the most intensive study of technological progress yet conducted—Project Hindsight. Although that study was limited to one user of technology—the Department of Defense—and one portion of the process of technological innovation—the research-development phase—it offers valuable guidance on the relevance and effectiveness of research activity, the selection of research goals, and a methodology for exploration of technological innovation in industry and government.

A Sociologist
Looks at
Technical Prediction

S. C. GILFILLAN

An effective way to learn about and improve the art of forecasting is by studying the most successful practitioners from the past. By carefully identifying and analyzing the methods of such men, the author has been able to extract many useful lessons and principles of successful forecasting. Two of the many points which are highlighted are the equivalence of invention (the fact that there are many possible ways to achieve the same function or capability) and the relationship of effort to technological progress.

Dr. Gilfillan has probably been concerned with the subject of technological forecasting for more years than any other individual. He has been studying or practicing technological prediction, social-technological interactions, and history of invention, since 1907. He is the author of important books and articles on these subjects.

In his "Discovery of the Future," a paper written in 1901,[1] H. G. Wells pointed out that less than a century before, the world's whole prehistoric past seemed forever lost behind an impenetrable curtain drawn by Time. Even the best scientific minds had been saying that, for knowledge of all that had happened in the world before the invention of writing, one must either accept the few statements provided by Holy Writ, or resign himself never to know: for, if no one had observed and written down what had happened, and the time was too remote for tradition to be reliable, how could anyone

---

[1] "Discovery of the Future," *Smithsonian Annual Report, 1902*; pp. 375–92, and *Nature*, Vol. 65.

H. G. Wells

possibly know, except by divine inspiration? Nevertheless, in the last century, as the result of many men devoting brains and much time to the sciences of geology, astronomy, paleontology, biology, archeology, and philology, so much has been learned about the world prior to recorded history that whole libraries can be filled with reliable information, even accurately dated thousands or millions of years back; and a child can understand the evidence.

Also in 1901, Wells pretty clearly foresaw the characteristics of the automobile age, although motorcars were then only occasional oddities disturbing horses.[2] He also did fairly well on future war and aviation; but in technological fields, his lack of information about contemporary engineering and the social sciences deprived his foresight of distinction. His finest note was to sound the call for a science of the future (future-lore or Futurology, one might call it) which would be equal to the sciences of the prehistoric past that a century of work had created.

[2] *Anticipations of the Reaction of Mechanical and Scientific Progress upon Human Life and Thought,* 1901.

There are, fundamentally, just two basic methods for predicting the future—two logical reasons for anticipation. One is the extrapolation of a trend or a cycle which one sees, or thinks he sees, in the past. Cycles, like those of the weather, are mostly of astronomical origin and are little involved in the difficult kinds of prediction examined here; trends are far more common tools. The procedure for their extrapolation is familiar and better handled by statisticians; however, it is worth mentioning an experiment for testing people's skill at extrapolation which does not necessitate waiting for future years to supply the proof—experiments the author proposed and Ogburn tried and reported in his *Social Effects of Aviation.*[3]

[3] W. F. Ogburn (assisted by J. L. Adams and S. C. Gilfillan), *Social Effects of Aviation* (Boston: Houghton Mifflin Company, 1946). For prediction by correlation, see pp. 41–43; for bias, pp. 50–52. This book, written in 1943, is a very good source, not only on the future of aviation, but also for its two chapters on "Predicting the Future" and "Predicting the Social Effects of Invention." Ogburn had a particular interest in prediction, and was the best man ever on the social effects of invention. He was my friend for forty-five years, and often my employer—extraordinary luck for me, who aspired to improve the profitless trade of the prophet.

W. F. Ogburn

In the experiment, only the first part of the recorded growth of an invention was plotted, concealing the last ten years, and statisticians were asked to extrapolate the last period from the earlier data, without knowing what invention they were dealing with. "For a ten-year projection there were 16 over-predictions with an average error of 74%, and 14 under-predictions with an average error of 43%." The statisticians could have done much better, of course, had they some knowledge of the invention's past, as predictors always do, and probably also if they had taken more trouble to draw the trend curve first.

Some people compute these curves by mathematics; a line of least squares, or a parabola perhaps, or a logistic curve. In the case of inventions it is more sensible to use a freehand curve. A mathematical curve or line assumes the value of time to be zero—the researcher's time. And it assumes that all the forces bearing upon the invention preserve either the same relationship throughout, or a foreseen steadily changing relationship; but with inventions this is never so.[4]

2. The Method of Causality and Chances

The method of extrapolation does not consider causation and uses no reasons, but simply extends a past trend (or cycle) into the future. Obviously one might do better if he understood the causes. In some cases, there may be little or no known data on past progress of an invention which can be used to plot a trend and extrapolate. Or one may not hope to graph the course of an invention's future, but only seek to predict whether a certain discovery will be made at some time or other in the future. An example is levitation: Will man ever learn to control gravity? So far there is no progress to plot. Possibly Galileo's and other later measurements of acceleration from gravity, and Einstein's theory of gravity, represent progress; but it is difficult to see how to plot these using one parameter, and how to extend the graph into a comprehensible future. Similarly, will the transplantation of major organs from one human to another (not an identical twin) be achieved, and if so, when?

For predicting such unprecedented events, and for much better assurance in every other kind of prediction, the second method of prediction is required. This can best be called the Method of Causality and Chances, or less precisely, The Method of Opportunity. It seeks to understand the expected invention(s), its causes, its goals and incitements; the milieu of prior art and

[4] The rates of advance of many inventions up to 1929, together with the date of their commercial success, were supplied by this writer for Ogburn's very useful chapter entitled "The Influence of Invention and Discovery." W. F. Ogburn, ed., *Recent Social Trends in the United States*, 1933, Vol. I, Chap. 3. See note 12 and pp. 163–66.

all other circumstances from which it will proceed; the difficulties of making or improving the invention; the amounts of creative talent and laboratory facilities which are available; the strength of motivation and financial support for the enterprise; and the obstacles of every sort that hinder its discovery or its use.

All of these are reasons for an event (an invention) to take place or to fail to do so. But if these are sufficient, why do events not take place at once? How does Time get into the act? It is because a succession of chances are involved. There are countless unknown or erroneous elements in the calculations, however well based, including the workings of the minds of all the potential inventors, in teams or in isolation. Will one of them think of some golden idea, or miss it by some unfriendly chance or (most likely) because he continues to think along familiar paths? And the requisite steps, whatever they will be, must occur in a certain order; b after a, c after b, and so on, perhaps for hundreds of steps. These all take time, and the time adds up, leading to the familiar statistical principle—the predictability of sums of many chances, as in the calculation of insurance rates. This may permit estimation, with high accuracy, of the dates when future inventions will arrive at each stage of development and use. Familiar examples are the scheduling of each future stage of the man-on-the-moon or the supersonic transport projects, involving promised delivery of inventions and discoveries yet to be made. So this predictive method of Causality and Chance, while it ignores the time dimension to begin with, in the end may achieve a high accuracy of timing. But it can succeed in thus timing the future only in those quasi-statistical cases where there are a large number of items which can be mentally grasped and organized, either through elaborate understanding of the case, or through the efforts of many inventors.

In examining the method of Causality and Chance, two points have been considered: first, the recognition of a need to accomplish some social or private function; and, second, the possibilities of fulfilling the need by invention. There is also a somewhat different possibility, in reversed order: the inventions, or a discovery, or a whole new branch of science, may appear first, whereupon the predictor strives to foresee what uses will be found for them and what social effects these uses will have. He will count on the inventors or discoverers to help the process along. Current breakthroughs in science that seem likely to have wide and largely unforeseen consequences, first on thought, then successively on invention, industry, and society, were listed in 1949.[5] The list contained: genetics of microorganisms, trouble-free electronic units, high-polymer chemistry and physics, fluorine chemistry, enzymology, virology, cosmic rays, the evolution of the universe, photosyn-

[5] Richard L. Meier, from an outline of a seminar course given at the University of Chicago, June, 1949, by this eminent atomic and social scientist.

thesis, microscopy, chromatography, isotopes, nuclear electrodynamics, meteorology, physiology of the nervous system, jet propulsion, and the sonic barrier. Two years later, the following were added: clear fused quartz, silicon chemistry, titanium, the photoelectric cell, microfilm, television, the walkie-talkie, the homing instinct of animals, together with clairvoyance and telepathy, lie detection and scientific mind reading, and rotary aviation.[6] Time has treated both of these lists for progress very well.

Ogburn [7] held that there is a third method of prediction—by Attention to Correlation: that is to say, if two things tend to move in unison, with either a positive or negative correlation (especially if one precedes the other), and if the first appears, the arrival of the other can be predicted without an understanding of the causation (as in the application of extrapolation). For many centuries people used the observed correlation of the moon and the tides to predict the tides, although it was not until Newton that they understood the cause of the correlation. This correlative method is a variety of Causality and Chance, since wherever correlation exists, a causal link must also exist, whether it be that A→B, or B→A, or C→both A and B. In any case, this method is rather rare in prediction, save where a causal link is at least hypothesized. It is most characteristic of medicine and other biological sciences, where, for example, scientists know that chemicals of one class are apt to be harmful to creatures of a second class, although they do not know why; so hopes are built on experiments along this line.

THE STAGES OF INVENTION

Some proof and assistance for the problem of timing a future development may be found in averages which were computed in *The Sociology of Invention* [8] and "The Prediction of Technical Change." [9] These covered the stages of development of 75 inventions of the 1900–1930 period, the 19 inventions which were voted "most important" by *Scientific American* readers for the twenty-five-year period prior to 1913, the 12 marine inventions thought to be most fundamental for the era beginning with steam and ending in 1935,[10]

---

[6] Gilfillan, "The Prediction of Technical Change" (from a paper for the Princeton Conference on Quantitative Description of Technologic Change, April, 1951), reprinted in James R. Bright, ed., *Research, Development, and Technological Innovation* (Homewood, Ill.: Richard D. Irwin, Inc., 1964), pp. 738–54.

[7] *Social Effects of Aviation.*

[8] S. C. Gilfillan, *The Sociology of Invention* (Chicago, Ill.: Follett Publishing Co., 1935), pp. 95–96. (A revised edition has been completed.)

[9] Gilfillan, *Review of Economics and Statistics*, 34 (1952), 371.

[10] Gilfillan, *The Sociology of Invention*, 1st ed., pp. 95–96.

Group of Inventions	Elapsed Time from 1st Thought to 1st Plan	Then to Practical Use	Then to Commercial Success	Then to Important Use
1900–1930			33 Med	
Scientific American 1888–1913	176 G	24 G	14 G	12 G
12 Marine 1808–1926			41 G, 90 Med, 86 A	9 G, 9 Med, 11 A
209 Inventions { Started 1787–1900			37 Med, 117 A	9.7 A
209 Inventions { Started 1900–1935			10 A	9.7 A

NOTE: G = Geometric mean
Med = Median
A = Common average (arithmetic mean)

Figure 1. Maturation Stages of Important Inventions (in years)

and 209 of the 500 civil inventions most important socially between the years 1787 and 1935 (a list prepared for Schumpeter).[11]

Figure 1, which combines the various averages, shows that during the latter part of the last century, and up to a generation ago, the most successful and important inventions took approximately twenty-five years to move from their first patent or definite plan to their application in practical use, then another generation or so to achieve commercial success, and then an additional nine to twelve years to reach important use. A comparison of the last two rows indicates that, in the latest period, there has been a great shortening of the time required for an invention to progress from the first plan to commercial success. This is explained both by the brevity of the time period which is examined, and probably by a real shortening of the stage, brought about by modern laboratories and staffs, and support by governments and great corporations.[12] In any case it is certain that the number of years of maturation-time which inventions require vitally depends upon how bounteously the developmental work is supported.

An invention already in abundant use will tend to have more improve-

11 Gilfillan, "The Prediction of Technical Change," p. 371. My lists of 75 inventions for *Recent Social Trends*, and of 500 inventions for Prof. Joseph Schumpeter, have not been published. The 2d and 3d Groups listed in our Table 1 are mentioned in my *Sociology of Invention*, and in par. 330 of my *Invention and the Patent System* below.
12 Gilfillan, *The Sociology of Invention*, Principle 18.

ments made on it than one which is only in trial use, let alone one for which utilization is only the hope of a few people.[13] The more an invention is produced, and the more it proves to be a source of profit, the more people will work to improve it. The supreme illustration of what effort can do, even without current utilization, is the atom bomb, which in just four years was rushed from abstract speculation to devastating success, through a totally new field of greatest difficulty, as a result of the expenditure of two billion dollars.

These statistics on maturation stages are highly inaccurate because of the difficulties of selecting and defining the inventions to count, dating their stages, and deciding which kind of average is the most appropriate. But they are better than no statistics at all to indicate the seriousness of the delay in development. Exceptional cases on the quick side (i.e., those winning wide use in short order) never occurred in the earlier periods examined. In most recent times we find in addition to the atom bomb its lethal follower, the H-bomb; the atom-powered warship; space navigation; and the transistor. All but the small and simple transistor have been military weapons, crash-produced by the U.S. government.

A very small and simple invention may occasionally win prompt perfection and success, but this is hardly ever true of a fundamental invention, unless it is done through a bottomless military budget. This is most serious for such basic new inventive starts as the voice-operated writing machine, the print reading machine, hydroponics, the fuel cell, magnetohydrodynamics, the convertaplane, the indexing of voices and handwritings, the telharmonium and other music in the just intonation, the home radio-printed newspaper, cheap clear fused quartz, etc.[14] These are civilization's orphan babies; born, but useless as yet and almost unable to grow because no institutions are adapted to support them. The patent system will not help, since its seventeen-year protection will have run out long before abundant sales can bring returns under present conditions. Commercialism without patents is similarly helpless. Neither government nor philanthropy will help these "orphans" because someone hopes, however deludedly, to make money from them, and they are not for war. So they languish for decades and often for centuries, with little support for their maturation. Their situation is like that of science, which languished for centuries and millennia because it could not pay its own way, until at last the universities and then governments saw that they must support the sciences.

---

[13] *Ibid.*, Principles 15, 18, 21 and 22.

[14] Gilfillan, *Invention and the Patent System*, Chap. 8. "Fundamental Inventions—Nobody's Baby"; also "The Hard Starting of Fundamental Inventions," *The Sociology of Invention*, N 8, Chap. 5.

Still worse retardation, amounting practically to prohibition of inventive progress, confronts the potential host of inventions which contravene a standardization enforced by unorganized custom, especially characteristic of Communication. In the case of one of the greatest inventions, the alphabet, no important improvements have been allowed for twenty-eight centuries past, except for special uses which can escape the standardization, such as shorthand, telegraphy, computers, and the successively improved alphabets for the blind. In these, invention has been permitted to display its more usual, far-reaching and glorious progress.[15]

One result of these considerations is that, for fairly short-range predictions of important inventions or effects, say for the next thirty years, one never thinks of a wholly new invention. Instead one starts with inventions already known, but insufficiently developed or adapted.

COMBINATIONS OF METHOD

The complete distinctness of the two predictive methods is not commonly understood, because the two are constantly used in combination, as is very desirable. For instance, the helicopter clearly is going ahead. One can easily plot its progress along various parameters of power, efficiency, and employment. By the second method, one can see many important functions that helicopters might fill, such as exploitation of forests, mountains, swamps and deserts, and handling of all traffic without the restriction of airports. There are no physical laws barring progress in such directions. Governments and great corporations are interested, capable, and working on the invention. There are no vested interests with power to block developments. So, according to both methods, helicopters must advance in certain directions and at certain rates.

Checking one method by the other is very desirable, since the concurrence of differing sources and types of reasoning on the same conclusion is very reassuring. For instance, any extrapolation of a trend, even using free-hand curves, embodies an implication that the same forces, or the same progressive changes in the forces, will hold true throughout the future period. But reasoning from causality may identify new forces (e.g., from a new but foreseen development) and correct the projection. Also, many more considerations can be included than just those of the invention itself—considerations and graphs of rising wealth, population and education, and competence with machinery (but probably with less frequency of inborn ability). By combining all available evidence on the future, both from such

15 *Invention and the Patent System*, Chap. 8, and par. 215–21.

extrapolations and from the Causality principle, one may be able to plot a future path for an invention where no sufficient basis for an extrapolation has been provided by the past. Then, using mathematical principles, one might wisely smooth the graph of the future.

Ogburn was inclined to extrapolate with logistic, long S curves, applying the idea that nothing continues forever at the same geometric rate of increase; if it did it would reach the absurdity of overfulness. Some years ago, an extrapolation of the number of automobiles (which would have yielded a steep, straight line on the ratio chart) would have indicated that, ultimately, there would be more cars than families. A predictor would have said that such a situation would be absurd. Yet today's wealth has resulted in many families that have two or more private cars, in addition to another motor vehicle used in business. An extrapolator of the future speed of airplanes might have said that the steep upward zoom of the speed of the graph would have to flatten off as it approached the speed of sound. But a forecaster with more faith in the power of invention might have predicted that that barrier would yield to effort, as it already had to the rifle bullet.

To be sure, studies of inventions have indicated a tendency for a decline after inventions reach a plateau of stability,[16] and once in decline, inventions hardly ever are revived in the same form. The reason for this is probably semantic rather than real. All talk about an invention begins with a definition of that invention. The definition makes the invention. When one talks about the future of the airplane, it makes a big difference whether the convertaplane (half helicopter), and the mail- and perhaps the passenger-carrying rocket are included. If they are not, then the airplane is destined to decline. But this decline will be semantic rather than real. The engineering realities will go right on expanding, speeding, and refining; their protean reality will, in time, squirm out of the definition of airplane, which will then, like the empty chrysalis of a larva turned butterfly, be left behind, though the creature keeps on living.

The two methods of predicting may also be worked backward in time, from result to cause, just as any natural law that is perfectly understood can be reversed. One may reason historically that the effect B must have been caused by A, and apply similar reasoning to the future. Suppose that an extrapolation of the graph of past maximum speeds of travel lead to the conclusion that by the year 2000 man will be traveling at N thousand mph. What vehicles will be required? Such speed certainly could not be attained by a railway, motorcar, hydrofoil boat, or a low-flying airplane. The only possibilities remaining are a stratospheric airplane or rocket, or possibly an electromagnetically levitated train in a very expensive evacuated tube. This should provide a basis for the prediction of one of those three inventions

[16] Gilfillan, *The Sociology of Invention*, Principles 9 and 12.

with all its requisite accompaniments. The story of the invention's forth-coming development can be left to be worked out between now and the year 2000.

HOW THE ART OF PREDICTION MIGHT BE RAISED TO A SCIENCE

Suppose one were setting out to advance any art to a science, say the art of sculpture or that of picking employees. Would it not be well to start by studying the present art as practiced by the experts, i.e., by those whose work is proved most successful? Something, to be sure, might be learned from the failures of the unsuccessful. But there are countless ways to blunder and only one or a few ways to succeed; and success is what is sought. So it is most economical to study directly how the best was produced, as art students always do.

Next, how should one identify the best predictors? Obviously, by the outcome: Were their predictions fulfilled? The past must be searched for such predictors, even centuries back if they had predicted for centuries ahead. And one should consider not the best-fulfilled single predictions, since these might have been mere luck, but the best predictors, using whole books, or at least articles containing enough separate predictions to give a valid statistical average of success. Having thus found the best practitioners of the art, one should examine the methods they used, the subjects they considered, the degree of success they won, and what sort of men they were —"men," not "people," because the prophets never come from the conservative sex.

If this historical-bibliographic method for establishing a science is un-usual, it is because there are few other fields in which it is so appropriate and needed. In most sciences, the would-be improver can test his idea and see if it works, either by a physical experiment or, as in the nonexperimental sciences like sociology and geography, by running a schematic test and cor-relating facts known today, regardless of when or by whom they were dis-covered. But in the proposed science of prediction, there is no way to get these desired facts, these verified predictions, except by going back in time, roughly as many years as the predictions were dated ahead, to the predictors who made them. So the historical-bibliographic method seems necessary. If one tried his own experiments as scientists ordinarily do, he should have to wait ten to one hundred years to see if they succeed.

The author started a project on past predictors' procedures in his Master's Essay,[17] beginning at the very dawn of prediction among the

17 "Successful Social Prophecy in the Past" (unpublished Master's thesis in Sociology, Columbia University, 1920).

prophets who helped stir up the French Revolution, and continuing the study through the predictors of 1951. The findings of his extensive study are valuable, both for what they reveal about the methods of the most successful and because the history of an art is instructive to those who would practice in it.

The French publicists of the eighteenth century were the real originators of prediction. Their earliest predecessors called "prophets" were religious exhorters, or mere soothsayers. The classical world usually saw only continuing moral degradation in the future, perhaps accompanied by some technical progress. For Medieval and Renaissance thinkers, the future was heaven and hell. Roger Bacon's statements in 1256–66 that "art can construct" submarines, flying machines, etc., were remarkably prescient, although not exactly predictions; nor were the later utopias of Francis Bacon and others predictions, despite the inventions mentioned in them.

The first general predictor was d'Argenson,[18] a marquis and foreign minister of France. Especially in his private journal, written from 1729 to 1752, he exhibited much daring and sound foresight of future political developments. But like his successor prophets, he cared and wrote little about technology. None of these men mentioned the steam engine, although it was contemporary with them all, and had reached, by the time of Condorcet (1794), almost modern form at the hands of Watt. And, except Condorcet, none had mentioned electricity as a meteorologic phenomenon to be measured, although it had been employed in wire telegraphy and, by induction, in wireless.

Next came the famous statesman Turgot, who in 1750, when only twenty-three years old, delivered a remarkable Latin discourse which included the first philosophy of progress.[19] He partly appreciated the importance of technology, the cumulation of knowledge, and the fact that inventions depend both on the number of men trained to think and on the sporadic occurrence of genius in the artisan class. The independence of the Americas, many political reforms, and the doctrine of perfectibility were well foreseen.

This was followed by the two fantastic utopias of Tiphaigne de la Roche and, especially, of Mercier.[20] Nominally a description of Paris seven centuries in the future, Mercier's utopia was mainly a tract against the abuses of the "ancien régime." Having received the best of classical education, he knew nothing of the modern world outside Paris, nor of industry; yet he managed some hits in the inventive field, including the phonograph, experimental cross-breeding, and the swivel chair which we ascribe to Jefferson. His chief

[18] René Louis de Voyer de Paulmy, Marquis d' Argenson, 1694–1757.
[19] A. R. J. Turgot (1727–81) 2nd Discourse at the Sorbonne.
[20] Louis-Séb. Mercier, *L'An 2440*, 1770, trans. as *Memoir of the Year 2500*.

Marie-Jean-Antoine-Nicolas Caritat, Marquis de Condorcet

clue was simple optimism; e.g., predicting that Paris hospitals would have as many beds as patients, would be resorted to for cure, not for free burial, and would not dump their wastes into the Seine above the points where half of Paris got its drinking water. Reading Mercier's predictions to three graduate students, the author averaged their judgments of Mercier's prophesies as: 38 percent justified, 28 percent still destined, and 36 percent erroneous, against a percentage of errors to be expected by mere chance of perhaps 60 percent.

Next came that imposing French nobleman, Condorcet [21]—philosopher, mathematician and one of the leaders in the Revolution—a Girondist. When the Revolution ran wild he had to hide for his life in a garret. There, without even a reference book, he wrote his *Sketch for an Historical Picture of the Progress of the Human Spirit,* predicting a glorious future advance of democracy. And then the *demos* got this nobleman and he died, but his book did not. In the social field, nine students rated his forecasts right in three-quarters of the cases, as opposed to a probable success by mere chance of one-third. He formally originated and used the extrapolative method of

---

[21] M. J. de Caritat, marquis de Condorcet, *Esquisse d'un tableau historique des progrès de l'esprit humain,* 10th epoch, On the Progress of the Human Spirit, and *Fragment sur l'Atlantide,* both in 1794.

prediction, and was one of the first to make conditional predictions. Condorcet wrote:

> The application of the calculus of combinations and chances promises to the social sciences progress doubly important, since that mathematical science is the only means of giving either a mathematical exactitude, or an exact knowledge of the amount of uncertainty. . . . This science of statistics . . . should bring new information in the social sciences, as inexhaustibly abundant as the combinations, relations and facts which can be submitted to it.

He studied, by mathematics, the probability of obtaining truth by majority votes. (Perhaps the developers of the Delphi method could find something in that.) He said that with agricultural inventions, population will grow, and that if necessary, population in a secular state could be checked by birth control, and that it might be fed by synthetic food.

In any case, as Turgot had foreseen, more population would mean more inventors, especially when universal education uncovered the 98 percent of the people who were then submerged without a chance to become inventors. Few people today appreciate this mathematical principle for prophecy as well as that great mathematician Condorcet did. (This is number 22 of the Social Principles of Invention.[22]) Condorcet also foresaw statistical sampling and census taking; the developments of meteorology, including testing the air at different heights by unmanned balloons, and a climatology of health; eugenics; the emancipation of women; a time capsule; a universal language. All this he dashed off while hiding for his life without a book! How much better could this genius have done with the normal facilities of a scientist?

After Condorcet, the French were long busy hammering out the future on the anvils of Mars. Yet there were more futuristic utopias; notably that of the German Johann K. Friederich, who, between 1826 and 1846, predicted endless applications of steam, including airships. In a humorous article of 1826, an Imperial American air fleet wipes out Tokyo a hundred years from then—too near the truth of 119 years later.

In 1846 Souvestre, in France,[23] turned on the optimists with contempt, and satirically predicted his own socialist utopia, in which steam and electric machines would free the hands from working, the mind from thinking, and the heart from feeling. Although this was written with scorn, Souvestre sketched the future pretty well, with household contrivances eliminating servants, with pneumatic tubes, wired television and news, doors that opened themselves, inador beds, steep-flight aircraft, subway railroads, photographic

---

22 Gilfillan, *The Sociology of Invention*, Prin. 22.
23 Emile Souvestre, *Le Monde tel qu'il sera dans l'an 3000*, 1846.

passports, etc. Many later novels have followed the same plan, notably Aldous Huxley's *Brave New World*.

In 1870, Harting, a Dutch physicist, wrote a passable utopia which was primarily concerned with invention.[24] He predicted that the future city would be roofed over but would not be a monecopolis (a single building). He added familiar marvels, including transoceanic telephony and sound recording some years before Bell and Edison. Bellamy's *Looking Backward,* 1888, was a much read socialist utopian novel of this type, and, to the writer's knowledge, the first American writing in this field.

Jules Verne is always thought of today as a prophet, yet he predicted deliberately in only a couple of minor publications. He was a science fiction writer but did not even believe in the feasibility of a submarine, although submarines had been built since 1624. In his case and in many others, it is evident that a writer may speak sooth and foretell the future aright, while only repeating the dreams of optimists, perhaps to scorn them or just to play at putting ideas together to make a pretty picture while not believing his own words—"Na woulden it be luverly?" For such have been the advancing powers of scientific man that, what one generation fondly, facetiously, or satirically imagines as being desired, is apt to be accomplished by its grandchildren.

Farcical prediction, yet brilliantly successful, was Robida's 1883 illustrated story of future war.[25] With great slaughter and gusto, the future would use tanks, gas shells and masks, liquid fire, biological warfare, minelaying by submarines, railway guns, new types of artillery, dirigibles, airplanes, air torpedoes, anti-aircraft artillery and observation posts, and airplane-to-ground telephones (using a trailing wire while the plane circled about). In short this article foretold almost all the novel instruments of the the world war thirty years later, except that radio substituted for the trailing wire which Robida proposed for the airplane telephone.

Most remarkable for its prediction of invention was a German book by Plessner in 1892.[26] It discussed the future of electrical *Fernsehen,* (seeing at a distance), by using the power of a selenium cell to translate light into electric current, which could then be reproduced as sight or sound, after transmission through space by electric wire, or through time by a phonographic or a photographic recording. So, seventy-five years ago, Plessner gave elaborate directions for telephotography and facsimiles; the optophone to make audible all visible things such as print; the then realized photophone;

---

24 Pieter Harting, *Anno Domini 2071,* by Dr. Dioscorides, 1870 Engl. tr.

25 A. Robida, in *La Caricature,* of which he was artist and editor, Oct. 27, 1883; reviewed in *New France,* 2 (June, 1918), 107–102.

26 Max Plessner, *Ein Blick auf die grossen Erfindungen des 20. Jahrhunderts, I, die Zukunft des elektrischen Fernsehens.*

the sound-on-film phonograph; the voice-operated writing machine with a suitable alphabet; the movie; the talkie; television by electric wire; and the mechanical analysis and identification of voices and colors. To be sure, the selenium cell has been found too slow for most of these uses; it has been replaced by the fast photoelectric cell, and some of the wires have been replaced by radio. (In accord with Principle 34 [27] of equivalent invention, when predictors try to start their own inventions, as Plessner did, they always fail. But they can still succeed as to the function, through the principle of equivalence.) Plessner further described the uses of these inventions, all of which have been or will be achieved. These forecasts were made with great competence and no errors three-quarters of a century ago. In the same year, the famous physicist Sir William Crookes did very well on radio and other inventions.[28]

Then came H. G. Wells's greatest fiction, the *Time Machine* (1895) and *When the Sleeper Wakes* (1899), both of which looked ahead two or more centuries. They are not only great stories and great science fiction, but also in the nature of political tracts, warning against certain political tendencies of our time.

Various minor prophets were now indulging in the art, and 1897 saw the first sober criticism of the prediction of inventions—an article by William Baxter.[29] He deplored the extravagant claims and ignorance of physical principles which characterized many of the predictors, and pointed out that they had been reading each other and following fashions, promising first of all electricity direct from coal or the like, then from the sun, tides, waves or wind. We see that later the fashion turned to television, the airplane and the airship; then to the helicopter and lightplane. Then, as the stubborn shortcomings of these two aircraft became evident, interest in their future waned. Now it is revived again for the whirlybird.

Fashion, or a unanimity of interest and agreement among the experts, is an attractive but insecure guide to prediction. It heightens the probability of truth, but proves nothing. The predictors may agree only because they have been facing the same problems of their day, thinking up remedies from the same contemporary science, and reading each other's discussions. It is hoped that the authors of the Delphi method are aware of this, and of the wry humor in the proverb, "Forty million Frenchmen can't be wrong."

The turn of the century called forth numerous forecasts, and engineers and their like began to write them. Sir William White, long chief designer of the Queen's Navy, did very well—one might say perfectly—at foreseeing the marine power plants of the next forty years; but he made no attempt to

[27] Gilfillan, *The Sociology of Invention.*
[28] "Some Possibilities of Electricity," *Fortnightly Review*, 57 (1892), 173–81.
[29] "Forecasting the Progress of Invention," *Popular Science Monthly*, 51 (1897), 307–14.

name them sixty years ahead.[30] He believed especially in the turbine, high pressure, oil fuel, nickel steel, noncorroding aluminum alloys, and larger ships.

R. H. Thurston,[31] historian of the steam engine, graphed the engine's past progress and made predictions which have been well justified since. Another technologist, Charles Sewall,[32] charted the "Future of Long Distance Communication." George Sutherland's 1901 work, *20th Century Inventions,* described in "The Prediction of Inventions," [33] rated 64 percent right. And yet for submarine and air navigation he could foresee nothing but failure, since he was not enough of a technologist.

Finally, at the turn of the century, H. G. Wells turned to serious prediction with his *Anticipations.*[34] This book focused on the automobile age, and was well justified and popular. Wells voiced a strong plea for making prediction a science:

> And now, it has been possible for men by picking out a number of suggestive and significant looking things in the present, by comparing them, criticizing them and discussing them with a perpetual insistence upon why? without any guiding tradition, and indeed in the teeth of established beliefs, to construct this amazing search-light of inference into the remoter past, is it really, after all, such an extravagant and hopeless thing to suggest that by seeking for operating causes instead of for fossils, and by criticizing them as persistently and thoroughly as the geological record has been criticized, it may be possible to throw a search-light of inference forward instead of backward, and to attain a knowledge of coming things as clear, as universally convincing, and infinitely more important to mankind than the clear vision of the past that geology has opened to us during the 19th century? [35]

There followed in the same year, and before Wright's first powered flight, a very intelligent forecast of aviation by B. F. S. Baden-Powell,[36] army

---

30 "The Progress in Steam Navigation," presidential address, reprinted in *Smithsonian Annual Report, 1899,* pp. 567–90.

31 "A Century's Progress in the Steam Engine," *Cassier's Magazine,* 17:191–99, reprinted in *ibid.,* pp. 591–603.

32 "The Future of Long Distance Communication," *Harper's Weekly,* 44:II (1900), 1262–63.

33 Gilfillan, "The Prediction of Inventions," pp. 15–23, in U. S. National Resources Committee, *Technological Trends and National Policy,* 1937, Part I, Sec. II.

34 *Anticipations of the Reaction of Mechanical and Scientific Progress upon Human Life and Thought.*

35 "Discovery of the Future," pp. 375–92.

36 "Recent Aëronautical Progress, and Deductions to Be Drawn Therefrom, Regarding the Future of Aerial Navigation," presidential address reprinted in *Smithsonian Annual Report, 1902,* pp. 121–31.

"TO WANDER THRU THE LOUVRE WITH
WILLIAM M. CHASE"

The Future
Home Theater

BY S. C. GILFILLAN

officer, president of the Aeronautical Society, and brother of the Boy Scout Founder. T. B. Russell's *100 Years Hence, The Expectations of an Optimist* (1906) [37] rates 74 percent right. In 1908, the distinguished inventor Hudson Maxim [38] became the first predictor from the inventor's craft, but he was not very successful. Two years later the first symposium on the future was held. It seems to have been well done and prescient.[39] Then in 1911 and 1913, the well-informed science editor Waldemar Kaempffert [40] looked into the future. His two articles contained twenty-five correct predictions, three not fulfilled by 1941, and three which were in error.

The next predictor is the author himself. Any fellow who claims to know something about prediction should prove that he has something on the ball —his crystal ball. In 1912 and 1913, three of my articles were published in

[37] Russell was English, like most predictors of this period.

[38] "Man's Machine-made Millennium," *Cosmopolitan,* 45 (1908), 569–76.

[39] *The New York World,* "Looking into the Future," 1910 issue; reviewed in *Popular Mechanics,* 63 (1935), 362–67.

[40] *The New Art of Flying,* 1911. "The Future of Flying," *Country Life,* 20 (July 15, 1911), 23 ff. and "Aircraft and the Future," *Outlook,* 104 (1913), 452–60.

the *Independent:* "Future Housekeeping,"[41] "The Future Home Theater,"[42] and "The Size of Future Liners."[43] They were not exceptional in prescience. They reflected diligent reading of the previous predictors (since I had started a book on the future), and showed the deficient technological information of a youth of twenty-three with a literary education. But they teach some lessons about prediction.

The first article expected the minimization of housework by various devices, including the delivery of cooked meals (and everything else) to each home by pneumatic tube. Instead, housework is being reduced by frozen and otherwise ready prepared food, and ready-made clothing. This again illustrates the principle of equivalent invention. The article on "The Future Home Theater" predicted this development by two different inventions: the home talkie, and television distributed over the telephone wires. Instead, the event came overwhelmnigly through a third invention, radio. In my youthful ignorance in 1912 I did not think of radio telephony, although it already had been accomplished and experimental broadcasts had been conducted. Technical ignorance and optimism also made me much too sanguine about the early perfection of techniques, including good color and stereoscopy, leading to my estimate that half the homes would be served by 1930. I also predicted such intellectuality of programs as we have yet to see even

41 "Housekeeping in the Future," *Independent,* 72 (1912), 1960–62.
42 "The Future Home Theater," *Independent,* 73 (1912), 886–91.
43 "The Size of Future Liners," *Independent,* 74 (1913), 541–43.

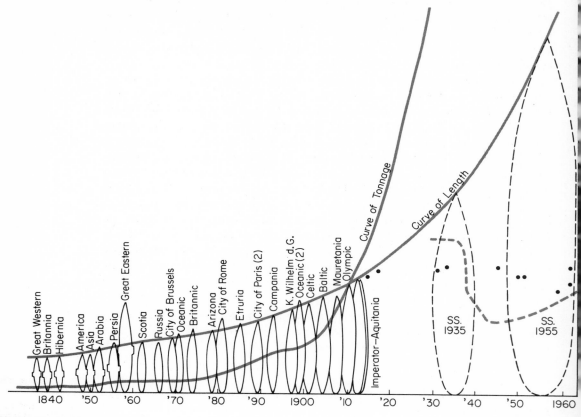

Figure 2. Lengths of Ships.

on educational TV, including: grand opera; documentary lectures by the greatest scholars; and a history of Greece which would be shown on prime time for a quarter-hour every evening for a year. Batman, the westerns, and alluring cigarette ads, I never thought of. Yet the overwhelming psychological influence of the home theater, for good or ill, was correctly anticipated, again showing how the *effects* of inventions can be foreseen more easily than the inventions themselves, or even their uses.

My third article, "The Size of Future Liners," was based first on extrapolation of the maximum length and tonnage of ships, using the chart shown in Figure 2. Simple extrapolation of the curves, from the 883 feet *Imperator* of 1912, would soon lead to the inconceivable monsters shown in dotted lines as *SS 1935* and *1955*. So I invoked the Principle of Causality, and reasoned that a check would be imposed about 1925, at 1175 feet, followed a decade later by an abrupt decline to 520 feet, which in turn would be followed by a gradual rise to 735 feet by 1965. Dots have been added to indicate the length of the few big liners built since then. As the graph shows, the prediction was pretty much in accord with the actual events. The recent growth of enormous tankers is something I never imagined, and my predictions were only for liners. The reasons given for the foreseen shrinkage included the competition of aircraft (carefully not specified as either airplanes or airships) and the halving of the Atlantic voyage time on routes to Newfoundland from Ireland. This latter development did not take place, but the air competition did, and so the prediction succeeded. I know of but one other prediction of a decline in the size of ships.[44] A prediction of the dimensions of ships is highly desirable, in order to plan canals, locks and port-works for future utility. The designers of the Panama Canal succeeded perfectly in this when they made their decisions (about 1907).

The next predictors of note were the great inventors Edison [45] and, especially, Steinmetz.[46] Steinmetz's forecasts were approximately 88 percent right. His later predictions of 1922 and 1923 should also be noted.

The best of all the predictions which were found in 1936 (during research for *Technological Trends*) was an editorial, written in 1920, by three editors of *Scientific American*.[47] Their predictions seemed 78 percent right at the time, and 79 percent today; 62 percent were verified and 17 percent seem still destined. A report of a small symposium conducted by inventors, published by *Popular Science Monthly* in May 1922,[48] included successful forecasts by Edison and Tesla.

From 1923 through 1927, there appeared in England a series of little books [49] which dealt with the future. These bore mythological titles and included: Bertrand Russell's *Icarus or the Future of Science;* Captain

[44] Archibald M. Low, *The Future*, 1925. See also his *Wireless Possibilities*, 1924, and *Our Wonderful World of Tomorrow*, 1934.

[45] Thomas A. Edison's predictive interviews are in *Independent*, 68 (1910), 15–18; *Cosmopolitan*, 50 (1911), 294–306; *Today & Tomorrow*, 77 (1914), 24–27 and *Popular Science Monthly*, May, 1922, pp. 21ff.

[46] Charles P. Steinmetz, "You Will Think This a Dream," *Ladies Home Journal*, September, 1915, p. 12; "100 Years from Now," *Nation's Business*, September, 1922, pp. 11–13, "Steinmetz Predicts 4-hr Workday," *New York Times*, Aug. 20, 1923, pp. 1, 9.

[47] 123 (Oct. 2, 1920), 320–21: "The Future as Suggested by the Developments of the Past 75 Years," unsigned, but by A. C. Lescarboura w. coll. as noted in Gilfillan, "Prediction of Inventions," p. 15. The figure there given of 38 percent for predictions already fulfilled should have been 48 percent.

[48] Symposium on pp. 21, 22, 26–28.

[49] *Today & Tomorrow Series*, published by Kegan Paul, Trench, Trubner & Co., London. The prophetic works of the series were reviewed in a closing volume, *Sibylla*, by C. A. Mace, a psychologist who pays little attention to invention.

Liddell Hart's good *Paris or the Future of War;* the notable booklet of J. B. S. Haldane, *Daedalus, or Science and the Future;* and E. Fournier d'Albe's *Quo Vadimus?* A. M. Low, D.Sc., inventor and engineer, contributed *Wireless Possibilities.* Low also wrote *The Future* (1925), a book with little genius and much prejudice, yet with a remarkably high score of hits because of his competence in science.

In 1926 the German A. B. Henninger produced *Predictions*—an ordinary sort of book. In the same year, Ferdinand Foch,[50] the great French generalissimo, drew a pretty accurate picture of the next war, dating it in 1946. He missed parachutes and underground civilians; he expected poison gases, burning phosphorus shells, air torpedoes and radio-controlled tanks; and he doubted high-speed and dreadnought tanks. Again in 1926, Hale's predictions on chemistry [51] and Parsons' on general invention can be cited.[52] In 1930, General Electric's eminent Whitney [53] predicted successfully and easily, on the basis of inventions already started. A symposium in 1932 [54] asked eminent inventors to write about the next, or the most needed, inventions. Unfortunately these inventors wasted their special skills by proposing mostly political remedies. The year 1935 brought J. N. Leonard's *Tools of Tomorrow,* which was competent in science and alive to the resistances to progress. C. C. Furnas,[55] a chemical engineer and university president, wrote about the future with verve and some competence, although he did not apply the social sciences. Kettering,[56] the eminent laboratory director for General Motors, came next. Chubb,[57] director for Westinghouse, limited his predictions to ten years.

In 1937, this writer contributed two chapters about the art of prediction to Ogburn's *Technological Trends and National Policy.*[58] These also contain a review or citation of all of the significant writings which were found up to

---

[50] Interview in *The New York Times Magazine,* Aug. 8, 1926, pp. 1, 20.

[51] William J. Hale, "Prophecy of a Chemist," *Science Monthly,* 22 (February, 1926), 161–66.

[52] Floyd W. Parsons, "New Things and Better Ones," *Saturday Evening Post,* Sept. 18, 1926, pp. 12ff, and "Facts and Fancies, New Industries, a National Remedy," *Gas-Age Record,* 65:II (1930), 731ff.

[53] "Dr. W. R. Whitney Answers the Question: What Won't They Do Next?" interview, *American Magazine* 110 (October, 1930), 34ff.

[54] *Science News Letter,* 21 (1932), 239–40; "Leaders of Invention Tell What the World Needs Most."

[55] *The Next 100 Years: The Unfinished Business of Science,* 1935. And "Prospects & Perils of Research," *Vital Speeches,* 5 (1938), 135–38.

[56] Charles F. Kettering, Interview in *Good Housekeeping,* 100 (January, 1935), 16ff.

[57] L. W. Chubb, *Scientific American,* 147 (1932), 12, 13.

[58] "The prediction of Inventions," pp. 15–23 and "Social Effects of Inventions," pp. 24–38. See also B. J. Stern, "Resistances to the Adoption of Technological Innovations," pp. 39–66.

1936. Any student of prediction can find useful material here or in the main part of the book. The book consists of articles by specialists, reviewing recent progress in their fields but voicing little prophecy. Like most scientific men, these specialists could hardly be induced by the editor, Ogburn, to take the risk of bold forecasts of the future. The book was reviewed, with comments on prediction, by the radical English scientist Lilley ten years later.[59]

My own later work on prediction included a manuscript of short book length which further expands the history and theory of prediction.[60] Finally, there is my paper of 1951 for the Princeton Conference on Quantitative Description of Technologic Change, most of which was printed as "The Prediction of Technical Change." [61]

Most of my publications have been on other social science aspects of invention. An example is *The Sociology of Invention*, a revised edition of which has been completed. This work, which largely expounds thirty-eight Social Principles of Invention, can help the predictor of technology, since it identifies the social factors that foster or hinder invention. Another book, *Invention and the Patent System* [62] measures American inventing since 1880 and contains a chapter on "Fundamental Inventions, Nobody's Baby," a subject discussed above. It emphasizes how scandalous it is that these greatest, most needed inventions, which open new lines of progress, have no direct and effective means for their development unless they are used for the military. Since 1941 I have not tested any more predictors fully or competently, but I have gathered notes on numerous individual and group forecasters of all periods.[63]

The year before the outbreak of the Second World War brought several articles worthy of mention. These were written by Bryson [64] (on the future of plastics), Chorlton,[65] Teague,[66] and Kaempffert.[67] Kaempffert, science editor of the *New York Times*, wrote that man may someday telegraph the

[59] S. Lilley, "Can Prediction Become a Science?" *Discovery*, November, 1946, pp. 336–40; this is primarily based on Ogburn's *Technological Trends*.

[60] Gilfillan, "The Literature of Prediction, etc.," unpublished (prepared for Ogburn in 1941).

[61] *Review of Economics and Statistics*, 34 (1952), 368–85. Reprinted in Bright, *Research, Development, and Technological Innovation*, pp. 738–54. The rest of this paper was mimeographed.

[62] Published by the Joint Economic Committee of Congress, 1964, ff.

[63] "The Literature of Prediction."

[64] H. C. Bryson, in *Discovery*, n.s., 2 (1939), 3–7 and 55–60.

[65] F. O. L. Chorlton, "Invention in the Future," *Mechanical Engineering*, 60 (1939), 256–67.

[66] W. D. Teague, "Planning the World of Tomorrow," *Popular Mechanics*, 74 (1940), 808ff.

[67] W. Kaempffert, "Look What's Ahead—" *American Magazine*, 127 (May, 1939), 14ff; and *The New York Times Magazine*, Feb. 18, 1940, pp. 12ff.

senses of taste, touch, and smell. Soon after the outbreak of World War II he considered the time required to bring novel weapons into use and concluded that no wholly new devices would be used in the war. He was almost right.

In 1939, a new technique was introduced by Pendray of Westinghouse [68] —the anonymous symposium. He asked fifty outstanding scientists and engineers what new developments in their workshops were most likely to affect life during the next twenty-five years. He then wove their anonymous answers together, necessarily infusing his own judgment as well. The product was both readable and predictively excellent. The technique was modified by Bruce Bliven,[69] editor of the *New Republic,* who cornered distinguished men, pushed them into the realm of the future, an area uncongenial to most scientists, and edited out the repetitive, trite, foolish, and extraneous from their impromptu thinking. He did not eliminate U235 as a source of power. Again in a 1941 article, that universal scientist, Kaempffert [70] (under whom I helped organize the Museum of Science and Industry at Chicago) looked ahead ten to fifty years (and very well) at how American life ought to be organized, with a half-way monecopolis and many inventions.

Clarke's bibliography,[71] lists nearly nine hundred titles, from 1733 to 1960, although it is confined to British books of fiction or utopism and omits all articles and discussions. Britain was decidedly the leader in prediction through the first third of this century.

Only a few of the outstanding predictors are covered here (the same is true of the critics who are examined in the next section). More thorough treatment is in the manuscripts previously mentioned.

ON THE CRITICISM OF PREDICTION

It has already been mentioned how, in the early nineteenth century, Souvestre and others turned with contempt again the "Zukunftmusik" of futuristic socialist utopias, yet made, in their parodies, pretty good predic-

[68] G. E. Pendray, "The Crucible of Change," *North American Review,* 247 (1939), 344–54; condensed in *Reader's Digest,* Vol. 35, July, 1939, 81–84.
[69] "The Men Who Make the Future," *New Republic,* 103 (1940), 681–83, 629–32, and 104 (1941), 47–50, 202–6.
[70] W. Kaempffert, "Tomorrow has arrived, picture of American life as it could be lived if we put our present tools and discoveries to work," *American Magazine,* 131 (March, 1940), 45ff.
[71] I. F. Clarke, *The Tale of the Future,* from start to 1961. A bibliography with brief annotations, on British books of fiction, satire or utopia. See also his *Voices Prophesying War, 1763–1984,* 1966.

tions of inventions themselves. Baxter has been mentioned as the first sober critic of predictors, and was especially critical of their addition to fashions. Shanks,[72] in 1919 and 1923, criticized prophetic fiction.

My own unpublished works of 1911 and 1920 were perhaps the first to propose a method of improvement by study of the most successful predictors.

Not until 1930 does one find another constructive study, when Israeli [73] and other social psychologists began investigating the influence of wishful thinking upon college students' judgments of future events. But they used near-future events for tests (for example, "will Hitler last another year?"), in order to avoid long delays for verification. As a result, the judgments depended more on understanding the present than the future, and the proposed science of Futurology was helped very little. As one would expect, the investigators found the influence of wishful thinking to be strong when the rational indications were ambiguous (i.e., a toss-up). But Israeli did approach this quest by proposing [74] a "Museum of Future History" which would be a collection of predictions for future verification. There has been no lack of prognosticators.

Cantril in 1937,[75] and McGregor the next year,[76] followed similar lines. Cantril circulated, among intelligent specialists in various lines, a questionnaire pertaining to seventy predictions. He then compared the different groupings and the influence of wish, but inventions were not considered. The impartiality of social scientists was much impugned. General intelligence was found to help much less than specific information, and the influence of wish was found to vary with its intensity, as one would expect. So future inventions should be an especially good field for prediction, since they involve less self-interest, emotion, and allegiance, and much specialized and objective knowledge.

In 1932, Helton [77] was utterly against the predictors, but he presents some useful thoughts. He cites how, to Victor Hugo, tomorrow was "a region where dreams come true," as exemplified by Hugo's prophecy that "by the 20th century there will be neither dogmas nor frontiers." Helton adds, "*We live in his paradise. It is a salutary thought.*" Still, such predictions as

---

[72] Edward Shanks, *First Essays on Literature*, 1923, with chapters on Wells and Sweet Bodements.

[73] Nathan Israeli, in *Journal of Social Psychology*, 4:92–115 and 201–22; *Journal of Applied Psychology*, 16:584ff; *Brooklyn Teacher*, 15:11, 12, and *Psy. Excg.*, 4:163–65. All about 1933–36.

[74] N. Israeli, *Journal of Abnormal and Social Psychology*, 28:181–93; and especially 25:121–32.

[75] H. Cantril, "Prediction of Social Events," *Public Opinion Quarterly*, 1 (Nov. 4, 1937), 83–87.

[76] Douglas McGregor, in *Journal of Abnormal Psychology*, 33 (1938), 179–204.

[77] Roy Helton, "Perils of Prophecy," *Harper's Magazine*, 165 (1932), 74–83.

Hugo's were not based on physical, social or any other science or method, save optimism.

Ogburn was constantly envisioning the future from 1928 onwards. In 1935, he called for the establishment of a predictive science,[78] and wrote well on its principles, as mentioned earlier.[79] He has done the finest work to date on the social effects of invention, although he overdoes the effects of particular inventions (neglecting the principle of equivalence), and over-claims invention as the main cause of social change. The true relationship has been better shown elsewhere.[80]

SUMMARIZING HISTORY AS TRENDS

The kinds of predictors and their interests

The earliest predictors were eminent statesmen or publicists, like Condorcet, interested in social welfare, not invention. Then came lesser figures —the utopian dreamers and their satirists, and novelists and science fictionists. Invention, rapidly progressing in their world, invaded their future worlds. Then, in the twentieth century, eminent scientists and inventors expressed their views on the general future of science, invention, and social affairs. Finally, in the most recent generation, specialized scientists and engineers, of less fame but with more thorough knowledge in their own departments of vastly proliferating and specializing science, became the chief spokesmen.

Their predicting tends to merge with the *planning* of man's work, which has always been a concern of the world's better minds. As prediction falls into the hands of specialized planners, the reach (the future limit date) tends to shorten, and the starting point tends to be inventions already started. Furthermore, the trends have moved from the social to the physical-science fields; from the general to the specialized; and from the single predictor to the person reading the works of others, on to the symposium, and, finally, to the team of cooperating specialists.

Their intents

At first, magicians tried to work the future. Then soothsayers and astrologers tried to dodge or take advantage of fate, and religious prophets used

---

[78] "Prospecting for the Future," *Social Frontier,* 1 (April, 1935), 20–22.
[79] *Social Effects of Aviation.*
[80] Gilfillan, *Social Implications of Technical Advance,* No. 4 of *Current Sociology,* Vol. I (1953), especially 192–203.

threats and promises of the future to control present conduct. Then came the utopist with his "future-music" so reminiscent of Heaven. Then the social reformer, and last, the scientific predictor, striving with increasing success to foretell, without bias, hope, or propaganda, but with proof and useful guidance. Prediction has passed through Comte's three stages—the religious, the philosophical, and the positive or scientific. It can be seen progressing from personal and subjective judgment toward objective conclusions from multiple scientific evidences which are judged by numerous minds.

Their countries

Prediction, as we have seen, began in France. It later appeared occasionally in Germany, moved chiefly to England beginning in the 1880's, and to the United States in this century.

The procedures they have followed

The predictors have said very little about their methods,[81] and what they do say does not instruct us further. The two basic methods—Extrapolation, and Causality with Chances—have always been used but have not been distinguished. Extrapolation has become more explicit and mathematical with the growth of statistical thinking in the world and the collection of more statistics to work on. The method of Causality has likewise grown in conscious definiteness. In the earlier periods, this growth may have resulted solely from *Optimism*, as was noted anent the prophets around 1890— optimism which had a passable logic, that whatever both writer and many people want, some people in the future will invent and provide. Optimism is also useful in liberating scientists from their drilled-in caution and conservatism, and in helping one to cope with the future. For one must have hope to deal with what lies ahead, even if it be only the hope of mitigating disaster. Also, the past two centuries have been an age of rapidly advancing invention, general civilization, and even humanitarianism and democracy, so that optimism as to material culture has been pretty well vindicated, even if there have been disappointments in the social sphere.

As the business of prediction has expanded, it has been undergoing Spencerian Integration—specialization with cooperation. Men come to predict in their own science rather than all over the map of the future. They cooperate in symposia, and more recently, in organized teams. But when somewhat ordinary scientific men take over, instead of the rare, inspired prophets like Condorcet and Wells, they bring an element of

---

[81] Gilfillan, "The Literature of Prediction."

Figure 3 — Time-Tested Predictors, 1770–1920

1. Author and Brief Title	2. Date	3. Success	4. % Right	5. Optimism	6. Trends Observed	7. Tendentiousness	8. Fiction	9. Future Scope, Years	10. Soc. Causation	11. Specialization	12. Compares Views	13. Own Inventions	14. Age of Predictor
Mercier: L'An 2440	1770	4	64	8	–	8	x	670		1	–	–	30
Condorcet: Esquisse	1794	8		9	7	7	–		5		–	–	51
Souvestre: Monde	1846	5		1	3	8	x	1254	1		–	–	40
Harting: Anno 2070	1870	5		7		7	x	200		1	–	–	58
Robida 20th Cen. War	1883	9		2	6	1	x	110	1	9		x	35
Fuller: A.D. 2000	1890	2		8	3		x			1		9	39
Plessner: Blick	1892	9		7	2	2	–		1	9	3	–	
Crookes: Possibilities	1892	7		7	3	1	–		1	8	8	–	60
White: Steam Navigation	1899	9		5	9	1	–	20?	2	9	–	–	54
Wells: Sleeper Wakes	1899	3		4	5	8	x	200?	2	1	1	–	33
Sewall: Future Communication	1900	7		7	6	1	–	50	2	7	4	x	45
Sutherland: 20th Cen. Inv.	1900	7	64	7	3	2	–		5	1	4	x	
Wells: Anticipations	1901	7		7	5	6	–	100	3	2	4	–	35
Baden-Powell: Aviation	1902	8		6	5	2	–			9	6	–	42
Russell, T. B.: 100 Years Hence	1905	8	74	8	5	6	–	100	2	1	–	–	55
Maxim, Hud.: Man's M.M.	1908	9		9	5	1	–		3	3	2	x	34
Kaempffert: 2 aviation articles	1919	9	87	7	6	3	–			9	3	–	
Gilfillan: Housekeeping	1912	5		5	7		–		6	8	–	3	23
Gilfillan: Future Home Theatre	1912	8		9	5	1	–	28	3	9	–	–	23
Gilfillan: Future Liners	1913	7		3	9	1	–	48	7	9	–	–	23
Steinmetz: You Will Think	1915	8	88	9	3	2	–		1	3	–	–	50
Sci. Am.: Future as Suggested	1920	9	78	6	8	1	–	75—	2	3	7	–	29+
Average		6.86											43

Figure 3. Time-Tested Predictors, 1770–1920

excessive scientific caution, a demand for proof, and a fear of making mistakes or seeming to be absurd dreamers. As a result they shorten the time span of their predicted futures and begin predicting late, starting with inventions that have already begun, as Ogburn and others have found. One tongue-starter is the idea of Pendray's—anonymity to veil the audacity of vaticinations that may prove false. Another remedy is authority—a boss in a corporate or government research organization who compels his staff to wade into the future. The best and final remedy will be to build up such a science of Futurology that scientists who are armed with it will have no more hesitation about predicting than they feel today amid the sciences of prehistory.

Figure 3 attempts, however subjectively and imperfectly, to set down the various characteristics and methods used by the chief predictors mentioned above. Where a column consists of single digits from one to nine, the digits indicate an evaluation of how characteristic the writing was of the trait named at the head of the column (e.g., Optimism). "One" rates it as least characteristic, and "Nine" as most. Note that after the nineteenth century, there is a notable decline in the ax-grinding "Tendentiousness" trait. Column 11 concerns the degree of Specialization of the subject covered; 12, the predictor's attention to others of the craft; 13 identifies the predictors who attempt to foresee just how it will be done (a rash procedure which always fails—yet the average "Success" of predictors who were scored positively in Column 13, 7.3, was a little better than the general score of 6.9). In Columns 13 and 8, "Fiction," an "x" indicates the trait was present, a dash, that it was absent. A blank indicates no judgment, or inapplicable.

Age

None of the predictors was over sixty, or under twenty-nine, except for the present writer and Turgot who were twenty-three. The average age was forty-three.[82] The information of the young is too scanty, and that of the old is too out-of-date, and their imaginations probably not bold enough.

The student of Futurology can analyze these statistics in various ways according to his hunches. For instance, one might make a spot chart, as in Figure 4, by plotting "Success" in the vertical direction and "Attention to Trends" in the horizontal. A third dimension can be introduced if the size of the spots is varied according to the publication's importance.[83] Then a trend line can be drawn among the spots, paying most attention to the

[82] Counting myself once and Wells twice.
[83] I attempted to rate this in the manuscript study of note 82, including "Generality of Scope" as one trait of importance.

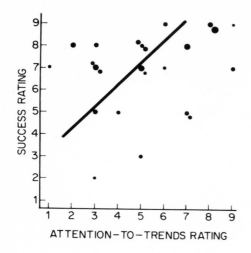

NOTE: SIZE OF DOT INDICATES IMPORTANCE

Figure 4. Correlation Between "Success" and "Attention to Trends."

larger spots. The result is a demonstration of strong correlation between the two traits of "Success" and "Attention to Trends." One might, if he thought it worthwhile, work out mathematically the correlation from the trend line, be it straight or curved. Stouffer, professor of Statistics at Harvard, thought this was a new and sound variety of Correlation.[84]

Similarly, Figure 5 shows a weighted and trended spot chart for "Success" vs. "Tendentiousness," which indicates, by its downward slope, a strong negative correlation. The element of time enters here, since "Success" has increased somewhat as the years have gone by, while "Tendentiousness" has been declining. So time, with all that it has brought, might be the whole explanation of the correlation.

Further data were gathered on the professions of predictors. These are summarized in Figure 6, which tabulates seventy-seven vocations that were identifiable for fifty-three predictors. (Their age averaged forty-two to forty-three in each period). The later period, 1921–41, shows an increase of scientific men (which would have been more marked had the researcher continued to later periods), and less concern with social science.

The statistics may be disappointing in their meagerness and, often, their unreliable, subjective basis, since the amount of forecasting has been immense. For two centuries forecasts have been recorded in objective print, and they are open to assessment of veridicality by anyone who desires to do

---

[84] Explained in Gilfillan, *The Sociology of Invention,* footnote 43 or 45.

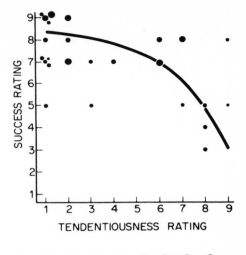

Figure 5. Correlation Between "Success" and "Tendentiousness."

• • • • • • • • ● ●
NOTE: SIZE OF DOT INDICATES IMPORTANCE

so. The excuse for presenting such faulty statistics is only that some quantified idea of magnitudes is better than none; that no one has presented *any* such statistics before; and that a positive, quantified assessment of the proved merits of the various methods and types of forecasters seems a highly appropriate and necessary step toward the creation of an urgently needed new field of science—Futurology.

Let us "prévoir pour pouvoir"—mapping the future for which we must

Figure 6. Professions of Predictors—A Comparison of Earlier Writers with Those of 1921–1941

Profession	Before 1921	1921–1941
Phys. science, math & engineering	6	12
Chemistry & chemical engineering	1	9
Inventors	3	6
Technical writers	3	5
Other physical scientists	6	4
Total with physical science	19 (68%)	36 (74%)
Literary writers & journalists	4 (14%)	4 (8%)
Other non-scientific men	4 (14%)	5 (10%)
Social scientists	1 (4%)	4 (8%)
Grand total of vocations	28 (100%)	49 (100%)

plan, just as we have mapped the prehistoric past: Posthistory to match Prehistory. It will be a hundredfold more useful, as Wells said.[85] Developed thus, with each prediction checking others, the structure of prophecy will not become like a chain, subject to total loss through failure of a single link, nor like a tangle of separate, independent threads of arguments, each serving but its own purpose and lending neither strength nor weakness to the other. Rather, the science of Futurology will become a mixture of these—a network wherein each strand is supported by several adjacent ones, so that if one fails, the rest are not undone but only weakened. It is by cross-checking evidence from many sources that the structures of the prehistoric past and of all the other sciences have been figured out. Thus Futurology can and must grow until, as the playwright said of history:

> The which observed, a man may prophesy,
> With a near aim, of the main chance of things
> As yet not come to life, which in their seeds
> And weak beginnings lie intreasured.
> Such things become the hatch and brood of time.[86]

---

[85] "Discovery of the Future."
[86] Shakespeare, *Henry IV*—Part II, Act III, Sc. 1.

Technological Forecasting Lessons from Project Hindsight

RAYMOND S. ISENSON

Project HINDSIGHT is probably the most extensive study of technological progress to date. This study analyzed the past history of weapon systems development to identify significant factors in the growth and application of defense technology. Its findings indicate that the major stimulus to technological growth is need, and that such growth is usually a composite of many small accomplishments instead of one well-defined achievement. The study emphasizes the need for increased inter-personal and interdisciplinary communication to accelerate technological change.

Colonel Isenson, head of Army-wide research planning for three years, moved to the Office of the Director of Defense Research and Engineering in May, 1965. He has been directing Project HINDSIGHT and interpreting its significance to the Defense Department's research. He was responsible for the development of fore-casting procedures and for the preparation of the Army's long-range technological forecasts during his assignment to the Army research planning activity.

In 1965, the Department of Defense (DoD) undertook a retrospective analysis of its utilization of science and technology. That study, called "Project HINDSIGHT," was intended to supply answers to several management questions that were of particular interest to the Department. By the summer of 1966, the effort had progressed to the point where the most pressing questions could be answered, and an interim summary report was published.[1] Research has been continued since the release of the first report.

---

[1] C. W. Sherwin and R. S. Isenson, *First Interim Report on Project HINDSIGHT,* Office of the Director of Defense Research and Engineering, Clearinghouse for Scientific and Technical Information #AD 642–400, June 30, 1966; revised, Oct. 13, 1966.

During the course of what is now well over a 50 man-year effort, a considerable amount of data has been collected, much of which provides insight concerning the processes of technological growth, thus offering possible lessons for technological forecasting.

This chapter reviews the objectives of the HINDSIGHT study and its methodology, in order to describe the data base. It then analyzes the data and indicates lessons which are relevant to technological forecasting.

The HINDSIGHT study involved descriptive rather than normative research. It looked at a particular environment—the U.S. defense technology environment—and a specific time period—essentially from 1945 to 1963. The findings of the study probably can be extrapolated into a more general situation, but there are limits which should not be exceeded.

HISTORY, OBJECTIVES, AND DATA BASE

Project HINDSIGHT was established in July, 1965, at the direction of Dr. Harold Brown, then Director of Defense Research and Engineering. The study, a joint effort of the three services, was intended to determine which, if any, policy-controllable factors could markedly influence the efficiency of the Department's Research and Exploratory Development programs. In addition, the study was to measure the return on the DoD's needs for knowledge by answering the question: "In view of the increasing support for scientific and technical investigations by the other departments of the federal government, as well as industry, could not the level of support offered by the DoD be decreased?

The approach taken was rather pragmatic. Operational objectives were established, and the research effort was designed to accommodate them. The objectives, which also defined the limits of the first phase of the study, were:

1. To establish the extent to which new weapon systems are dependent upon the results of recently conducted research in science or technology for an increase in system effectiveness, a decrease in cost, or an increase in cost-effectiveness ratio (as compared to a predecessor system);

2. To determine that portion of the utilized new scientific or technological knowledge that was a result of DoD-financed programs;

3. To determine significant management and other environmental factors, as seen by the research scientist or engineer, that are uniquely correlatable with a high degree of utilization of results.

The field investigations essentially had the following steps:

1. A new weapon system, or end item equipment, which was already in or committed to inventory, was selected for study. Criteria for selection assured that the study would include a representative sampling of equipment types.

2. A team consisting of five to ten scientists and engineers was appointed. The team members generally were from the DoD's in-house laboratories, and were chosen for their expertise in technical areas relevant to the selected system.

3. The team dissected the system into its subsystems and components, to assure thorough analysis. It examined each of these smaller items for novelty and for importance to the system. The purpose of this step was to identify those ideas, devices, materials, fabrication techniques, etc., which, in the judgment of the team, were clearly important to increased performance, reliability, or maintainability and which, for lack of contemporary knowledge, could not have been available five, ten, or fifteen years earlier. Clearly, the team was identifying technological growth. In making these judgments, the analyzing teams worked with the weapon system design engineers.

4. Once an item was judged to be novel and significant, it was assigned to one of the team members for further study. He traced the evolution of the idea, component, or material backward in time, identifying the principal contributors, the organizations with which they were working at the time, the nature of the work (i.e., science or technology), the approximate cost, the funding sources, motivations, and similar information. This information was recorded in a standard format, and it constitutes the primary data bank.

Although there were some misgivings at the onset of the study about the ability of physical scientists and engineers to accomplish a job that might better be done by historians, the results demonstrated that, with reasonable effort, the origin of a technical contribution can be traced to a specific time and to specific individuals.

An example of such a trace was the series of activities leading to the availability for switching purposes in radar of a rugged, high-power, hydrogen thyratron. Early in radar history, switching for microwave pulse formation was accomplished through the use of crude spark gap wheels, in which the ionizing medium was air. These early switches had very poor jitter characteristics, poor recovery time, and very short operating lives. The rapidity of deterioration of the electrodes led to the construction of fixed spark gaps in glass envelopes, using various gases, at elevated pressures, for the ionizing medium. The second generation devices, although better than their predecessors, still suffered from rapid erosion of the cathode and build-up of the anode, which changed the breakdown characteristics of the gap. (This problem is closely analogous to the wear-out of the breaker points in automobile ignition systems.) It was clear that a much better switching device was needed. This need was satisfied, and the historical trace developed by the study reveals the following sequence:

1. In 1942, K. Germeshausen, then at the MIT Radiation Laboratories, developed the boxed anode structure which made the basic high-voltage thyratron possible.

2. In 1943, to prevent depletion of the hydrogen gas resulting from capture of the hydrogen ions by impurities in the electrodes, the International Nickel Company, working with Germeshausen, developed an electrolytic refining process for nickel.

3. In 1944, Marsh and Rothstein, of the Army Signal Corps Laboratories, calculated the theoretical internal electric field, identified the source of the internal breakdowns which resulted as the operating voltages were increased, and pointed the direction to new electrode design practices.

4. In 1945, Germeshausen, in collaboration with Marsh and Rothstein, conceived and demonstrated the practicality of the titanium hydride reservoir to compensate for the residual hydrogen clean-up, even with the pure nickel electrodes.

5. During the period 1951–55, Martin, Goldberg, and Riley, all of Edgerton, Germeshausen & Greer Company, as a result of a detailed theoretical and experimental study of the hydrogen gas discharge phenomenon and its effect upon tube life, were able to design a much smaller, more rugged, long-life tube.

6. Finally, in 1957, this latter group developed the high-temperature, metal and ceramic, long-life tube that was used in the AN/SPS-48 radar and so significantly contributed to that radar's performance and reliability.

The actual trace moved backward in time. It started with an examination of the AN/SPS-48 radar, and continued until Germeshausen's original invention was identified.

Each of the individual advances in this series was carefully documented by the study team and each was called an "Event." The set of six Events is quite representative of the type of work which leads to improved system performance. Within the example, it is possible to identify several characteristics which appear to be associated with the growth of technology. First is the overwhelming influence of need orientation. In each case, the identified performers were aware that a technical deficiency existed in equipment that already had been developed or was in the process of being developed. Second, the same names appear over a long time period, which, in this case, exceeded fifteen years; thus a certain degree of stability of personnel is suggested. Third, a number of separately identifiable and discrete activities occurred, and it was the combination of these activities that resulted in the improved capabilities. Fourth, and this may shock the science-oriented person, these very practical, even "pedestrian," technical efforts were credited with a major role in improving weapon systems. These thoughts afford guidance for analysis of the total data base for relevant lessons.

EVENTS

The quantifying unit for the study was the Research or Exploratory Development (RXD) Event. The Event is simply the birth of new or important scientific or technical information, or the synthesis of information into an important new technological capability. Perhaps the concept of the Event is somewhat more clearly defined in the following manner: Picture an individual or a small group of scientists or engineers busily at work in routine duties. Suddenly, one of them, in a burst of creativity, recognizes a previously obscured phenomenon or invents a new material or a new device. This process can be considered as having two separate phases—the conceiving of the idea, and the test of the validity or feasibility of the idea— or the two can be taken together, as was done in Project HINDSIGHT, and called an "Event."

Figure 1 lists the systems that were studied, the number of such Events that were fully analyzed, and any predecessor systems. Of the Events originally identified by the analing teams, about 30–90 per cent, depending upon the system, were studied in detail. The Events which apparently had the greatest impact on the system were studied first. In each system, study was continued until analysis showed a relatively unchanging pattern among the parameters of interest. The twenty systems contributed a total of 835 analyzed Events of which 710 were distinct; i.e., 125 Events were identified in more than one system.

Confidence in the sample is high. The properties of the sample have not changed substantially from the time the data base had fewer than 100 Events, taken from seven systems. Further, the use of thirteen autonomous teams, generally from in-house laboratories, but also including a significant number of individuals from industry and nonprofit corporations, served to minimize the consequence of biases.

System	Number of Events	Predecessor System
Hound Dog ASM (Air to Surface Missile)	23	——————
Bullpup ASM	42	——————
Polaris A-1 SLBM (Sea Launched Ballistic Missile)	49	——————
Minuteman I ICBM (Intercontinental Ballistic Missile)	47	——————
Minuteman II ICBM	31	MM I
Sergeant TBM (Tactical Ballistic Missile)	20	Corporal
Lance TBM	127	Honest John
Mark 46 MOD 0 Torpedo Mark 46 MOD 1 Torpedo	48	Mark 44
M-102; 105MM Howitzer	2	M2A1 Howitzer
AN/SPS-48 Radar	86	SP Radar
Mark 56 Sea Mine Mark 57 Sea Mine	144	Mark 9 Mark 10
Starlight Scope	18	——————
C-141 Aircraft	81	C-130
Navigation Satellite	26	——————
M-61 Nuclear Warhead * M-63 Nuclear Warhead *	26	——————
XM-409; 152MM Heat MP (Artillery Round)	16	——————
Fadac Computer	49	——————

Total Events—835
Discrete Events—710
* Non-nuclear components only

Figure 1. Systems Studied

LESSONS FROM PROJECT HINDSIGHT

These data suggest several points that might be relevant to the processes of technological growth. First, in describing the example of the growth of the thyratron technology, note was made of the influence of need orientation. The need orientation factor was studied in depth because it was so obviously relevant to the matter of uniqueness of the DoD's needs for knowledge. For example, the performers of the RXD Events, or their immediate supervisors, were asked: "What was the objective of the work?" or "What led you into this area of research?" The results of an analysis of their answers are shown in Figure 2. Most significant is the fact that, in the case of both science and technology, a DoD need was usually cited as the motivational factor.

Next, weapon systems tend to evolve through one of two general patterns. Some go through an extended period of system concept attention and pre-

	Science	Motivated by DoD Need
Applied—DoD oriented research	7.0%	7.0%
Applied—Non-DoD research	2.0%	
Undirected research	(.1%)	
	9.0%	
Technology		
Generic—DoD oriented	27%	27%
A system in advanced development or a system-concept	41%	41%
A system in engineering development or operational system development	20%	20%
Non-DoD oriented	3%	
	91%	95%

Figure 2. Research Objective

prototype development. Operational objectives or specifications are established, and an optimum configuration is gradually developed to satisfy those specifications. In the other class, an assessment is made of the technological state of the art; judgments conclude that a system can be built to satisfy some operational objective; and a well-defined system development contract is let.

Figure 3 depicts the Event distribution for a system that has gone through the extended development route. Relevant scientific and technical

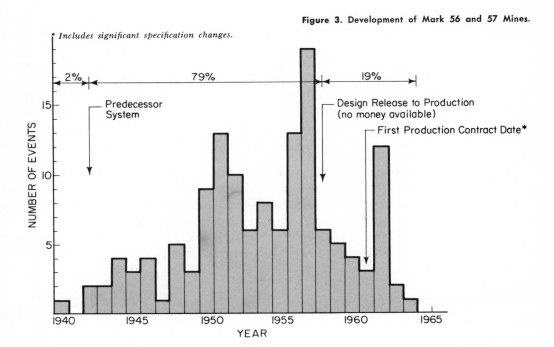

Figure 3. Development of Mark 56 and 57 Mines.

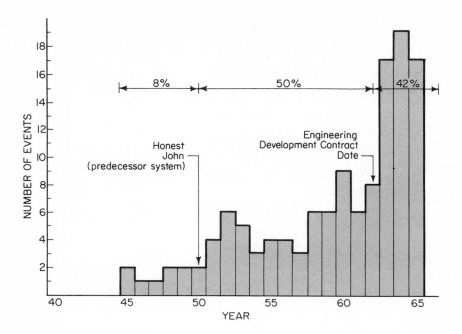

Figure 4. Lance Missile System.

knowledge was accreted at a gradually but steadily increasing rate until a demonstration prototype was in hand. This was followed by a rapid drop, until a decision was made to go into manufacturing. The spike in 1962 correlates with a marked change in specifications, doubling the operating depth of the mine and introducing a need for much stronger nonmagnetic materials, new lead seal techniques, new test techniques, and the like.

Figure 4 depicts the other class of systems. To the extent that there was some system concept attention, some focus was provided. However, as compared with the preceding figure, the relatively slow rate of accretion of knowledge prior to the letting of the development contract and the doubling of the rate of progress within a year after the contract date clearly suggest a different forcing function at work, or a different response to a forcing function.

In order to avoid the dangers of inferring too much from single examples, the entire data base was presented in the format shown in Figure 5. To develop the figure, the systems were separated into two groups: those which evolved through an extended period of pre-prototype development, and those which essentially moved directly from a technological base to final system development. The data were normalized to a time zero—the date at which each system went into the system development phase. The upper curve describes the accretion of knowledge where system concept attention was allowed to spur and provide focus to the development of the knowledge. The lower curve describes the consequence of a more random process in which individual technologists were permitted to determine what would be important to steer the technology programs. It is clear that where a systems engineering approach was taken for the definition of technological goals, the rate of accretion of utilized knowledge was faster.

Where the pre-prototype developments which provided information for the upper curve had been funded, where an attempt was being made to design and fabricate a useful equipment, or where real problems were being encountered in the process, a set of needs were, in a sense, being established. The response to these needs resulted in the better-focused technological growth.

Figure 5. Technical Confidence Level (Time Before or After Engineering Development Decision Date).

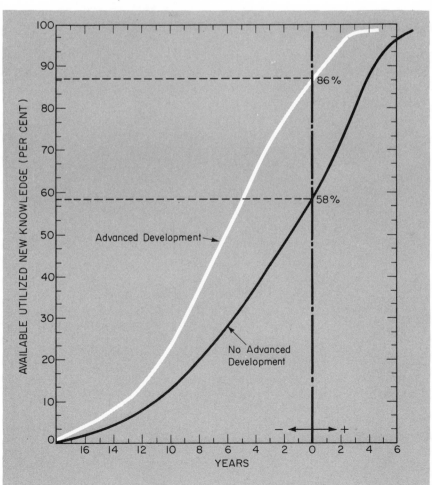

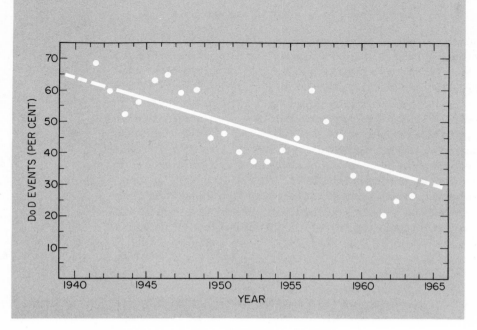

Figure 6. DOD In-House Activity (Percentage of All Events vs. Time).

The first conclusion of the study is that real needs result in accelerated technological growth. Conversely, in the absence of real needs, technological growth is inhibited.

A factor of interest, suggested by the thyratron example, was the characteristics of the scientists and engineers involved in the growth of technology. The task of coming to grips, meaningfully, with this factor required a somewhat circuitous course; in fact, the first clue was obtained rather serendipitously. Figure 6 is a time-dependent plot of the relative contributions of the in-house laboratories to the new science and technology being utilized. The curve suggests that the in-house laboratories have played a decreasingly important role. Early in the period they were contributing about 60 per cent of the new knowledge. This percentage gradually decreased so that by the end of the period their contribution was about half that.

The interesting information is really behind the curve. During the time frame, the strength of the in-house laboratories was constrained to a growth factor of about two. In terms of professional strength, the laboratories were about twice as strong in 1963 as they were in 1945 or 1946. Meanwhile, if one accepts Professor Derek Price's analyses,[2] the entire population of the

---

[2] D. J. de Solla Price, "A Calculus of Science," *International Science and Technology,* March, 1963, pp. 41ff.

R&D community increased by a factor of four. This suggests that the decrease in relative productivity of the in-house laboratory is a measure, not of change in the relative quality of these laboratories, but of the relative quantity of available scientific and engineering personnel.

The suggestion was tested by examining the absolute productivity of the in-house laboratories. The results are shown in Figure 7, which indicates a correlation between the increase in absolute output and the increase in manpower. Thus, *the second conclusion of relevance to technological forecasting* which emerges is that the growth of knowledge relates directly to the number of scientists and engineers involved in the relevant technical areas. The expression "growth of knowledge," rather than "growth of technology," has been used deliberately because, as will be shown later, the two are not necessarily the same.

Some refinements of the second conclusion can be made. During the course of the field investigations, detailed résumés were collected from the individuals who were identified as having been productive. These résumés were compared with other available data in the following ways. First, a distribution by level of education was made. In Figure 8, the findings are compared with those of other similar studies. The comparisons suggest that, not only are the number of scientists and engineers important, but also their relative levels of educational achievement.

Next, the mobility of the productive scientific and engineering group was

Figure 7. DOD In-House Activity (Number of Events vs. Time).

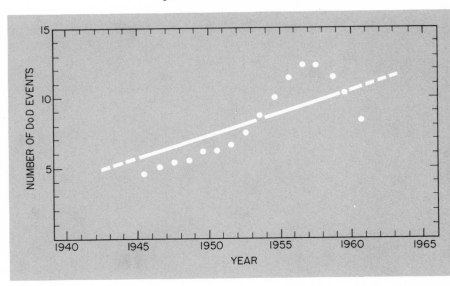

Highest Degree Held	Hindsight	NORC [1]	SRI [2]	NSF [3]	EJC [4]
PhD	10.5%	3.1%	1.2%	3.8%	( )
MS	22.5%	8.6%	7.2%		(63%)
BS	57.0%	34.6%	47.0%		( )
Some college	6.8%	39.5%	( )		( )
			(44.6%)		(37%)
No college	3.2%	14.2%	( )		( )

Notes:

[1] Worker and Marsh, *The Education and Training of America's Scientists and Engineers, 1962*, NORC, University of Chicago, 1965, p. 17.

[2] A. Shapero, R. P. Howell, and J. R. Tombaugh, *An Exploratory Study of the Structure and Dynamics of the R&D Industry,"* Stanford Research Institute, June, 1964, p. 31.

[3] *Profiles of Manpower in Science and Technology,* National Science Foundation, NSF 63-23, Library of Congress No. 63-60092, 1963, pp. 17ff.

[4] "How Many Engineers?" Engineering Manpower Bulletin #5, Engineers Joint Council.

Figure 8. Educational Level of Identified Performers.

examined. Figure 9 displays the distribution of the number of employers of each of the individuals identified in HINDSIGHT, from the onset of their professional careers until the date in 1966 when their résumés were collected. Considerable discussion within the R&D community about mobility of professional personnel suggests that the distribution of Figure 9 represents an unusually stable portion of the community. The median length of employment of this group at the time their résumés were collected was sixteen years. The median age at which the individual had made his contribution was approximately thirty-five (about 10–12 years after going to work). Thus,

Figure 9. Employee Mobility.

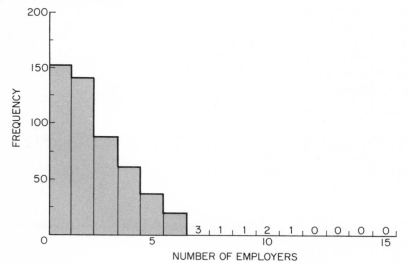

FREQUENCY

NUMBER OF EMPLOYERS

the fact that 60 per cent had two employers or less could not be explained by the possibility that these employees were very young and did not yet have time to move.

Shapero, Howell, and Tombaugh report, in their studies of defense industry R&D personnel in the Boston and Los Angeles areas, that over 75 per cent of the professional personnel currently employed have had two or more employers.[3] The median age of their sample was about ten years lower than that of the HINDSIGHT sample. This comparison certainly supports the hypothesis that the HINDSIGHT-identified performers tended to come from the relatively more stable population.

Introducing the education and stability factors into the second conclusion, the lesson becomes: the growth of knowledge relates directly to the number of stable, better-educated scientists and engineers involved in the relevant technical areas.

Some interesting analyses are possible in regard to the relationship of the growth of knowledge to the growth of technology. Of the twenty systems investigated by Project HINDSIGHT, ten had reasonably well-defined predecessors for which it was possible to make first order approximations of relative cost-effectiveness ratios.[4] Figure 10 is a regression curve demonstrating the relationship between the relative product improvement, the sophistication of the predecessor equipment, and the number of increments of new knowledge that were identified as being responsible for the cost or performance difference between the successive generations of equipment. Sophistication of the predecessor was measured in a rather common fashion, by noting its procurement cost in dollars per pound.

If each Event is the equivalent of an increment of knowledge (and from the definition, this appears to be reasonable) and technological growth is measured in terms of relative cost-effectiveness, then there appears to be a logarithmic relationship between the growth of knowledge and the growth of technology. If it were possible to identify "increments of knowledge actually utilized in the systems," rather than only "recently acquired knowledge," the predecessor sophistication factor would probably not be needed as a correction factor. Unfortunately, there is no obvious way of testing such an hypothesis.

The finding of a logarithmic relationship between knowledge and system capability is not surprising. A typical experience is that successive improvements in any effort tend to be increasingly difficult to achieve. According to

---

[3] A. Shapero, R. P. Howell, and J. R. Tombaugh, *The Structure and Dynamics of the Defense R&D Industry; The Los Angeles and Boston Complexes,* Stanford Research Institute, November, 1965, pp. 45–49.

[4] Note that the actual ratio calculated is the measure of effectiveness divided by the cost.

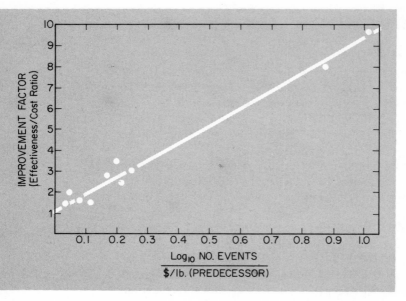

Figure 10. Increased Cost-Effectiveness as a Function of Knowledge Added.

the old and apparently valid cliché, "one approaches perfection asymptotically."

The particular analysis described above was limited to cases of successive, similar systems, and the analysis tended to look at relatively well-established technologies. Thus, a provisional conclusion can be offered: for relatively well-established technologies, a constant rate of growth in relevant knowledge will result in a decreasing rate of growth in technological capability. This suggests a corollary hypothesis for new technologies: the rate of growth of technological capability exceeds the rate which might be inferred from the rate of growth of knowledge.

Having identified the relationship shown in Figure 10, it is possible to calculate the number of Events that should be required to achieve a given increase in cost-effectiveness for predecessor-successor pairs of equipments. Interestingly enough, where the successor uses a completely different technology or set of technologies than did its predecessor (to achieve the same type of operational capability), the calculated "required number of Events" greatly exceeds the number actually identified by the study. For example, the curve suggests that, in order to progress from the cost-effectiveness of the World War II vintage, active, infrared night-viewing devices to that of the new image amplifier, Starlight Scope, approximately a thousand Events would be required. Actually, Figure 1 noted that eighteen Events were adequate, perhaps as a consequence of the technological shift. This example is far from sufficient to demonstrate the validity of the corollary hypothesis, but it does identify the limited applicability of the Figure 10 relationship.

Thus, *the third conclusion of apparent relevance to technological forecasting* is better stated thus: where increased operational capability is dependent upon advances in an unchanging set of technologies, a constant rate of growth in relevant knowledge will result in a decreasing rate of growth in operational capability.

In addition to identifying and studying the RXD Events leading to the twenty systems, Project HINDSIGHT is using the identified Events for a number of behavioral science studies. These studies, underway at the Sloan School of Business at MIT and at Northwestern University, are considering such matters as: idea flow, information retrieval, skill development, task selection, and the like. In general, there was no attempt to include these matters in the Phase 1 study from which the previously described data were drawn, and only a limited amount of attention was given to them.

For most Events, it was possible to establish gross characteristics of the idea flow mechanism. As an idea progressed from one Event to a succeeding Event, in some way the second individual, or group, learned of the activities of the first. Figure 11 displays the distribution of transfer mechanisms. The interesting factor is the relative dominance of the informal person-to-person confrontation as the propagating mode. Surprisingly, even in the case of science, the informal link is about as important as the published paper. This observation suggests that the growth of technology is sensitive to the relative ability of the involved scientists and engineers to communicate freely. It also suggests that technical publications are not adequate to provide the requisite degree of communications.

The in-house laboratories of the military services have a number of responsibilities in the general scheme of things: they conduct scientific and technical investigations; they provide consultant services to the military staffs on technical problems; and they are expected, encouraged, and funded to maintain close personal communications with the national scientific and

Figure 11. Idea Transfer Mechanism.

Activity	Personal Contact	Publication or Report	Seminar or Symposium
Science	45%	53%	2%
Technology	64%	33%	3%
Engineering (design)	79%	21%	0
Engineering (mfg. technique)	77%	23%	0

Number of Events	In-House Laboratory	Industry	University
One	25% *	64%	11% **
Two or more	31%	56%	13%
Four or more	36%	52%	12%
Six or more	50%	29%	21%
Eight or more	45%	36%	19%
Ten or more	60%	20%	20%

* Figures are percentiles of rate class (horizontal rows).
** Including university research centers.

Figure 12. Event Participation Frequency by Organization Class.

technical community so as to provide the Department of Defense with a window into science.

Because there are relatively few in-house laboratories (compared to the number of industrial organizations that are involved in military research and development), the opportunities for informal, person-to-person communications for determining needs or for passing ideas are more concentrated in government organizations. Thus, if these informal communications links are important, the productivity per organization should be greater in the in-house laboratories.

A count was made of the number of Events that had occurred in each of some 300 identified organizations and an analysis was made of the frequency of participation for each type of organization. The resultant distribution is shown in Figure 12. The hypothesis is supported. Even though industry, as a class, contributed a greater total number of Events than did the in-house laboratories, an individual in-house laboratory was far more likely to contribute heavily, if it contributed at all.

Unfortunately, factors other than communications undoubtedly are accountable for part of this distribution unbalance. For example, there is a greater stability, as a rule, among the civil servants of the in-house laboratories than is typical within industry. The apparent importance of the stability factor was previously noted. Thus, although the hypothesis is supported, its validity has not really been proven. At least, however, this proposition can be offered: The rate of growth of knowledge is directly related to the relative level of informal, person-to-person communications in the flow of problem statements and solution ideas.

Finally, there are two interrelated thoughts that tend more to describe what constitutes technological growth than to identify forcing functions. Nevertheless, they appear to be important because they describe the process itself.

Having observed the ease with which 50 to 100 Events were readily identified through each of the larger systems, and having examined the interrelationship between these many Events, the Project HINDSIGHT report concluded: "Engineering design of improved military weapon systems consists primarily of skillfully selecting and integrating a large number of innovations, from diverse technological areas so as to produce synergistically, the high performance achieved."

At the onset of the pilot studies that preceded Project HINDSIGHT, it was believed that it would be possible to identify a few, really key ideas or Events to which the advanced capability of a new weapon system could be attributed. The eventual realization that, in terms of a weapon system, the concept of relative value among contributing Events has little merit, did not come easily. But this certainly appears to be the case. It is the many Events, or their equivalents, all working in unison, that makes the difference. As an example, transistor technology is credited with being responsible for size reduction in electronic equipments. However, without the development of such ancillary technologies as tantalytic capacitors, high core-permeability chokes and transformers, printed circuits, dip soldering, nickel-cadmium batteries, and silicon solar cell power supplies, the electronic equipment chassis would be only marginally (perhaps 10 per cent) smaller than a vacuum tube version.

It is clear that all those technological advances, properly integrated, resulted in a small chassis. From the point of view of the circuit designer, all were important. From the point of view of the technological forecaster, as long as he was referring to the entire chassis, all were important also. But there is another aspect of this situation. The transistor was the first of these technologies to appear. In a sense it preceded and forced the development of the others. In fact, the early history of tantalytic capacitors and ferrites demonstrates a marked lack of interest until the advent of the transistor and the realization that oil or wax electrolytic capacitors and iron core transformers had to be replaced in order to exploit the small size of the new signal amplifying device.

In the previously described example of the hydrogen thyratron, Germeshausen's invention of the boxed anode provided a somewhat different sort of precursor. Without that anode, the thyratron would not have been. But, given the anode without the other identified Events, the AN/SPS-48 radar might never have been, or, at least, would have been considerably different.

Earlier in this chapter it was noted that HINDSIGHT had analyzed 710 of the apparently more important Events leading to advanced weapon system capability. Note was also made of the fact that this was considerably less than an exhaustive analysis. Estimates suggest that a greater effort could track down at least as many more. Thus, one might be able to find some 1,500 Events. It is not likely that the larger data base would result in sig-

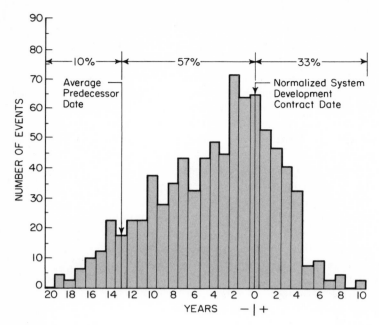

Figure 13. Technological Growth Pattern.

nificantly different conclusions because, as has previously been noted, the properties of the 710 Event sample are very similar to those of the first sample of 100.

Figure 1, listing the systems that were studied, suggests that most of the important technologies of the current weapons inventory were considered. Included were aircraft, liquid and solid propelled missiles, radio and inertially guided missiles, radars, computers, nuclear warheads and conventional high-explosives, night vision devices, tube artillery, mines and torpedoes. Except for ships and boats, and tanks and other land vehicles, the spectrum of types of military systems is reasonably complete. Thus the 710 Events appear to constitute a fairly good-sized sample of the militarily useful technological growth between 1945 and 1963.

A composite histogram of the growth of these technologies is shown in Figure 13. The reference point is the year in which a development contract was let, for each of the systems examined. The histogram records the total number of Events which occurred in the "zero year" for all of the systems and the total number of Events for each predecessor and successor year. The figure shows that the median Event occurred about five to six years before the knowledge was used in a system design. Apparently, it takes about thirteen years, on the average, to accrete enough new knowledge to warrant developing a new design for a successor system.

The primary lesson to be gained is that advancing technology is made up of many relatively pedestrian advances. Each takes time and each takes money. The forecaster must allow for both. However, there are precursor advances that should suggest to him the direction in which technology is most likely to move. These, more than anything else, provide guides for useful technological forecasting.

In 1964, Arthur D. Little, Inc., received a Department of Defense contract to investigate management factors affecting the utilization of the results of research and exploratory development. The effort eventually became part of the pilot studies that led to Project HINDSIGHT. Perhaps the most significant observation made by the A. D. Little participants was:

> "In nearly all Events, the burst of successfully utilized activity constituting the (RXD) Event started only when the following three elements were present:
>
> 1. An explicitly understood need, goal or mission;
> 2. A source of ideas, typically a pool of information, experience and insight in the minds of people who could apply it;
> 3. Resources, usually facilities, materials, money and trained and experienced men, who could be committed to do a job." [5]

Their statements appear to describe the pacing factors of technological growth very succinctly. At no point does the HINDSIGHT study refute their contentions; instead, it demonstrates, amplifies, and enforces their observations. If the technological forecaster seeks measurable criteria upon which to base his projections, the Arthur D. Little statement identifies at least three which are very important.

In summary, Project HINDSIGHT has developed a great deal of quantitative information relevant to the growth and utilization of new science and technology. An analysis of the data provides several lessons which appear to be meaningful to the technological forecaster:

1. Real needs result in accelerated technological growth. In the absence of such needs, technological growth is inhibited.
2. The rate of growth of knowledge is directly related to the rate of change in the number of stable, better-educated scientists and engineers in the relevant technical areas.
3. For relatively well-established technologies, a constant rate of growth in relevant knowledge results in a decreasing rate of growth in technological capability.

[5] G. Raisbeck et al., *Management Factors Affecting Research and Exploratory Development,* Arthur D. Little, Inc., April, 1965.

4. The rate of growth of knowledge is directly related to the relative level of informal, person-to-person communications in the relevant technical areas.

5. Advancing technology is made up of a number of precursor Events and a far greater number of pedestrian accomplishments. The direction of technological growth can be inferred from the former, but the rate of growth will be dictated by the latter.

TECHNIQUES OF TECHNOLOGICAL FORECASTING

PART TWO

By what methods might technological progress be predicted? In this section leading practitioners describe their concepts; most of which are based largely on trend extrapolation or on relationship of a technical parameter to indicators that foreshadow the phenomenon under study. The one exception—the Delphi method—is based on getting a consensus of expert opinion.

Trend extrapolation can be both criticized and defended on the same grounds—realism. Objectors point out that trend extrapolation assumes that past conditions will continue. Technology is treated as a variable independent of the world around it. Neither assumption is true for most technology.

Defenders reply that trend extrapolation is very realistic over limited periods of time because historical data show that society does indeed make progress gradually. The forces influencing technology may affect the *rate of change* in a given technology or the *timing* of introducing a new technology; but they do not change the *evolutionary character of progress.*

Trend extrapolation, therefore, is appropriate for predicting the progress of a given technological element. One author suggests that trends also be used to predict the coming of new capabilities, although not necessarily the nature of the new devices that will achieve these capabilities.

Philosophically speaking, trend extrapolation suggests that technological progress moves through history with a grand sweep, scarcely disturbed by the environment of the times. The discontinuity so apparent to the daily practitioner disappears when viewed over decades. The abrupt, order-of-magnitude gains of recent years then are seen only as points on steeply ascending curves.

The Delphi consensus technique evokes another philosophical concern: Protagonists hold that no forecast could be potentially more promising than the collective wisdom of experts. The opposition replies that the shaky part of the assumption is the belief that experts do indeed have any forecasting wisdom. Collected errors, though mathematically manipulated and elegantly modified, are still errors, they say.

The closing chapter, which compares major known forecasting techniques, makes it clear that all of us are groping toward attempts at understanding technological change. Forecasting is only in its infancy.

Forecasts of Exploding Technologies by Trend Extrapolation

RALPH C. LENZ, JR.

One of the most useful techniques for technological forecasting is trend extrapolation. Devices can be considered as systems of functional characteristics, and the future potential of such characteristics, or capabilities, often can be identified by trend analysis. This chapter deals with the exponential nature of most growth trends, trend construction methodology, and the advantages to be gained and the pitfalls to be avoided when applying this technique.

Mr. Lenz is Technical Director for the Deputy for Advanced Systems Planning, Aeronautical Systems Division, Wright-Patterson Air Force Base. Since 1954, he has been engaged in planning and anticipating the impact of technological progress for the Air Force. His government monograph "Technological Forecasting" is considered to be a landmark in the field.

The views expressed herein are those of the author and do not necessarily reflect the views of the U.S. Air Force or the Department of Defense.

THE MYTHS OF TECHNOLOGICAL FORECASTING

In every age man has bitterly and justly complained that Nature hurried and hustled him . . . Fifty years ago science took for granted that the rate of acceleration could not last . . . [it] encouraged society to think that force would prove to be limited in supply. . . . nothing short of radium fairly wakened men to the fact . . . that force was inexhaustible. . . . the new American—the child of incalculable coal-power, chemical power, electric power, and radiating energy . . . must be a sort of God compared with any former creation of nature. At the rate of progress since 1800, every American who lived into the year 2000 would know how to control unlimited power. He would think in complexities unimaginable to an earlier mind. He would deal with problems altogether beyond the range of earlier society.[1]

As contemporaneous as they sound, these words were written by the eminent historian Henry Adams in the first decade of this century. To Adams, the pattern and force of technological advance were explosive, as evidenced by the following:

> One might use the formula of chemical explosion [for the measurement of progress]. The force evolved seemed like explosion, and followed closely the curve of steam [power increase]. . . . the man of science must have been sleepy indeed who did not jump from his chair like a scared dog when, in 1898, Mme. Curie threw on his desk the metaphysical bomb she called radium. . . . So long as the rates of progress held good, these bombs [of progress] would double in force and number every ten years.[2]

These quotations should dispel the myth that this generation is the first to face the problem of rapidly advancing technology.

Somewhat more difficult to deal with in the practice of technological forecasting are two moral mythologies from engineering and religion. That part of engineering education which demands, and pretends to supply, absolute answers is often the basis for rejecting technological forecasts, which cannot be proven right or wrong, except uselessly, after the fact. Religious education tends to reserve knowledge of the future for the Deity. This results in superstitious attitudes toward all forecasts and particularly toward forecasts of scientific discoveries, which are considered impious in themselves. Lying between engineering prediction and religious prophecy, the technological forecast is neither; as Professor Warren Bennis has said: "It lacks the empirical foundation of the former and the divine guidance of the latter." [3]

The myth that progress is dependent upon the chance occurrence of individual genius has been thoroughly disposed of by Dr. Gilfillan and others. It continues, however, to be invoked in the deification of scientific folk heroes. Another myth, dealt with below, charges semilogarithmic graph paper with the possession of occult powers which distort honest data and extort false forecasts.

Adherence to these myths is reflected in the case histories of many companies. Although explicit forecasts often are not available for examination,

---

[1] Henry Adams, *The Education of Henry Adams* (New York: The Modern Library, 1931), pp. 493–96.

[2] *Ibid.*, pp. 452, 491, 492, 494.

[3] Warren G. Bennis, "Organizational Developments and the Fate of Bureaucracy," *MIT Industrial Management Review*, Spring, 1966.

actions which determine the future of a company may be used to deduce the type of forecast implicit in those actions. A few typical examples will illustrate methods of forecasting which should be avoided. The weaknesses of these methods of forecasting seem painfully obvious, and the consequences almost self-evident, yet these practices are found often enough to indicate that further warning is needed.

FORECASTING METHODS TO BE AVOIDED

The first of these examples, the actual case of "no forecast," occurs in transient situations where actions are unrelated to past experience, the present situation, or future probabilities. It is based on the idea that many discoveries have been and will continue to be made, but that no pattern can be discerned. As one moves from the "development" end of the scale toward the "research" end, an increasing tendency toward the "no forecast" situation may often be observed. This is difficult to rationalize, except for the case of the self-supported researcher working alone, since the commitment of resources is ordinarily based upon expectation of improvement. A long and loud insistence that no forecast of improvement is possible may well result in withdrawal of resources.

Second is the group of forecasts implicit in actions based on some knowledge of odds and stakes, with the assumption that external forces are randomly controlled. Such forecasts are successful in the event of a lucky run by a gambling management. This forecast is a random walk: it produces spectacular successes and equally spectacular failures. Characteristic of the failures is the commitment of large funds to development efforts, without understanding either the trends of prior progress or the present status of the technology. Examples of failure tend to be controversial; however, mechanical scanners for television in the 1920's and 1930's, jet engines for automobiles in the 1950's, the Comet jet transport, vertical takeoff fighter aircraft in the 1950's, and variable-sweep aircraft in the 1935–1955 period may be examined for evidence of this type of forecasting error.

In the third type, the forecast is characterized by the use of precedent as a basis for decision—in memory of a glorious past. A tradition-bound management implicitly acknowledges this forecast. When plotted, the forecast shows little recognition of past progress and negligible progress in the future. Oddly enough, some R&D organizations making this type of forecast are most demanding and insatiable in their requests for funds. Decisions based on the precedents of a glorious past err either by underestimating the rate of progress which could be attained by a new approach or by commitment of large funds for marginal improvements in exhausted areas of technology. Thus, no amount of money spent for research on candles would have made them competitive with Edison's incandescent lamp, nor would the efficiency of nylon for sails have overcome the advantages of steam. More recently, part of the money spent in reciprocating engine development during the late thirties might have been more equitably apportioned to jet engine research and development.

Fourth is the forecast that current circumstances will continue, leading to "panic button" management. This type of forecasting provides a new problem every day. If a company survives, the situation may be tolerable, since the constant supply of new problems eliminates the need for solutions of the old ones. A plot of this forecast shows multiple, concurrent, and divergent predictions, subject to frequent and erratic change. The "panic-button" environment permits little time and support for research. This environment also wastes time and money in development, by funding for the clearly impossible, followed by continual redirection and eventual termination of projects.

Fifth is the forecast that existing "trends" will continue. This is "window-blind forecasting"—an extension of existing abilities to go higher, faster, further, bigger, and better, with more of everything being the characteristic adjective. When plotted, this forecast errs by extending short-term trends, and forgetting common sense. The rising popularity of technological forecasting has produced, in the popular and technical press and in many companies, more or less sophisticated forecasts based on continuation of existing trends. Often these projected trends are products of accretion instead of progress. It is as if a man were to plot the increase of his waistline as a measure of his growing strength, or the recession of his hairline as a measure of increasing intelligence. Frequently, the forecasts assume continuation of recent rates of advance, with blind avoidance of long-term trend implications.

The sixth type involves intuitive forecasting on the basis of individual genius or competence. This method is effective, but impossible to teach and expensive to learn. It is essentially an autobiography of remembered events and pronouncements by the oracle of events to come. If a certified forecasting genius is available, he should be used. If he is president of the company, there may be no other choice. However, thought should be given to the possibility that a series of past successes in forecasting may not be proof of infallibility. Also, in the case of irrevocable commitment to the genius method, some thought should be given to the replacement problem.

FORECASTING BY TREND EXTRAPOLATION

Forecasting by trend extrapolation, if carefully done, offers a useful way of avoiding the errors just discussed. This paper examines the basis for using trend extrapolation in technological forecasting, and the premises which govern the rules to be used.

Henry Adams observed that the speed of progress after 1500 was "as though it were the acceleration of a falling body," [4] and that "one might tentatively carry back the same ratio of acceleration to the year 1400." [5] Others have also presented evidence of such rates in technological progress, and one might, therefore, reasonably assume that exponential progress is an inherent characteristic of Western civilization. However, this pattern need not be accepted solely on the basis of empirical evidence, since the process which leads to such progress can furnish an explanation. The clue may be found in our use of *biological* terms to describe almost every facet of discovery, invention, and innovation. Such terms as "conceptual phase," "father of the idea," "embryonic phase of the development," "technological maturity," "body of thought," "fertile inventor," and "technological growth," should seem strange and awkward. However, common usage of these terms indicates an intuitive understanding of the existence of biological analogies for technological progress.

One of the biological analogies is the process of cellular growth. In this analogy, as shown in Figure 1, each invention gives rise to another. Two then exist. They, in turn, divide, giving four, and so on in an exponential increase. This holds true for the first fifteen years of patents in several technical fields, such as cotton machinery, the airplane, and radio, and in the production of scientific papers.

Exponential growth tapers off when the technical area becomes so large that it competes seriously with other areas for funding, or when the technical field becomes "mature." As one aspect of maturity, Dr. Gilfillan has noted that, when a technical field becomes specialized, standardized, and over-organized, limits are placed on improvement in that field.

Pearl's method of population forecasting uses the growth of biological organisms as an analogue for the growth of population within a given geographic area. This analogue may also be used for predicting technical progress. The characteristic feature of this approach is the forecasting of exponential growth which tapers asymptotically to an upper limit. In the absence of a known, unalterable, upper limit, Pearl's formula reduces to a constant exponential increase. Thus, technological progress generally may be forecast as an extension of established exponential trends, in the absence of known or evidential limiting restrictions.

The taboos commonly invoked against semilogarithmic graph paper have been mentioned previously. However, if it is accepted that the common rule of progress is exponential increase, then it is only logical to plot the time-series data on semilogarithmic paper where such trends are observed as straight lines.

---

4 *The Education of Henry Adams*, p. 484.
5 *Ibid.*, p. 492.

BIOLOGICAL GROWTH		TECHNICAL IMPROVEMENT

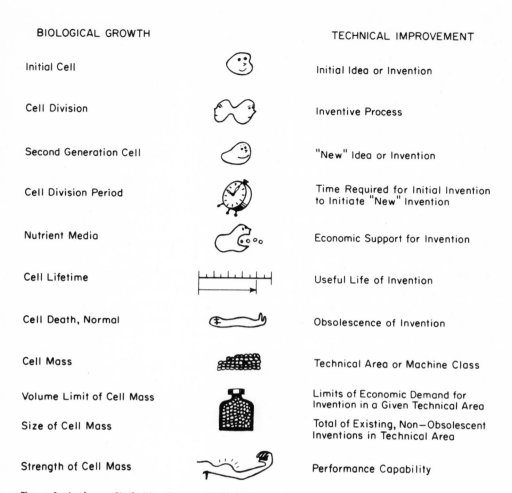

BIOLOGICAL GROWTH	TECHNICAL IMPROVEMENT
Initial Cell	Initial Idea or Invention
Cell Division	Inventive Process
Second Generation Cell	"New" Idea or Invention
Cell Division Period	Time Required for Initial Invention to Initiate "New" Invention
Nutrient Media	Economic Support for Invention
Cell Lifetime	Useful Life of Invention
Cell Death, Normal	Obsolescence of Invention
Cell Mass	Technical Area or Machine Class
Volume Limit of Cell Mass	Limits of Economic Demand for Invention in a Given Technical Area
Size of Cell Mass	Total of Existing, Non–Obsolescent Inventions in Technical Area
Strength of Cell Mass	Performance Capability

Figure 1. Analogue Similarities Between Biological Growth and Technical Improvement, on the Basis of Cellular Division.

With these general rules in mind the selection of parameters for forecasting may be considered. For most organizations the selection should start with determination of product or service objectives. A company that has an objective to produce better light bulbs may select parameters which differ from those of a company whose objective is to provide devices for illumination of work, study, and play areas. Once the product or service objectives are known, knowledgeable persons should be asked to identify characteristics of the product or service which have been, or can be, improved. The characteristics should be as broad as possible so that a minimum number will encompass the objectives, but they must be capable of quantification and measurement. Thus, progress in illumination might be measured by the parameters of lumens per unit of energy and cost per lumen.

When agreement has been reached on the principal parameters that are identified with progress, "demand" factors related to these parameters should be listed for subsequent regression analysis. Demand factors might include production hours, disposable time and income, educational levels, and other factors related to use of illumination. This should be followed by the selection of a structured set of parameters which contribute to progress in the principal parameters. These secondary parameters may be viewed as "supply" factors, and should be considered in terms of possible contribution to the principal parameters selected. Examples of secondary trend factors in illumination might be cost per unit of energy, energy conversion efficiencics, and properties of materials at high temperature.

One other set of parameters must also be identified—the category of "competitive" trends. The number of such competitive trends is inversely proportional to the narrowness of scope of the original objective and its associated principal parameters. If the objective is better light bulbs, competitive trends must be identified for other sources of illumination. If the objective is devices for illumination, the trends for sources of illumination become "supply" trends, and the external competitive factors are those which eliminate or reduce the need for illumination.

Obviously, this process produces a long list of parameters for which trends may be established. To start with the overall parameters at the top may be most difficult, but if the trend of progress is unknown at the general level, then definition of trends at sublevels may be quite misleading. In practice, each echelon or segment of the organization is probably best qualified to establish trends in the product elements for which it is responsible. Trend data should flow in both directions; i.e., broad parameters should be dissected to identify component trends, and trends in subelements should be synthesized to obtain major trends. The primary guide in parameter selection at any level is the utility of the trend for guidance in decision making. The most beautiful trends are useless unless they contribute to a necessary decision.

When useful parameters have been selected for trend extrapolation, the next problem is the gathering of data. Time-series data are plentiful for parameters which can be quantified by counting, such as numbers of people, dollars, automobiles, and kilowatts. Time series for performance parameters such as speed, horsepower, energy, strength, payload, and resolution, which must be carefully measured under standard conditions, are scarce. Certified record performances, although accurate, are often useless because they are accomplished by freak equipment under artificial conditions, and therefore fail to represent the true state of technology. Arduous searching and careful checking are usually required to insure that performance data represent the achieved performance for the specified point in time.

At the gross level, the *Statistical Abstract of the United States,* the *Historical Statistics of the United States,* and their source documents provide some useful time series. These time series may be used both as a source of basic data and for practice in the techniques of trend forecasting. However, most forecasts require original research, and will continue to until a body of reliable and accepted data is established.

The first point of data to be obtained is that which satisfactorily identifies the present level of capability for the selected parameter. Men who can readily identify the principal parameters of progress in their field are not uncommon, but men who can quickly and positively state current capabilities in those parameters are surprisingly rare. Once current capability is determined, and an appropriate unit of measurement is agreed upon, the next step is *not* to extrapolate from this point. To the statistician, such an error should be obvious; to some forecasters, it seems to be the primrose path.

Once the present level of capability has been determined, the next step should be the gathering of capability data as far back toward the origins of the selected parameter as possible, but at least as far into the past as the forecast plans to extend into the future. Sources of performance data in any technical area are usually known to the experts in those fields. If records of performance for the selected parameters are available, the problem of data gathering is simple. Often, however, performance must be derived from indirect evidence and known relationships. As an example, average installed efficiencies of thermal power plants can be derived from statistics for fuel consumption and electrical power production. These average efficiencies can be converted to efficiencies for new installations, for specified years, by correcting them for average installation life-times. Whatever this process lacks in accuracy is compensated for by the smoothing of otherwise erratic data which may not reflect sustainable rates of progress. Where data are not available for early periods of a technology, it is often useful to extend trends backward to these periods on the basis of rough approximations. Thus, if recent history indicates doubling of a given capability in seven years, and the technology is twenty-one years old, the present capability may be divided by eight (2^3), and the resultant value checked to see if it represents a reasonable threshold figure for the initial performance at a useful level.

When satisfactory time-series data for the selected parameter have been gathered, the next step is to plot the data on semilogarithmic graph paper. The trend is that straight line which, to the expert in the field, matches the data points in a manner best describing the trend of attained progress. In establishing the trend line, deviations from the straight-line exponential trend generally invalidate any subsequent extrapolation, unless fully explainable. For example, a regular decrease in rate of progress, as a result of maturity or boundary conditions, may justify an extrapolation which continues the diminishment of the rate of increase. If a straight-line trend has been established, the forecast is accomplished simply by extension of the trend. If a regular change in the exponential rate has been established, the continuation of this regular change may be used to calculate future values.

A most common error at this point is the tendency to hedge the forecast by establishing a broad-band trend which can be used to absolve the predictor of blame for a bad forecast. The forecast may, of course, include conditional "ifs" to provide alternate forecasts. Even so, if the forecasts are to be useful for decision-making purposes, they should be as precise as the nature of the decision requires.

An application of these general rules may be demonstrated by the trend of average horsepower per automotive vehicle. It may be argued that an increase in horsepower for the average automobile is not necessarily a mark of progress, yet the regularity of increase in this time series, as shown in Figure 2, indicates both significant demand and continuing effort to fill this demand.

Figure 2. Average Automotive Horsepower (Data Points Derived from Total Horsepower Divided by Total Vehicles).

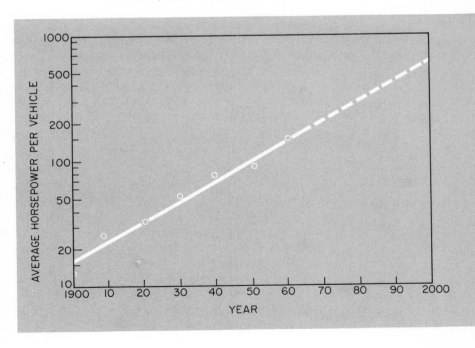

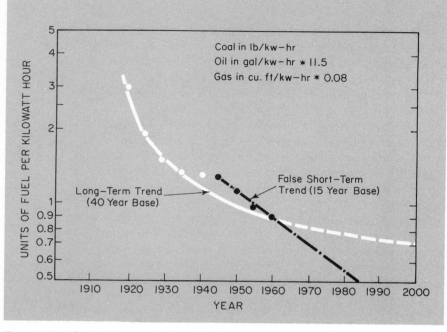

Figure 3. Specific Fuel Consumption-Electrical Generating Plants.

Figure 4. Speed Trends of U.S. Combat Aircraft.

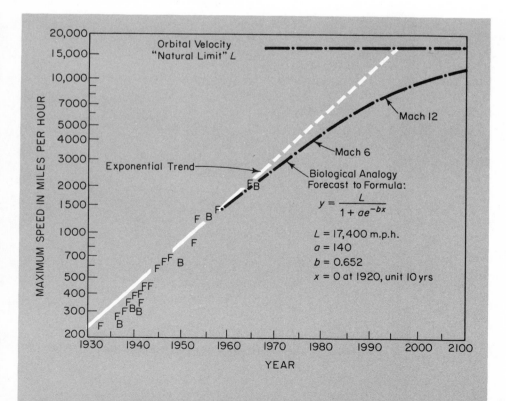

Figure 3 showing the trend of power plant fuel consumption, demonstrates the characteristic of a regular decrease in rate of progress, as shown by the long-term trend from 1920 through 1960. It may also be noted from this figure that the data for the most recent fifteen-year period (from 1945 to 1960) show a constant exponential rate of progress. Since the slowing of progress from 1930 to 1945 may be accounted for by the effects of economic depression and war, the long-term trend would appear to have greater validity for trend forecasting purposes.

Aircraft speed trends may be examined for an application of the biological analogy. To provide a comparison of the exponential trend method with the biological analogy, both are shown in Figure 4. The fixed growth limit is chosen as the speed representing orbital velocity at 100 miles altitude. This may be assumed to be the point at which spacecraft become fully competitive with aircraft, or alternatively, the point beyond which the vehicles cease to be aircraft. As shown, application of Pearl's formula results in an extrapolation asymptotic to this limit. According to this forecast, Mach 6 performance would not be expected until 1979. Mach 12 performance would not be achieved until 1995, ten years later than predicted by the exponential trend.

Some trends may be extrapolated on the basis of events which have already happened. The "lead trend" or "lead event" technique has three major elements. The first is a definite causal relationship between the "lead" and "follower" trends. The second is the existence of nonvariable restraints in the relationship. The third is the accurate establishment of the "lead trend."

To exemplify the lead-follower trend extrapolation method, the relationship between commercial transport aircraft speeds and combat aircraft speeds may be used. In this case the transport speeds follow the combat aircraft speed trends with some degree of regularity and consistency. As shown in Figure 5, the transport speed performance is approximately 52 per cent of the combat aircraft speed trend at any given point in time. The causal factor in this relationship has been presumed to be the dependence of transport development upon military expenditures for pioneering research and development. Possibly a more important causal element has been the proof of advanced technology and the definition of associated cost factors provided by military aircraft. The most apparent restraint in this relationship is the time required to develop and produce the commercial transport after a development decision, based on military aircraft demonstration, has been made. If the established trend of combat aircraft speed is accepted, then Mach 2.2 transport speeds should be expected by 1972, Mach 2.7 by 1975, and Mach 6 about 1994. It may be noted that the transport trend, in lagging behind combat speed trends by 48 per cent, has a regularly increasing lag in terms of years, so that the nine-year lag in 1930 increased to ten by 1950, to eleven years by 1970, and to thirteen years by 1990.

The most effective employment of trend extrapolation lies in the use of multiple, interdependent relationships among as many trends as possible. Where known physical relationships exist between two or more factors, the trend curves may be adjusted to the time series for each factor so as to maintain the proper physical relationship.

A simple example of such a forecast is the relationship of passenger capacity, passenger-miles, load factor, and total plane miles for domestic trunk airline operations. Trends for each of these four factors may be extrapolated independently. However, the four factors are not independent

Figure 5. Speed Trends of Combat vs. Transport Aircraft, Showing Lead Trend Effect.

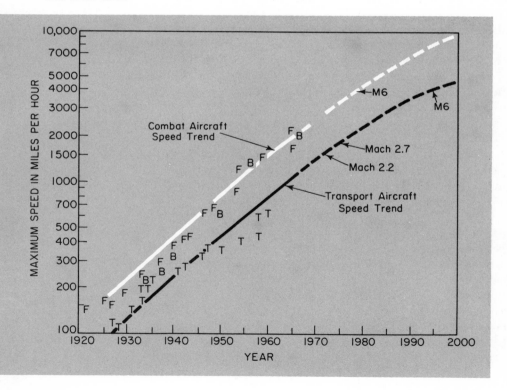

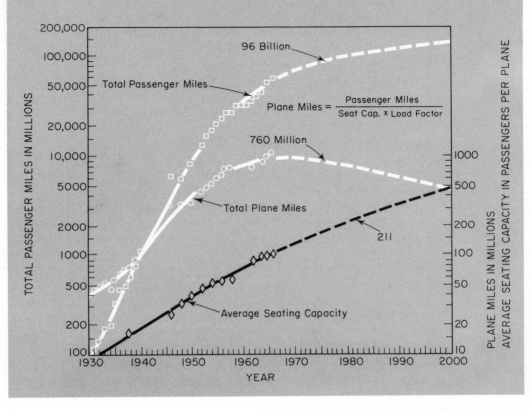

Figure 6. Domestic Trunk Airlines—Multiple Trend Forecast.

but are related as shown in Figure 6. Load factor must be kept within narrow limits for economical operation, so long-term forecasting may assume a single value (60 per cent) for this variable. The passenger-mile trend has been quite consistent in the long term, and the economics of aircraft operation have produced a steady increase in aircraft size. Therefore, total plane miles becomes dependent upon the trends of the other quantities. Somewhat surprisingly, this results in a reversal in the trend of total plane miles, leading to a long-term decline after 1970. The important point is the fixed relationship of these trends, so that extrapolation of any one of the factors must include consideration of the effects of that factor on the trends of the others.

Outline Case Study: Automotive Engine Development

Assuming that the Sterling Motor Company wishes to maintain a profitable position in manufacturing and sales, it must first determine its long-range objectives. The company may decide that its basic objective is the manufacture and sale of devices for the overland transportation of small groups from multiple points-of-origin to multiple destinations, on a nonscheduled basis. Since such devices have been produced and used over some period of time, data concerning capabilities and use should be available. The company may determine trends for such factors as time spent in travel, percentages of disposable income spent on travel, group sizes, and number of vehicles per capita. These trends may be extrapolated to determine possible futures affecting the company and the decisions necessary with respect to those futures.

The Sterling Motor Company may determine, from the trends of vehicles per capita and horsepower per capita which are shown in Figure 7, that satisfaction of per capita horsepower requirements is significant to the company's future. Therefore, it should know how much increase in vehicle horsepower will be necessary if the company is to remain competitive at

Figure 7. Automotive Trends (Horsepower Per Capita and Vehicles Per Capita).

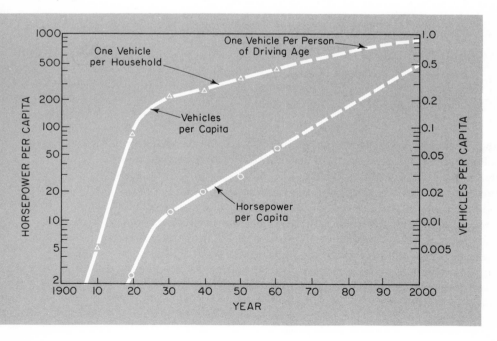

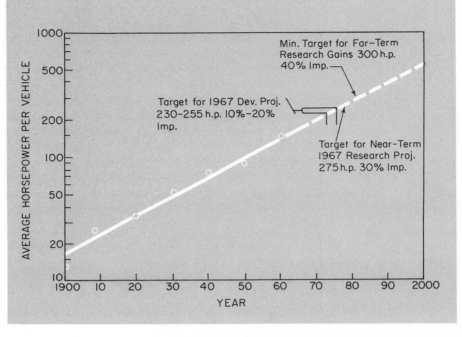

Figure 8. Average Automotive Horsepower (Data Points Derived from Total Horsepower Divided by Total Vehicles).

specified times in future markets. Then efforts may be initiated to attain the required increase. The relationship of the type, quantity, and timing of improvements required indicates the Sterling Motor Company's need for extrapolation of trends in technology.

As previously noted, the time series of average horsepower per vehicle has increased exponentially, doubling every nineteen years. Extrapolation of this trend should provide a forecast of future increases in average horsepower. However, the Sterling Motor Company would do well to examine other trends such as combustion chamber efficiency, engine horsepower-to-weight ratios, and similar performance measures, to determine if some single factor can be identified which clearly leads the average horsepower trend.

Other time series which might be considered for forecasting of interdependent relationships include total automotive fuel consumption as related to total automotive horsepower, specific fuel consumption (miles per horsepower per gallon), and total automotive mileage. Using the horsepower trend shown in Figure 8 as an example, appropriate actions for the Sterling Motor Company may be examined. Since this trend includes all existing automotive vehicles, regardless of age, the average horsepower lags behind the horsepower average of this year's production by 3–4 years. Furthermore, horsepower is set by a "design freeze" some 2–3 years in advance of production, and development must precede "design freeze" by 1–2 years. Therefore, the company must set goals for current short-term development so as to match the predicted trend levels at least 6 years and as much as 9 years in the future. Such development projects should increase average horsepower from 10 per cent to 20 per cent over present production levels, while maintaining current displacement and specific fuel consumption. Research goals for early application should result collectively in increases of not less than 30 per cent, with longer-term research goals resulting in collective gains of 40 per cent or more. If totally new engine concepts must be applied to achieve any predicted power level, without increase in engine weight, then research and development projects on these concepts must be initiated at such times as to enable attainment by the predicted date.

Outline Case Study: Cargo Aircraft Development

The decision process which results in production and use of a new aircraft for cargo transportation involves large numbers of people in the engineering, manufacturing, operating, certifying, and ultimate user agencies. Therefore, this case study does not imply that the technological forecast presented here has been a major factor in any decision leading to a specific aircraft program. Rather it is presented to show how such a forecast may aid in establishing development objectives for such programs.

The characteristics of cargo aircraft which are generally considered to reflect technological progress include size, payload, cruise speed, and range. These and other factors may be combined to obtain job-related figures of merit, such as ton-miles-per-hour and cost-per-ton-mile.

Ton-miles-per-hour is a figure of merit for transportation utility which reflects the combined parameters of speed and payload. Since a regularity of increase exists in this factor, it may be extrapolated to aid in setting development objectives for new aircraft. The time series reveals an exponential trend with groups of new aircraft occurring at roughly $12\frac{1}{2}$-year intervals, as shown in Figure 9. Each such group approximately triples the ton-miles-per-hour capability of the prior "generation." Secondary factors affecting the ton-miles-per-hour figure of merit include speed, payload, range, takeoff and landing characteristics, lift coefficients and many others. Aircraft designs to provide cargo-moving capability are also affected by production and operating costs, by unit costs of cargo, and by many similar factors. Trends of such factors, which are related to the ton-miles-per-hour capability, should also be extrapolated to determine if they will bring about changes in the ton-miles-per-hour trend.

Certain conclusions may be deduced on the basis of extrapolation of the ton-miles-per-hour figure of merit. First, the development objectives for the "jumbo jet" aircraft and for the supersonic transport programs are consistent with the established trend. Secondly, the efforts required to achieve the capabilities of the following (1985) generation of transport aircraft can be estimated. If major technological advances are required to achieve this capability, the demonstration of such advances should be in hand not later than 1977. Thus, only a short ten years is available for formulation, initiation, and completion of the research and development programs which will demonstrate the feasibility of the new technologies.

As noted earlier, this forecast cannot be cited as having been a major factor in decisions leading to specific programs. However, the consistency of the forecast with current transport aircraft program objectives may lead to speculation: (1) that similar forecasting approaches influenced the establishment of these objectives; (2) that intuitive knowledge of this trend is reflected in the objectives; or (3) that the cumulative total of technological

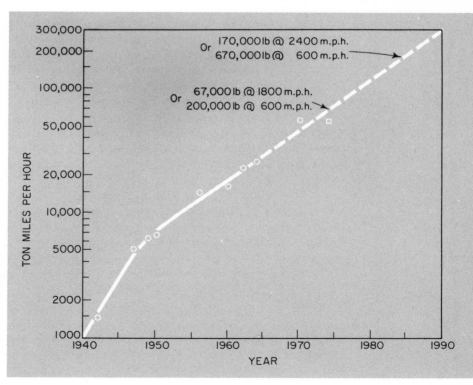

Figure 9. Cargo Aircraft Productivity.

advances and economic requirements operated as an "invisible hand" to bring about programs with these objectives. If supposition (3) is chosen, the argument may be advanced that trend extrapolation can indeed be a valid predictor of the future.

Influences and Guide Lines in Application of Technological Forecasting

Among the factors which influence the trend forecasting process are the social and psychological patterns developed within an organization. These factors determine whether or not any forecasting process will be adopted, what parameters will be selected for forecasting, and which forecasts will be used in decision making.

Foremost among the psychological considerations is the effect of forecasting on the personal security of those who will participate in, or be affected by, the forecasts. In any organization, those people whose involvement in forecasting is essential have usually fared quite well without formal technological forecasting, and they may feel that they will not do as well with a new technique. Selection of objectives and related forecasting parameters is significantly conditioned by the fundamental interests of the decision makers. If a man's entire career and the careers of his friends have been based on development of steam locomotives, it is almost impossible to expect him to participate in a prediction that diesel-electric locomotives will completely displace steam within fifteen years. A man whose greatest rewards have come from sailing ships is emotionally constrained from extrapolation of trends in steam power. Battleships versus aircraft, and horse power versus motor vehicles, are part of a long list of such conflicts. To the extent that a man views his career contribution not only as his life but as his claim to immortality, he resists any prediction which makes that contribution obsolete, since such predictions amount to ego-suicide.

On the other hand, a finding that trends in competitive technology will overcome an organization's existing product or service does not necessarily imply that the organization can or should convert to the new technology. Sailors may be both unhappy and unproductive in the engine room; cavalry generals may be poor tank corps commanders; and aircraft engine manufacturers may move slowly into rocket engine production.

The forecasts that are used in decision making depend largely upon the background of the key executives involved. The executive trained in the sales division is inclined to favor or dispute trends most obviously related to marketing. The former test pilot, now manager, may ignore the economic and social factors which impede the adoption of fascinating new aircraft and may make decisions on the basis of optimistic technical trends. The engineer, in management, is sometimes inclined to emphasize technical sophistication in a product, giving insufficient consideration to the actual needs of the user. This emphasizes trends of increasing complexity.

Environmental factors primarily affect the choice of objectives and trend parameters according to the manner in which the decision maker relates his organization's function to the larger world. For instance, the man who views the construction industry as a rebuilder of cities will use a different set of trends from the man who sees the industry as a service agent to individual buyers.

SUMMARY

Technological forecasting is concerned with establishing outlines of technological advance and may be defined as "the prediction of future characterestics of useful machines," or as "the prediction of useful technological capabilities." Such predictions are necessary and useful only to the extent that they relate to actions which are or should be undertaken. By this criteria, the forecasts of interest are those which may be used to plan current actions.

The principal problems in using trend extrapolation for technological forecasts are the identification of parameters of progress, and the obtaining of time-series data. The major pitfall is the plotting of trends on the basis of arithmetic progression or on linear scales. The identification of parameters which truly reflect progress seems incredibly easy, until it is tried, whereupon it becomes unusually difficult. In particular, the generally accepted parameters of progress, which should be related to established objectives, often are found to have little connection with these objectives. Obtaining time-series data will be difficult until ways and means are found to compile such data on a national basis, at least for parameters of major interest.

Plotting trends of arithmetic progression is, at best, a waste of time, and, at worst, dangerously misleading. Forecasts of arithmetic increase either fail to identify actual potential or conceal the onset of maturity and obsolescence. The plotting of trends against a linear ordinate results either in an almost vertical slope for rapidly advancing technologies, in a failure to recognize exponential increase when short-term time series are plotted, or in a complacent satisfaction with arithmetic progress when possibilities for greater progress should be evident.

The technological forecast should be arrived at consciously and deliberately, should have a separate identity from plans and objectives, and should identify economic, political, accretion, and technical factors insofar as possible. Even when the forecaster is most enamored of his trends and extrapolations, a continuous watch must be maintained for trend-changing discoveries and events.

A final caution may be offered. This, roughly translated, is Dante's warning in the Divine Comedy: that all forecasters must circle endlessly about a bottomless pit in Hell, with their heads turned backward on their shoulders, so that their copious tears will flow down the cleft of their buttocks because they tried to look too far ahead.

Envelope
Curve
Forecasting

ROBERT U. AYRES

Envelope curves are hypothetical curves that describe the maximum performance available for any particular functional characteristic, regardless of the configuration of the device which is employed. As such, they are extremely valuable tools for the technological forecaster. This chapter discusses both rules for the application of the curves and problems which are to be avoided when they are used. It also illustrates these points with examples from an application of envelope curves to a current study of the potential of the electric automobile.

Dr. Ayres has been studying technological forecasting intensively for the past two years. He is author of a book on technological forecasting and long-range planning soon to be published by McGraw-Hill.

The contents of this chapter are solely the responsibility of the author, and no opinions, statements of fact, or conclusions contained herein can be attributed to the Hudson Institute, its staff, its members, or its contracting agencies.

Envelope curves have long been known to technologists as tools for technological forecasting. Frequently, however, their potential usefulness has been overlooked or greatly underestimated. This chapter examines such curves and primarily considers the questions:

1. What are the criteria for choosing the curves to extrapolate?
2. When is it safe to extrapolate a rate-of-change naïvely, and when must points of inflexion, or changes in the rate of change, be anticipated?

DEFINITIONS

The definition of an envelope curve is best presented by means of an illustration. Figure 1 plots the maximum energy available from high-energy particle accelerators (atom smashers). Typically, each new type of machine takes the lead for a short period and then, because of inherent limitations, it reaches the end of its phase of rapid improvement while a newer invention escalates to a higher level. The "envelope" is a curve which approximates the general trend and is tangent to the individual performance trends.

At any given moment, particle accelerator designers are tempted to think that the particular machine then in vogue is the "ultimate" and that future progress will be controlled by the machine's particular constraints. A fore-caster from the traditional school almost automatically projects a future curve which "saturates" and levels off rapidly. He does this because he knows that the problems of his particular configuration will not yield readily, and he is unwilling to predict a totally new invention (or a new configuration) because he cannot imagine what it might look like. If he could imagine, he

Source: M. Stanley Livingston, Introduction to The Development of High Energy Accelerators *(N.Y.: Dover Publications, Inc., 1966), reprinted by permission.*

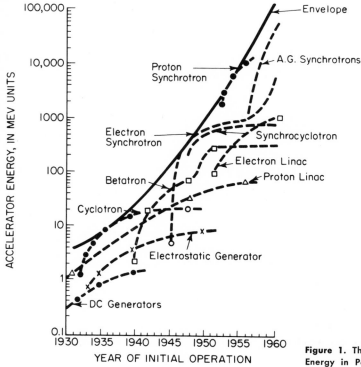

Figure 1. The Rate of Increase of Operating Energy in Particle Accelerators.

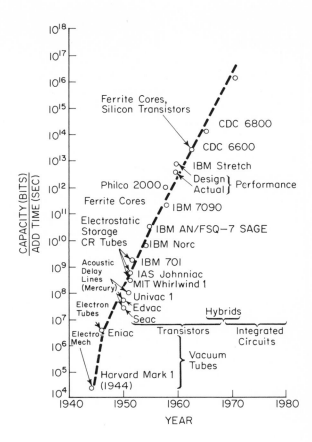

Figure 2. Computer Trends.

would probably invent it himself! But this hypothetical forecaster puts himself into a peculiar position: he has to assume an asymmetry between the past and the future. He knows that inventions have been occurring at a regular rate in the past, but he assumes that in the future there will be no more. This chapter presents the thesis that projecting the envelope itself is the safest thing to do—in the sense of being least likely to introduce an error—because such a projection is tantamount to assuming a continuation of the past rate of invention. It does not assume an inexplicable break between the past and the future.

Although envelope curves may *not* continue in the future as they have in the past, in the absence of specific reasons to the contrary, it is useful to assume that such curves are likely to continue in a smooth and steady progression. The reason is that once a rate of change has become established, it acquires a sort of inertia. In other words, the curve is self-reinforcing. This can be explained with the help of Figure 2. This graph depicts the progress of modern computers as measured in terms of a composite variable especially invented for the purpose—high-speed memory capacity (in bits), divided by add-time (in seconds). Computer manufacturers typically try to increase the number in the numerator and decrease the number in the denominator. This curve is self-reinforcing because the people charged with setting the technical performance specifications for XYZ corporation's next generation of electronic computers have two worries: (1) they do not want to aim too low and have a competitor beat them badly, and (2) they do not want to try to achieve too much and fail (although they would very much like to beat their competitors). The best guide for steering successfully between this Scylla and Charybdis is the envelope curve. It indicates the increments of progress which have been achieved successfully in the past. Hence, there is a very good chance that XYZ corporation will aim for a point right on the extension of the curve—neither below it nor above it—which, in turn, maximizes the probability that the curve will continue.

Two points fall noticeably *above* the envelope in Figure 2. These correspond to the IBM "Stretch" and the Philco "2000." The Stretch never achieved its design performance and was withdrawn from the market. The Philco machine was also a commercial failure, for reasons having to do with the difficulty of programming and operating it. Both computers were unsuccessful attempts to outpace the rest of the industry. These are very convincing arguments for using envelope curves to set program objectives. Even if a company chooses to try to do better than the curve suggests, it will at least have some sense of the odds of success.

The trick in dealing with the forecaster's dilemma is to find a method of extrapolating which takes into account the continuation of invention (as opposed to mere engineering development), without requiring the anticipation of the details of the future invention. Lack of detail is the key. What are needed are rather general indices of performance—or "figures of merit" —which are sufficiently aggregative so that they do not specify how the performance is achieved. These can be called "macrovariables."

The distinction is relative, like the distinction between strategy and tactics. Just as every military officer tends to feel that his own responsibility lies somewhere between the two (his superior being mainly a strategist while his subordinate is strictly concerned with tactics), every variable may be encompassed under all-inclusive macrovariables, while within the variable one can always find subsidiary and more particular measures which are clearly microvariables. A major problem is the determination of the proper variables with which to work.

RULE NUMBER ONE

Any salient variable may be chosen which can be defined independently of a particular narrowly defined class of devices. Thus, *energy conversion*

Energy conversion efficiency (e.g. electric generating efficiency).
Information transmission through a specified channel.
Efficiency of harvesting crops.
Efficiency of recovery of metal from ore.
Efficiency of use of materials in fabrication, e.g., machining, stamping.

Pressures close to zero (high vacua).
Temperatures close to absolute zero.
Speeds close to the Einstein speed (velocity of light).
Efficiency of a heat engine or refrigerator (close to Carnot efficiency).

Maximum traffic flow per lane.
Maximum speed of elevator or escalator.
Minimum time between 2 points by plane.
Maximum velocity in atmosphere.
Minimum time to circumnavigate globe.

Figure 3. Constrained Variables.

efficiency is clearly a macrovariable whereas *compression ratio* and *octane rating* are microvariables. Similarly, *specific thrust* is a macrovariable whereas *muzzle velocity* and *combustion chamber temperature* are microvariables. However, even the best of rules leaves some grey areas. The variable in Figure 2, describing computer performance, might really be a macrovariable. Even though it certainly can be described independently of any specific computer design, it still refers to calculating machines.

Ambiguities of definition appear to pose less of a problem, however, than do *constraints*. There seem to be two quite different types of constraints. The type most easily recognized, and easiest to describe, is an absolute physical limitation, such as *absolute zero* (temperature) or the *speed of light* (Einstein velocity), or an intrinsic bound like 100 per cent (the upper limit on all ratios of output to input, whether of energy, mass, volume or dollars). The second type of intrinsic constraint is imposed by limited capabilities of the human body, or by the characteristics of the earth. Thus, all means of mass transportation in which people are permitted to stand are limited to 3 mph/sec acceleration, or about 0.15 g. On the other hand, physically fit test pilots in special seats may tolerate up to about 10 g. In both instances, the limits are imposed by the nature of the human organism and its interaction with the existing environment. (On the moon these limits would probably be different.) The list contained in Figure 3 presents further illustrations.

An *intensive* macrovariable is one which is approaching an intrinsic or basic physical constraint. By contrast, an extensive macrovariable is one which is not immediately subject to this sort of limitation. If such a variable can be said to be constrained, the constraints typically would be economic; e.g., the constraints on speed indicated in Figure 4. "Economic" refers to

Medium	Constraint
Interstellar Space	Einstein speed (c).
Solar Space	Escape velocity from the solar system.
Earth's Atmosphere	1. Escape velocity from the earth. 2. Friction heating and strength of materials. 3. "Economics."

Figure 4. Constraints on Vehicular Speed.

trade-offs between development, procurement, deployment, and indoctrination costs and the degree of departure from existing technology; and trade-offs between size, turnaround time, load factors, safety regulations, noise limitations, takeoff power altitude, and speed.

RULE NUMBER TWO

Determine whether the macrovariable is extensive or intensive. If the former, it is possible that a change of the magnitude being forecast would tend to push the variable from one category to the other. In many cases this step is a simple formality, since there is usually little doubt, but in others there *is* some doubt. Figure 5 is a rather crude, year-by-year plot of the maximum energy conversion efficiency obtained in thermal power plants

Figure 5. Efficiency of External Combustion Energy Conversion Systems.

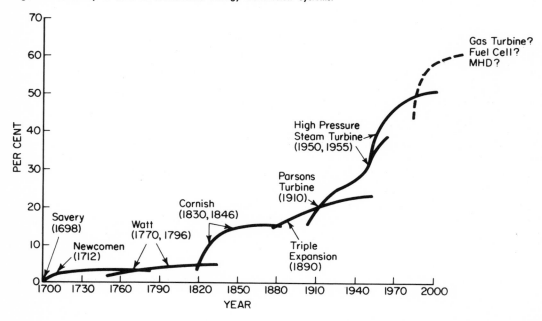

Improvement	Factor	Time Lag
Watt	1.5	85 years
Cornish	3.2	50 "
Triple expansion	1.3	40 "
Parsons turbine	1.5	35 "
High pressure turbine	1.6	30 "

Figure 6. Improvement in Efficiency of External Combustion Energy Conversion Systems.

since 1700. The curve has escalated in typical fashion from 1 per cent or 2 per cent to about 44 per cent where it stands today. Increases have occurred rather sharply and have been of the order of 50 per cent each time (see Figure 6). But they have come at steadily decreasing intervals. Extending the trend, one might expect to achieve a maximum operating efficiency of 55–60 per cent somewhere around 1980. Few people would be prepared to make a definite prediction of this event, especially in view of the long lead time of a commercial power plant; however, efficiencies of this magnitude are probably feasible, using several devices (fuel cells, gas turbines, MHD) which are under active development at the present time. Increases after 1980 pose a problem, however, since only one more improvement factor of 1.5 would bring efficiencies up to 90 per cent and further absolute improvement at the same rate is clearly impossible.

Up until now (and possibly until 1980), efficiencies have been constrained by economics and ignorance. The rate of invention, which determines the state of our ignorance, is not itself technologically determined *in toto,* but is very much subject to the economic winds that blow, particularly where research requires heavy investments. However, after 1980 one can hardly ignore the fact that further incremental improvements become harder and harder to achieve. In fact, one might say that the curve "feels" the looming presence of an intrinsic and absolute upper limit.[1] At some time between now and 1980, the energy conversion efficiency curve will make the transition from an extensive to an intensive category.

[1] It has been observed repeatedly by many authors that technological trends tend to follow exponentially rising curves (i.e., straight lines on semilog paper), as long as the number of scientists in the field remains constant or changes slowly. However, when the parameter begins to approach a constraint, a different sort of behavior is observed: the curve bends over (into an "S" shape) and tends to approach the limit asymptotically, roughly as the (negative) exponential function of the difference. However, this is only an approximation and does not suggest a reliable method of predicting the point of inflexion of the "S-curve." Such a criterion is, however, explicit in the method presented by A. L. Floyd in Chapter 5.

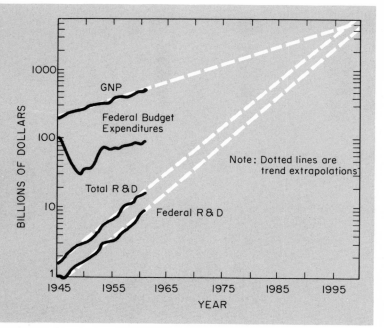

Figure 7. Dollar Growth of R&D and GNP.

Source: Reprinted from Science & Technology, *December, 1963, by permission.*

Figure 7 illustrates another similar situation. The rate of increase of R&D, relative to GNP, is bound to decline sometime soon. A more detailed examination would probably indicate that this has begun to happen already.

Interdependencies among variables may also act like constraints, as in the case of trends in automobile ownership. Extrapolating the time-series data on the number of private vehicles on the road leads to a simplistic forecast. However, the variable in question is certainly correlated with personal income, the per cent of family income spent on transportation, and the costs of automobile ownership (including the costs of highways and gasoline). In fact, the variable can be considered the product of the first two, divided by the third. By projecting these three parameters separately, and combining the results, a forecast of the numbers of automobiles can be obtained by using another route. Assuming all changes in all variables were linear, there would be no difficulty in reconciling the two forecasts, but a non-linearity or saturation phenomenon in *any* of the component variables would result in discrepancies. A saturation—for example, in the per cent of family income spent on transportation—would constitute a "hidden constraint" on the total number of automobiles on the road, albeit a fairly obvious one. Trends in total transportation demand, the proportion of all trips taken by automobile, the total amount of time spent traveling (per capita), and the amount of travel attributable to automobiles could also be considered. A rapidly declining air travel time between cities contrasts more and more sharply with a stable or increasing terminal-interface time. If further improvements in highways do not materially reduce terminal-inter-face time by automobile (as seems likely), then new approaches and new systems will probably be tried. Here is another and somewhat more subtle hidden constraint which may put further expansion of the auto industry into the *intensive* category.

RULE NUMBER THREE

Rule three modifies such naïve extrapolations to take this change into account: when a variable moves from an extensive to an intensive category, *the scales on which the performance data are being recorded should be changed.* A logarithmic scale [2] can always be found in which the constraint is mathematically transformed into a more convenient form or effectively eliminated. Thus, instead of recording absolute efficiencies of future energy conversion, the negative logarithms of the fractional energy *losses* in conversion might be recorded. An efficiency of 60 per cent implies a fractional loss of 0.4, which has the negative logarithm 0.916. As efficiency increases to 80 per cent, the fractional loss declines to 0.2 and its negative logarithm jumps to 1.61—or about an 80 per cent increase! As the efficiencies approach 100 per cent, the negative logarithms approach infinity, and the inconvenient constraint has been removed by a mathematical artifice.

This kind of trick is actually useful in "real" forecasting and is a customary method of handling the better known physical constraints. Measuring *losses* instead of *efficiencies,* in the case just described, is tantamount to defining a new scale which sets zero at the absolute constraint rather than at some other point (which, more than likely, resulted from an historical accident). This can be illustrated by the familiar example of temperature scales.

The centigrade scale has its zero at a fairly natural place—the freezing point of water. The temperature at which water boils (at sea level) is set at 100. Unfortunately, on this scale the absolute physical limit turns out to be minus 273 degrees! Lord Kelvin made the obvious change: he set zero "Kelvin" at −273 centigrade. On the Kelvin scale, water freezes at +273°K and boils at +373°K. But suppose 273°K was set equal to 1 degree on the "Ayres" scale. Then temperature landmarks would appear as in Figure 8.

This scale measures not what has *been* achieved, but what is left to be

---

2 On such a scale, the asymptote of the "S-curve" would tend to approach a straight line, if classical behavior occurred.

	Temp. °A	
Water freezes	1(°A)	(= 273°K)
Neon boils (or liquefies)	10^{-1}	(= 27.2°K)
Helium 4 boils (or liquefies)	1.5×10^{-2}	(= 4.2°K)
"Lambda point"	0.8×10^{-2}	(= 2.186°K)
Lowest temperature achievable by boiling He3 at reduced pressure	10^{-3}	(0.3°K)
Lowest temperature achievable by adiabatic demagnetization of paramagnetic salts	10^{-9}	(0.0000003°K)

Figure 8. Temperature Landmarks in Natural Units.

achieved. Furthermore, the real measure of this residue is the *negative power of ten*. In a very important sense, the lowest point on the scale shown in Figure 8 is six "orders of magnitude" (i.e., six powers of ten) more difficult to achieve than the next lowest point, and this corresponds quite closely to the scale of effort involved.

A similar situation prevails for pressure measurement. Instead of using a scale with zero at zero pressure and unity in the obvious place (atmospheric pressure), vacuum technologists measure in terms of a much smaller and less natural unit, the torr, which is the pressure exerted by a 1 mm column of mercury (1 bar = 760 torr).[3] The quality of a vacuum—the absence of pressure—is normally measured in negative powers of ten (torr) as shown in Figure 9. Some sense of the enormous strides in technology which these differences represent can be obtained from the negative logarithmic scale, whereas, on a *linear* scale, the difference in terms of pressure between an ordinary high vacuum and an interstellar vacuum is not merely negligible,

[3] 1 atmosphere = 1 *bar*.

Figure 9. Pressure Landmarks in Natural Units.

Atmospheric pressure (at sea level)	1 bar (= 760 torr)
Pressure at 150,000 ft. altitude	1.3×10^{-3} (= 1 torr)
"High Vacuum"	$\sim 10^{-9}$
Limit of technology, 1950	$\sim 10^{-12}$
Limit of oil diffusion pumps (1965)	$\sim 10^{-14}$
Limit of ion pumps	$\sim 10^{-15}$
Interplanetary space	$\sim 10^{-17}$
Limit of technology (1965) (helium cryopump)	$\sim 10^{-18}$

but unreadable. Thus, the logarithmic scale not only removes the inconvenient constraint but corresponds more closely to subjective reality.

There are several factors which can, and often do, make envelope-curve forecasters look silly. It is a sad fact that drastic changes in the political, cultural, military, or economic environment can often be far more potent in determining what particular technology will be developed, and at what pace, than the internal social dynamics of the "research, invention and development system" itself. The overwhelming influence of war needs no laborious documentation. A very large number of the technologies which seem woven into the fabric of our civilization today were stepchildren of World War II and the Cold War which followed. It is, however, worth stressing that even minor shifts in the strategic concepts governing defense policy, or in the crosscurrents of international relations—or even in religious dogma—may have an immense and often unsuspected impact on what subsequently happens in technology. The three examples which follow illustrate this point.

The civilian jet airliner and its successor, the future SST, are examples of a technological development which profited immensely from a particular —and by no means historically inevitable—decision in the Department of Defense; namely, the decision to rely on manned long-range bombers long after the Soviet Union had switched its entire effort to missiles (thus giving rise to the original "missile gap" and the shock caused by Sputnik 1 in 1957). If the United States had abandoned its reliance on bombers when the Russians did, it is questionable whether civilians would be flying much in jet airliners today, and it is extremely doubtful that a supersonic transport would be contemplated seriously by the U.S.

As for the influence of international relations, the nuclear test ban treaty led, eventually, to a cutback in our entire nuclear weapons program and its "atoms for peace" stepchild, PLOWSHARE. It is now doubtful whether the use of nuclear explosives for such purposes as digging canals or tunnels will ever be sanctioned, although this might have happened if international politics had developed differently. On the other hand, the test ban also led to project VELA—the government program to develop technology pertinent to detecting nuclear tests anywhere on, under, or above the earth. For several years, VELA has been the major sponsor of basic research in seismology—which might accelerate the day, in the not too distant future, when destructive earthquakes can be predicted or even prevented.

A third example, hypothetical but worth postulating, relates to the influence of religion. Any substantial liberalization of current Catholic doctrine on birth control will probably be followed, within a year or two, by a very sharp increase in the level of research on chemical means of contraception.

The most important hazard of forecasting is the problem of taking changes in the external environment into account. Many people stop at this point, arguing that, for periods of time over five or ten years out, the political-military-international-economic uncertainties far outweigh any other considerations. This view must be respected; certain types of technology are almost totally unpredictable more than a few years ahead because exogenous factors are so overwhelmingly important. On the other hand, some technologies seem to be comparatively insulated from, or independent of, external influences. It is important to distinguish which is which, and where the particular technology under scrutiny fits. Technologies relating to food, medicine, and weapons seem to be examples of the most environment-sensitive type, whereas those connected with communications and energy conversion, for instance, appear to fit into the less sensitive category.

RULE NUMBER FOUR

Determine the sensitivity of the particular macrovariable to the state of the outside world. This is by no means simple, and it is very easy to overlook even obvious interactions. Nevertheless, the exercise can be extremely valuable if done systematically. A checklist such as the following is very helpful:

1. What are the "constituencies?" (Who is helped, and who is hurt by changes in the technology? How influential are they? What kind of influence do they have: votes, money, the power to strike or obstruct, the power to agitate?)

2. Is there a strong prospect that legislation will affect the macrovariable one way or the other? Would it be as a result of subsidy, regulation, or otherwise?

3. Is current research in the field broadly or narrowly supported? Is it being supported for its own sake or incidentally, as the result of some other program (as seismology is supported by project VELA)? Could a shift of strategic priorities affect the sources of funds? Would R&D in this field be speeded up or de-emphasized in the event of greater or lesser tension between the U.S. and the U.S.S.R. (or China)?

4. Would the level of support be greatly affected by any conceivable

natural disaster, such as a great drought, storm, or flood, a great earthquake in a populous area, an epidemic of a new type, or a deep famine?

Going through a list of questions like these and answering them as completely as possible develops some feeling for the depths of the difficulties which lie ahead, and the number and nature of the caveats which must accompany the final forecast.

RULE NUMBER FIVE

The last and most interesting issue relates to the way technological change affects technological change: specifically, *examine the developments in other technologies that could affect the macrovariable being studied.* Such impacts may be either competitive or complementary. An example of a competitive situation comes from the history of the automobile. If a closed cycle steam "flash" boiler had been invented and applied to automobiles in 1910 (instead of 1924), today's complaints about air pollution would probable be directed at the external combustion engine instead of the internal combustion engine. A forecaster in that era would also have had to worry about the possibility of a breakthrough in battery technology, since the electric car was also a strong contender at the time. The fifth and last rule of envelope-curve forecasting calls for an extension of the forecast—at least to first order—to include related technologies which would notably advance or retard the rate of change of the particular technology under consideration.

To recapitulate, the five rules are as follows:

1. Choose appropriate macrovariables (independent of any narrowly defined class of devices).
2. Identify constraints and determine whether each variable is in an *extensive* or *intensive* category.
3. If the variable is intensive, transform away the absolute constraint by a suitable change of scale.
4. Determine the degree of sensitivity to the "state of the world" (political, military, international, etc.).
5. Iterate the procedure for "obviously" interacting technologies. Now extrapolate!

AN EXAMPLE

A question Hudson Institute has been considering in some detail, during 1966–67, is "What are the prospects for a practical electric automobile by

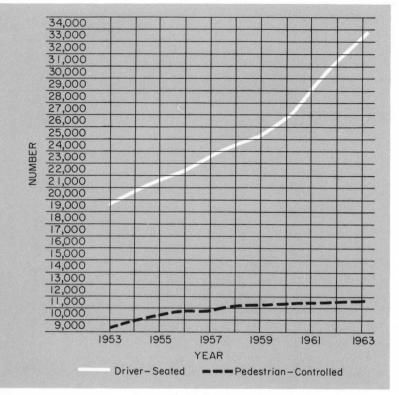

NUMBER

34,000
33,000
32,000
31,000
30,000
29,000
28,000
27,000
26,000
25,000
24,000
23,000
22,000
21,000
20,000
19,000
18,000
17,000
16,000
15,000
14,000
13,000
12,000
11,000
10,000
9,000

1953   1955   1957   1959   1961   1963

YEAR

—— Driver–Seated   ▬ ▬ ▬ Pedestrian–Controlled

Figure 10. Number of Electric Road Vehicles.

Source: Electric Vehicle Association, London.

1980–85?" In order to approach this question systematically, Rule #1 calls for a selection of appropriate macrovariables. Figures 10 through 12 illustrate a number of possibilities. For contrast, two parameters (Figures 13 and 14) which fall into the category of microvariables are included. (It is interesting to observe how the increased pace of R&D in recent years has affected even the old standbys: the lead acid automobile storage battery and the Edison-type nickel-iron reserve battery. The most spectacular gains [Figures 11 and 12] have come from the introduction of new types of batteries—a trickle since World War II that has become a flood in the last five years).

Regarding constraints, it is clear that sales and research expenditures are not approaching saturation in any sense, since the number of electric vehicles now in service is infinitesimal and the research being done in the field amounts to a negligible share of the total research effort of the nation—a much smaller effort than currently goes into high-energy nuclear physics, for instance. On the other hand, battery and fuel cell performances are

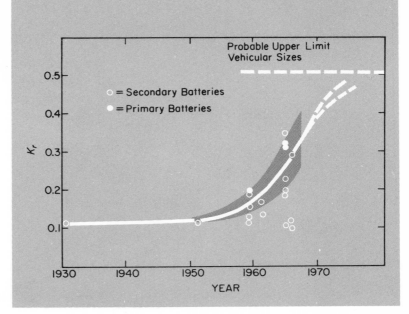

Figure 11. Trends in Reactant Efficiency Ratio (K_r) of Batteries.

Source for Figures 11 and 12: R. U. Ayres and R. McKenna, "Technology and Urban Transportation: Environmental Quality Considerations," Hudson Institute, HI-949/1, 2-RR, January 11, 1968.

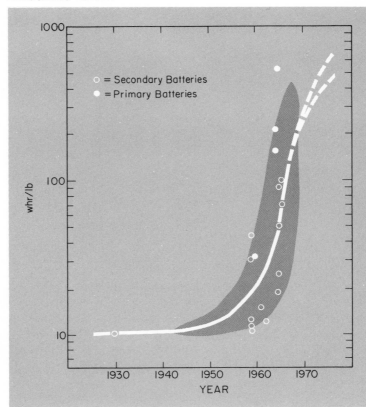

Figure 12. Trends in Actual Energy Density (whr/lb) of Batteries.

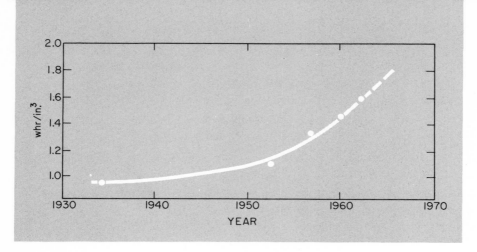

Figure 13. Improvement in Lead-Acid Storage Batteries (Automobile). Theoretical Limit $= 9.3$ whr/in.^{3}

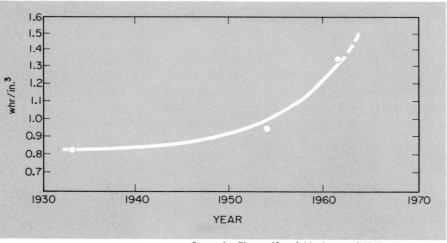

Source for Figures 13 and 14: Ayres and McKenna, op cit.

Figure 14. Improvement in Edison-Type Nickle-Iron Reserve Batteries (whr/in.^{3}).

constrained. The maximum energy output for a given cell is limited by the theoretical energy content of the reactants.

A measure of design efficiency is the reactant efficiency ratio (K_r)—the ratio of weights of active materials (anode, cathode) to inactive components (containers, separators, connectors, grids, tubes, pumps, electrolyte, etc.). At the present time, most batteries are only about 20 per cent efficient by this measure. The absolute upper limit is, of course, 100 per cent. It is impossible to say how close to 100 per cent manufacturers may ultimately reach, but, as Figure 11 indicates, 50 per cent would be a plausible figure. In this regard, it would seem that batteries are rapidly approaching, but have not yet reached, the *intensive* category (although fuel cells probably are still far from this point).

According to Rule 3, a scale transformation might be required prior to extrapolating the "reactant efficiency ratio" to 1985. However, this transformation can be dispensed with for the present, since efficiencies are still relatively low and the trend curve is by no means well defined.

Rule 4 asks how sensitive the electric car is to military, social, and political phenomena. Public and congressional interest in the electric car at the present time probably is almost entirely attributable to the air pollution situation, and this concern, which temporarily ebbs and flows, probably will continue to intensify. The automobile industry hopes to "short-circuit" the electric car by reducing the air pollution problem in other ways.[4] Its chance of succeeding is a very salient point, and part of the issue revolves around the question of how much atmospheric pollution can be tolerated without serious worry. The answer rests partly on matters of fact (such as the cumulative toxicity of oxides of nitrogen over long periods of time, and the extent to which various air pollutants are implicated in such illnesses as lung cancer, asthma and emphysema) and partly on matters of preference (such as how much it is worth, and to whom, to reduce the general unpleasantness and dirt associated with pollution).

The electric car depends on military issues as well. Thus, the space program provided the major impetus for fuel cell research in the United States, and the needs of the military have stimulated most of the advanced battery research. The results which are beginning to flow from this research —*not* the current wave of publicity—make an adequate electric car look feasible within twenty years or so. Anything resulting in a substantial change, either up or down, in the current level of government support for battery and fuel cell research would affect the likelihood of an electric car. A drastic cutback in NASA's activities might have such an effect, for example.

Another kind of external affect is the possibility of a substantial evolution, or revolution, in the conditions of automobile ownership. A great increase in the prevalence of rented cars, or an extension of the rental industry into the field of "U-drive it" taxis, would open a new market for electric vehicles, since large fleet owners are in a much better position than private owners to trade off a higher initial cost for the longer-term operating economy of electric vehicles. An incursion of electric utilities or other finan-

---

[4] It is probably not unreasonable to expect a good deal of obstruction and foot-dragging from both the automotive and the petroleum industries.

cial institutions into the field of battery rental might also open up a new market.

The fifth rule is to look for technological interactions. What possible developments in other disciplines might have a major impact on the outcome? One development which would almost certainly forestall the electric car for many years (if not permanently) would be a really nonpolluting type of engine. It seems certain at this time that no engine based on internal combustion can fully eliminate *both* unburned hydrocarbons and carbon monoxide on the one hand and oxides of nitrogen on the other. However, it is interesting to note that the Philips Stirling cycle engine, now in an advanced development stage, offers not only fuel consumption efficiencies which are apparently better than diesel engines (for comparable horsepower) and much better than Otto-cycle (gasoline) engines, but also produces less than 1 per cent as much carbon monoxide and unburned hydrocarbons as conventional Otto-cycle engines. It also yields substantially smaller amounts of oxides of nitrogen, although the differences here are not as great.

There are three major revolutions in the offing which might have a great impact on the electrical side:

1. A breakthrough in understanding and synthesizing cheap, efficient oxidation catalysts (particularly types which would have low activation temperatures) would completely change (for the better) the outlook for progress in fuel cells. Since the phenomenon of catalysis is very dimly understood at present, such a discovery cannot be ruled out, although it would be risky to bet heavily on it.

2. A breakthrough in the cost of producing hydrazine in bulk—now $10 per gallon—would be another avenue to achieving practical, low-temperature fuel cells. However, an improvement factor of 50 would be required, and this seems somewhat remote.

3. A sharp reduction in the cost of manufacturing high-power, high-speed, silicon control rectifiers ("thyristors")—or the equivalent—would make it possible to convert direct current into variable, high-frequency AC, suitable for driving very lightweight, relatively inexpensive induction motors. This development would greatly improve the cost and performance characteristics of electric cars vis à vis the likely competition.

The transportation study is not yet finished, nor are the conclusions in final form.[5] However, it does present an illustration of the application of envelope-curve forecasting and the use of the rules outlined above.

[5] The study is being performed under a grant by Resources for the Future, Inc., and review copies will be circulated by Hudson Institute in early 1968. Final publication is expected in 1968.

A Methodology for
Trend-Forecasting
of Figures of Merit

A. L. FLOYD

An extremely useful approach to technological forecasting is the projection of "figures of merit" for parameters that are under study. These figures of merit serve as a basis for measuring progress in particular areas of technology. A methodology is described which, by use of a mathematical model, permits trend extrapolation of figures of merit and identifies the probabilities associated with the trend. Incorporated in the projections are not only historical data but estimates of the effects of competitive technologies.

Dr. Floyd is Senior Scientific Adviser for Lockheed Aircraft Corporation. He has conducted numerous studies of technological progress for his firm and has been experimenting with figure of merit forecasts.

The use of historical trends to forecast future technology and "figures of merit" has been the subject of considerable study.[1] Lockheed Aircraft Corporation has been experimenting with one such technique which is based on mathematical simulation of the development process and its effect on industry.

BASIC APPROACH

The technique focuses on the usual types of figures of merit such as: thrust to weight and thrust to rate of fuel consumption for aircraft engines,

---

[1] See, for example, items 1, 2, and 4 in the appended list of references.

efficiency of energy conversion, or inventory requirements. The basic approach is to calculate the probability of improving the figure of merit through applied effort.

The probability of one worker improving a figure of merit, in one try, from an initial level to another higher level, f is given by:

$$(1) \qquad P(f, 1) = \frac{X}{M},$$

where X is the number of techniques available that would be successful and M is the total number of possible techniques or approaches that could be considered.

Expanding this to include the average number of workers W performing N attempts per unit of time to improve the figure of merit, the probability of exceeding a given level of the figure of merit in a time span of Δt is given by

$$(2) \qquad P(f, \Delta t) = 1 - \left(1 - \frac{X}{M}\right)^{\overline{N}\,\overline{W}\,(\Delta t)}$$

Equation (2) states that the probability of making the improvement in the figure of merit is given by one, minus the probability of not making the improvement.

The value of $\frac{X}{M}$ can be estimated in terms of the figure-of-merit values. Figure 1 approximates the relationship between available techniques and the figure-of-merit values. The figure of merit can be improved from its

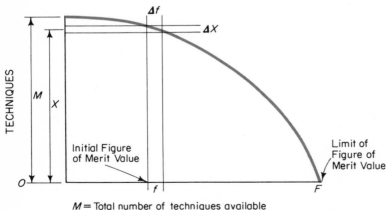

$M =$ Total number of techniques available
$X =$ Number of "successful techniques"
   (i.e. capable of raising the figure of merit)

Figure 1. Techniques vs. Figure of Merit.

initial value by any one of the available techniques. As small improvements are made in the figure of merit, the number of "successful techniques" which remain decreases only slightly. However, as the limit of the figure of merit is approached, the number of successful techniques which are still available must rapidly go to zero. Although this curve could take many forms, it is usually similar in nature to the curves for absorption phenomena. Therefore, for a first general approximation, the following assumption is made:

The rate of change of successful techniques available to improve a figure of merit is proportional to the number of techniques absorbed to achieve the value of the figure of merit, or,

(3)
$$\frac{\Delta X}{\Delta f} = -k(M - X),$$

where Δf is the change in the figure of merit and k is constant.

Integrating equation (3) between f and the limiting value of f, defined as F, and between $X = X$ and $X = 0$, the following is obtained:

(4)
$$\int_X^0 \frac{dx}{M - X} = -k \int_f^F df,$$

or

$$\frac{X}{M} = 1 - \exp[-k(F - f)]$$

Equation (4) does not consider changes in X and M with time, and the constant k could be time-dependent. The value of X/M from equation (4) can be substituted into equation (2), giving

(5)
$$P(\Delta f, t) = 1 - \exp[-(F - f)k\overline{N}\,\overline{W}(\Delta t)]$$

This is equivalent to stating that the probability of achieving f for any total time t is given by multiplying the probabilities of not achieving f, and subtracting this value from 1 $[1 - \overline{P}(t)]$:

(6)
$$P(f, t) = 1 - \exp[-(F - f) \int_{-\infty}^t kNW \, dt]$$

Equation (6) replaces the sum of all of the $k\overline{N}\,\overline{W}(\Delta t)$ elements by the integral. This would allow probability calculations if the integral could be evaluated; however, generally it cannot be. The situation can be improved by examining the variables within the integral. The quantity k can be expected to vary with time; however, k is dependent upon the general growth in technology and, therefore, should not vary widely. Similarly, N, the number of tries per unit time, should be a well-behaved function of time, depending on the nature of the technology and overall improvements in technology, i.e., computers and general automation. However, the number of workers W can be varied at will, within limits, especially for military programs, and wide variations must be considered in trend forecasting.

There is another type of variation that should be considered in a more general way. The introduction of a new technology generally brings a shift of workers from the old technology to the new. This shift brings a rapid advance, due both to the build-up of activity and to the transfer of technology; e.g., the shift of engineers working in vacuum tube technology to transistor technology after the development of the transistor. This shift should affect the growth of those trend curves in electronics that are associated with efficiency and package size. The exact form of the rate of this shift is not known. However, it seems reasonable to assume that it is a function of the difference between the value of the figure of merit for the new technology f and that for the competitive technology f_c, or

$$(7) \qquad W = W(f - f_c)W_0(t),$$

where $W_0(t)$ represents the relatively constant growth of total workers available. The value of f_c can usually be estimated (e.g., for electronic package sizes). Although the exact form of the function $W(f - f_c)$ cannot be determined, the first order approximation $(f - f_c)$ can be used. Thus, the assumption is made that

$$(8) \qquad W = (f - f_c)W_0(t)$$

where $W_0(t)$ is a slowly varying function of time.

Placing this value in equation (6) yields

$$(9) \qquad P(f,\, t) = 1 - \exp[-(F - f) \int_{-\infty}^{t} (f - f_c)T(t)\ dt],$$

where

$$(10) \qquad T(t) = k(t) \cdot \overline{N}(t) \cdot W_0(t),$$

and the function $T(t)$ is a slowly varying function of time.

For trend forecasting we are interested in keeping the probability $P(f,\, t)$ constant at the 50 per cent value and determining how the figure of merit varies with time. Under this requirement the integral in equation (9) can be evaluated by separation of variables (see the appendix at the end of the chapter). Thus

$$(11) \qquad P(f,\, t) \equiv 0.5 = 1 - \exp\left[\frac{-0.6931(C_1 t + C_2)}{Y + \ln(Y - 1) + C_2}\right],$$

where

$$Y = \frac{1 - f_c/F}{1 - f/F}$$

$$C_1, C_2 = \text{constants},$$

$$t = \text{time},$$

and the integral of $T(t)$ has been replaced by a constant times the change in time for finite ranges of time considered.

Equation (11) is the basis of the trend forecasting methodology. Three values must be determined to use it. First, F, the limit for the figure of merit, must be calculated. Second, f_c must be estimated. Third, the value of the constant C_1 must be determined from at least two data points.

Equation (11) can be put in simpler form for plotting by setting $P(f, t)$ equal to a constant and taking the logarithm of both sides. Thus

(12a)
$$Y + \ln(Y - 1)^{tc_2} = -(C_1{\cdot}t + C_2),$$

or

(12b)
$$Y + \ln(Y - 1) = C_1{\cdot}t$$

For convenience, a universal nomograph can be constructed from equation (12a). Figure 2 shows a plot of $Y + \ln(Y - 1)$ or $C_1 t$ vs. f/F. This curve rep-

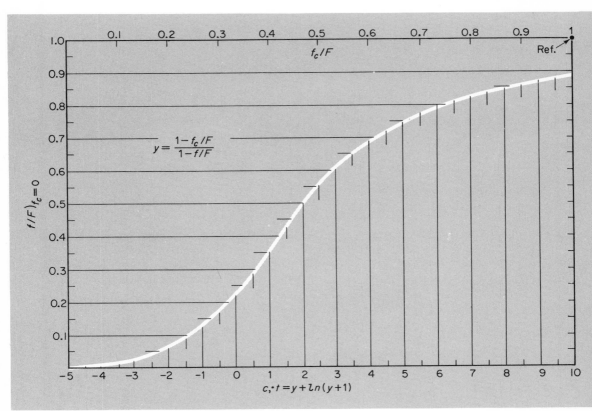

Figure 2. Trend Nomograph.

resents the general technology trend curve if f_c/F, the competitive technology figure-of-merit value, is zero. The ratio f_c/F acts as a scaling factor for f/F. The value of f_c/F has been plotted across the top of the graph shown in Figure 2, with the value of 1 labeled as reference. This nomograph is used as follows: The value of f_c/F is determined and a line parallel to the $(f/F)_{f_c=0}$ axis is drawn through this point. The value of f/F is plotted on this line. A straight line is then drawn between the reference point and the plotted point, and is extended until it intercepts the $(f/F)_{f=0}$ axis. The point at which it touches the axis is the scaled value of f/F. The scaled value is then projected onto the curve, and the value of $C_1 \cdot t$ corresponding to the figure-of-merit value is used. The value of C is then determined by calculation or by plotting actual data vs. $C_1 \cdot t$ and fitting the best straight line. The trend curve can be plotted by the reverse process.

For very small values of f/F, or for very large values of F, the logarithmic term dominates in equation (12b), and a semilog plot of the difference between f/F and f_c/F vs. $C_1 \cdot t$ is a straight line. This is shown in Figure 3.

The trend line developed by this process represents estimated values at a 50 per cent probability level. However, the latest actual figures do not always fall on this trend line. In addition, the establishment of estimated probabilities spreads, such as the trend for 20 per cent and 80 per cent

Figure 3. Trend Nomograph.

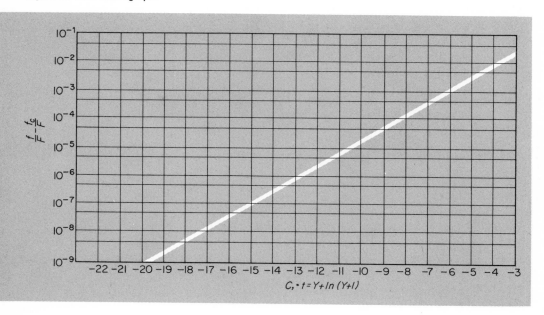

probability levels, is desirable. This can be accomplished through application of the rules for conditional probability.

Thus:

$$(13) \qquad P(f/f_0, t) = \frac{P(f, t)}{P(f_0, t)},$$

where f_0 is the latest data point.

The calculation of the probabilities used in equation (13) can be made directly from equation (9) for any fixed value of f over time. As f_0 is fixed, and the time integral was previously evaluated by equations (11) and (12a), equation (9) becomes

$$(14) \qquad P(f_0, t) = 1 - \exp[-0.6931(F - f_0)(f_0 - f_c)(C_1 \cdot t + C_2)]$$

where t is the new time. Noting that on the trend curve $P(f_0, t_0)$ is 50 per cent and using equation (12b), equation (14) can be written:

$$(15)$$
$$P(f_0, t) = 1 - 0.5\exp\{-(F - f_0)(f_0 - f_c)[Y + \ln(Y - 1) - Y_0 - \ln(Y_0 - 1)]\}$$

where y is evaluated from the trend curve at the new time and y_0 is evaluated at the time on the trend curve corresponding to the figure of merit f_0. Equation (15) can be used to calculate the probability of trend figures. In general, it allows calculation of the probability that the trend will occur with time, by dividing that calculated number into 0.5, as indicated by equation (13).

Several examples have been chosen to illustrate the application of this approach and some of the problems encountered in using it. These are based on simple and well-known figures of merit.

Example 1

The first example relates to the problem of maintaining inventories of crude oil which are sufficient to meet demands. Available data [2] are recorded in terms of days of crude oil stock on hand. While short-term variations of this parameter may be due to demand variation, the long-term effort to reduce inventory investment represents primarily a technological problem. The objective is to minimize the inventory of crude oil. For this example, a limit has been set at one day. This represents no inventory (i.e., $F = 1$). The figure of merit is the inverse of the number of days of supply on hand [i.e., $f = (1,$ divided by the number of days)]. Thus, for ten days of available crude oil, the factor f/F would be 0.1. No comparative systems are known; thus f_c/F is zero. Using these values and published data, the trend curve

2 The data are taken from Table 63 of a report entitled *Petroleum Industry of the United States—1965*, U. S. Department of The Interior.

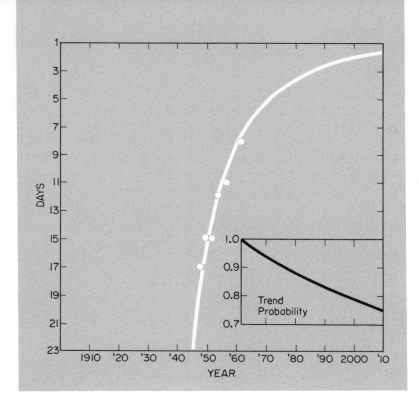

Figure 4. Days Supply of Available Stocks of Crude Oil in U.S. Data from the Petroleum Industry of the United States, January, 1965, U.S. Department of the Interior, Table 63.

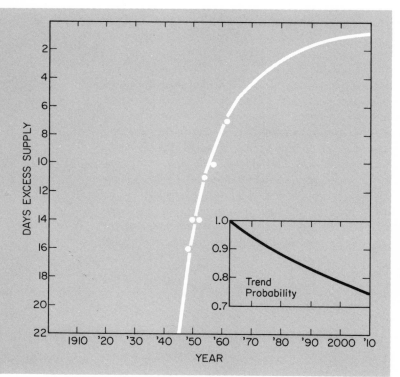

Figure 5. Days Supply of Available Stocks of Crude Oil in U.S. Data from the Petroleum Industry of the United States, January, 1965, U.S. Department of the Interior, Table 63.

shown in Figure 4 is obtained. The actual data points are shown by the heavy dots. Using the conditional probability rule, we can show the probability of the trend in the insert on Figure 4.

This trend curve illustrates a particular problem in interpreting trends. The problem becomes apparent if an attempt is made to change the scale from "Days Supply of Available Stocks of Crude Oil" to "Hours Supply of Available Stocks of Crude Oil." Under the latter conditions, the limit would be one hour. However, Figure 4 shows that one day, twenty-four hours, is the maximum limit. This problem can be resolved by changing the scale to "Days of Excess Supply of Available Crude Oil," as shown in Figure 5. Both curves will now agree. While this scale problem may seem trivial, its occurrence can be overlooked and misleading results can be obtained.

Example 2

The speed-trend problem illustrates another type of difficulty encountered with the figure-of-merit approach. Using data developed by D. G. Samaras, the trend curve can be derived for mechanical-powered vehicles, as shown in Figure 6. In this very general form, the competitive system is animal-powered vehicles, and the ultimate and competitive limits are the speed of light and the Pony Express, respectively.

As can be seen, the curve for missiles does not fall on this trend line. Changing the competitive limits, within reason, or weighting the data points does not alter the trend line to improve the fit. All of the data, except that for missiles, seem to fit the derived trend well. (The future supersonic transport will also fall on the trend line, as shown in the figure.) If one assumes that this trend technique is valid, two possible explanations could be considered.

First, an extraordinary amount of effort could have accelerated the growth trend in the period from 1949 to the present. An increase in effort by a factor of four or five during this period could have produced this result. Data on national expenditures for missiles seem to confirm that at least this amount of increased effort was applied. Future budget figures indicate a slowing of this effort to maintain a constant percentage of the national budget. Thus, based upon this explanation, the maximum speed trend would be expected to parallel the trend curve drawn, starting at the missile level.

A second explanation is that missiles are not the same type of elements which were used to develop the rest of the trend curve. As an example, the muzzle velocity of bullets has not been included. In addition, free space flight can use energy other than mechanical, e.g., gravity. If this explanation is accepted, the missile data should be removed, and the trend curve will give the speed trend for commercial transport vehicles.

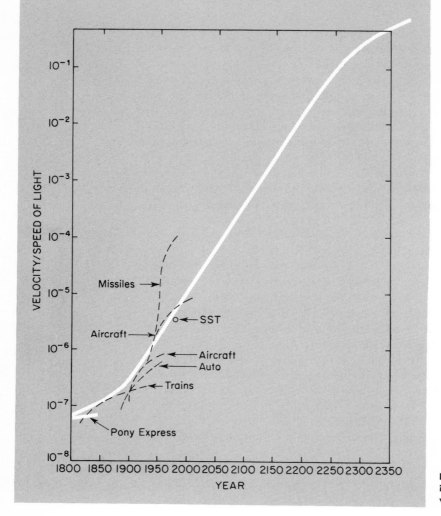

Figure 6. Speed Trend (Mechanical Powered Vehicles). Data developed by D. G. Samaras.

This example illustrates a general problem of trend forecasting—mixed missions. When choosing a figure of merit, such as speed for commercial transport vehicles, it must be remembered that many other parameters will grow as improvements occur in the chosen figure of merit. Consistent data are only obtained if the same mission is examined. If different missions are used, the associated requirements will be different and the trend data can become inconsistent.

Another type of problem is also illustrated by this data. In addition to a fundamental limit on speed there are competitive limiting effects. Automobiles compete against trains. Aircraft compete against both. Thus, progress in automobiles results in slower progress with trains. The calculation accounts for the increased rate due to the transference of activity from a less favored competitor, but it does not allow for this decreased rate of progress on the competitors. Such information is not considered because the future competitors are usually not known; therefore, the trend represents the progress which is expected under a continuation of present conditions. Where required, such data can be included in the calculations by modifying equation (7); however, the additional complexity it introduces does not usually seem to be warranted.

Example 3

The last example relates to the efficiency of fuel-burning electric utility power plants in the United States. Considerable historical data are avail-

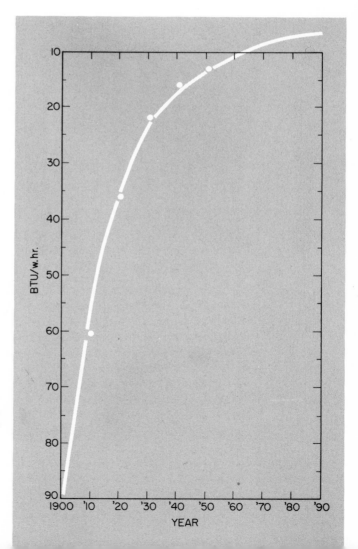

Figure 7. Efficiency of Fuel Burning Electric Power Plants (Ultimate Limit = 3.4 BTU/whr; Competitive Limit = 0).

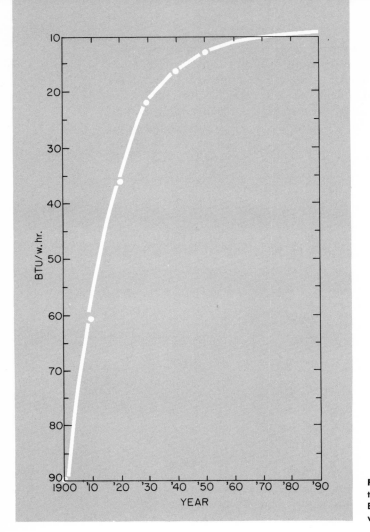

Figure 8. Efficiency of Fuel Burning Electric Power Plants. (Ultimate Limit = 7.8 BTU/whr; Competitive Limit = 230 BTU/whr).

able.[3] The figure of merit used is BTU's of energy consumed per watt-hour of electricity generated. The ultimate limit is the conversion factor, 3.4 BTU/watt-hour. No competitive system has been identified, although there must have been some type of competitive power. The trend curve shown in Figure 7 was developed from the nomograph, using infinity as the competitive limit. The actual data points are shown on the figure. The S configuration of these data points about the trend curve indicates that the limits chosen may not have been the best for the data. Thermodynamical con-

[3] *McGraw-Hill Encyclopedia*, Vol. 10, 558.

siderations indicate that high temperature strength of materials is the controlling limit for this technology.

Using 7.8 BTU/watt-hour as the ultimate limit, and 230 BTU/watt-hour as the competitive limit, the trend curve shown on Figure 8 is obtained. This fits the data better and illustrates the importance of the limits, which are the scaling factors of the nomograph. The particular estimates used in Figure 8 are still very rough and a better fit could be obtained; however, since the data are distributed about the trend, wherever possible, these limits should be calculated, rather than estimated from the best fit of the trend curve.

SUMMARY

The technique described can be employed to develop trend curves for figures of merit where:

1. An ultimate limit can be calculated or estimated;
2. The competitive technology limit can be estimated;
3. At least two data points are available.

The accuracy of the trend curve depends on:

1. Accuracy of estimates of ultimate and competitive limits used;
2. Accuracy of data;
3. Consistency of environment.

The time variation of the probability of achieving given values of a figure of merit can be calculated from the trend curve using the rules of conditional probability. It should be noted that the accuracy of the trend curve has not been considered in this calculation. However, if data are scattered, this effect should be included in probability calculations. The technique can easily be modified to allow calculation of the additional effort that would be required to achieve given probability levels of a figure of merit by a fixed time. This has application in planning research and development activities for future systems and equipment.

Caution must be exercised in choosing the figure of merit. Some figures of merit are not applicable in their usual form because of design trade-offs which can be made; e.g., the trade-off between fuel consumption and thrust-to-weight for aircraft engines. Under these conditions a figure of merit which allows for this trade-off must be used.

Although this methodology is not entirely new and considerable experimentation and improvements are required before forecasters will have confidence in its application, the approach seems to have value for figure-of-merit trend forecasting. The main modification that is required is some means for incorporating the acceleration effect which results from extremely high work inputs.

APPENDIX

The evaluation of equation (9) can be accomplished as follows:

$$P(f, t) = 1 - \exp[-(F - f) \int_{-\infty}^{t} (f - f_c)T(t) \, dt]$$

Let

$$P(f, t) = 0.5.$$

Then

$$0.5 = \exp[-(F - f) \int_{-\infty}^{t} (f - f_c)T(t) \, dt],$$

or

$$\ln 0.5 = -(F - f) \int_{-\infty}^{t} (f - f_c)T(t) \, dt.$$

Differentiating both sides with respect to time, this equation becomes

$$- \frac{df/dt}{(F - f)^2} = (f - f_c)T(t),$$

or

$$\int^{t} \frac{-df}{(F - f)^2 \, (f - f_c)} = \int^{t} T(t) \, dt.$$

The left side of this equation can be written

$$\int^{X} \frac{dX}{X^2 \, (X - \beta)} = \int T(t) \, dt,$$

where

$$X = F - f, \qquad \beta = F - f_c.$$

Using partial fractions this becomes

$$- \frac{1}{\beta^2} \int^{X} \left[\frac{\beta}{X^2} + \frac{1}{X} + \frac{1}{\beta - X} \right] dX = \int T(t) \, dt,$$

or

$$\frac{1}{\beta^2}\left[\ln\frac{\beta-X}{X}+\frac{\beta}{X}\right]+C_2=\int T(t)\,dt.$$

Letting

$$Y \equiv \frac{\beta}{X}=\frac{F-f_c}{F-f}=\frac{1-f_c/F}{1-f/F},$$

this becomes

$$\frac{1}{\beta^2}\left[\ln(Y-1)+Y\right]+C_2=\int T(t)\,dt.$$

Since the integral on the right is taken over very large values of t and since the time function is varying slowly, the integral can be approximated by a constant times the time interval plus a second constant, or

$$\frac{1}{\beta^2}\left[\ln(Y-1)+Y\right]+C_2'=C_1'\,t+C_2'$$

where C_1' and C_2' are constants. Thus, for the 50 percent probability trend,

$$P(f,\,t)=0.5=1-\exp\left[-0.6931\,\frac{C_1t+C_2}{\ln(Y+1)+Y+C_2}\right]$$

where the constant β has been included in C_1 and C_2. Along the trend line the function of Y and t is always unity.

It should be noted that the equation can also be integrated for cases where $(f-f_o)$ has exponent values greater than unity. The general solution is

$$\int\frac{dx}{X^2\,(\beta-X)^n}=n\ln\left(\frac{\beta}{X}-1\right)-\frac{1}{\beta^{n+1}}\sum_{S=0}^{n}\frac{n!}{(n-S)!\,S!\,(1-S)}\left(\frac{\beta}{X}-1\right)^{1-S}$$

$$=n\ln(Y-1)+\frac{1}{\beta^{n+1}}\sum_{S=0}^{n}\frac{n!}{(n-S)!\,S!\,(1-S)}(Y-1)^{1-S}$$

The additional terms generated are inverse values of $Y-1$, and they can be neglected with small error, except for values of Y near 1, or values of f/F near f_c/F. Thus, only the first term has been used, i.e., $n=1$.

REFERENCES

1. Bagby, F. L., D. L. Farrar, G. W. James, R. F. Badertuscher, H. C. Cross, *A Feasibility Study of Techniques for Measuring and Predicting the State of the Art*, Columbus, Ohio: Battelle Memorial Institute, July, 1959.

2. Isenson, R. S., "Technological Forecasting in Perspective," *Management Science*, Vol. 13, No. 2 (October, 1966), B-70.

3. Lenz, Ralph C., Jr., *Technological Forecasting*, Ohio: Wright-Patterson Air Force Base, June, 1962.

4. Prehoda, R. W., "Technology Forecasting and Space Exploration," *QED*, October, 1966, p. 16.

Techniques for Measuring Uncertainty in Technological Forecasting

FRANK J. HUSIC

Technological forecasting is, by definition, an area intimately concerned with uncertainty. However, too often the forecasts that are presented to decision makers fail to include an explicit description of the inherent uncertainties. Three techniques are described that can be used to convey such information to decision makers. They are based on probability theory and permit the build-up of uncertainty distributions of total projects from the distributions of individual parameters.

Mr. Husic is a member of the technical staff of the Research Analysis Corporation. The techniques which he describes are being used at RAC by Mr. Husic and his colleagues.

The mission of technological forecasting is to ". . . help evaluate the probability and significance of various possible future developments so managers can make better decisions." [1] The future contains an almost infinite number of threats and opportunities that could be relevant for a decision maker. Technological forecasting attempts to project those of greatest probability and potential impact. This requires (1) a projection of stages of technical development and (2) a projection of potential needs or demands.

To be useful for planning, such projections must be explicit in terms of

[1] James Brian Quinn, "Technological Forecasting," *Harvard Business Review*, March–April, 1967, p. 89.

the impact of uncertainties associated with the projections. Unfortunately, present techniques do not provide all of the information that is available concerning these uncertainties, but there are new techniques that effectively present such data.

Projections are often presented to decision makers as single-point estimates. However, such analyses have severe limitations because of the uncertainties associated with the variables being forecast and the often large dollar implications of deviations from those estimates. To circumvent these problems a form of sensitivity analysis has become popular. This technique identifies the impact of variations of input parameters on forecasts. Thus, if a model relates total future demand for a particular product to population growth, sensitivity analysis would involve running the model utilizing various growth rates. Presumably, these rates would be the user's assessment of "reasonable" values.

Such an analysis, however, still confines itself to single points, not ranges. It allows for no statements as to the probability of deviations and no measures of the uncertainty inherent in the projection. Thus, while an analysis may illustrate that a 4 per cent growth in population will generate demand of $9 million in the future, and that a 6 per cent increase will generate $30 million, it makes no statement as to which is most likely or whether either is really likely at all. The decision maker is forced to make judgments about the more probable growth rate or to accept the equal likelihood of both.

In the context of a simple model such as the one described above, the decision maker may be able to judge which is the more meaningful growth rate; but in more complex models, the increased number of variables and relationships makes the use of judgment extremely difficult. The objection to this type of analysis becomes even stronger when projections of stages of technical development are considered. First, these projections are often dependent upon the development of selected critical parameters; e.g., payload per gross weight, for personal flying belts. Second, the individuals best informed about the parameters are, in most cases, not those who will be making the decisions. This emphasizes the need to tell the decision maker all that is known about probable states of development of critical parameters.

Considerations such as these have focused attention on new techniques based on probability theory that can better develop and portray the information on uncertainty necessary for decision making. Three techniques have been developed and are being tested at the Research Analysis Corporation (RAC).[2] The basic assumption of each of these techniques is that forecasting inputs, like growth rates, R&D costs, and stages of development of technical parameters, can be considered to be random variables which have

[2] For more details, see Frank J. Husic, *Cost Uncertainty Analysis*, RAC P-29, May, 1967.

probability distributions. The techniques then combine these distributions in accordance with the equations of the particular forecasting model to produce probability distributions instead of single-point estimates for demand and/or capability projections. The techniques, which differ only in method of combination of distributions, are enumerated and briefly described below.

1. Derivation of Moments

A distribution curve has a set of mathematical properties called moments, which can completely define a particular curve. Moreover, these can be combined by certain mathematical formulae to produce corresponding moments for any combination of sums and products of curves. The derivation of moments technique can be used to: (1) convert user-specified parameters to the moments of their distributions; (2) combine these moments in the manner specified by the forecasting model; and (3) reconvert this combination of moments to the distribution it describes.

2. Monte Carlo

In this method, many iterations of the same forecasting model are run, each of which changes the inputs of the model in accordance with random values drawn from the probability distributions of the inputs. After a number of such iterations, a frequency curve can be developed for the model's outputs.

3. Symmetric Approximation

This method employs the same basic approach as the derivation of moments technique, but utilizes certain approximating relationships to determine the moments of the distributions.

To date, tests have been run utilizing Beta distributions. This is a type of distribution which, in its symmetric form, resembles a bounded normal distribution. However, it differs from the normal in that it can reflect skewness or flatness—traits which often prove valuable for expressing uncertainty.

For all three techniques, the user must select a most likely value (presumably this would correspond to the input that the user would specify if producing only a single-point projection), the high value, and the low

Low Value   Most Likely   High Value   **Figure 1. Beta Distribution.**

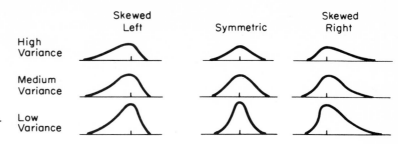

Figure 2. Sample Set of Distributions.

value. These are illustrated in Figure 1, which shows one type of Beta distribution.

In addition, the user selects a type of distribution from a fixed set of distributions which can be described qualitatively in terms of skewness and variance. Figure 2 illustrates a sample set of nine distributions.

With these user-specified parameters as inputs, each technique can produce probability distributions for the projections which result from the particular forecasting models. An example will help to illustrate the way these techniques can be used by a firm for technological forecasting.

Suppose a manager is interested in estimating the costs of a missile airframe. The missile is not yet designed or built, so no production-cost data are available. A cost estimating relation (CER) has placed the airframe cost at approximately $32,000, but the design group has warned that additional sophistication might raise costs above the CER prediction, and that improvements in some manufacturing techniques hold the promise of lower costs. Quick calculations provide estimates as low as $26,000 and as high as $45,000. Each of these calculations is based on a set of assumptions concerning labor and overhead rates, material costs in the future, and design details which are not yet firm and are subject to some uncertainty. After each factor is considered, the analyst enters his final estimate as $36,000. Obviously, with a single-point estimate the analyst is not telling the hypothetical decision maker all he needs to know to make a rational decision.

If the reasoning that fixed the relevant range of costs at $26,000 to $45,000 could yield information on the probabilities of occurrence, the techniques described above could develop the missing information. From this information, a probability distribution for costs of the airframe could be developed. When combined with similarly determined distributions of other cost components, total missile cost could be obtained, or even total system cost if other equipment is to be costed. The techniques would produce statistical measures of the distribution of total missile cost, including the mean and variance. Most important, it would provide a graphical display of the total cost range implied by the uncertainties associated with the input parameters. This is illustrated in Figure 3.

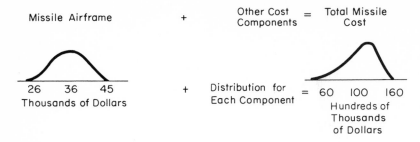

Figure 3. Obtaining Total Project Cost Distributions.

The development of combinations of probability distributions need not be limited to costs. This reasoning can be applied to any aspect of the firm's technological forecasting for which (1) explicit statements of the relationship of variables can be made; and (2) the necessary input parameters can be determined. Moreover, the ultimate use of such techniques appears to be in models to project probabilistic measures of return on investment for different product markets. In these kinds of models, the example described above would be just a minor component, the output of which would feed into other relationships and finally lead to the establishment of distributions for total costs.

The techniques described here are part of an ongoing research effort at RAC. At present, research is being conducted to enable the use of distribution types other than Beta. Other efforts are aimed at incorporating time phasing so that forecasts can be developed probabilistically on a year-to-year basis. Moreover, these techniques, or an adaptation of them, probably can be used in conjunction with other technological forecasting techniques to provide probabilistic, as opposed to deterministic, projections for a total research and development planning system.

Caution is necessary, however, in using these techniques. Certain assumptions are made that may not be valid in every situation. Two of these are especially important. The first is that the user can, in fact, specify a distribution type and the required parameters of that distribution. This does not assume that the user has a distribution that has been mathematically determined from a large set of data, but that he can construct a distribution using subjective judgments about parameters. This assumption, moreover, highlights the twofold nature of the problem the decision maker faces. He must first obtain the inputs required for distribution specification and then he must process the distributions into a form which is useful for decision-making. The nature of the two aspects is vastly different; the latter is a purely mathematical process, while the former involves subjective judgments and thus has psychological implications. Much research remains to be done to develop useful tools for eliciting the inputs required for a distribution. Second, the techniques assume that the input variables are independent or that their dependence can be made explicit. Research in this latter area has produced a number of ways of determining such explicit relationships but has not eliminated this constraint altogether.

Techniques such as these do not eliminate uncertainty from forecasting. They are valuable tools because they furnish measures of uncertainty which would not otherwise be available. Therefore, while limitations exist and caution must be exercised in their use, there is cause for optimism about the utility of such techniques in a wide range of forecasting problems.

Analysis of the Future: The Delphi Method[1]

OLAF HELMER

Many of the elements involved in projecting future developments do not lend themselves to quantification. Instead, the opinions of experts must be combined in some meaningful way so that their collective knowledge and judgments can be brought to bear. The Delphi technique is gradually evolving as a way of systematically combining individual judgments to obtain a reasoned consensus. Its unique feature and potential merit lie in requiring the experts to consider the objections and concepts of other group members, in an environment free from bias caused by personalities.

Dr. Helmer developed the Delphi method in collaboration with Norman Dalkey. Together with T. J. Gordon of Douglas Aircraft, he applied it to a major long-range forecasting study under the auspices of the RAND corporation, where he is a Senior Mathematician. Dr. Helmer has done a great deal of work in the area of technological forecasting and has published a book and a number of articles on the subject.

The decade of the Sixties has brought an important change in the intellectual climate throughout many parts of the world. A new attitude toward the future has become apparent in public and private planning agencies as well as in the research community. This change has extended

[1] Material for this paper was drawn from several of the author's published articles. This paper has also appeared in Italian translation in *Rivista Italiana di Amministrazione Industriale*.

customary planning horizons to a more distant future and replaced haphazard intuitive gambles, as a basis for planning, by sober and craftsmanlike analysis of the opportunities the future has to offer.

The change in attitude toward the future is manifesting itself in several ways: philosophically, it has brought a new understanding of what it means to talk about the future; pragmatically, it has fostered a growing recognition that it is important to do something about the future; and methodologically, it has stimulated new and more effective ways of doing something about the future.

The change in philosophical attitude means that the exploration of the the future is no longer equated with fortune-telling or with crystal-ball gazing. Instead there is a growing awareness that a great deal can be said about future trends in terms of probability, and, moreover, that through proper planning, these probabilities can be influenced considerably. In other words, fatalism has become a fatality. The future is no longer viewed as unique, unforeseeable, and inevitable; there are, instead, a multitude of possible futures, with associated probabilities that can be estimated and, to some extent, manipulated.

The new pragmatic attitude, which is beginning to be noticeable in government as well as in industry, is due to the fact, that not only technology and the environment are undergoing change, but also the pace of change is accelerating. No longer does it take generations for a new pattern of living conditions to evolve. Instead, the present generation is going through several major adjustments, and its children will have to accept continual adaptation as a way of life. For such adaptation to occur without major psychological or economic disruption, it is becoming mandatory to anticipate changes in the environment instead of attempting to deal with such changes belatedly and inadequately, after they are obviously upon us.

The recognition of this need for anticipation has had visible effects. Until recently, systematic efforts at long-range governmental or industrial planning were in bad odor in the capitalist countries, because they were associated in the public mind with what many considered to be the worst aspects of state-controlled socialism. This view, fortunately, is now outdated, and there is a general awareness that in the competition between Western capitalism and the Communist bloc, the former cannot hope to prevail unless the quality of its long-range planning is unsurpassed. Confirmatory evidence can be found in several recent developments, in the areas of labor, industry, and government. Labor unions show growing and explicit concern, not just over the near future, but over the long-term social implications of automation and other causes of increased productivity. Industry also shows a noticeable change in attitude, inasmuch as it is beginning to take a hard look at the possible long-term future of our society in order to formulate appropriate guidance for the conduct of operations. Finally, the various departments of the U.S. federal government are undergoing a thorough reorganization of their planning methods. This is the consequence of a directive from President Johnson to introduce, throughout the government system, so-called program-budgeting procedures which were first used successfully only in the Defense Department.

The growing ability to do something about the future is enhanced by the fact that the so-called soft sciences are on the verge of a revolution. The traditional methods of the social sciences are proving inadequate to deal effectively with the ever-growing complexity of forecasting the consequences of alternative policies. This situation is rapidly being remedied by the introduction of new methods developed primarily as operations research techniques. These include the construction of mathematical models, the use of simulation procedures, and a systematic approach to the utilization of expert opinions. In addition to these techniques, new uses of computers, with automated access to central data banks, will provide the soft sciences with the same kind of massive data-processing capability that created the breakthrough in the physical sciences which led to the development of the atomic bomb.

Among the new methods that are under development is one that has become known as the "Delphi technique." It attempts to make effective use of informed intuitive judgment. It derives its importance from the realization that projections into the future, on which public policy decisions must rely, are largely based on the personal expectations of individuals rather than on predictions derived from a well-established theory. Even when a formal, mathematical model is available—as is the case, for example, for various aspects of the national economy—the input assumptions, the range of applicability of the model, and the interpretation of the ouput are all subject to intuitive intervention by an individual who can bring the appropriate expertise to bear on the application of the model. In view of the absence of a proper theoretical foundation and the consequent inevitability of having, to some extent, to rely on intuitive expertise—a situation still further compounded by its multidisciplinary characteristics—two options are available: hands can be thrown up in despair and policy decisions can be postponed until adequate theories are available to deal with socioeconomic and political problems as confidently as problems in physics and chemistry are handled, or the most can be made of an admittedly unsatisfactory situation and attempts can be made to obtain the relevant intuitive insights of experts and then use their judgments as systematically as possible.

The best that can be done when expert judgments have to be relied upon is to make the most constructive and systematic use of such opinions. In dealing with experts, there are basically three rules which ought to be followed: (1) the experts must be selected wisely; (2) the proper conditions under which they can perform most ably must be created; (3) if several experts forecast a particular subject, considerable caution must be used in deriving a single combined position.

Much depends on how expert the experts are. Their proper selection presents many problems. There are difficulties in defining qualifications and measuring relative performance of experts. It is far from obvious what is meant—or should be meant—when somebody is labeled an "expert." Even given reasonable criteria of "expertness," it may not be easy to obtain adequate data for determining a person's degree of expertise.

The second rule, that an expert should be placed in the right conditions in order to perform well, means that communication should be facilitated as much as possible. The prior formulation of an appropriate model, even a very tentative one of the operations-analytical kind, serves to communicate the problem to the expert with clarity and permits the receipt of his answer without risk of misinterpretation. The expert's performance is aided greatly if he has ready access to relevant information that may exist elsewhere. (In this regard, rapid progress in data processing may open up new possibilities by which the present "swamping with irrelevancies" will eventually be replaced with push-button availability of pertinent data in the form of automated libraries.) Also, in order to provide access to intuitive knowledge that may not have been recorded yet, an expert's performance is enhanced most significantly if he is placed in a situation where he can interact with other experts in the same field or in fields related to other aspects of the same problem.

A particularly effective way of encouraging interaction among experts is to place them in a laboratory situation where they are required to participate in a simulation exercise. In a simulation model a kind of conceptual transference takes place. Instead of describing a situation directly, each of its elements is simulated by substituting mathematical or physical objects for the real ones and simulative relationships for those that actually exist. As an example, a policy planning operation can be simulated by a set of make-believe decision makers who, playing roles in a laboratory "game," might go through the decision-making motions that their real-life counterparts would be expected to carry out in actuality.

In a simulation model, instead of directly formulating hypotheses and predictions regarding the real world, they can be formulated with reference to the model. Any results obtained from an analysis of the model, to the extent that it accurately simulates reality, can later be translated back into corresponding statements about the real world. This interjection of a model has the advantage of "pseudo-experimentation" ("pseudo" because the experiments are carried out in the model, not in reality).

Past experience with simulation models suggests that they can be highly instrumental in motivating participants to communicate effectively with one another, to learn more about the subject matter by viewing it through the eyes of persons with backgrounds and skills different from their own, and, above all, to acquire an integrated overview of the problem area. This stimulating effect of collaborating on the employment of a simulation model is particularly powerful when the simulation takes the form of an operational game where the participants act out the roles of decision- and policy-making entities. The exposure, within a simulated environment, to a conflict situation involving an intelligent opposition, compels the "player," no matter how narrow his specialty, to consider many aspects of the scene that might not influence his opinions significantly if he worked in isolation.

The traditional and, in many ways, the simplest method of achieving a consensus of experts has been to conduct a round-table discussion and ask for a statement of a group position. This procedure is open to a number of criticisms. In particular, the outcome is apt to be a compromise between divergent views, arrived at, all too often, under the undue influence of certain psychological factors such as specious persuasion by the member with the greatest supposed authority, or even merely the loudest voice; the unwillingness to abandon publicly expressed opinions; and the bandwagon effect of majority opinion. The Delphi technique is designed to overcome these difficulties. In its simplest form, it eliminates committee activity among the experts altogether and replaces it with a carefully designed program of sequential, individual interrogations (usually best conducted by questionnaires). These are interspersed with information and opinion feedback.

The principles involved in this procedure can best be described by referring to a particular example. During an inquiry into the future of automation,[2] each member of a panel of experts was asked to estimate the year when a machine would become available that would comprehend standard IQ tests and score above 150 (where "comprehend" was interpreted, behavioristically, as the ability to respond to printed questions, possibly accompanied by diagrams). The initial responses consisted of a set of estimates spread over a sizeable time-interval, from 1975 to 2100. A follow-up questionnaire fed back to the respondents a summary of the distribution of these responses, stating the median and—as an indication of the spread of opinions—the interquartile range (i.e., the interval containing the middle 50 per cent of the responses). The respondents were then asked to reconsider their previous answers and revise them if desired. If a new response lay outside the interquartile range, the particular respondent was asked to state his reason for thinking that the answer should be that much lower, or that much higher, than the majority judgment of the group.

Placing the onus of justifying relatively extreme responses on the re-

[2] As part of a long-range forecasting study conducted with the participation of Theodore Gordon under the auspices of the RAND Corporation; a report on this study appeared as an appendix to *Social Technology* by O. Helmer (New York: Basic Books, Inc., Publishers, 1966).

spondents had the effect of causing those without strong convictions to move their estimates closer to the median, while those who felt they had a good argument for a "deviant" opinion tended to retain their original estimates and defend them.

In the next round, responses (now spread over a smaller interval) were again summarized, and the respondents were given a concise summary of the reasons presented in support of extreme positions. They were then asked to revise their second-round responses, taking the proffered reasons into consideration and giving them whatever weight they thought was justified. A respondent whose answer still remained outside the interquartile range was required to state why he was unpersuaded by the opposing arguments. In a fourth and final round, these criticisms of the reasons previously offered were resubmitted to the respondents, and they were given a last chance to revise their estimates. The median of these final responses could then be taken as representing the nearest thing to a group consensus. In the case of the high-IQ machine, this median turned out to be the year 1990, with a final interquartile range from 1985 to 2000. The procedure thus caused the median to move to a much earlier date and the interquartile range to shrink considerably, presumably influenced by convincing arguments.

This convergence of opinions has been observed in the majority of cases where the Delphi approach has been used. In a few of the cases where no convergence toward a relatively narrow interval of values took place, opinions began to polarize around two distinct values, so that two schools of thought regarding a particular issue seemed to emerge. This may have been an indication that opinions were based on different sets of data, or on different interpretations of the same data. In such cases, it is conceivable that a continuation of the Delphi process, through several more rounds of anonymous debate-by-questionnaire, eventually might have tracked down and eliminated the basic cause of disagreement and thus led to a true consensus. But even if this did not happen, or if the process were terminated before it had a chance to happen, the Delphi technique would have served the purpose of crystallizing the reasoning process that led to the positions which were taken and thus would have helped to clarify the issues even in the absence of a group consensus.

The illustration given above is intended to describe the basic essentials of the Delphi technique. Refinements can be made to fit each particular case. Two such refinements are discussed below.

One is the introduction of weighted opinions. If it were easy to measure objectively the relative trustworthiness of different experts, greatest, if not exclusive, weight would be given to the opinions of those who were most trustworthy. In view of the absence of such measurements, experiments have been carried out to test the degree of reliance that may be placed on the experts' self-appraisal of their relative competence, and the results have been quite promising. This device was used in November, 1965, when twenty members of the faculty of the Graduate School of Business Administration at the University of California (Los Angeles) made forecasts of ten economic and business indices for the last quarter of 1965 and for the entire year 1966 (twenty answers altogether). The procedure was as follows: In addition to going through four rounds of Delphi arguments, the respondents were asked to rank their relative competence with regard to each of the ten indices. Then, instead of using the median of all twenty final responses as the group consensus for each index, only the responses of those individuals who had ranked themselves relatively most highly competent for that particular index were used. Subsequent evaluation showed that this select median, compared to the median of all responses, was closer to the true value of $13\frac{1}{2}$ out of the 20 cases.

Second, a slightly more sophisticated application of the Delphi approach can be made where it is used in conjunction with a simulated decision-making process of the kind mentioned earlier. A typical situation to which this mode of using expertise is applicable is one in which budgetary decisions have to be made on the basis of cost-benefit estimates. When costs and benefits are clearly measurable objective terms, there is no need to resort to the use of mere opinions. But in practice, the benefits resulting from the choice of a given policy alternative almost never can be measured unambiguously. Even in the case of cost estimates, usually only the dollar expenditures are closely predictable, and social costs may be as elusive as the benefits. In such cases, a consensus of judgments made by experts may be helpful in obtaining an appraisal.

In a recent experiment conducted in the course of a project concerned with educational innovations, expert opinions were used in a context of this sort. Applying the Delphi process, a list of potential educational innovations, together with rough cost estimates, was first obtained. Experts were grouped into several panels and each panel was asked to go through a simulated planning process to decide how a given budget should be allocated to the educational innovations contained in the list. In order to make these allocations in a rational manner, the participants had to engage in an intuitive, cost-benefit appraisal of each item. A Delphi synthesis of individual opinions proved to be the most effective means of achieving a group consensus.

These examples are intended merely to illustrate the potentialities of the Delphi technique. Many additional experiments need to be carried out to test the extent of its validity and to refine it to the point where it may be fully accepted as one of the standard tools for the analysis of the future and, in particular, for policy applications in the general area of social technology.

The Delphi Method—
An Illustration

One way to understand the concepts, potential, and limitations of a technological forecasting method is to try it. Dr. Olaf Helmer, assisted by Mr. T. J. Gordon, conducted an interesting audience participation session at the Conference on Technological Forecasting. Although limited by time and selection, this simple illustration quickly and effectively familiarized participants with the attributes and theory of the Delphi method.

The following example is presented as an illustration of the Delphi method. It describes a Delphi session which was conducted by Dr. Olaf Helmer and was evaluated by Dr. Helmer and Mr. T. J. Gordon at the First Annual Technology and Management Conference. The session was intended to give conference delegates an experience in the Delphi technique, and the participants were selected at random, not on the basis of their expertise in regard to the session's subject matter. Consequently, attention should be directed toward the methodology, not the results. Under ideal conditions, each of the participants would have been selected for his particular knowledge of the fields for which projections were being made.

STEP 1

Questionnaire 1 (see Exhibit 1) was distributed to over one hundred conference participants and each was asked to complete the form and return it to Dr. Helmer. In addition to giving his answers, each participant was asked to rank his expertise to deal with the particular questions. A "one" was to be placed in the box beside that question which the participant felt most competent to answer, and a "seven" alongside the question about which he believed himself to be least competent. Each of the remaining questions was to be ranked so that every number from 1 to 7 was used exactly once. Although questions were raised concerning biases in the wording of the questions, for purposes of the illustration participants were asked to accept the questions exactly as they were presented on the form.

EXHIBIT 1.

QUESTIONNAIRE #1

This is the first in a series of four questionnaires intended to demonstrate the use of the Delphi Technique in obtaining reasoned opinions from a group of respondents.

Each of the following six questions is concerned with developments in the United States within the next few decades.

In addition to giving your answer to each question, you are also being asked to rank the questions from 1 to 7. Here "1" means that in comparing your own ability to answer this question with what you expect the ability of the other participants to be, you feel that you have the relatively best chance of coming closer to the truth than most of the others, while a "7" means that you regard that chance as relatively least.

RANK	QUESTION	ANSWER *
☐	1. In your opinion, in what year will the median family income (in 1967 dollars) reach twice its present amount?	☐
☐	2. In what year will the percentage of electric among all automobiles in use reach 50 percent?	☐
☐	3. In what year will the percentage of households reach 50 percent that are equipped with computer consoles tied to a central computer and data bank?	☐
☐	4. By what year will the per-capita amount of personal cash transactions (in 1967 dollars) be reduced to one tenth of what it is now?	☐
☐	5. In what year will power generated by thermonuclear fusion become commercially competitive with hydroelectric power?	☐
☐	6. By what year will it be possible by commercial carriers to get from New York's Times Square to San Francisco's Union Square in half the time that is now required to make that trip?	☐
☐	7. In what year will a man for the first time travel to the Moon, stay for at least one month, and return to Earth?	☐

* "Never" is also an acceptable answer.

Please also answer the following question, and give your name (this for identification purposes during the exercise only; no opinions will be attributed to a particular person).

CHECK ONE:

☐ I would like
☐ I am willing but not anxious   } to participate in the three remaining questionnaires
☐ I would prefer not

NAME (block letters please):

. . . .

From among those participants who indicated on the returned questionnaires that they would like to participate in the remaining sessions, Dr. Helmer selected twenty-three. The selection attempted to achieve a uniform distribution of the number of "expert ratings" (i.e., those who ranked themselves "1" or "2," etc.) for each of the questions, but was otherwise random. Each of the twenty-three participants then received Questionnaire 2 (see Exhibit 2), containing a summary of the results of Questionnaire 1 (derived from the responses of the entire group of conference participants). Each participant's Questionnaire #2 also listed the estimates he gave on his Questionnaire #1.

The completed Questionnaires #2 were returned to Dr. Helmer and analyzed, and each participant then received a copy of Questionnaire #3 (see Exhibit 3). The participant's Questionnaire #2 was also returned to him.

The completed Questionnaires #3 were returned to Dr. Helmer. These were analyzed and each participant then received a copy of Questionnaire #4 (see Exhibit 4). The participant's Questionnaire #3 was also returned to him.

The series of questionnaires were analyzed by Dr. Helmer and Mr. T. J. Gordon, and the results were presented to the entire group of conference participants. The results are summarized in Exhibits 5–8.

Participants found the session to be extremely educational. It also raised a number of questions relating to the importance of proper question formulation, the selection and ranking of experts, and the tendency to move toward the interquartile range to avoid extra effort (i.e., the justification of one's position in writing). Such illustrations were believed to be very valuable for imparting knowledge of the technique, even though the results of the forecasts, in this case, were not expected to be particularly reliable.

EXHIBIT 2

QUESTIONNAIRE #2

This is the second in our series of four Delphi questionnaires.

The same seven questions that had been posed in the first questionnaire are repeated below, together with information on the median and the interquartile range (IQR) of the first-round responses. [The IQR is the interval containing the middle 50% of the responses.]

Please reconsider your previous estimate, and change it if you wish. Whenever your present answer is outside the IQR, briefly state your reason why you think the answer should be a year that much earlier (or later) than that given by the majority of respondents. (No such reason needs to be given when your answer is inside the IQR.)

Question	Median	IQR	Your Old Answer	Your New Answer	Reason Why Your Answer Is Below or Above the IQR
1. In your opinion, in what year will the median family income (in 1967 dollars) reach twice its present amount?	85	80–92	F		
2. In what year will the percentage of electric among all automobiles in use reach 50%.	90	85–2012	I L L		
3. In what year will the percentage of households reach 50% that are equipped with computer consoles tied to a central computer and data bank?	2000	90–2075	E D		
4. By what year will the per-capita amount of personal cash transactions (in 1967 dollars) be reduced to one tenth of what it is now?	90	82–2000	I N B Y		
5. In what year will power generated by thermonuclear fusion become commercially competitive with hydroelectric power?	90	79–2005	D R.		
6. By what year will it be possible by commercial carriers to get from New York's Times Square to San Francisco's Union Square in half the time that is now required to make that trip?	80	75–85	H E L		
7. In what year will a man for the first time travel to the Moon, stay for at least one month, and return to Earth?	77½	75–85	M E R		

NAME: ....

EXHIBIT 3

QUESTIONNAIRE #3

The same familiar seven questions are restated below, together with the medians and interquartile ranges (IQRs) or the 23 second-round responses. Also included are some brief arguments as to why the estimates should be either earlier or later than those within the IQR.

Please reconsider your previous estimates (which are attached), and revise them if you wish, giving the stated reasons for raising or lowering them what weight you think they deserve. (If there is no change in your previous response, please re-insert it under "Your new answer.")

If your present answer lies outside the indicated IQR, briefly state in the last column why you think the argument that had been given in favor of an estimate on the opposite side of the IQR from your own is unacceptable. (In other words, if your estimate is high, refute the argument for a low estimate; if your estimate is low, refute the argument for a high estimate.)

Question	Median	IQR	Argument in Favor of An Earlier Date	Argument in Favor of A Later Date	Your New Answer	Your Critique of Arguments Unacceptable to You
1. In your opinion, in what year will the median family income (in 1967 dollars) reach twice its present amount?	1985	1980–1990	There is a 10% annual inflation. Union demands will bring this about sooner, through amendments to the "guide posts." The number of workers per family will rise. Income will grow faster than GNP as wage earners take a greater share of productivity earnings due to new technology.	The GNP goes up only 4% per year. There will be a decrease in the number of hours worked per family. Increasing inflation will devaluate the dollar. A major business depression may be expected. Real family income rose only 50% in last 25 years. The productivity per family will not grow so fast because neither the size of family unit nor productivity per family will.		
2. In what year will the percentage of electrical among all automobiles in use reach 50%?	1995	1985–2020	The first use will be for local travel, which will rapidly exceed 50%, in view of urban development. Developments in nuclear-power cost/effectiveness and energy storage point to an earlier date.	Pollution will force improvements in the combustion engine. Batteries don't provide enough power or range. Battery recharging is too inconvenient. The oil industry will resist this.		

EXHIBIT 3

QUESTIONNAIRE #3—Continued

Question	Median	IQR	Argument in Favor of An Earlier Date	Argument in Favor of A Later Date	Your New Answer	Your Critique of Arguments Unacceptable to You
3. In what year will the percentage of households reach 50% that are equipped with computer consoles tied to a central computer and data bank?	2010	1985–2100	The technology is here now. This will be combined with your telephone. Computers are getting cheaper fast. We need to reduce the volume of mail. Progress in computerization in commercial and social organization will require individual computers in homes; 15 years should do it (analogy: TV in 1945–60).	Electric cars will be too expensive. Natural-gas fuelled turbines have a better chance. There are enormous problems in economic conversion to electric energy in small packages, hence delay until fossil fuels exhausted. The social demand will not be great enough, considering the high cost. The main use would be for education and reference; we are several generations away from the intellectual level that can use such teachers and librarians. Cost-effectiveness of personal data banks and decentralized computers will rise, and they are preferable because of privacy. Who needs instant bank statements that badly?		
4. By what year will the per-capita amount of personal cash transactions (in 1967 dollars) be reduced to one tenth of what it is now?	1985	1985–1990	Everyone will soon be assigned a combination credit card and social security card. Studies by the banking industry are already underway to computerize monetary transactions. Connecticut already has a state-wide credit card.	We seem to be already approaching the minimum now, and therefore may never reach that low a level in the near future.		
5. In what year will			Water shortage within 10	Fixing-generated		

...desalination, will rapidly become so great that thermonuclear power production will be generally accepted.

Decentralization of population centers and cost of distribution favor nuclear power.

The next drought will be world-wide.

problems to overcome.

There is little economic incentive since electric power is cheap.

Tidal power is yet untapped.

The cost of hydro-electric facilities is shared, there is no fuel cost, and maintenance is lower.

Efficient containment of thermonuclear energy seems to be completely out of the question.

	1976	1975–1980		
6. By what year will it be possible by commercial carriers to get from New York's Time Square to San Francisco's Union Square in half the time that is now required to make that trip?			Rapid transit approaches to the airports will be set up. Baggage will be handled faster. The Concorde will appear on U.S. schedules by 1973, and a U.S. SST by 1975.	Supersonic flight is not possible over land barriers. Now it takes 15m + 4h 30m + 30m = 5h 15m; with SST it would take 10m + 2h 15m + 20m = 2h 45m, which is more than 50%. Increase in aircraft speed alone will not achieve this so soon; other developments (vertical take-off etc.) will be required, which will take somewhat longer.
	1977	1975–1980		
7. In what year will a man for the first time travel to the Moon, stay for at least one month, and return to Earth?			After a first successful landing, only about 3 years will be required to develop life-cycle equipment for an extended stay. The capability will exist in the early 70s, national prestige and curiosity will dictate the decision. Mission profiles compatible with Apollo/LEM hardware/payload capabilities will be available in the early 70s.	Regular Moon trips will not occur until 1980, and a Moon station not until after 1990. The rise in cost will force a slowdown in the Moon program, especially in view of alternative goals (e.g. oceanographic research).

EXHIBIT 4

QUESTIONNAIRE #4

This is the last in our series of four questionnaires. Together with each of the seven questions, restated once more below, you are given the third-round median and IQR of the 23 responses received, as well as a summary of statements critical of the reasons that had been given in response to the second questionnaire.

Please reconsider (and possibly revise) your previous estimates once more in the light of arguments (see attached Questionnaire 3) and counter-arguments that had been advanced for and against raising or lowering them.

Question	Median	IQR	Counter-Arguments in Defense of An Earlier Date	Counter-Arguments in Defense of A Later Date	Your Final Answer
1. In your opinion, in what year will the median family income (in 1967 dollars) reach twice its present amount?	1985	1980–1990	The GNP rose 4.3% before the "guide posts" were removed; now it will go up faster. Advanced skills will sharply increase income. A major depression (as opposed to a healthy recession) is very unlikely under current and future federal safeguards. Family size is not of critical importance; husband and wife are the essential income producers.	Even if income grows faster than the 4% rate of GNP, it will not double in 20 or 30 years. Greater productivity of direct labor is largely offset by indirect labor due to maintenance etc. of more sophisticated equipment. The inflation argument is beside the point since the question is phrased in terms of 1967 dollars. The Union bargaining position has been weakened by strikes; federal intervention is more likely to be demanded in future. The number of workers per family will not rise, because as income increases, families tend to subdivide into new units.	
2. In what year will the percentage of electrical among all automobiles in use reach 50%?	1995	1985–2011	The later-date arguments overlook the political pressure. Battery and fuel cell improvements will, in the 1970s, provide sufficient power and range (cf. e.g., Ayres's envelope curves). Inconvenience will be minimized because recharging can be automatic upon garaging. Resistance of the oil industry can be countered by positive response of electric utilities. The later-date proponents seem to overlook the possibility of the car to tie into a power grid.	If it were not for pollution, this would occur even later than 2000. Energy storage would have to improve by 10 orders of magnitude. Consumers buy cars for long-distance high-speed driving.	
3. In what year will the percentage of households reach	2010	1995–2075	Social demand can be generated artificially.	The computerization argument fails to establish why home computers are required.	

Question	Year	Range		
to a central computer and data bank?			the bank-statements statement is irrelevant. The argument for later occurrence ignores the credit card, which means computerized banking, of which the event in question is a logical extension.	the poor, of which there will always be lots, have no need for the service provided, nor is there an economic incentive to provide it for them.
4. By what year will the per-capita amount of personal cash transactions (in 1967 dollars) be reduced to one tenth of what it is now?	1985	1985–1990	The statement about our approaching a minimum now is not based on fact.	Credit will not be extended so generally, i.e., not until bank accounts and payrolls are tied into the system, and this will take more time. "Studies" do not mean immediate implementation. Only 5% of my present expenditures are in cash; this would be hard to reduce to one tenth. The greatest portion of personal cash transactions today is in the lower income groups, and the impact of the earlier-date arguments on them will be minimal.
5. In what year will power generated by thermonuclear fusion become commercially competitive with hydroelectric power?	1985	1980–2030	Pressures regarding this on government and industry will escalate exponentially. The "out of the question" statement is of the form "airplanes will never fly."	Technical feasibility of plasma containment is not demonstrated or in sight. The earlier-date argument merely supports the case for fission-generated power, —which may be the real competitor, rather than hydroelectric power. The drought argument is too speculative for comment.
6. By what year will it be possible by commercial carriers to get from New York's Time Square to San Francisco's Union Square in half the time that is now required to make that trip?	1976	1975–1980	The airlines have identified ground transportation and "people handling" as their top priority assignment. Many downtown rooftop airports will be built for fast local air transport. Supersonic flights take place daily over the southwestern U.S.	High-speed land transportation will take longer to develop. The rapid-transit argument is not good enough, not until we have something faster than the SST under development. Rapid ground transit already exists; increased air traffic will further increase time on the ground.
7. In what year will a man for the first time travel to the Moon, stay for at least one month, and return to Earth?	1977	1975–1980	We are still competing with the Russians. Regular Moon trips will occur in the early 1970s; a Moon station is not required for a month's stay. "Regular Moon trips" was not part of the question. (Analogy: no regular transatlantic flights right after Lindbergh's flight.)	The argument for an earlier date is excessively optimistic as to resources to be devoted to this project by the U.S. or Russia. Reliability demands will cause delay. Growing use of cost-effectiveness analysis in government funding will slow development of necessary hardware in view of competing goals.

EXHIBIT 5

SUMMARY OF OUTCOME

	Inter Quartile Range	Median	"Expert" * Median
1. Family income doubled	1982–90	1985	1985
2. Electric autos 50%	1985–2000	1995	1997
3. Home computer consoles	1985–2075	2010	1985
4. Credit card economy	1985–90	1985	1987½
5. Economical fusion power	1985–2030	1990	1987½
6. N.Y. → S.F. in ½ time	1975–80	1976	1975
7. Man on moon one month	1975–80	1977	1975½

* Median of the 8 individuals who ranked themselves highest. The cutoff point was usually 2 or 3.

EXHIBIT 6

CONVERGENCE OF RANGE WITH SUCCESSIVE QUESTIONNAIRES

(Heavy Lines — Range, Dotted Lines = Final Median)

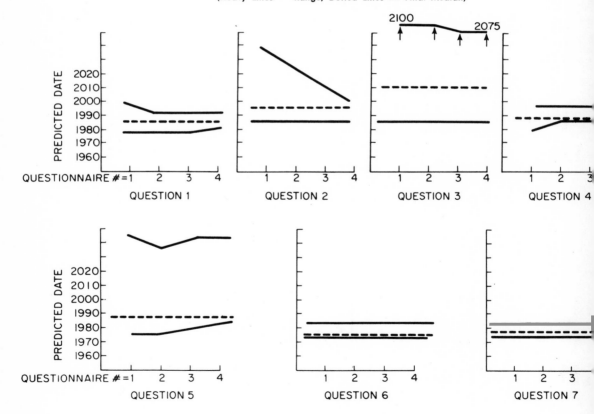

EXHIBIT 7

COMPARISON WITH OTHER STUDIES

(Medians)

	Present Conference Forecast	RAND * Pretest	1963 ** LRF Study	
1. Family income doubled	1985	1985	——	
2. Electric autos 50%	1997	1988	——	
3. Home computer consoles	2010	2002	2005	Facsimile magazines in home
4. Credit card economy	1987	1995	1974	Credit link bank to stores
5. Economical fusion power	1988	1990	1986	Controlled fusion achieved
6. N.Y. → S.F. in ½ time	1975	1980	——	
7. Man on moon one month	1976	1980	1975	Two men on moon one month

* A 1966 Delphi pretest, using 23 RAND employees as participants.
** A 1963 RAND Long Range Forecasting Study. A report of this study appeared as an appendix to *Social Technology*, by O. Helmer (Basic Books, 1966).

EXHIBIT 8

FORECAST PRECISION

(Note: Numbers on Graph Refer to Questions Asked)

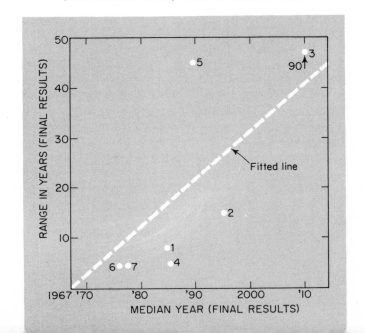

New Approaches to Delphi

T. J. GORDON

The Delphi method is a new and still evolving technique. The author describes a number of modifications which are being developed to eliminate some of its shortcomings and improve the usefulness of its results. Described are adaptations to situations where questions are not independent and the incorporation of computer capabilities within the Delphi procedure. Great emphasis is placed on the importance of careful selection of the "experts" who comprise a Delphi panel.

Mr. Gordon is Director of Space Stations and Planetary Systems for the Douglas Aircraft Company. Together with Dr. Olaf Helmer, of The RAND Corporation, he is an author of the Delphi technique. He has also designed the game "Future," for Kaiser Aluminum Company, which permits players to estimate likely future events which are interlinked with each other, and to influence the future through investment policies.

In their milestone paper, "An Experimental Application of the Delphi Method to the Use of Experts," Olaf Helmer and Norman Dalkey described the philosophical basis of the Delphi system for combining expert opinions into a group consensus.[1] The technique recognizes that in non-exact disciplines, expert opinion and subjective judgment must, of necessity, substitute for the exact laws of causality found in the physical sciences.

The Delphi method has proven extremely useful for long-range forecasting of expected technological and sociological developments. Several

[1] *Management Science*, Vol. 9, No. 3, April, 1963.

corporations and government agencies have recently completed future-oriented Delphi studies covering such inexact domains as political alliances,[2] technological potentials,[3] war prevention techniques,[4] and economic indices.[5] Results generally have been satisfactory; i.e., in most cases, consensus seems to have been achieved and the potential developments which were described provided a basis for subsequent planning action.

The method is being sharpened through the use of computers and as a result of interaction with other methods of operations analysis. These new approaches promise to bring additional flexibility, speed, and accuracy to this powerful technique. Some of these new approaches have been successfully demonstrated; others are being planned. Ideas will be described here to indicate the diversity of analyses which can be applied, not only to nonexact problems, but also to non-analytic problems.

CROSS CORRELATIONS

The Delphi technique has been criticized because it yields a set of "linearly independent" estimates of the future, with the probability or date of each item estimated independently of the others. When a participant, for example, considers an item such as "widespread acceptance of personality control drugs," other factors are subordinated to this item, and he must write his scenario for the world surrounding the use of drugs. Convergence of other items in the set of related subjects which contains "personality control drugs" proceeds independently from the eventual outcome of the drug items. This picture is not very satisfying. One should be able to view the future as an immense set of interrelating and interlocking paths. The pursuit of one path in this matrix, or the realization of certain items, should make certain other alternatives more or less probable.

Suppose that a list of developments are forecast, with varying levels of probability, to occur prior to the year 1984. If these developments are designated $D_1, D_2, \ldots D_n$, with associated probabilities $P_1, P_2, \ldots P_n$, then the question can be posed: "If $P_i \rightarrow 100\%$ (i.e., D_i happens) how do $P_1, P_2, P_3 \ldots P_n$ change?" If there is a cross correlation, the probability of individual items will vary either positively or negatively.

[2] Joseph Martino, *An Experiment with the Delphi Procedure for Long Range Forecasting*, USAF, AFOSR 670175, 1967.

[3] Harper North, *Technological Forecast*, Thompson Ramo Wooldridge Report, 1966.

[4] T. J. Gordon and Olaf Helmer, *Report on a Long-Range Forecasting Study*, Report P-2982, The RAND Corporation, Santa Monica, Calif., 1964.

[5] Robert M. Campbell, Ph.D. Thesis, UCLA, "A Methodological Study of the Utilization of Experts in Business Forecasting," September, 1966.

By way of illustration, if the following developments and probabilities have been forecast for a given year:

Development, D_i	Probability, P_i
1. 1-month reliable weather forecasts	.4
2. feasibility of limited weather control	.2
3. general biochemical immunization	.5
4. crop damage from adverse weather eliminated	.5

then these might be arranged in matrix form as shown in Figure 1. (The arrows indicate positive cross correlation.)

Thus, if D_2, "the feasibility of limited weather control," were to occur, D_1, "one month reliable weather forecasts," and D_4, "elimination of crop damage from adverse weather," would become more probable as noted by the upward arrow. The extent of the increased probability can itself be determined by Delphi processes. The process is not reversible; in other words, while the probability of D_4 will increase if D_1 happens, D_2 will not increase if D_4 happens. In exploring the relationship between forecasted developments, it has become apparent that certain classes of developments can be categorized as "provoking" (i.e., demanding subsequent innovation or policy action) or "enabling" (i.e., improving the feasibility or removing policy objections to other developments).

This cross correlation concept was employed by the author in a forecasting game designed for Kaiser Aluminum and Chemical Corporation (Figure 2).[6] Here sixty items forecast for the year 1986 were deployed around

[6] Inquiries about this game should be directed to Mr. Al deGrassi, Kaiser Aluminum and Chemical Corporation, Oakland, California. Dr. O. Helmer of RAND was a co-inventor of the game.

If this Development Were to Occur:	Then Probability of			
	D_1	D_2	D_3	D_4
D_1	╳	—	—	↑
D_2	↑	╳	—	↑
D_3	—	—	╳	—
D_4	—	—	—	╳

Figure 1. Matrix of Development Probabilities.

Courtesy: Kaiser Aluminum Company.

Figure 2.

a central square. Each item had an initial probability indicated by markers. One item, selected at random, was determined; i.e., its probability was shifted to either zero or 100 per cent depending on the roll of a die. The predetermined cross correlations were brought into play and the probabilities of the other items were adjusted accordingly. The design of the game also permitted adjustment of initial probabilities by investment of fiscal resources. Chance elements were introduced by randomizing the order in which each item would be examined, by using a die to determine the outcome of the item under scrutiny, and by introducing "unforeseen items" which independently affected the play and were beyond the control of the players. These "unforeseen items" were analogous to the unexpected breakthroughs of real life which can so greatly affect progress in many fields but are sudden and mutant deviations from current research anticipations. In the interest of the game, these were "tongue-in-cheek" events (see Figure 3 for an example).

In order to construct the game described above, a 60 x 60 matrix was reviewed for item cross correlations. Clearly, more extensive models would benefit from the use of machine memories. Suppose that 1,000 possible developments were listed, rather than 60, and that initial probabilities for each of these were established for a given year. Suppose further, that the 10^6 cross correlations could be constructed by some objective means. Then a

NEWS EVENT C

ADVANCE IN GENETIC MANIPULATION MAKES POSSIBLE CHOICE OF COLOR OF ONE'S PROGENY

New York: A spokesman for the Skyscraper Foundation announced here today that any parents could now treat their genes in such a way as to have babies of any color. Many parents already have selected colors such as chartreuse and mauve. As styles are beginning to crystallize, a new professional organization of "Posterity Decorators" has sprung into being to offer guaranteed color-scheme coordination service. . . .

Courtesy: Kaiser Aluminum Company.

Figure 3.

computer might be used to map out most probable combinations of these developments. In other words, automated scenarios would be produced, each with an overall probability ranking in respect to its neighbors. A computer could do this rather simply by starting with any item at random, determining its accomplishment or rejection based on its probability and a random number selection, and then adjusting the probability of the remaining 999 items according to the programmed cross correlations. The next item would then be selected at random, determined, and remaining items adjusted in probability. The beauty of this method would be that the effect of individual investment strategies could be tested quite simply by raising the initial probability of one or several items (simulating an allocation of resources) and determining the effect on the probabilities of the various scenarios observed. The author plans to experiment with this technique within the next year.

The problem of correlating developments is very complex. Real correlations are not digital. Instead, connections are subtle and vary widely in strength, depending on the developments being considered. Figure 4 shows some of these considerations. The four circles on the left represent classes of developments which influence D_1; the circles on the right represent the developments affected by D_1. The probability of each of the developments is composed of at least two major elements: the probabilities of feasibility

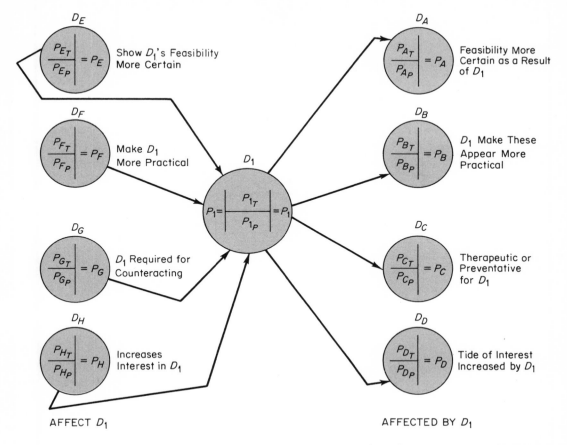

Figure 4. Relationship of Event D_1 to Other Events.

(subscript T) and of pursuit (subscript P). These components interrelate as shown in the figure.

SEQUENTIAL SCENARIOS

The future must build on the present, and the present is a summation of the past. Similarly, an image of the future can be constructed in steps, using the results of a single study or group of studies which define a near term world, as the base point for longer-range forecasts. Thus a twenty-year forecast might be constructed from four five-year forecasts—each succeeding study being built on the consensus of the prior study. This approach has proven to be particularly valuable in exploring alternative future policies which, necessarily, must be based on prior developments.

COMPUTER CONTROLLED FEEDBACK

At RAND, the JOSS computer has been used to control a series of simple Delphi studies. JOSS is a centralized, general purpose computer which is programmed to accept English language instruction and has tele-typewriter input/output stations at several remote locations in the RAND building.

Figure 5. An Example of a Page from a JOSS Controlled Delphi Run.

```
3.  What was the percentage of housing units in Arkansas in
1960 which had all plumbing facilities sound?  'All plumbing
facilities sound' means hot and cold running water inside the
structure for the exclusive use of the people in the unit.

    60.
    45.
    35.

            A = 55

4.  What was the percentage of housing units in California in
1960 which had all plumbing facilities sound?

    85.
    84.
    80.

            A = 85

That is a high estimate compared to others given.

You should type a short note giving your reasons in the
form of paragraph 43.  When you finish, type 'Go.' and the
experiment will continue.

I don't think that I considered the itinerant Mexican workers homes as housing

Please limit lines to 78 strokes.  Say again:

43.1  My estimate is high because I forgot about the itinerant workers.

Go.

5.  How many people were executed for murder in 1960?

    440.
     80.
     10.

            A = 220

There will be a short pause now.

Round three will be like round two, except that in addition
to all the answers given, you will be presented with some
of the reasons which participants had for them.
```

The computer was instructed to pose the same question to several isolated participants who were seated in rooms in different parts of the building. The computer asked for opinions on the questions posed, and the participants typed in their numerical estimates. (The questions were all of the type which could be answered numerically.) The computer scanned the answers and requested, from the players with the highest and lowest estimates, brief explanations of the reasons for their choices. These were automatically fed back to the players along with requests for re-estimates, etc. A partial reproduction of a JOSS run is shown in Figure 5. Typically, a six-question study, involving four participants and four feedbacks, required one and a half hours to complete.

The participants in these computer runs felt as if they were on intimate terms with JOSS, particularly since it assumed a first person identity. The computer had a personality—albeit an impatient and slightly arrogant one. Presumably, slight revisions in programming will make the machine somewhat more pleasant.

It is presently feasible to include participants located almost anywhere in the world in such computer controlled interactions. This offers the opportunity for relatively fast studies involving widely separated participants, and focusing important questions of the moment.

The computer itself might be used to perform auxiliary functions during the consensus determination; for example, it could serve as a data bank, available to all participants on call. Perhaps, as Dr. Marvin Adelson of the Systems Development Corporation has suggested, *banks* of models might be stored, ready to be called upon by the participants to aid in answering the machine-posed Delphi questions. Simliarly, through time-sharing facilities, computers used to control interpersonal communications might simultaneously perform auxiliary computations for the participants. During a recent JOSS run, one of the players, when asked a question by JOSS, instructed the machine to perform certain computations. Thus, he caused the machine to generate the answer to its own question.

THE USE OF EXPERTS

In September, 1964, Bernice Brown and Olaf Helmer, of RAND, prepared a short Delphi study to test the effect of self-appraisal of the participants' expertise on the outcome of a Delphi consensus study.[7] In this experiment twenty questions, all having numerical answers, were submitted to twenty-three respondents from the RAND research staff. All questions

[7] Bernice Brown and Olaf Helmer, *Improving the Reliability of Estimates Obtained from a Consensus of Experts*, Report P-2986, The RAND Corporation, Santa Monica, Calif., September, 1964.

had obscure but exact answers. For example, one question was: "What was the average price received by the U.S. farmer for a bushel of apples in 1940?" The subjects were told to give each of their answers within a few minutes, without the use of reference material. Each respondent was asked to evaluate his own degree of expertise on each question, ranking himself in a scale of 1 through 4. The opinions were fed back by a standard Delphi process through four rounds of questionnaires.

Not only was consensus achieved, but in most of the cases the median answers to the questions approached the true answer as the questioning process progressed. Furthermore, the consensus was, in all cases, superior to the opinions of the median participant. A comparison of the final round consensus with the estimates of the best individual respondents in the final round showed that the consensus was closer to the true answer 7½ times out of 20. When the median was compared to the estimates of the worst respondents, it was closer in 17 of the 20 questions.

An elite group could be defined as those respondents who rated themselves as experts. The consensus produced by this group was better than the answer of the best respondents in 12 cases out of 20, and better than the answer of the worst respondents in 18 cases out of 20. Thus, the elite produced a considerably more accurate estimate than that of the group as a whole. In the words of the authors, "the use of self-appraised competence ratings to form a consensus [appears] to be a powerful tool for increasing the reliability of group estimates." As a test of absolute accuracy, a "ball park" was defined as an answer lying within 25 per cent of the correct answer. The first round of questionnaires produced 6 median answers out of the 20 which were in the "ball park." By the fourth round this had improved 50 per cent, to 9 out of 20. The elite medians of the last round placed 14 out of the 20 within the 25 per cent bound.

MIXED FORECASTING TECHNIQUES

Studies are being performed or are being planned which mix various forecasting techniques in order to take advantage of the peculiar benefits of each approach. As an example, a game simulation designed to explore the relationship between technology and value change was performed in September, 1966, at the University of Pittsburgh.[8] The basic format of this study involved role-playing, with the participants simulating policy makers and segments of society which would evaluate the effect of technological change on values. In the process of this game, however, it was necessary to

---

[8] Symposium on Technology and Values, sponsored by the Carnegie Corporation and organized by the Department of Philosophy, University of Pittsburgh, September, 1966.

reach a consensus on certain investment policies. The participants were instructed to reach this consensus using Delphi techniques. This was accomplished in open discussion rather than through use of written questionnaires, to save time. The Delphi format provided a well-ordered approach to this conference-style interaction. Each participant was asked to provide independent estimates for questions posed by the moderators. The answers were supplied to the moderators in written form. The moderators reviewed these answers for a consensus and asked for oral explanations of extreme opinions. The participants, after hearing the explanations, were asked to reassess their positions and provide new estimates. These new estimates were rapidly collated by the moderators, and the group consensus was announced. This technique is referred to as "embedded Delphi."

Similarly, a gaming or simulation study can be an integral part of a Delphi simulation. A study currently being outlined at RAND involves the use of formal Delphi procedures. Midway through the study, the tentative results will be introduced in a simulated planning exercise, using a gaming format. The results of this planning exercise will be included in subsequent feedbacks to the Delphi respondents. This will permit the introduction of policy-oriented information to the process of obtaining consensus.

CONCLUSIONS

These techniques, built around the basic Delphi concept, provide a new set of approaches for the forecaster and a new flexibility for approaching problems which are not accessible to more direct methods of analysis. Taken together they indicate that the methodology of forecasting is only now being formulated. In the decades immediately ahead, the analytic methods of social technology will be sharpened, tested, and used in the objective search for man's best world.

An Evaluation and Appraisal of Various Approaches to Technological Forecasting [1]

MARVIN J. CETRON
THOMAS I. MONAHAN

The acceptance of the concept of technological forecasting is only a first step for successful planning. The potential user must also be aware of the advantages and disadvantages of the various techniques which are available to him and of how he can best use them to obtain what he needs to know. He must also decide whether he must develop a means for appraising the data his forecasts provide. Above all, however, he must remember that technological forecasts are decision-aiding tools, not decisions in themselves.

Mr. Cetron is the head of the Technological Forecasting and Appraisal Group, Exploratory Development Division, in the Headquarters of the U.S. Naval Material Command and has been engaged in various technological planning roles in laboratories, Navy Headquarters and in the Department of Defense for more than fifteen years. He has published extensively in the fields of operations research, R&D planning and resource allocation, as well as technological forecasting. Mr. Monahan is in charge of Long Range Planning and Forecasting for the U.S. Naval Applied Science Laboratory. He was a member of the committee which determined the desirability and format of the U.S. Naval Technological Forecast for the Chief of Naval Material, and has had extensive experience in technological planning methodology and applications.

The views expressed are those of the authors and do not necessarily represent those of the Navy Department.

[1] The authors wish to acknowledge the advice and assistance they received from many individuals, and especially from Ralph Lenz, Colonel Raymond Isenson, James Sterling, Major Joseph Martino, and Lewis Roepcke.

144

Many approaches and techniques are being applied to both "exploratory" and "normative" technological forecasting. Each has certain advantages and disadvantages vis-à-vis the others, and it is useful for the forecaster to be fully aware of the selection available to him and the characteristics of the various methodologies. To provide this information, the following questions must be answered:

I. What are the advantages and disadvantages of various forecasting procedures? What should be considered in selecting a method?

II. What does the user want to know? How may it be presented?

III. What advantages will accrue to the laboratory or technical portion of the organization performing the forecasting?

IV. What is "normative" forecasting?

V. How and where does forecasting fit into the decision-making process?

VI. What factors may be used in developing appraisal systems to aid in the decision-making process?

VII. What are the opinions of the users (or potential users) of normative forecasts?

WHAT ARE THE ADVANTAGES AND DISADVANTAGES OF VARIOUS FORECASTING PROCEDURES?

Introduction

At present, there are at least five definable categories of technological forecasting techniques. The classification system chosen is somewhat arbitrary; however, it does provide a means of grouping related methods and a structure for meaningful discussion.

The available techniques are listed as follows:

1. *Intuitive Forecasting*
   a. Individual or "genius" forecasting
   b. Consensus
      (1) Polls
      (2) Panels
      (3) Delphi
2. *Trend Extrapolation*
   a. Simple extrapolation
   b. Curve fitting with judgment modifications
   c. Trend curves
   d. Systematic curve fitting
3. *Trend Correlation Analysis*
   a. Precursor events
   b. Correlation analysis
   c. Regression analysis
   d. Correlation coefficient

4. *Analogy*
   a. Growth analogy
   b. Historical analogy

Evaluation of Forecasting Methods

1. INTUITIVE METHODS

One of the most direct and widely used methods of generating a forecast is to sample the opinions of one or more persons who are knowledgeable in the specific technology or technical area under consideration. When more than one forecaster is involved, the forecast is built from a consensus or a composite of estimates.

a. *Individual or "genius" forecasting.* There is considerable merit in a forecast made by a single individual who is expert in his special area and has both depth in the underlying scientific disciplines or technologies and also a synoptical view of the functional area to which his expertise has direct application.

b. *Consensus.*

(1) Polls

To overcome the difficulty inherent in a single estimate which may be poor, it may be well to combine the judgments of several individuals who are active in the field. It is presumed that a realistic forecast can be obtained by cancelling out the errors of individual predictions, but this may not necessarily be true, especially if the sample is poorly drawn.

(2) Panels

The panel approach to technological forecasting brings individual experts together and provides for a desirable interaction of their different opinions. "Project Forecast," of the Air Force, and "Project Seabed," of the Navy, are two interesting examples of successful panel operations.

(3) Delphi technique

The Delphi technique is directed toward the systematic solicitation of expert opinion. Instead of using the traditional approach toward achieving a consensus through open discussion, this technique "eliminates committee activity altogether, thus . . . reducing the influence of certain psychological factors, such as specious persuasion, unwillingness to abandon publicly expressed opinions, and the bandwagon effect of majority opinion." [2] It re-

[2] See O. Helmer and N. Rescher, "On the Epistemology of the Inexact Sciences," *Management Science*, June, 1959, p. 47.

places direct debate by a carefully designed program of sequential individual interrogations (best conducted by questionnaires), interspersed with information and opinion feedback derived from consensuses which are computed from earlier parts of the program. Both inquiries concerning their own reasons and subsequent feedback of the reasons adduced by others may serve to stimulate the experts to consider points which they had inadvertently neglected, and to give more weight to factors they had dismissed as unimportant on first thought.

2. TREND EXTRAPOLATION

a. *Simple extrapolation.* The most obvious method of technological forecasting is to assume that whatever has happened in the past will continue to happen in the future, provided there are no disturbances. While this is not a very accurate method, it has the advantage of objectivity.

The method is applicable to forecasting functional capabilities. If the field of interest to the forecast centers on man's ability to communicate, appropriate data sets might be "frequency spectrum exploitable," or "number of intelligence bits per hour, per mile of separation between communicators." Such data are not explicitly concerned with whether the desired function is to be accomplished by cable, microwave, teletype, or a Telstar satellite. One or more of these techniques must be implicitly involved. The growth is considered in terms of cumulative time or calendar years.

b. *Curve fitting with judgment modifications.* Technological progress, as we are currently witnessing, more than likely proceeds in an exponential manner, similar to the law of acceleration under the influence of gravitational forces, or to the phenomenon of biological growth. Initially, the technique tends to experience a period of slow growth. Finally, its potential is recognized, money and work are poured in, problems are resolved, and accelerated growth occurs. Eventually, limiting factors are encountered, the growth rate decelerates, and the curve asymptotically approaches some upper value that should be defined when the limiting factor is known.

c. *Trend curves.* Several types of trend curves may be described:

1. Linear increase with flattening, as a limit is approached
2. Exponential increase with no limit in the time frame under consideration
3. S-shaped curve (the normal characteristic of specific maturing technologies)
4. Double-exponential or an even steeper increase, with subsequent flattening (characteristic of some functional capabilities in areas of concentrated research and development)

5. Slow exponential increase followed by a sudden, much more rapid, increase, and then eventual flattening

d. *Systematic curve fitting.* To calculate and project trends quantitatively, one or more empirical equations can be used:

1. Straight line or first degree polynomial, in instances where growth is characterized by a linear increase or decrease:

$$y = a + bx$$

2. Parabola or second degree polynomial, in instances where growth is characterized by one bend, either upward or downward:

$$y = a + bx + cx^2$$

3. Exponential, where growth is a geometric function with respect to time (or other controlling parameter):

$$y = ae^{bx}$$

If the empirical data to be used in making the projection are reliable, the above equations may be used, together with the technique of least squares, to project future values of significant parameters. To determine the parameters (constants) of the desired polynomial, a set of "normal" equations is derived by a squaring and minimizing procedure.

3. TREND CORRELATION ANALYSIS

The trend of a technical parameter which is complex and difficult to predict by itself may be more easily expressed as a result of its relationship to two or more other trends. Whereas time-dependent trend extrapolation attempts explicit forecasting, interrelationships between parameters can be explored on a much more general level if they do not have to fit into an explicit time frame. Nevertheless, they may represent extrapolations of reality beyond present capability or estimates, in the instance of future technologies.

In order to use two or more trends to determine a third, the predictor must have available a number of primary trends which are related to the technical field of interest. To these he must add a knowledge of probable relationships that might arise from combinations of such variables. The predictor may then select the relationship and the primary variables which influence the desired technical improvement. The trends of the primary variables may be projected on the basis of any techniques which appear appropriate. The prediction is then completed by projecting the unknown variable on the basis of the relationship between the primary variables.

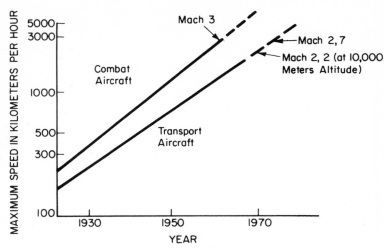

Figure 1. Relationship Between the Speeds of Combat and Transport Aircraft.

Source: *Department of the Air Force, ASD-TDR-62-414.*

a. *Precursor events.* Forecasting by analysis of precursor events uses the correlation of progress trends between two developments, one of which is leading the other. But it must be obvious that the two developments are logically related to each other. For example, the research and development effort applied to combat aircraft eventually also bears fruit in the air transport sector (see Figure 1).

b. *Correlation analysis.* "Correlation" covers problems dealing with the relationships between two or more variables, and specifically, the degree of a certain special type of relationship among them. In practical problems, it is often more important to find out what the relationship actually is, in order to estimate or predict one variable (the dependent variable) from knowledge of another (the independent variable). The statistical technique appropriate to such a case is called "regression analysis," or "least squares." When consistent correlations can be found, the method offers an objective approach to forecasting.

When more than two variables are involved, "multiple correlation" can be used. Any number of "causal" factors can be handled by multiple correlation, as long as there are more observations than factors. While the procedure cannot be described graphically for more than two causal factors or independent variables, the formulas and ideas are essentially the same. It is most desirable that all factors which have a bearing on the outcome be considered, and that any relationships among two or more which are known a priori be defined in advance.

4. ANALOGY

According to Lenz, attempts to develop a theory explaining why technical progress should proceed in an exponential manner date back at least as far as 1907 to the theory advanced by Henry Adams.[3] Adams compared the acceleration of progress with the effect of a new mass which is introduced into a system of forces (previously in equilibrium) to accelerate the system's motion until a new equilibrium is established. The accumulated information is analogous to the distance traveled by the new mass; the rate of information gain is analogous to the speed; and the second derivative of information over time is analogous to an acceleration (assumed constant).

a. *Growth analogy.* To support his thesis on the analogy of population increases with the growth of biological organisms, Pearl includes the rate of increase of fruit flies within a bottle, the rate of increase of yeast cells in a given environment, and the rate of cell increase within white rats. De Solla Price includes technological forecasting within the larger framework of all growth phenomena in science, including the number of scientists or papers, etc. This analogy has some merit in that it normally gives a symmetrical curve, without further assumptions. Ayres proposes autocatalytic chemical processes as a model. Hartman derives his model from a simple analogy with reaction processes in a gas. In Hartman's "gas," the molecules are scientists and pieces of information, both occurring at a given volume density. The "scientist molecules" do not move significantly, whereas the "information molecules" move with assumed constant velocity in random directions. A useful reaction (i.e., the generation of new information) is supposed to occur when the scientist molecules have a "reaction cross-section" upon being hit by the information molecules. A criticism of Hartman's model relates to his basic assumption that information gain is proportional to the amount of existing information ($dI/dt = kI$). This holds only where ideal communication between all investigators and all sources of information can be assumed, and every opportunity presented by this communication can, in fact, be exploited. The model may be a useful approach to research and development in a specific field or within a small or medium-sized research group.

b. *Historical analogy.* To study the impact of a new technology on functional capability, it may be desirable to consider lessons from history. As an example, General Electric Company (TEMPO)[4] has forecast the relative contributions of various power sources to the energy input of the United

---

[3] *The Education of Henry Adams* (New York: The Modern Library, 1931).
[4] J. C. Fisher, *Energy Input of the United States, 1800–2060: History and Forecast*, Report 66 TMP-26, General Electric Company, Santa Barbara, Calif., 1966.

States, by decades, up to the year 2060. TEMPO estimates the contributions which nuclear fuels will make to electricity by using the same type of growth curves observed in the relationship of fossil fuels to hydroelectric power during the period from 1800 to 1960.

WHAT SHOULD BE CONSIDERED IN SELECTING A METHOD?

The technique which is best depends upon the circumstances under which the forecaster is working; his needs; the reliability, completeness and quantitative precision of the data base; the purpose of the forecast; the length of the forecast period; and the time available for generating the forecast. Furthermore, the technique should be compatible with and adaptable to the information available; i.e., a micrometer should not be used to measure a sewer pipe.

On the other hand, there is a very real need for improvement in the level or degree of sophistication with which many technologies are treated by forecasters. As an example, the most unsophisticated forecasting technique is obviously the genius type. It has been estimated that 80 per cent to 95 per cent of all forecasting done by the military services is of this type. Frequently, insufficient historical data preclude the use of more sophisticated techniques; however, in many other instances, substantial quantities of reliable data are available for analysis but are not used. As a result, the levels of confidence which can be ascribed to the forecasts are frequently lower than desirable.

When valid data are not fully utilized because of an unsophisticated forecasting technique, a Type I forecasting error has been made. If, on the other hand, a sophisticated technique is applied to imprecise and incomplete data, a Type II forecasting error has been made. In either case, a wrong decision or error in judgment has occurred, and the resulting forecast is of questionable value. Of the two types of forecasting errors, Type I is far more common, especially when subject matter specialists are called upon to prepare inputs to forecasts.

The major requisites of good forecasting can be reduced to: (1) a reliable data base, which normally consists of the knowledge of scientific and technical specialists in the subject matter area, as well as any supporting data; (2) astute judgment and common sense on the part of the forecaster; and (3) an understanding of available forecasting techniques and how and when to apply them. The primary gain from the use of such techniques is a greatly improved insight into the nature and interrelationships of influencing factors and the sensitivity of solutions to factor variations. These techniques also provide the possibility of evaluating, within a consistent frame of reference, distinct alternative technical solutions to a given operational problem. In effect, the techniques provide the tools whereby the technical knowledge and judgment of the forecaster can be applied to logical, systematic thinking about the pattern of development of the particular technology.

WHAT DOES THE USER WANT TO KNOW?

Suggested Forecast Forms

The format of a forecast should be flexible and should be largely determined by the personnel preparing the forecast and the user. Each area forecast should include the following:

1. BACKGROUND, INCLUDING PRESENT STATUS

The background should highlight the evolution of the technology being forecast, with emphasis on relevance to the firm's goals or military technological needs. The present status should include the state of the art of the category.

2. NEW CAPABILITY OR TECHNICAL APPROACH

The proposed functions, characteristics, or concepts of any new item should be presented, including limitations which may exist. Where appropriate, tabular or graphical presentations should be used to show the merits of competing items. Functional diagrams should be included in the description of the technical approach.

3. FORECAST

The forecast should display, graphically, a projection of anticipated advances of the item as a function of time, up to twenty years in the future. This projection should be a quantitative expression of achievable parametric limits showing, where possible, the level of confidence in the validity of the projection. Supporting and qualifying narration should be minimized.

4. POTENTIAL SIGNIFICANCE TO THE FIRM OR THE MILITARY

Where appropriate, the value of the items forecast should be appraised in light of the company's requirements or military relevance. As an example, yield strength/density can be expressed in relation to time. This is meaningful to the scientific community. However, a more meaningful expression for the operational community would be collapse depth versus time (see Figure 2). (The values in Figure 2 are hypothetical and are presented for illustrative purposes only.)

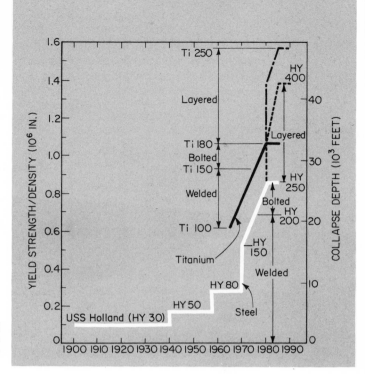

Figure 2. Strength Levels of Steel and Titanium with Corresponding Hull Collapse Depth (Based on Weight/Displacement Ratio of 0.6).

5. REFERENCES

For the convenience of the user who may want to obtain further information, the reference section should list associated R&D organizations making important contributions, names of outstanding experts, and references to reports or literature supporting the forecast material.

For the technological forecast to be utilized, it must be credible. Indeed, the more credible the forecast, the more it will be utilized. It is important to identify the individual or organization that generates the forecast because the credibility depends on the good professional judgment of the forecaster(s) and of his organizational segment. The forecaster must not become involved with the socioeconomic implications; he must forecast what is feasible in a given time frame. This means he must address himself to a technological area—and only to the technological area—leaving the social implications to the sociologist.

TECHNIQUES FOR PRESENTING TRENDS

Words without pictures are as weak as pictures without words. In the first instance, the reader is asked to visualize what is spread out in rhetoric and probably exists in the mind of the writer. In the second instance, pictures imply a logic which may not be identical with that of the accompanying syntax. The technological forecast should be a proper combination of the two modes of expression.

Time-Dependent Trends

Figure 3 depicts a *time-dependent trend*. The payload ratio of flying belts is shown as it is expected to increase in the future. Conventional fuel is a barrier at one level of performance and exotic fuels at another. The improvements between barriers are those expected in the usual history of moving from the demonstration of feasibility to the futility of incremental improvements. The figure implies that new fuel research would break out in 1963. It also implies that between 1965 and 1970 competition will exist between the underdeveloped new configuration and the overdeveloped old configuration. The broad areas indicate the confidence interval. Real time in this case, as the independent variable of progress, makes a certain amount of sense.

Figure 4 is a similar set of curves which identifies anticipated results if selected special circumstances occur. Figure 5 shows the trend of a critical parameter (in this case the thrust-to-weight ratio of lift engines). Uncer-

Source: Army Long Range Technologcial Forecast.

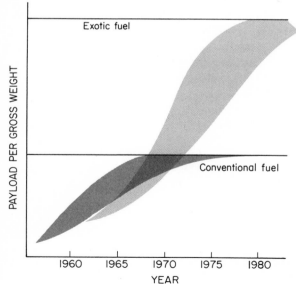

Figure 3. Time-Dependent Trend (Example: Personal Flying Belts).

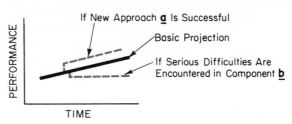

Figure 4. Identification of Anticipated Results if Selected Special Circumstances Occur.

Source: Pardee, Research Program Effectiveness.

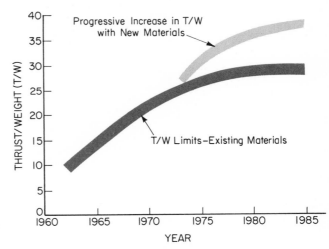

Figure 5. Trends in Thrust-to-Weight Ratio of Dependent Lift Engines.

Source: Army Long Rang Technological Forecast.

tainty (because of technology or funding limitations) is shown by the broad line. The impact of new techniques (in this case, materials) is also shown.

The case of a development involving the projection of two critical parameters is shown in Figure 6. In this instance, the graph depicts power gain band-width and system noise of solid state amplifiers.

The projection of a critical parameter in technology, in which specific milestones in research and development are identified, is shown in Figure 7. The actual and anticipated gains in certain characteristics of air cushion vehicles are reported. Air cushion vehicles (ACV) performance, in terms of a factor of merit, is projected for a vehicle with a bare bottom and with a skirt and trunk system. Significant improvements in ACV performance have resulted from the development of skirts and flexible jet extensions. Aerodynamic problems associated with these developments have been largely resolved, but finding suitable materials for the air cushion devices is a continuing problem.

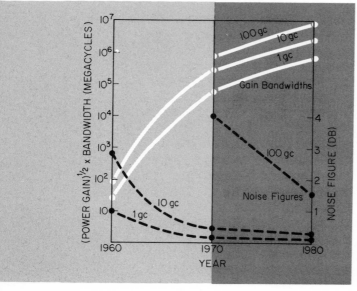

Source: Army Long Rang Technological Forecast.

Figure 6. Projected Development of Solid State Amplifiers.

Source: Naval Ship Research and Development Center.

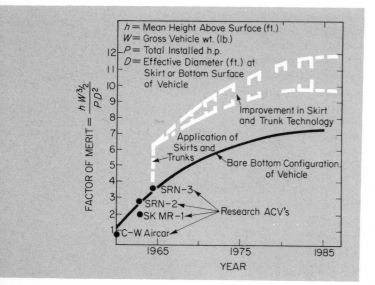

Figure 7. Air-Cushion Vehicle (ACV) Performance.

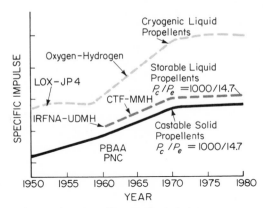

Figure 8. Predicted Improvements in Specific Impulse.

Source: Army Long Rang Technological Forecast.

The projection of the critical parameters in each of several alternative techniques, showing specific developments in perspective, is shown in Figure 8. As shown, considerable improvements in specific impulse have been made in solid and liquid propellants, especially in recent years. However, no one parameter in itself can be used as a basis for comparison of the various propulsion systems. Solid propellants have lagged behind liquid propellants in specific impulse values for years. This trend will continue, because of the need for compromising performance in order to attain certain physical and ballistic properties in the solid-propellant grain. Solid-propelled motor designs, however, are less complex and lighter in weight than liquid-propelled systems. Consequently, overall advantage can result from the selection of somewhat less energetic solid-propellant combinations.

Parameter-Dependent Trends

In other cases, the identification of real time is less precise. Often the real times of occurrence of steps of progress are dependent on one or more factors (parameters or variables). Figure 9 depicts a *parameter-dependent trend*. Gal/day of desalinized ocean water is hard to put on a time scale of expected progress. Many factors affect this progress, two of which are the cost of power and the diffusion rates of membranes. These effects are not independent. Their joint occurrence would determine the performance characteristics of constructable diffusion desalinization plants, but no one has enough confidence to predict the separate parameters as time-dependent trends.

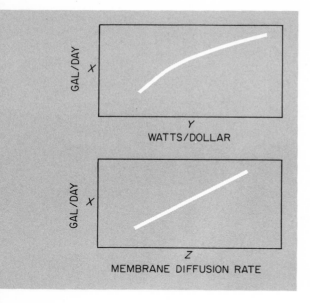

Figure 9. Parameter-Dependent Trend (Example: Desalinization of Water).

The plotting of parameter-dependent trends is full of problems. In the first place, partial and contingent dependency is poorly represented graphically. For instance, the rule of combination of the partial effects of y and z on x is not necessarily the addition which is implied by the chart. There may be complex relationships between diffusion rates and power in specific design applications because of such factors as induced potentials. On the other hand, if x, y, and z are graphed together in a three-dimensional pictorial to account for this specific-design interaction, the general, nonspecific design direction of effects may be obscured. The specific functionally related curves are basic to systems design, whereas the trends provide the engineeringly imprecise but directionally correct information for planning. The engineer cannot use what is useful to the planner and the planner cannot use what is useful to the engineer.

The problem here is not trivial. It bears on the whole issue of the feasibility of forecasting in terms of time and probability. Almost all forecasting, if examined in detail, involves parameter-dependent trends as elemental pieces. Time as an independent variable increasingly takes the role of a modulus, not real time. Again, the correspondence between real and psychological probabilities in predicting R&D products is called into question. With little physical basis for making probability estimates, should the available physical elements be combined or should an overall estimate of probability be made by the forecaster? If the latter makes more sense, the forecaster's projections, in probability terms, can be logically combined by planners who are not predictors but who deal with even larger aggregates and who need to know their probabilities.

Figure 10 shows performance characteristics of microwave tubes over the past twenty-five years and as projected through the next fifteen years. The trend of a critical parameter may also be presented in bar graph form, as shown in Figure 11.

The projection of a critical parameter in terms of other constraining parameters is shown in Figure 12. In order to resist the intense temperatures, high pressures, shear forces, corrosion, and erosion of exhaust gases, the uncooled nozzle on the solid-propelled rocket has, of necessity, been undesirably heavy. The flame temperature of 1960 exhaust products ranges between 5,700°F and 5,900°F (Figure 12). As of the time of the preparation of the forecast, these temperatures soon were expected to exceed 6,300°F, and to approach 7,000°F by 1970. This would require the development of nozzles which function by other than heat-sink methods, since the highly refractory metals, hafnium, tantalum, and tantalum-zirconium alloys, have melting points around 7,000°F.

Figure 10. Progress in Capacities of Microwave Tubes.

Source: Army Long Rang Technological Forecast.

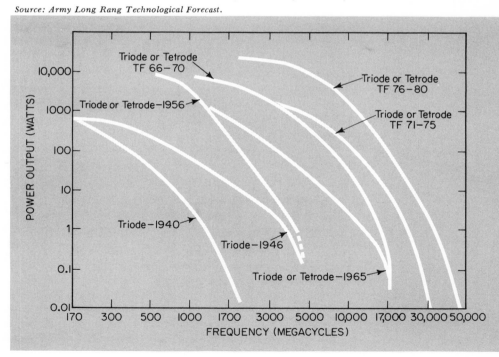

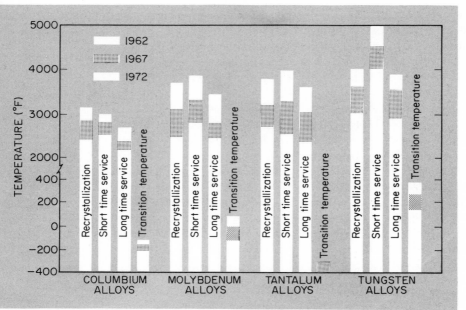

Source: *Aerospace Industries Association of America, Inc., Forecast.*

Figure 11. Refractory Metal Alloys.

Source: *Aerospace Industries Association of America, Inc., Forecast.*

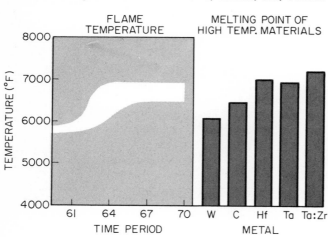

Figure 12. Projected Propellant Flame Temperature.

A forecast of projected functional capabilities in terms of the technical state of the art is shown in Figure 13. The advantages of combined sensors for tracking become obvious because each is most effective in a given portion of the trajectory. Infrared, for example, is probably the most used, and generally the most efficient, sensor for air or space-borne use in tracking a missile through its powered phase and upon re-entry. Ultraviolet is extremely effective for detection and tracking in the powered or mid-course portion of the trajectory, but only from a space platform when the target is above the O_3 layer. Electro-optical techniques are usable in any part of the trajectory if the target is self- or solar-illuminated. Active electro-optical techniques (i.e., incorporating a laser transmitter for illumination of the target) will provide tracking capabilities under more varied conditions.

Performance requirements for certain technologies, as a result of related system developments, can be identified as in Figure 14. Interference control specifications will have to be expanded to meet the critical requirements of the aerospace age. Frequency coverage of interference measurements and analysis of conducted and radiated electrical energy will have to be ex-

Figure 13. Tactical ICBM Trajectory Showing Optical Tracking Capabilities in Various Spectral Regions.

Source: Air Force Technology for Tomorrow.

Figure 14. Expanding Frequency Coverage for Vulnerability Reduction.

Source: Army Long Range Technological Forecast.

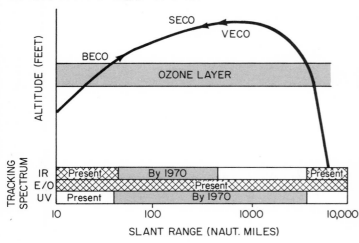

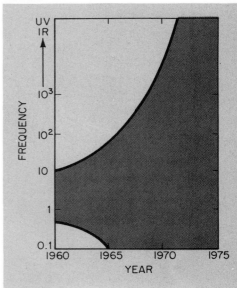

tended downward to direct current and upward to the infrared, visible, and ultraviolet spectra, as shown in Figure 14.

In some areas of investigation it becomes necessary to define requirements for research and development in several elements of the area under consideration. It is possible to project the state of the art in the various disciplinary areas and to estimate their relative importance during the forecast period in terms of operational requirements. From these two trends, it is possible to establish research requirements and associated resource (personnel, funding) needs during the period under examination. For example, Figures 15a–c were prepared to define a desirable Nuclear Weapons Effects Research program for the projection of aircraft and air crew in 1962 and following years, assuming an extended moratorium on atmospheric nuclear weapons effects tests. Figure 15a, indicating relative research requirements (RR), combines relative importance (RI) from Figure 15b and predictability (P) from Figure 15c (which is stated in terms of per cent of total requirements) as follows:

$$RR = \frac{RI \times (1 - P)}{RI \times (1 - P)} \times 100$$

Figure 15. Desirable Nuclear Weapons Effects Research Program.

(a) NWER Requirements.

Source: Air Force Technology for Tomorrow.

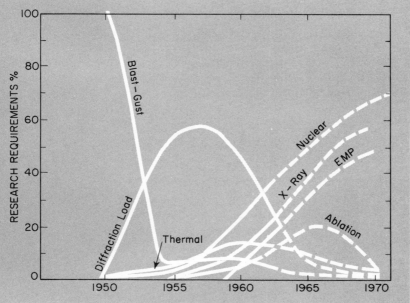

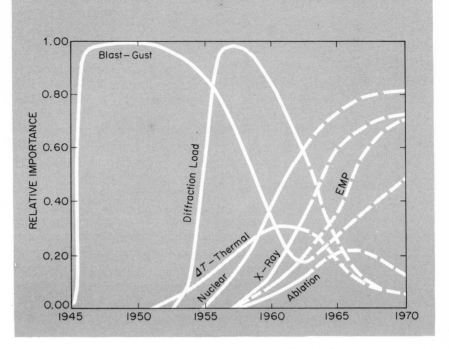

(b) Relative Importance Trends.

(c) Predictability Trends.

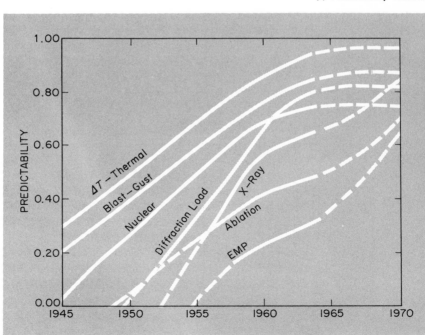

WHAT ADVANTAGES WILL ACCRUE TO THE LABORATORY OR TECHNICAL PORTION OF THE ORGANIZATION PERFORMING THE FORECAST?

A survey of the various government and nongovernment research and development activities, to determine views on forecasting, showed that the forecast helped the laboratories by:

1. Providing them with a means of making their capabilities known to potential sponsors. This was a sales technique which aided the laboratories in presenting new programs to higher management. In fact, in two cases the laboratories said it was a way of bypassing middle management and informing top management of what the laboratories were doing.

2. Improving interlaboratory communications. Most laboratories did not care to look at other forecasts in their own area of expertise because they felt they knew their own areas well enough from technical society meetings and publications, and believed that they would suffer from "inbreeding" if they looked at such information. However, in activities oriented more toward research and exploratory development, the engineers and scientists looked at the forecasts from other disciplines, to see whether some of the new innovations or theories could be applied in their own fields. (It should be noted that most breakthroughs which occur in science today happen not in depth in one technology but where two or more disciplines come together, such as biomechanics, electrometallurgy, and electrochemistry.)

In the test and evaluation centers, on the other hand, the engineers and technicians read forecasts with a different view in mind; primarily, they looked for "what was coming down the pike." In other words, what could they expect to see in the future so that they might order the proper test equipment to evaluate prototypes when they become available? It was especially helpful in the government to be able to "justify" military construction funds early, since it might take four to five years from the time of the original submission until a facility was operative. Considerable lead time was also attributed to private companies, and forecasts would aid in justifying the procurement of proper test facilities.

3. Providing data for feasibility studies. Most laboratories advised that they received requests, on an average of once a week, to provide parameters (usually in a specific format) for utilization by a specific organizational segment. The laboratories felt that if the most important parameters of each functional capability were forecast in a standard format, the information would satisfy many users and thus eliminate the need for considerable repetitive paper work.

4. Aiding in the justification of budgets and the development of long-range plans. One laboratory director said that, while his laboratory did

forecasting, at least implicitly, he was a little afraid to commit these forecasts to paper for fear that some "headquarters type" would turn the forecasts into plans and commitments. The authors are inclined to agree with this particular laboratory director on both counts: (1) they are presently forecasting in the laboratories, because forecasting is essential in carrying out their work, and (2) they have a right to fear that some of the "not-so-knowledgeable" managers in the higher echelons are apt to utilize these forecasts as plans rather than inputs to the planning procedure.

In specific studies in which the laboratories were called upon to evaluate both the current state of technologies and what could be expected, such as the Air Force's Project Forecast and the Navy's Project Seabed, the laboratories felt that the "need orientation," without constraints on technology, made it possible to generate forecasts which were appropriate to the specific goals of the study in question. Generally speaking, laboratories would have preferred not to prepare formal forecasts; however, they did cooperate when their managements requested them to do so.

WHAT IS "NORMATIVE" FORECASTING?

In developing both short- and long-term plans, the planner must structure his forecast on a sound data base. Operations research, in its narrowest sense, is an essential ingredient of the planning process. In its broadest sense it may well pervade the entire forecasting process. By analyzing the data in terms of its short-run as well as its long-range potentialities, and its relevant environment, a pattern for the future may be established. If the approach to technical forecasting is purely sequential, it is called "exploratory."

When the forecast is "needs oriented," it is termed "normative." In the normative forecast, goals, needs, objectives, or desires are specified, and the forecast works backward to the present to see what capabilities now exist or could be extrapolated to meet future goals. In some cases the goal may even force technology. Indeed, the remoteness of the goals and the priority they have may well determine how many concurrent approaches are pursued to meet the goal. Two good illustrations of normative forecasting are the Navy's "Polaris" Program and NASA's "Man on the Moon" Program. It should be noted that in both cases in which a needs-oriented forecast was involved, resource availability was not the major problem.

Normative forecasting may be formalized and usually is. In fact, normative forecasting probably should be called "goal oriented planning." Most appraisal techniques that are utilized fall into two categories: those which use the decision theory approach of rating (subjectively or objectively) various criteria for success in order to arrive at an overall figure of merit, and those which are based on economic analysis. Actually the two are not that different. In the military, the term "military utility" or "value" is multiplied by the probability of success (or a suitable risk factor) to determine an expected value. If this expected value were divided by dollars, a "desirability index" could be obtained. In the economic area, the methods generally involve computation of the discounted net value or present worth of a discounted cash flow, using a selected interest rate. A maximum expenditure for the project can then be justified. This is the discounted net value times the probability of success. The ratio of this figure to the estimated project cost can be used as an index of "project desirability."

The advantage of both of these systems is that totally dissimilar projects or programs can be compared; therefore, such methods have relevance to policy planning at both the national and corporate level. It must be remembered that, in both of these systems, the data plus the *analysis,* either manual or computerized, furnish only *information.* The manager must use the information, and it is information plus judgment that renders a *decision.* As L. B. Mullet of the British Ministry of Technology pointed out:

> Several examples of decision theory systems can be identified in British firms. In one case involving shoe machinery, decision theory is coupled with deliberate concentration of effort on a selected number of projects rather than diffusion of effort over all possible projects. The system has been operating for some time and is eminently successful, not only in project selection but in indicating the optimum level of research and development expenditure and in showing up quite detailed deficiencies.[5]

On the other hand, during recent discussions in Paris, M. H. de L'Estoile explained that he had developed a system which provides a logical, objective determination of future requirements and which indicates the research and development activities necessary to meet these requirements. His procedure, which is mission oriented and displays future technical capabilities, assists operational planners in better expressing their desires in terms to which the "technical types" can respond.

HOW AND WHERE DOES FORECASTING FIT INTO THE DECISION-MAKING PROCESS?

There is a need for improvement in communications between the operating and technical communities within the military. The technological forecast is designed to provide a vehicle that can partially fulfill this need.

---

[5] *Forecast, Planning and Decision Making in the Context of the Ministry of Technology (UK),* published under the serial code of RDSU 3 (1967), February 22, 1967.

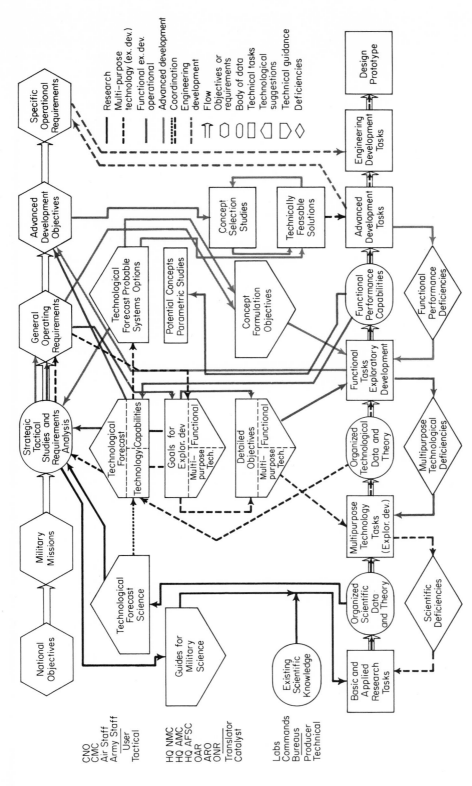

Figure 16. Tactical-Technical-Dialogue and Flow.

Figure 16 illustrates the framework whereby the tactical-technical dialogue takes place through an upward flow of technical capabilities, forecasts, and system concepts which are to be mated with the constraining downward flow of missions, technological goals, and operational requirements. The scientific community "proposes" technological capabilities while the operational community "disposes" to fulfill strategic and tactical needs.

A technological forecast of scientific and technical capabilities can constitute a vital part of the overall tactical-technical dialogue. The forecast can assist in establishing guides for military science and goals for exploratory development by pointing out capabilities leading to conceptual systems and new operational requirements. Figure 16 indicates that the goals translate tactical requirements into technical objectives and that the forecast translates technical capabilities into strategic possibilities. The forecast and the goals form a two-way street. Ideas and desired capabilities which are pointed out in developing the goals might not show up in the forecast. Conversely, potentials which would otherwise be overlooked in the plan will show up

Figure 17. A Proposed R&D Sequence.

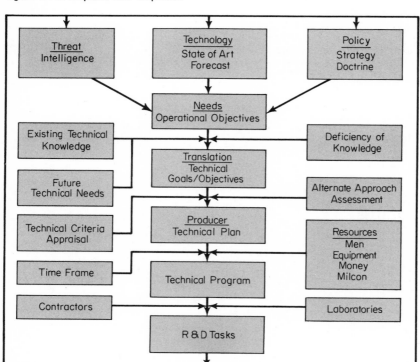

in the forecast. If the forecast is good, it can be a repository of avenues of technical approaches from which choices can be made in developing the goals.

It can be seen from the proposed R&D planning sequence in Figure 17 that technology, including technological forecasting and threat and policy determinations, plays a major role in developing operational objectives. An analysis of these operational objectives and current and projected technology results in goals for exploratory development and/or technical objectives. The goals/objectives are then appraised technically, and alternate approaches are considered prior to incorporation into the technical plan. This technical plan should serve as a basis for the procurement of resources and for the generation of the technical program. The procurement and program generation should go on concurrently in order to reduce sharply the time frame. The technical program is broken down into R&D tasks which are executed either by government or contractor groups. The crucial point in this R&D planning system is the feedback concept in which the technical information generated in the R&D tasks is fed back into threat and policy, from which it may affect the operational objectives. In other words, the planning sequence is iterative, and dynamic technological forecasting is not only an ingredient but also a catalyst.

It is fairly obvious that, by changing "threat" to "competition" and "needs" to "corporate goals," and by adding economic factors, the planning sequence in the nonmilitary sphere becomes quite similar to that of the military group (see Figure 18). Economic factors are not included in the military flow charts because the budget constraint is implicit in the military. If internal economic and environmental factors are balanced against each other, corporate goals can be defined. The finest engineering achievement is worthless, however, if no one will buy it. Consequently, market research may well play a major role in determining company and technical goals. The extent of its role depends on the type of firm. If the product is a shelf item, or if the firm knows what the consumers want, then the marketing department will call the shots. If, on the other hand, the company is going to sell something that has not been produced before, the research department must exert the major influence.

Prior to developing production objectives, however, the corporation must consider all constraints, including the resources required, the resources available, and any unique requirements. At this point in the cycle, the production objectives are appraised technically and economically, in order to develop the most cost-effective production cycle. After a decision has been reached on the materials to be used, an experimental model is built and tested, and the results are used to modify and build the prototype. The test results from the prototype are then incorporated into the preproduction plan. In a strictly sequential design analysis, one step would be fully com-

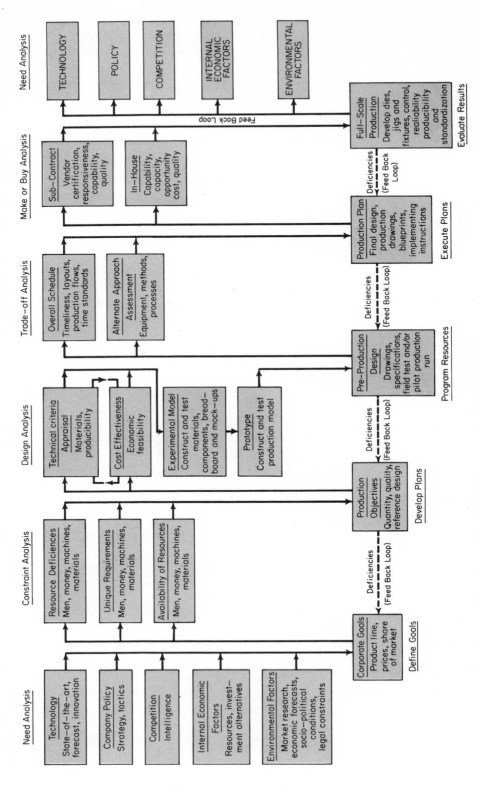

Figure 18. Graphic Portrayal of a Manufacturing Firm's Planning and Design Process.

pleted prior to the start of the next step and there would be no feedback from later to earlier steps (no iterations). In the real world, it is improbable that a purely sequential process is ever carried out. Modifications and readjustments in the design are made regularly, as a result of evaluations, analyses, tests, and prototype fabrications.

A trade-off analysis should address itself to alternative approaches to producing the product. The results of this analysis should produce a product plan which, when approved, should serve as a basis for developing detailed drawings, procuring resources, and specifying fabrication procedures. This plan should also include the schedule. Another comparative analysis should be performed at this stage. It should address itself to the question of whether the firm should "make or buy." This should include, but not necessarily be limited to, the capability, capacity, availability, quality, and opportunity costs of its own facilities as compared with those of a contractor, and should also consider the responsiveness of certified vendors. Even after production is underway, it is a good idea to review the results of such analyses on a regular basis, since it is possible to find marketable products in those items which a firm can make cheaper than it can buy. While such new products usually involve competition with one or more existing manufacturers, there is an advantage in having a captive market (i.e., the company itself).

It is at this point that the firm should go into full-scale production or fabrication. Full-scale production must consider production planning and control techniques, in addition to quality control, dies, and jigs and fixtures which are required. Here again, after the results are evaluated, a critical reappraisal should take place and the results should be "fed back" to influence future policies, competitive tactics, or other factors which ultimately affect corporation goals. In this sequence, technological forecasts are dynamic inputs which act as catalysts to lead the total operation.

The research or development project is viewed as a sequential acquisition of knowledge and may be described as an ordered series of events with a probability of success (P_s) (based on the technological forecast), a value of utility (V), and an associated cost (C). These projects are evaluated by quantified subjective judgments of these "P_s's", "V's", and "C's." These criteria, which seem to be almost universal in project appraisal, are then manipulated in one of many ways: to maximize expected value in time, to minimize cost, to optimize the use of resources, or to achieve some combination of the three.

The simplified formula would be:

$$\text{VALUE } (V) \times \text{PROB OF SUCCESS } (P_s) = \text{EXPECTED VALUE } (EV)$$

$$\frac{\text{EXPECTED VALUE } (EV)}{\text{COST } (C)} = \text{DESIRABILITY } (D)$$

These techniques are not intended to yield decisions but rather to furnish information which facilitates decisions. Indeed, these techniques are merely thinking structures to force methodical, meticulous analysis. *Data* plus *analysis* equals *information* (this may be computerized information, but even so it is information). It is *information* plus judgment that come together to render *decisions*.

Many procedures are being developed and used in government and industry. Ultimately, the widespread installation of such procedures appears inevitable because of the strong trends toward organizing and mechanizing information for long-range planning and because of the growing number of persons who are interested in these procedures and are trained to use them. It is obvious that efficient planning and programming depend on the ability to handle large numbers of individual R&D projects in an efficient manner. Quantitative appraisal and selection techniques, along with the powerful computer, now give the decision makers additional information on which to base their decisions.

WHAT FACTORS MAY BE USED IN DEVELOPING APPRAISAL SYSTEMS TO AID IN THE DECISION-MAKING PROCESS?

Interest in quantitative methods of evaluation of R&D projects has become quite pronounced within the past few years, especially within the Department of Defense. The authors have conducted surveys of methods, both completed and ongoing, within industry and government. These have been evaluated, using a fixed set of factors. While the original purpose of this survey was to recommend a system for application within one of the military services, the results of the survey may well be of interest to others.

A total of fifteen different features were found which could describe the items of input and output of the various methods. No single method possessed all the features. The various features are described in some detail below.

1. *Utility measure:* Does the method include some measure of the utility or value of success of a particular R&D project? This measure may be a share of a market, profitability, military worth, etc.

2. *Probability of success:* Does the method explicitly take into account an estimate of the probability of success of each individual R&D project?

3. *Orthogonality of criteria:* Are the criteria used by the method mutually exclusive (orthogonal), highly correlated, or do they have a high degree of overlap?

4. *Sensitivity:* Has the sensitivity of the output to small changes in the input been checked? A high degree of sensitivity to small variations in input is undesirable, since the output then becomes unstable in the presence of minor perturbations in the input.

5. *Rejected alternatives retention:* When a project is rejected for funding, is it retained for later consideration in the event of a budget increase or other adjustment, rather than being rejected completely?

6. *Classification structure:* Does the method provide a structural relationship between the R&D project and a hierarchy of higher-level goals of the organization?

7. *Time:* Does the method take scheduling requirements into account, or provide scheduling information as an output?

8. *Strategies:* Does the method permit the user to consider several possible scenarios, world environments, market situations, etc.

9. *System cross support:* Does the method give a system development credit for support which it provides to another system development?

10. *Technology cross support:* Does the method give a system development credit for support which it provides to the advancement of other technologies?

11. *Graphical display:* Is the output amenable to presentation in some graphic form which gives the user a condensed picture of evaluation of various projects?

12. *Flagging:* Does the method flag problem areas, to bring them to the attention of the responsible management?

13. *Optimization criteria:* What criterion for optimization does the method use, and what constraints are considered? (All methods studied used either a composite score from a number of factors, to obtain a ranking, or some form of maximum [discounted] net value.)

14. *Constraints:* Constraints considered by the methods included budgets, available skills, available facilities, available raw materials, and competition efforts.

15. *Computerized:* Is the method capable of being implemented in a computer program? Is it a linear program or a dynamic program? (It should be noted that most techniques can be computerized if desired.)

Each method was evaluated according to several criteria which are related to ease of use. The criteria considered are described below:

1. *Data requirements:* While in general the more data a method uses as input, the more information it provides as output, the ease of use is affected by the amount of data required. Two factors entered into the amount of data required: the level of organization at which data are obtained (i.e., individual work unit, subsystem, system, etc.) and the amount of data required for each effort.

2. *Manual:* Is manual operation of the method possible or reasonable to consider?

3. *Computer program:* If a computer is required, has the method already been programmed for some machine?

4. *Running Time:* If the method has been programmed, what is the running time for one cycle of evaluation or allocation?

5. *Updating:* What is the ease of updating the system to take new information into account? Can it handle information which is developed periodically and new items which come in on an unscheduled basis?

6. *Proficiency level:* What level of proficiency is required of the operator (not the manager who is using the output)? Can the system be handled by a clerk? Does it require a skilled technician? Does it require a degreed professional?

7. *Outside help:* Is help or information required from persons outside the R&D organization to evaluate goals set by others (i.e., environments not under the control of the R&D organization, etc.)?

Few of the systems appeared to be applicable throughout the entire R&D spectrum. Some were more applicable to one portion of the spectrum than to others. The methods are rated as being applicable to research, exploratory development, advanced development, or engineering development.

Figures 19 through 21 list thirty techniques.[6] These are identified by the name or names of their originators and with the acronym used to designate the method. Their features, ease of use criteria, and areas of applicability are compared and displayed in matrix form. An entry of X in the matrix indicates that the method has the feature, satisfies the cri-

[6] Each of the 30 methods is explained in greater detail in the article entitled "The Selection of R & D Program Content—Survey of Quantitative Methods," *IEEE Transactions on Engineering Management*, March, 1967.

Method	Utility Measure	Prob. of Success	Orthog. Criteria	Sensitivity	Retain Rej. Atl.	Class Struc.	Time	Strateg.	Sys. Cross Support	Tech. Cross Support	Graph. Displ.	Flag	Optimiz.* Criteria	Con-straints**	Com-puterized
1. Mottley-Newton, 1959	X	X	X	X			X	X					1	1, 6, 7	X
2. Gargiulo et al., 1961	X	X	X	X			X		X	X			1	1, 2, 3, 4	
3. Pound, 1964	X	X								X			7	1	
4. Sobelman, 1958	X	X	X			X	X						7	1, 2, 3	X
5. Freeman, 1960	X	X	X				X						7	2, 5	X
6. Asher, 1962	X	X											7		X
7. Hess, 1962	X	X					X						7	1	X
8. Dean-Sengupta, 1962	X	X	X		X	X							7		
9. Disman, 1962	X	X											7		
10. Cramer-Smith, 1964	X	X			X	X			X					1	X
11. Esch, "PATTERN," 1963	X	X	X	X	X	X	X	X					1, 2	6	
12. Blum, 1963	X	X	X	X	X	X							6	1, 6	X
13. Bakanas, 1964	X	X	X	X	X	X							3	1, 6, 7	
14. Dean, 1964	X	X	X	X	X	X	X	X		X	X		4	1, 2, 3	X
15. Hill-Roepcke, 1964	X	X	X	X	X	X	X	X		X	X		2	1, 2	
16. Nutt, 1965	X	X	X	X	X	X						X	1, 2	1	X
17. Cetron, "PROFILE," 1965	X	X	X		X	X	X	X	X				3, 3, 4, 7	1, 6, 7	X
18. Rosen-Saunder, 1965	X	X	X	X	X	X	X	X	X	X			3	1, 2, 3	
19. Sacco, 1965	X	X		X		X	X						2		
20. Albertini, 1965	X	X	X	X	X	X	X	X		X	X		5	1, 6, 7	X
21. Berman, 1965	X	X			X	X									X
22. Sobin-Gordon, 1965	X	X	X		X	X	X	X			X	X	1	1, 2, 3, 7	
23. Albertini, 1965	X	X	X	X	X	X	X	X					2	1, 6, 7	
24. Wells, 1966	X	X	X		X									1, 7	
25. Cetron, "QUEST," 1966	X	X	X	X	X	X	X	X		X	X	X	1, 2	1, 7	X
26. Dean-Hauser, 1966	X	X	X	X	X	X	X			X	X	X	3		
27. Belt, 1966	X	X								X					X
28. De l'Estoile, 1966	X	X													
29. Martino et al., 1967	X	X	X		X	X	X	X	X	X	X	X	3	1, 7	X
30. Caulfield-Freshman, 1967	X				X	X	X	X					1, 2, 3	1, 7	

* Optimization Criteria
1. Ordinal Ranking
2. Expected Value
3. Cost-Benefit
4. Profitability
5. Incremental Costs
6. Composite Score
7. Discounted Net Value

** Constraints
1. Budget
2. Skills Available
3. Facilities Available
4. Competitor Efforts
5. Raw Materials Available
6. Risk
7. Program Balance

Figure 19. Features of the Methods.

	Rsch.	Expl. Devel.	Adv. Devel.	Engr. Devel.
1. Mottley–Newton, 1959	X	X	X	
2. Gargiulo et al., 1961		X	X	X
3. Pound, 1964		X	X	
4. Sobelman, 1958			X	
5. Freeman, 1960				X
6. Asher, 1962			X	X
7. Hess, 1962				X
8. Dean–Sengupta, 1962				X
9. Disman, 1962		X	X	X
10. Cramer–Smith, 1964	X			
11. Esch, "PATTERN," 1963		X	X	X
12. Blum, 1963		X	X	X
13. Bakanas, 1964		X	X	
14. Dean, 1964		X	X	X
15. Hill–Roepcke, 1964		X	X	
16. Nutt, 1965		X	X	
17. Cetron, "PROFILE," 1965		X	X	
18. Rosen–Saunder, 1965				X
19. Sacco, 1965		X	X	
20. Albertini, 1965		X	X	
21. Berman, 1965		X	X	X
22. Sobin–Gordon, 1965	X	X	X	
23. Albertini, 1965	X			
24. Wells, 1966			X	X
25. Cetron, "QUEST," 1966	X	X		
26. Dean–Hauser, 1966		X	X	X
27. Belt, 1966		X	X	
28. De l'Estoile, 1966		X	X	X
29. Martino et al., 1967	X	X		
30. Caulfield–Freshman, 1967			X	

Figure 20. Ease of Use.

terion, or is applicable to that area. For the "Data Required" column, the methods are coded "L" for little or none, "M" for moderate amount, and "C" for considerable amount. These evaluations are subjective but provide some guidance as to the ease of use.

Each method, within its capabilities and limitations, can provide assistance to the management of an R&D enterprise in appraising the worth of its R&D effort. In particular, the use of quantitative methods tends to eliminate bias, provides a degree of consistency, and forces managers to render their judgments more explicit in evaluating R&D programs. While some of the described techniques lack certain features, these usually can be added with some modification, if desired.

The value of any appraisal method is further limited by two factors: (1) The validity of input information supplied by the laboratory workers and management staff, and (2) The effective support and use of the system by higher management. If managers support a method, and make proper use of it, and furthermore insure that the input information is as valid as humanly possible, the methods can provide a very valuable tool for improving the management of an R&D organization.

Considering the limitations of the methods described, there is clearly

Figure 21. R&D Areas of Applicability.

	Data Req'ts	Manual Oper'n Poss.	Comp. Prog. Avail.	Comp. Run Time	Diffic. of Updating	Operator Profic. Level	Need for Outside Help
1. Mottley–Newton, 1959	L	X	X		L	T	L
2. Gargiulo et al., 1961	M	X				T	L
3. Pound, 1964	C	X				T	L
4. Sobelman, 1958	M	X					
5. Freeman, 1960	C	X	X			T	
6. Asher, 1962	C		X			T	
7. Hess, 1962	C		X			T	
8. Dean–Sengupta, 1962	C					T	
9. Disman, 1962	C						M
10. Cramer–Smith, 1964	M	X					M
11. Esch, "PATTERN," 1963	C		X	C	C	P	C
12. Blum, 1963	M	X			L	T	
13. Bakanas, 1964	C		X	M	L	T	
14. Dean, 1964	M	X			L	P	L
15. Hill, Roepcke, 1964	C			M	L	T	L
16. Nutt, 1965	C		X	L	L	P	C
17. Cetron, "PROFILE," 1965	L	X			L	P	M
18. Rosen–Saunder, 1965	C		X			T	
19. Sacco, 1965	C			L	L	P	L
20. Albertini, 1965	C		X	M	L	T	
21. Berman, 1965	C			C	L	T	
22. Sobin–Gordon, 1965	M		X	M	L	P	L
23. Albertini, 1965	C		X	M	L	T	L
24. Wells, 1966	M		X	L	L	P	C
25. Cetron, "QUEST," 1966	C	X			M	P	C
26. Dean–Hauser, 1966	C		X	L	L	P	L
27. Belt, 1966	M	X			M	P	L
28. De l'Estoile, 1966	C		X	C	C	P	C
29. Martino et al., 1967	C	X			M	P	C
30. Caulfield–Freshman, 1967	C	X			M	P	C

Symbol Keys

Computer Running Time		Need for outside help	
L—little	L—low	L—little or none	C—clerk
M—moderate	M—moderate	M—moderate	T—technician
C—considerable	C—considerable	C—considerable	P—degreed professional
Difficulty of Updating		Operator Proficiency	

much room for further refinement and improvement of quantitative methods for appraisal of R&D programs. However, even in the absence of these refined methods, the spectrum of existing methods can provide the R&D manager with considerable assistance in appraising his program.

WHAT ARE THE OPINIONS OF THE USERS (OR POTENTIAL USERS)?

There are differing opinions as to the applications of these techniques, but users fall into one of three categories:

1. The unbeliever
2. The strong advocate
3. The "noncommittal"

The unbeliever is illustrated in this statement by Professor Edward B. Roberts of MIT.

Although a number of industrial firms are striving to improve their R&D funding decisions, the Defense Department under McNamara is the first major organization to react definitively to this folklore approach. And the reaction is a somewhat characteristic overaction that produces a decision-making system that promises to be even more cumbersome, less realistic, and more ironclad in appearance than . . . The outputs thus derived emerge from the computer with the same factual appearance as does a payroll tabulation. Upon such illusory bases will fundamental research funds be allotted, if present DoD trends hold sway.[7]

A supporter and potential user of this appraisal information, Captain Edmund Mahinske, USN, stated in a management memo:

A planning appraisal system which operates on task area proposals . . . is a crucial necessity to our attempts to derive our program on a basis of relatively unimpeachable logic. . . . Remember our goal is to improve our management of the program *not* to perpetuate the "control we now exercise." [8]

[7] Edward B. Roberts, "Facts and Folklore in Research and Development Management," *Industrial Management Review*, May, 1967.
[8] Edmund B. Mahinske, HQ. Naval Material Command, *Memorandum on Exploratory Development Planning Appraisal System*, November 22, 1966.

Colonel Buck, Technical Director of the Air Force Flight Dynamics Laboratory, at Wright-Patterson AF Base, has used a computerized quantitative resource allocation system as an aid in planning his R&D program for three years. Perhaps the best answer to the question was given when Colonel Buck asked how he used the quantitative technique, replied, "Very carefully."

Professor Roberts is correct, if the choice is between any machine and the human brain. The brain would be selected because it has a marvelous feedback system that learns from experience. It also has an uncanny way of pulling out the salient factors and rejecting useless information. But it is wrong to say that one must select intuitive experience over analysis or minds over machines. They are not really *alternatives*. They complement each other. If the two are used together, the results are far better than if either is used individually.

One of the most pertinent statements in this connection comes from Paul Sturm, Assistant Director of Plans and Policy, Office of Director of Defense Research and Engineering:

> Attempts to quantify the unquantifiable, in the interests of satisfying the demands of an unyielding methodology, is a potentially stifling practice that could cause irreparable damage to our technological supremacy and the consequent ability to defend ourselves during the challenging decades ahead. At the other extreme, neglect of the quantifiable economics of defense materiel, in the interests of cost-free choices of action, is also a dangerous practice that could cause irreparable damage to our economic solvency and the consequent fiscal stability necessary during the challenging decades ahead. The prudent course lies between those two extremes.[9]

Perhaps the titles of these techniques, instead of "PATTERN," "PROFILE," "QUEST," or "TORQUE," should be "IMPACT," an acronym, standing for "*I*MPLEMENTATION *M*AY *P*ROVE *A* CONSIDERABLE *T*ASK."

[9] Paul J. Sturm, "Problem Mongers, Solution Mongers and Weapon System Effectiveness," *Defense Industry Bulletin,* July, 1966.

INTEGRATING TECHNOLOGICAL AND ENVIRONMENTAL FORECASTING

PART THREE

One viewpoint on forecasting is that technological progress cannot be predicted without anticipating the environment in which it will exist. If population, for instance, presses on food supply or causes pollution of the water and air, technology is called upon to ease these problems. Progress follows social needs, and will tend to be focused on those areas where society perceives the necessity of change. Future technology is essentially the result of society's present assessment and reaction to environmental changes—political, economic, social—as well as of technological activity. Therefore, technological progress and social needs must be examined concurrently in any forecasting effort.

A more extreme view is that the forecast of technology should begin with a projection of the total future environment. Since it is impossible to describe the precise environment that will exist, or even to select the dominant or controlling environmental factors, we should examine a number of possible alternative futures. From this study of "scenarios," the relative likelihood and importance of various technological developments may be projected.

Some technologists and believers in the statistical methodology described in Part II tend to reject this "Let's start with the future and see what we need" approach. However, there is a most significant fact that should be recognized: With the establishment of the NASA programs in the United States and now the major efforts in urban renewal, health, mass transportation, control of pollution and similar goals, a new influence has become involved. Our government is initiating major efforts to marshal technical resources for goals other than war. Political decisions to pursue these goals will indeed determine forecasts of technological progress. Hence, environmental forecasting will become more useful and more relevant to the technology forecast.

An Integrated Model of Technological Change

F. H. BUTTNER

E. S. CHEANEY

Technological change occurs as the result of attempts by many organizations to find a way to match scientific and technical progress with societal needs. The authors have developed a framework that assists the technological forecaster to identify the needs of society and match them with the technical concepts that must be developed to fulfill the needs. The methodology provides a means for determining the efforts required to develop the concepts and the manner in which they tie in with corporate goals.

Both Dr. Buttner, Fellow, Department of Economics and Information Research, and Mr. Cheaney, Chief of Battelle's Technical Planning Center, Department of Mechanical Engineering, have explored many techniques of forecasting in Battelle's numerous studies for industry and government clients.

Technological change does not just happen. It is managed by organizations, either private or government, which see enlightened self-interest in promoting and subsidizing specific technological improvements. The efforts of many organizations, together with many technological improvements, add up to technological change. As an example, the Bureau of Mines may observe that the national interest would be served by advancing the fortunes of the coal industry through foreseen technical innovations. Accordingly, the Bureau would subsidize research in an effort to realize those innovations. If successful, the innovations would serve society with an added or more economical energy supply. In the Bureau's enlightened self-interest, the successful research would be another achievement under its charter.

Industry obtains new profit opportunities from technological change as the result of cost reductions, or new products and services. Accordingly, it subsidizes research in selected directions, hoping to serve society better with newer and cheaper offerings, while increasing profits that encourage new investment. In so doing, industry manages technological change. These are real and important motivations.

The rate at which innovations occur depends heavily on the rate at which money is invested in their development. This, in turn, depends on the urgency with which social needs are pressing for the innovations. Organizational management actions are primarily responsible for integrating social need, opportunities, and capabilities so as to indicate the direction that timely technological change should take, and to motivate programs at a rate proportional to the sense of urgency.

Bypassing management decisions for the moment, the rate and direction of technological change depend upon the magnitude of four elements: the state of society, the evident rate of change in that state of society, the state of the pertinent technical art, and the potential rate of change possible in that state of the art. If society is pressed, or is willing to pay for a technological change, and if technology is capable of producing the change, innovation can be fairly rapid, if managed by an interested and able organization. If either need or capability is lacking, motivation will be weak and change will be slow. The purpose of this paper is to consider pragmatically the foregoing elements, their interrelationships, and how they interact in actual cases.

CONCEPTUAL FRAMEWORKS

The literature abounds with models describing technological change. These models are valuable for helping scientists and R&D managers find their way among the complexities that line the path to success. As a service organization to industry and government, Battelle has the mission to develop pragmatic approaches for planning useful R&D programs for sponsoring organizations.

This chapter describes a simplified conceptual framework which Battelle finds useful. The framework is next translated into working models, and examples of practical applications are finally discussed. Many familiar terms are used, such as technological forecasting, technical capability, state of the art, social and economic need, interaction between social need and technical capability. In addition, a few new catchwords are also introduced, such as science forecasting, socio-forecasting, state of society, and socio-economic forecasting. The chapter concludes with a description of results obtained from the environmental network, the objectives network, and the attainability technical forecast, through which Battelle develops specific plans for sponsor organizations.

Simplified Conceptual Framework

The simplified framework can be visualized as the inside of a room, as shown in Figure 1. This is a simple, three-dimensional room, with a grid marked off on the ceiling and on the floor. The ceiling is called the "Social Plane" and the floor is called the "Science Plane."

Each grid box in the Social Plane represents an area of social activity and its related needs. One box might be called medical needs; others,

Figure 1. Plane of Social Need in Parallel with Plane of Scientific Knowledge.

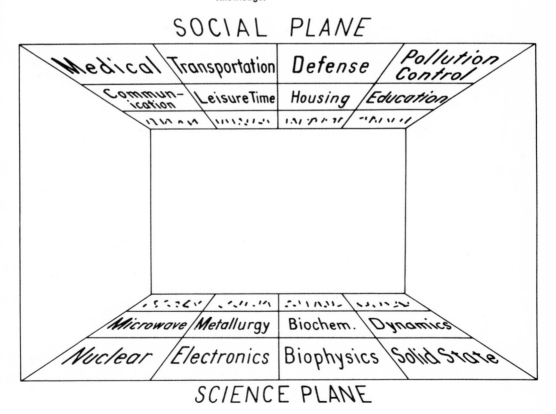

transportation needs, defense needs, pollution-control needs, communication needs, and so on. These cover a host of social areas in which needs now exist and in which new needs will arise as population expands.

In the Science Plane, each box represents an area of science in which scientists are making new discoveries. Boxes might be called: nuclear science, metallurgical science, biophysics, astronomy, solid state physics, microwaves, electronics, and so on, almost endlessly.

Out of each of the social areas, specific needs can be plotted in the form of arrows reaching downward, with the length of each arrow representing the maturity of the need; i.e., how well-defined the need is, how urgent it is, and how soon a solution to that need would be accepted by society. As an example, a cancer cure would be shown by a long arrow, because society is highly conscious of the problem and is eagerly awaiting a solution. An electric automobile, however, would be represented by a shorter arrow, because society is not yet sure about wanting it.

Correspondingly, from the Science Plane, upward-reaching arrows would indicate new capabilities or states of the art which stem from understandings in basic science. The length of these arrows would represent the degree to which the science has been oriented and progress has been made toward useful ends; i.e., satisfying some possible need reaching down from the ceiling.

If a solid arrow reaching upward represents a technical capability, or a "state of the art," then an arrow coming down from the ceiling represents a "state of society." Ultimately, the two arrows will meet. At that point, we will observe completion of another step in the progress of technology. (See Figure 2.) By predicting the joining of a pair of arrows, a technical forecaster would be conceptualizing how technology will progress in a certain technical field of interest. Thus, he would produce a technical forecast. Contemporaneously, a market forecaster would have assessed future markets for likely products from the same technical field of interest. He would have produced a market forecast. Putting the two forecasts together and making value judgments from them is *technological forecasting*—a step which is indispensable in planning a venture and is necessary for seeing the venture through to a conclusion.

Thus, the technological forecast is composed of five elements: (1) the state of the art at the moment, (2) the state of society at the moment, (3) the technical forecast, (4) the market forecast, and (5) value judgments as to the likely contribution this integration of possibilities might have to an organization.

Both the technical forecast and the market forecast are usually some kind of extrapolation. In the simplest form, the forecast is an extension from some basic time series. However, such extrapolations often are made

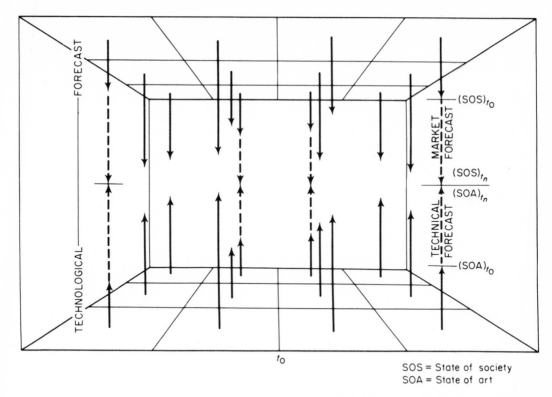

Figure 2. Technical and Social States Forecasted.

SOS = State of society
SOA = State of art

more sophisticated by introducing growth analogies and by combining several trends into new predictions. Market forecasting is a comparatively sophisticated art at the moment. However, technical forecasting is not. There are many different approaches to this task, and technical forecasting has some way to go before it is considered a reliable art in itself.

Figure 2 assumes fairly definable states of the art and states of society. Forecasts stemming from these states are fairly well charted by what has gone on before. These are most likely to lead to microinnovations; i.e., small improvements in present techniques, systems, materials, etc.

There are other kinds of forecasts which lead to macroinnovation, or revolutionary change, such as the replacement of lathes by electrolytic machining tools, or the substitution of hydrofoils for boats, or jet propulsion for propellor propulsion. Macroinnovations are rare because we are not very good at forecasting entirely new needs of society or entirely new scientific understandings. Such forecasting, called socio-forecasting and science forecasting, might be developed through rational processes based on evident long-term forces at work today. This is illustrated in Figure 3 wherein, at time zero, there is no tangible evidence of a new social need or a new scientific understanding. Then, somewhere down the road, at time "n," new capabilities and new social needs start to appear.

Battelle is presently working on a pioneering program in socio-forecasting called Aids to Corporate Thinking. It is well funded, primarily with Battelle money. Progress has seemed painfully slow, but promising results are now being shown, and there is great enthusiasm to press on with the program. Basically, forecasting is done by correlating trends which relate to many fundamental aspects of society and the people who compose it.

It seems that no one has really done anything similar in regard to science forecasting, at least beyond some initial conceptual thinking. The Delphi method is probably the most progressive technique in this area at the moment. It would appear that techniques which parallel socio-forecasting might very well apply in science forecasting.

In reference to Figure 2, it is rare for any pair of arrows to come together spontaneously. As an example, undeveloped countries have grievous social needs which could be satisfied with existing technical capabilities. Yet these technical capabilities seldom seem to join spontaneously with the social needs. Some kind of an organization must step in and draw these arrows together, by conceptualizing a technological forecast, planning action, and acting on the plan. In other words, the arrows must be *managed* to come together, by institutions which link technological progress with social need.

Figure 3. Long Term Forecasting.

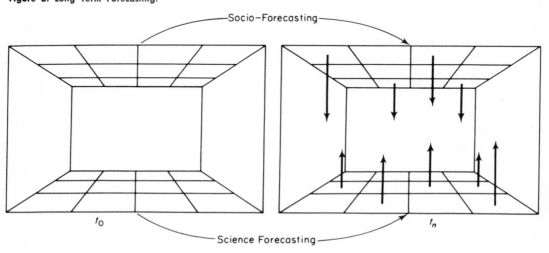

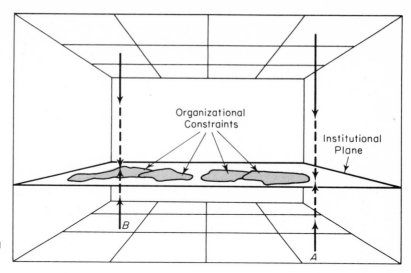

Figure 4. Institutional Plane and Organizational Constraints.

Figure 4 shows an Institution Plane, midway between, and parallel to, the ceiling and the floor. Specific organizations such as the DOD, General Electric, and Battelle, would lie in that plane, each covering only part of it. No single organization could cover the entire plane, simply because no organization can be all things to all people and to all sciences at the same time. Organizations having certain interests are bounded by certain constraints, shown as wiggly circles on the Institutional Plane. The organizations' hopes for the future might be shown as torroidal areas surrounding the original areas.

In a technological forecast, the technical economist integrates likely concepts of future technological development, shown in Figure 4 as dotted lines between the technical capabilities and the social needs. In this model, a dotted line intersects the Institutional Plane at some point on its surface. If the point of intersection lies outside a given organization's constraints, as does dotted line *A*, that linkage is of no interest to that organization, no matter how important it might be to society and to technology. However, those dotted lines that do intersect at a point within the organizational constraints and future aspirations, as does dotted line *B*, are things that the organization can do something about. Such points come within the organization's area of interest and automatically indicate possible objectives for business plans and for R&D. The value of any specific objective to an organization is the net value between what society will pay to have the need satisfied (social motivation) and what it will cost the organization to develop the capability to produce a product that satisfies the need (R&D investment).

This represents a simplified concept in graphic and theoretical terms. It suggests several practical questions: How does this framework apply to the real world? How can it be reduced to a working tool so that a forecaster can develop specific R&D plans against this background? These questions are answered in the application of the Environmental Network and the Objectives Network, which comprise the working tools of technological forecasting. Within these frameworks is a practical technical forecasting methodology called concept-oriented forecasting.

Environmental Network

The description of the environmental network begins with a title. This essentially carves out a section of three-dimensional space between the social and the science planes of Figure 1. The title might be "Coatings in Packaging," or "Manganese in Steelmaking," or "Automation in Machining." In general, it describes some kind of input (i.e., innovation, activity, or the like) for a going manufacturing or process operation. The title is important because it narrows the infinite universe of science and society to a sector of specific interest.

The environmental network next provides a means of drawing the arrows of Figure 2 within the identified section of space. It is comprised of seven sets of data, each set forming a link in a chain which is anchored to society at one end, and to science at the other. In general terms, these sets are titled: Environmental Factors, Basic Functions (unit processes, etc.), Present Systems (or component systems now used), Methods of Modifying Systems, Material Used, and Methods for Application. These terms become clearer with reference to specific titles. Figure 5 shows the seven sets described in terms specific to "Coatings in Packaging." The boxes to the right contain titles of information relevant to each set.

If boxes in each set are connected by vertical lines, the essential elements in an *objective* are automatically pinpointed. A *statement* of that objective is developed by reasoning out the connection. By digging into the information and data behind that statement, pictures are developed of a *State of Society,* an evident *change in that State of Society,* and an available *State of the Art;* and these suggest a *change in the state of the Art* which will make a linkage. This process gives meaning, through words and ideas, to the arrows of Figure 2.

Vertical lines can be drawn randomly in Figure 5, and an endless number of objective statements can be developed. However, a cursory examination of such lines reveals many which are absurd, as well as many sensible linkages which would otherwise be missed. So, with common sense and imagination, a long list of reasonable statements of objectives can be drawn up.

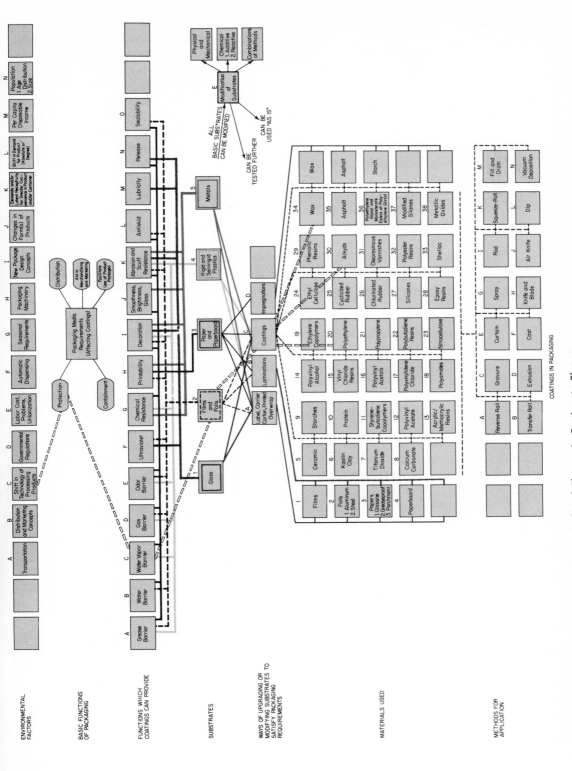

Figure 5. Pattern of a Graphic Model Relating Technical Changes in Coatings to Changes in the Environment.

The Environment

What has just been called the "State of Society," gives way, in the practical sense, to the so-called "Environment." The word "Environment" is more descriptive than "State of Society." From an organization's viewpoint, the Environment is that which goes on outside the organization's own realm of control. It is limited to those things in the State of Society that have direct bearing upon the fortunes of the organization. Thus, the Environment is essentially the state of only one segment of society, or that parish within society that comes directly into contact with the organization.

The Environment may be conveniently considered in three or four sectors: (1) Government, (2) Other Industries, (3) Technical and Technological Change, and sometimes, (4) Other Divisions of the same organization (see Figure 6). If the organization happens to be an automobile company, government safety restrictions would be outside and beyond the direct control of the company itself. In the realm of Other Industries, the company must be prepared to meet the challenge of changes wrought by other automobile companies in their manufacturing processes, their automobile designs or their business policies. Finally, technical change can affect an organization's operations in many ways by introducing new materials, new machines and equipment, and new maufacturing and testing techniques of all kinds.

Figure 6. Coatings in Packaging—Environmental Factors.

	Government		Industry		Technical Change		Other Divisions	
ENVIRONMENTAL FACTORS	FDA	ICC	Food Proc.	Meat Packing	Plastics	Fibers		
	IPH	HEW	Frozen Food	Transp.	Auto Mchy	Printing		
			Metal Parts Mfg	Tobacco				
			Other Mfg Ind					

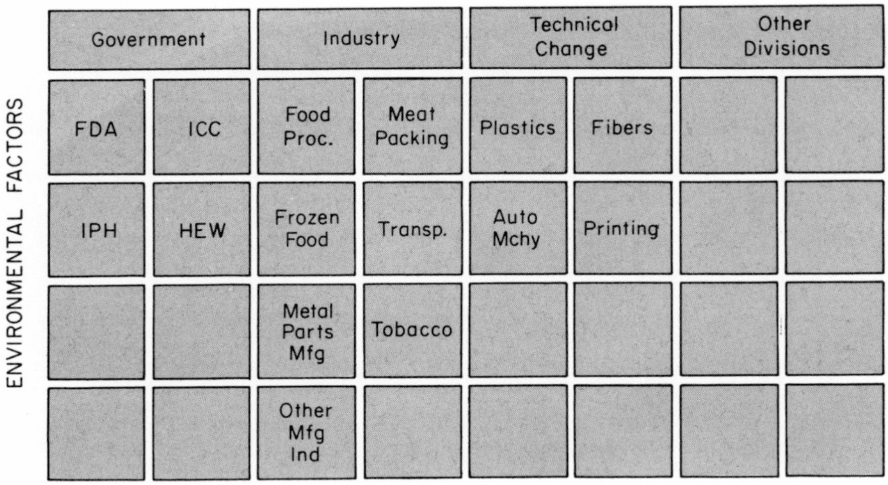

The fourth category of Environment Change enters when the focus is only one division of a larger corporation. Accordingly, the actions of other divisions within the corporation become part of the environment.

In the example of Coatings in Packaging, the Environment consists of a number of factors organized into the four categories just mentioned. The Environmental Factor boxes (see Figure 6) reflect specific items of change in these four areas. They represent a statement as to the State of the Society, but only so far as Coatings in Packaging are concerned.

The Institutional Plane

Figure 7 shows some of the organizational constraints within the Institutional Plane. These constraints consist of the basic functions of packaging, or the results which must be achieved for effective packaging. These functions are labeled: Protection, Containment, Distribution, Aid in Merchandising and Marketing, and Facilitate Use of Product in Package. These are not the only constraints pertaining to a packaging association or its member companies, but are the constraints which pertain to the design and manufacture of packages which are common to all member companies. Working at the association level, the many other specific constraints that would be encountered in working with a single company, such as financing, marketing, and preferences of individuals, could not be dealt with.

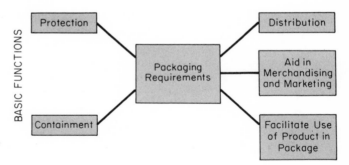

Figure 7. Organizational Constraints on the Institutional Plane.

For illustrative purposes, the fewer constraints to worry about the better. Later on, however, additional constraints, common to all member companies, will be shown in the Objectives Network. Also, as the findings of such a study at the association level become available to member companies, each one can temper the recommendations in the light of its own company constraints.

The subsequent rows of boxes in Figure 5 are too numerous to repeat here. However, they lead into the State of the Art as it presently exists, and then into speculations on possible changes in the State of the Art. In Figure 5, the existing State of the Art and its possible change concerns substrates upon which coatings are normally applied, methods for modifying substrates, materials used, and methods of application.

Basic function of coatings is a string of boxes pinpointing several barrier properties; resistance to ultraviolet and chemicals; various physical properties; and mechanical properties of packages.

Substrates includes glass, film, foils, plastics and metals.

Methods of modifying substrates includes lamination, coatings impregnation, labels, etc.

Materials Used includes 38 individual materials that have and could find their way into packages, such as wax, resins, shellac, polypropylene, cellulose, proteins, metals, metal oxide.

Methods of Application includes conventional and new application methods such as gravure, transfer rolls, squeeze rolls, cast, dip, vacuum deposition, spray.

In this case, there was no need to go into fundamental science. If there were, it would be quite permissible to add additional rows to cover various items of new technology that would apply.

The vertical line shown in Figure 4 links various boxes to present the following picture (see the dotted line on Figure 5):

Environment	Freeze Drying of foods is an advancing technology that is imposing many new demands on packaging,
Basic functions of packaging	particularly in the area of Protection. Packages are basically required to protect the contained dried food against—
Functions of coatings	—pickup of moisture. Thus, an important function of the coating is to provide a moisture barrier.
Substrates	This may be achieved by the judicious choice of substrates—in this case a foil material—
Method of modifying substrate	with a proper coating applied to it.

| Materials used | Coating materials of specific interest are polyethylene, alkyds, and wax. |
| Methods of Application | No particular variance from standard practices is expected in applying these coatings. |

The statement strung together in the right-hand column is a statement of a future technological situation. It needs to be reworded in terms of a technical objective and it implies alternate R&D investigations. Any number of similar statements can be constructed, either mechanically on a computer or by intelligent inspection. The second approach is usually sufficient to accumulate an overwhelming number of reasonable statements. The list of reasonable statements is then screened through the Objectives Network.

Objectives Network

The Objectives Network begins with a statement of *an* objective and, through a series of five levels of considerations, provides a framework for assessing the value of alternate courses of action which can lead to fulfillment of the stated objectives. In the Objectives Network, the reasonable statements of objectives are subjected to further constraints of the organization—the irregular area plotted in the Institutional Plane of Figure 4. Depending on the organization, the arrays of more specific constraints differ. An industrial organization might consider cost/performance ratios; compatability with existing plant equipment, with customer equipment, and with future plans; the investment required, etc. A government organization might seek maximum performance at any cost. In any case, the constraints establish the criteria by which the "reasonable" objectives are judged.

For illustration, Figure 8 restates the objective outlined in the description of the Environmental Network:

To improve the moisture barrier properties of freeze-dried food packages.

Although the method of developing moisture barriers in paper which is examined here involves the application of an impregnable coating, other alternatives are considered simultaneously. These include modifying the product; developing nonpaper substrates; and developing material combinations. These alternatives would also be explored for superior alternatives during a comprehensive study.

Level II objectives are alternative approaches for achieving Level I objectives. Figure 8 indicates at least six specific ways to achieve better

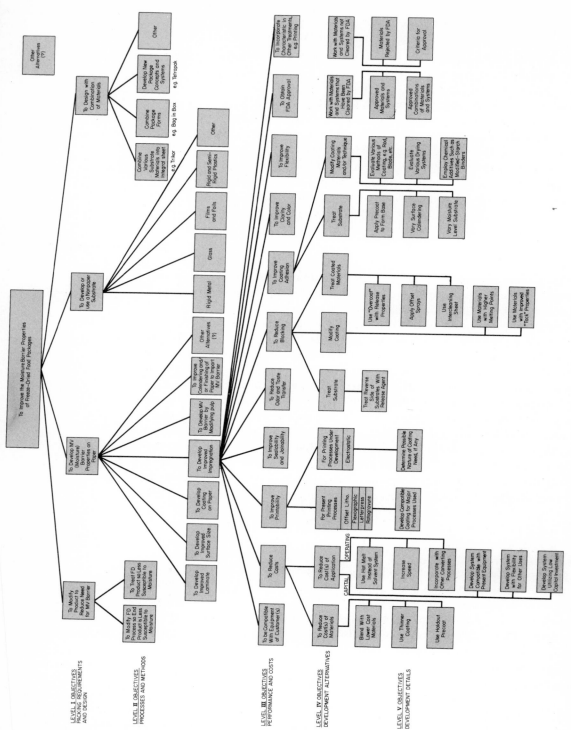

Figure 8. Typical Portion of an Objectives Network.

moisture-vapor barrier properties on paper. The technically competitive ideas also have a few alternatives at this level.

Level III objectives lead to more specific screening. These objectives list performance and cost criteria that are important to the sponsor's ability to maintain a profit position while satisfying the coming need of society. A similar array of performance and costs would exist for any of the other six alternatives listed in Level II objectives.

It should be noted that, to reduce costs, thinking is focused on reducing the costs of materials and applications (Level IV objectives). Level V lists alternative objectives which could achieve lower costs, e.g., by blending lower-cost materials, or using thinner coatings or a hold-out precoat. In keeping with the industrial constraints, any low-cost material chosen must be compatible with the lowest capital cost equipment and operating cost systems. It also must be compatible with the constraints listed to the right of "Level IV" and "Level V objectives."

At this point, the forecasting process begins to depart from exploratory and descriptive investigation. Networks have mapped the situation, outlined the many possibilities, and assisted investigators in forming an initial sense of scope. Beyond this point, the procedure begins to deal more strictly with technical alternatives.

To proceed with an assessment of the most likely direction of technological change, it is necessary to utilize methods that comprehend relative values and quantitative boundaries solely in the technical realm. Such methods have arisen from technical research and design direction, where practitioners are responsible for selecting specific corporate programs of research and development. The methods are centered on the generation and analysis of definite concepts; hence, the generic term "concept-oriented forecasting" has evolved. These methods lead to forecasts of the change in the state of the art to be expected from (1) the pressure of future need, and (2) the foreseen technical capabilities present today.

The following section illustrates the application of "concept-oriented" technical forecasting to a system in mechanical engineering. Similar applications might be made in electronics, space mechanics, or wherever proven physical and engineering principles are available to accurately predict cause and effect. Where such principles are lacking or poorly defined, as, for example, in alloy design and other materials areas, allowances in the basic "concept-oriented forecasting" scheme would be required.

CONCEPT-ORIENTED FORECASTING

Obtaining and evaluating concepts is the central activity of the engineering designer—not primarily the man designing parts at the drawing board, but the man who perceives the possibilities of new systems and devices and directs the many activities (including drawing board work) that go into bringing these perceptions to three-dimensional fruition. It is he who possesses the authority and responsibility to commit resources to programs arising from design decisions. When such an individual makes a design decision, a complex act of forecasting is involved. Engineering designers have been serving man for centuries—Da Vinci was a great designer—and the intellectual processes involved have been well defined, although, assuredly, they are not well understood. The methods of the engineering designer can be examined for guidance in ways to assemble useful forecasts.

The thought processes of the engineering designer who is confronted with a technological objective boil down to trying to answer four questions: (1) What, precisely, is needed? (2) What are some different physical ways in which the need can be met? (3) For each way, what seems to be the potential relative effectiveness for meeting the need? (4) What is the relative attainability of each? When the designer has obtained answers to these questions, he selects the option with the most responsive combination of effectiveness and attainability; that is, he makes a design decision. Such a decision is tantamount to a technological forecast of the specific concept. Its degree of refinement, and the confidence with which it can be accepted, depend on the scope, depth, and technique of inquiry used by the designer in seeking answers to his four basic questions.

Examinations of the design process have revealed definite patterns of approach to these questions which could almost be called methods, except that they are so intrinsic that they are practiced unconsciously by most designers. Several authorities[1] have attempted qualitative and analytical descriptions of engineering design, to improve engineering curricula and the performance of practitioners. In so doing, they have made available a wealth of insight about the way the four basic questions are structured and attacked. Some of this insight is especially relevant to technological forecasting.

The First Question—Needs Profiles

Any good designer continually probes and reflects on the situation he is studying, in order to increase the technical precision with which he expresses the need that he is endeavoring to meet. Tentative solutions often expose anomalies or omissions in the needs definition, and these must be rectified by investigations of various kinds. The statement of

---

[1] See the bibliography to this chapter.

need inevitably takes on a structure built around a hierarchy of wanted characteristics—a morphology—containing many value judgments.

Intuitively or otherwise, the engineering designer will construct the morphology of a proposition by asking himself what elements of performance combine to supply the need. If his scope of comprehension is limited to technical matters, his thoughts will center on mechanical performance, leaving out economic and social factors. The more competent designers recognize their larger role: to relate economic and social factors to the technical performance of products. Such designers will think of the cost of a product as part of its performance. Also, they will include even more abstract features such as aesthetic appeal, the excellence of field service backup for a product, the ease with which servicing can be done, and so on. The morphology, or list of wanted characteristics of an automobile air conditioning system, might be as follows:

Efficiency (thermodynamic coefficient of performance)
Compactness
Lightness
Flexibility of configuration
Control continuity
Operational economy
Low first cost
Good air distribution
Quietness and freedom from vibration
Reliability
Low useful power consumption

To make this list useful for forecasting or design, two things must be added. First, the range of variation from "poorest acceptable" to "best conceivable" must be determined for each characteristic. These extremes are difficult to locate. It is interesting and instructive to observe that knowledge of what constitutes "poorest acceptable" inevitably arises from the market place, whereas the "best conceivable" generally comes from the technical community. Thus, the market place can show itself willing to live with an energy cost of 7 horsepower to drive an auto air conditioner, but a technologist is required to perceive that waste heat from the engine exhaust could theoretically be used to power an air conditioner so that the *useful* power consumption could be reduced to zero. Thus the variation of this factor is from 7 to 0 horsepower.

The second thing that must be added to a morphology is a determination of the relative value of excellent performance in each characteristic. A typical question would be: Is it going to be more valuable in the market place to have an automobile air conditioner of low useful power consumption or one that is extremely compact? It is in the making of these value judgments that the real crux of the needs expression formu-

Performance Characteristic	Threshold Performance	Optimal Performance	Value Index Number
Low original cost (to user)	$250.00	$125.00	2.20
Comfort of air distribution pattern	Common minimum per- formance like under- dash add-on units	Low velocity No sensible draft No temperature stratification	1.85
Large capacity (for rapid pulldown and extreme ambient)	0.75 tons under specified test conditions	1.2 tons under specified test conditions	1.30
Low consumption of vehicle propulsive power	About 6 hp	0 hp (with waste-heat system)	1.00
Low maintenance cost	1¼¢/mile	0¢/mile (waste-heat or sealed system)	1.00
Uniformity of temp. control	Off-on control over a 7- deg. change in temp.	Smooth, continuous modula- tion producing constant temperature and humidity & fresh air under full- section range of ambients	0.75
Small size	1.0 cu. ft.	0.5 cu. ft.	0.60
Minimum occurrence of unexpected failure	0.9	0-not more than two components	0.55
Quietness and freedom from vibration	Like underdash add-on unit	Imperceptible	0.35
Lightness	80 lb.	40 lb.	0.20
Ease of Operation	Off-on control	As in "constant control" system	0.20
			10.00

Figure 9. Automobile Air Conditioner Needs Profile

lation and, indeed, of the whole forecasting process lies. Such judgments can be, and most often are, made intuitively by knowledgeable individuals. The performance characteristics that a designer struggles hardest to achieve are those he has put at the top of his importance list, either by explicit analysis or by undefined "feel."

The techniques of operation research have provided the design community with methods of value analysis that are rational and structured. These lead the analyst to a hierarchy of value which does not contain internal inconsistencies and which can be quantified. The method of

Churchman and Ackoff [2] is noteworthy here, since it imposes on the individual(s) making the value judgments an intellectual discipline which governs his research and investigations in a most demanding way. The discipline generates specific questions which require answers, and, in a sense, it forces the investigator to either answer them in an orderly way or be content with obviously wild guesses. One can imagine the sort of study and soul-searching that a responsible investigator would have to go through to produce a statement about vehicle air conditioning like that shown in Figure 9.

In this figure, the value index numbers are simple quantitative expressions of the relative importance of good performance for each characteristic. There are several profound philosophical assumptions and difficulties connected with the idea that value is quantifiable. These do not interfere with the usefulness of the method for regulating and organizing thought about concepts and for mobilizing the creative energies of designers. The meaning of Figure 9 is that the capability of manufacturing an air conditioner costing only $125 would be eleven times more valuable *to its manufacturer* than the capability of manufacturing one weighing only 40 pounds. The leverage exerted on the product design effort by a needs statement containing this kind of precision is obvious. Clearly, the same guidance is valuable to the technical forecaster.

The Second Question—Conceptual Research

A designer seeking concepts to fill a need is not trying to make an invention. In fact, as Marples points out,[3] he is, if anything, trying hard to avoid having to make an invention. Bringing an invention to life is a tedious, high-risk, and expensive project. It can seldom be justified if the designer is able to meet the need by a shrewd arrangement or refinement of existing art. If he cannot do this—if new technology seems necessary—then his search for concepts will become more of an out-and-out search for invention; but it will still be governed by the needs to be fulfilled. Many of our greatest and most significant technological innovations—long-span suspension bridges, jet aircraft engines, expansion steam engines—can be traced to the creative thought patterns of gifted designers endeavoring to fill a perceived and defined need.

The search for concepts is an activity of the individual designer's

[2] C. W. Churchman and R. L. Ackoff, "An Approximate Measure of Value," *Journal of the Operations Research Society of America*, Vol. II, No. 2 (May, 1954).

[3] D. L. Marples, *The Decisions of Engineering Design, IRE Transactions on Engineering Management*, Vol. EM-8 (June, 1961), 55–71.

imagination. He envisions ways to do the job and keeps a record of his ideas in the form of schematics, sketches, and mathematical relationships. His ability to generate concepts is determined by the combination of his imaginative fertility and the breadth of his technical knowledge. A man ignorant in the area of electricity will not generate electrical approaches to creating a needed effect—because he cannot.

This brings into focus the fundamental requirement imposed on a designer: he *must* be broadly qualified in the physical sciences. Recognition of this in recent years has had, and is still having, a profound effect on curriculum planning in our technical schools. But precisely the same requirement must be imposed on one who would produce technological forecasts. No man of narrow specialization can maneuver his way through environmental or objective networks. Nor can such an individual recognize a range of types of concepts which may be relevant to some need.

The Third Question—Relative Effectiveness

Engineering design and technological forecasting are not vocations for idealists whose satisfaction comes from perfect solutions and surefire predictions. All design concepts are compromises between the needed performance and the constraints imposed by the laws of nature and economics. Accordingly, all technological forecasts are expressed probabilistically, because there is no way to ascertain what the future will hold. Thus, the designer examines concepts to see which is likely to come the *closest* to filling the need. The forecaster does the same thing to choose the conceptual approach most likely to be used.

This evaluation is carried out by imagining the concept to be in completed commercial form and then measuring the effectiveness of this image with respect to each of the performance characteristics contained in the statement of need. Experienced designers can and do perform this measurement intuitively. As situations have become more complex and competition more intense, it has become useful to quantify this process. The range of variation of each characteristic can be set to a scale, and the effectiveness of a given concept with respect to weight, for example, can be expressed in terms of the scale. If the scale provides for dimensionless effectiveness ratings (e.g., from 1 for minimum performance to 10 for optimal), then the ratings can be multiplied by value indexes for each performance characteristic, to arrive at a score for the concept. The sum of the scores for each characteristic would be an overall figure of merit for the particular concept. The needs profile for the auto air conditioner provides a hypothetical example of the ideas expressed here. Figure 10 shows a set of values to illustrate how the process works. Although the example

Characteristic	Value Index	The Current Offering Eff.	Score	New Concept A Eff.	Score	New Concept B Eff.	Score	0 3 6 9 12 15 18 21 24
Low original cost	2.20	8	17.60	9	19.80	6	13.20	
Comfort of air distribution	1.85	3	5.55	7	12.95	5	9.25	
Large capacity (pull-down)	1.30	6	7.80	8	10.40	3	3.90	
Low useful power concept	1.00	4	4.00	7	7.00	4	4.00	
Low maintenance cost	1.00	7	7.00	8	8.00	3	3.00	
Uniformity of temperature control	0.75	8	6.00	7	5.15	9	6.75	
Small size	0.60	8	4.80	4	2.40	10	6.00	
Minimumun unexpected failure	0.55	6	3.30	3	1.65	5	2.75	
Quietness and freedom of vibration	0.35	5	1.75	5	1.85	9	3.15	
Lightness	0.20	8	1.60	2	0.40	9	1.80	
Ease of operation	0.20	5	1.00	2	0.40	10	2.00	
			60.40		70.00		54.80	

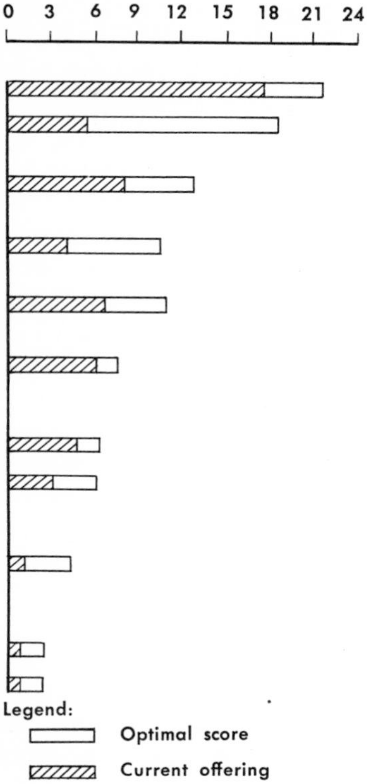

Legend:
☐ Optimal score
▨ Current offering

Figure 10. Concept Scoring Matrix

is based on a real-life situation, the value hierarchy and the effectiveness numbers are fictitious.

The example clearly shows the difference between need-oriented creativity and random creativity. New concept A is superior to the current product because its conceiver has concentrated on improved performance in the high-valued characteristics. Furthermore, he did this at a considerable sacrifice in compactness, weight, and the "fanciness" of the air conditioner control system. The conceiver of "B" accomplished great things with these latter characteristics, relative to the present offering, but he failed abysmally to produce a really competitive product because he concentrated on less significant characteristics. The bar charts at the right of the tabulation compare optimal performance with current performance.

The resulting white areas indicate, in a graphic manner, where the opportunities for superiority are located and how great the opportunities are thought to be. The significance of this for technological forecasting is that the conceptual configuration that most nearly meets a need is also most likely to appear in a relatively free and competitive market.

The Fourth Question—Concept Attainability

Any concept, even one involving a very modest rearrangement of existing art, evokes some doubt about whether or not it can be realized in a practical sense and some question about the magnitude of the resources required for realization. These issues take on supreme importance for planning and forecasting when the realization of concepts begins to depend upon advances in the commercial state of the art. How can one reliably forecast that a given idea for an invention will prove successful when it is tried? Or, stated another way, how can the amount of effort required to *make* an invention successful be predicted?

The engineering designer has repeatedly been confronted with this question. His approach is to break the concept into the elements of technical art required for success. Suppose a concept for a vehicle air conditioning system requires that the compressor be driven at constant speed. Then the art of constant-speed drives becomes a critical element. An air conditioning system contains many devices and processes, all interacting to produce the cooling effect. There are many elements of art involved. If an array of different concepts for an air conditioner is prepared, it is likely that many of the elements of technical art will be common to two or more of the concepts. For example, the compressors of concepts A and B may be quite different and run at two different speeds—one fast and one slow—but they both may be constant-speed devices. The art of constant-speed drives is common. More important, since no one has yet created a constant-speed drive of *any* kind that has proved to be economically feasible for vehicle accessories, this art must be advanced somehow, to make the concepts possible. Thus, this element of art is critical; it is necessary to the concepts and must be advanced if either concept is to be feasible.

Figure 11 illustrates the idea of critical elements of art with respect to a number of concepts. As shown in the figure, the designer-forecaster identifies the state of the art required to realize the individual concepts. The inputs are principally disciplinary, but they might also consist of ancillary concepts that would need to be analyzed themselves. An important part of this analysis is the identification of the critical factors—the indispensible art for each concept.

The critical factors are then subjected to analysis by experts to whom the designer has access. They use background and historical data to es-

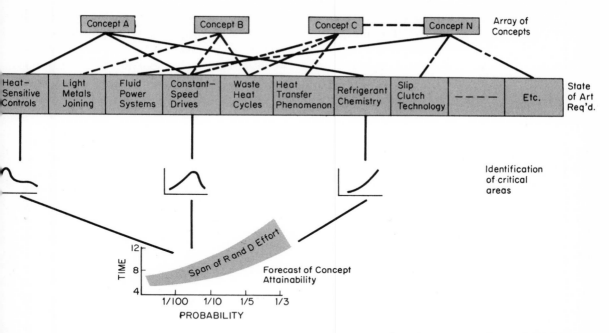

Figure 11. Flow Chart of Attainability Forecasting.

tablish trends and momentums of advance. Both the amount of research being done and the success in achieving advances are established. The ideas of pure technical forecasting—trend extrapolation, use of precursors, and amalgamation of expert judgment—are all brought into play. The outcome will be forecasts for the critical areas, expressed in terms of probable attainment of various levels in sequential time periods.

For each potential concept, the state-of-the-art inputs are integrated to provide an anticipation of the feasibility of the concept. The ideal mode of expressing this feasibility is in terms of probability at a given time period. This expression, in turn, has a breadth representing various levels of technical effort. The symbology in the lower part of Figure 11 represents such a prediction.

The integrating power necessary for making such implicit predictions is one of the facets of the experienced designer's mental equipment. Something of this integration goes into nearly every design decision, and many successful designers seem to have acquired a sort of sixth sense about it. In lieu of more explicit ways of making concept-oriented forecasts, recourse to the judgment of an experienced designer appears to be the only way open.

Methodologies for an explicit treatment of the subject have been prepared, but no evidence has been found that they have been systematically evaluated. The need to decide upon the feasibility of concepts has become so vital to our society and to our defense posture that it would seem wise to invest the resources necessary to develop an explicit method of concept-oriented feasibility determination. Such a procedure would:

1. Make the forecast applicable for envisioning the concepts of the future in terms of their form and functional capabilities;
2. Permit the placement of limits of pertinence on forecast technical areas, thereby avoiding the necessity for continuously forecasting the "technical universe"—an impossible task;
3. Maintain a baseline of forecasting realism in terms of the time to achieve conceptual feasibility and the effect of technical effort on achievability.

THE DESIGN DECISON—A CONCEPT-ORIENTED FORECAST

Studies of the kind described above leave a designer with an array of concepts, each of which has some potential for satisfying the need and some level of attainability. In other words, for each concept, the designer has developed an opinion concerning how good it is and how tough it is going to be to achieve. Now he must choose the one in which to invest.

This is an exercise in optimization. Obviously, concepts that are both poor and difficult will not be chosen. Instead, in each situation a balance must be struck between the risk of technical failure and the benefits of superior performance. All the methods of cost-benefit analysis under conditions of risk can be brought into play. In the real-life case, such explicit methods seldom are utilized. The superior concept is often clearly revealed without any necessity for elaborate optimization analysis. In fact, it is comparatively rare for more than one concept to be under serious consideration in the final stages of the design-based examination.

The form of the forecaster's decision is similar to that of the designer. The best overall concept is the one most likely to characterize the form of the product in the future. In addition, the forecaster can express this conclusion in probability statements and can include similar statements about all conceptual approaches that were considered.

BIBLIOGRAPHY

1. Asimow, M., *Introduction to Design*. Englewood Cliffs, N.J.: Prentice-Hall, Inc., 1962.

2. Churchman, C. W., and R. L. Ackoff, "An Approximate Measure of Value," *Journal of the Operations Research Society of America,* Vol. II, No. 2 (May, 1954).

3. Hoess, J. A., *A Discipline for Both Obtaining and Evaluating Alternative Product Concepts,* American Society of Mechanical Engineers Publication, 66-MD-87, June, 1966.

4. *Interim Report of the Committee on Engineering Design,* School of Engineering, MIT, November 3, 1955.

5. McCrory, R. J., *The Design Method—A Scientific Approach to Valid Design,* American Society of Mechanical Engineers Publication, 63-MD-4 May, 1963.

6. Marples, D. L., *The Decisions of Engineering Design,* IRE Transactions on Engineering Management, Vol. EM-8 (June, 1961), 55–71.

The Multiple Contingency Concept of Long-Range Technological Planning

ROBERT H. REA
PETER S. MILLER

One of the most difficult aspects of long-range planning is the selection of proposed research and development projects in view of the uncertainty of future environments. The basic thesis of this chapter is that not one but many possible futures should be examined. It discusses a computer assisted technique that combines the value judgments of management with historical data to generate a large number of scenarios (possible futures) within which R&D projects can be evaluated.

Mr. Rea, Vice-President of Abt Associates, has had broad experience in designing models for basic research planning and resource allocation. His work has involved the aeronautical sciences, political science, operations research, and education. Mr. Miller, Senior Operations Analyst for Abt Associates, has worked with Air Force space operations planning and the development of systems to assist the Air Force in obtaining effective future configurations of manpower and material.

The long lead time required in technology-based industries to transform research and development projects into delivery of new products is a serious problem. Decisions made today to support particular R&D projects often bind companies to future market positions which cannot be changed quickly. As a result companies have great need for techniques which can insure competent long-range decision making and thereby provide protection against major technological surprises by competitors.

One approach is to project the technological environment as far into the future as possible. This is *not* to say that, somehow, the single most probable future situation should be identified and the entire R&D program should be tied to it. Such projections are clouded with uncertainty, and it is unlikely that the specific environmental conditions will occur exactly as described. However, the cloud is neither totally shapeless nor infinite. It has boundaries that can be identified. These are formed by constraints placed on the rate of technological change, by gaps in basic scientific understanding and the inertia of development projects. But even within these boundaries, many situations can occur, and many of them should be explored. This can be done by:

1. Projecting into the future as many plausible situations as can reasonably be considered;
2. Developing contingency research and development plans for each situation;
3. Examining these plans to find the extent to which the number of different kinds of R&D projects changes with the number of situations considered (the curve shown in Figure 1 can be expected);
4. Planning current R&D projects around the areas of greatest overlap, hopefully covering most situations;
5. Being prepared to change the list of projects as new information is discovered.

The ability to perform these five steps depends on a forecasting and planning framework which can handle a large amount of data quickly. This framework should not be a complex "black box." Managers must fully understand and have confidence in the system before they will use it for guiding action. Elaborate computer simulation which attempts to take everything into account often leaves management immersed in a sea of entangling interrelationships. At the other extreme, blind intuition is often based on "experience" gained during past situations that will never recur. A happy medium is required. Intuition and judgment are clearly necessary, but they need help.

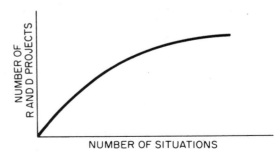

Figure 1. R&D Projects vs. Number of Situations.

THE TECHNOLOGICAL ENVIRONMENT

The products of the future must compete in a "technological environment" composed of three parts: (1) the world of basic science and engineering, (2) customers and their demand, and (3) competitors. These products cannot be defined in detail, but the functional characteristics which define the industry probably will not change dramatically. The following paragraphs describe the dimensions of this future environment and show how product characteristics can be related to this environment to provide guidance for choosing R&D projects.

Basic Science and Engineering

To avoid technological surprise and to generate as many alternative R&D projects for consideration as possible, it is necessary to keep up with those fields of basic science and engineering that could affect the functional characteristics of the products of an industry. There are several ways of doing this, including (1) periodically reviewing selected portions of the literature of many fields; (2) making in-depth studies of a few areas; (3) obtaining advice from consultants; and (4) using government-sponsored research and facilities. These methods can never provide complete coverage because of the sheer bulk of information. The problem can be reduced somewhat by limiting attention to those areas where there has been a flurry of recent activity. Items of great interest in the basic research community do not always provide opportunities for industry, but missing fruitful chances can be very expensive in the long run.

The purpose of "keeping up" is to generate a long list of R&D projects which can be sponsored by a company or can be followed closely if they are the work of other groups. These projects should cover as long a time period as possible and a wide range of both basic and applied work. Each should be directed toward improving or revolutionizing a functional characteristic of the industry's products, and estimates of potential improvement, as a function of time, should be made for each project. The feasibility of achieving any given improvement increases with time, and this fact should be reflected in any analysis.

Improved performance is only realized at some cost, and this cost should be stated for all phases of the work required to turn an idea into an improved functional characteristic for the market place. This cost information will be needed later to balance improved performance against customer demand, costs, and competitors' activity.

Customers and their Demands

The future will bring changes in product characteristics, and customers will respond differently to these changes. Anticipating customer response is both extremely important and very difficult. One approach is to analyze reactions to recent changes in product characteristics, to get a feeling for the sensitivity of change. *How much* did sales increase or decrease, and after *how big* a change? Since such changes result from the interaction of many interrelated social, political, and economic forces that cannot be identified readily, only correlations are feasible. Cause and effect cannot be traced quantitatively, and as these changed relationships are extended further into the future, the basis for historical correlations crumbles.

At this point, the influence of larger systemic changes must be considered. Changes in demographic characteristics, the influence of the national space program, international relations, the growing importance of service industries, and many other factors must be estimated. This requires the fine art of long-range forecasting. Where estimates of systemic changes can be based on data, they should be used. Where uncertainty in data is so great that there is a danger of serious error, the estimates should be made but used with caution. In this case, it is necessary to abandon data and substitute intuition and judgment.

Fortunately, only relative values are necessary to estimate differences in customer response to improved product characteristics. They can be assigned on the basis of structured judgment, using a not completely uncontrolled process. There are procedures that can impose helpful constraints on the problem. One such device is the Churchman-Ackoff Approximate Measure of Value procedure. This is a system for checking the internal consistency of initial relative weight assignments by asking questions about the relative importance of combinations of objectives or categories of product characteristics. It is surprising to discover how confining the discipline of internal consistency is and how little room it allows for arbitrary value assignment.

Where a group decision is required (as it often is), there are procedures, such as that developed by Mr. Howard Wells (of Bell Aerosystems), which will produce one. This may not coincide with the decision of any one individual in the group, but it will represent a "weighted consensus." [1]

The purpose of all of the various approaches is simply to provide a set of values that estimate the importance of improving each product characteristic. Insofar as estimates can be made in terms of the actual dollar volume of sales expected from each improvement, the estimates have some absolute value. But more importantly, the value of the approach for R&D project decisions depends only on the *relative* values of the estimates, and it does not matter greatly if all are wrong by the same amount.

[1] Mr. Wells points out that individual decisions may frequently be better than group decisions, and where such a situation can be anticipated, it is better to simply ask the individual. His method is a system which employs weighted secret voting, eliminates extremes, and includes periods for persuasion by group members.

The specific information that is desired for each product characteristic is the importance of being ahead of the market average, and the danger of being behind it. Sensitivity estimates are also needed to indicate *how much* more important it is to be *how far* ahead, and how serious it is to be how far behind. As an example, it is probably more than twice as important to be 20 per cent ahead than 10 per cent. It is also important to maintain consistency in value assignment among the characteristics. It is not only useful to know that a 20 per cent improvement is more than twice as important as a 10 per cent improvement in a single characteristic, but also that a 20 per cent improvement in one characteristic is twice as important as a 20 per cent improvement in another one. These numbers will be added later in the analysis, and if their *relative* values are not consistent, the sums will not be of much use.

Competitors

The term "competitors" refers to the rest of the industry. Distinctions between individual companies can be made if desired, but they become less meaningful as forecasting and planning are extended further into the future. This part of the technological environment is characterized by the extrapolation into the future of recent trends of product characteristics. This extrapolation takes the form of an increasingly widening band, not a single most likely line. The boundaries of this band are determined by several factors. First, there may be natural limits to how far the characteristic can be pushed. Second, major investments may be required for R&D, and these could eliminate profits. Third, government research may advance the state of the art, making information available to all competitors. At some point, the band will widen to the extent that currently conceived R&D projects cannot fill the gap. At this point, it might be prudent to allow the band to expand a little more, to account for unanticipated technology transfers and to remain constant thereafter.

When all of the important characteristics that could describe a product are considered simultaneously at some point in the future, there are many plausible situations or "scenarios" that could exist. Any combination of values within the characteristics band describes a scenario for which appropriate R&D project support decisions should now be made. The R&D program should be planned to cope with these "multiple contingencies." The program cannot, and should not, be optimized for any single scenario, but it can be planned to cover most of them. In any case, it is desirable to evaluate alternative R&D programs to determine those scenarios with which they can or cannot cope.

One way to limit the many scenarios to a reasonable number without limiting the value of the technique is to impose a "difference" criterion.

After the first scenario is generated, new scenarios are not examined unless they significantly differ from the first one. If a rule is adopted that the scenarios be as different as possible, the only scenarios that will be studied are those that contain the limits of the band of uncertainty for any given year. As the difference criterion is relaxed, more scenarios will result.

Once the three dimensions of the technological environment have been explored, it is necessary to determine how they interact, in order to move from forecasting to planning and action. The results of the basic science and engineering discussion are long lists of R&D project profiles that describe product characteristic improvements over time, beginning with basic and applied research and extending to product introduction into the market (Figure 2). Estimates of costs of achieving the improvements as a function of time are also included. The results of the discussions dealing with customers and their demand are estimates of relative opportunities and dangers of product characteristics that are ahead of and behind an industry (Figure 3). The results of the discussion on

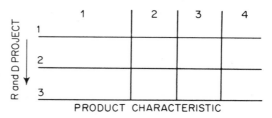

Figure 2. Basic Science and Engineering Profiles.

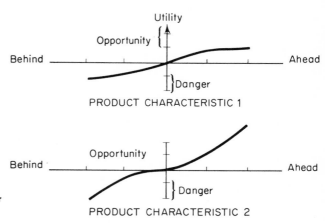

Figure 3. Customers and Their Demand—Customer Response Curves.

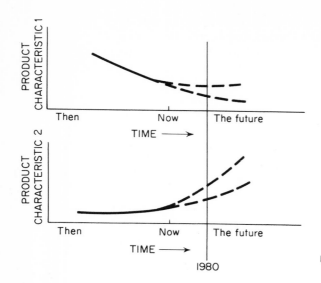

Figure 4. Competitors.

competitors are extrapolations of recent trends in product characteristics into increasingly widening bands of uncertainty (Figure 4).

The first step in integrating the three dimensions is the generation of scenarios for the planning year, e.g., 1980. This is done by selecting a single value for each product characteristic from the band of uncertainty as of that year. These values are combined and the set is treated as the industry average for one scenario. The results of the R&D projects show how far ahead or behind these averages a company could be. The customer response curves show how large the opportunities and dangers are if the company is ahead or behind.

Comparisons of these factors are converted to relative values for the R&D projects in the following way: For each project, the difference between the product characteristic value produced and the industry average, as given by the scenario, is multiplied by the importance of the characteristics, as derived in the customer response curves. These weighted numbers are then added for all of the characteristics. The final result is a table of R&D project values for every scenario. Later in the paper, various ways of resolving this table into specific decisions for project support are discussed, but first it is useful to look at an example of the process.

EXAMPLE

Suppose that someone in a company wants to use the forecasting model. He gathers data, in the form just described, and goes to the nearest dataphone or teletype console. (This person could be *anyone* in the company. He need not be a computer programmer.) He then dials a number. When the computer answers, he types in an identification code. The computer then begins typing out a question about the data that he has collected (in plain English) and waits for an answer. The person responds by typing in an answer and the computer goes on to the next question. When all of the questions have been answered, the computer types out the table of R&D project values and scenarios. The following is a hypothetical example. It is taken from a company in the light private aircraft industry which is planning its R&D program, which, in turn, will eventually determine the company's fortunes in the world of 1980.

This example was run at Abt Associates, using a computer program which performs technological forecasting through the consideration of multiple contingencies as described above. The functional portions of the program are:

1. Selection of the functional variables of interest;
2. Determination of the history of progress in these variables;
3. Establishment of the envelope of likely future progress for these variables;
4. The generation of scenarios based on extrapolated historical information;
5. Determination of the likely results of the alternate research projects which may be carried out by the company;
6. Evaluation for each variable of the importance of the company's position with respect to the industry as a whole;
7. The evaluation of each research project in each scenario;
8. The evaluation of the value matrix derived from the previous step to determine which program to fund.

The first step in the multiple contingency planning process is the selection of the functional variables of interest. These should be the variables which define the product under consideration. They should be sufficiently general so that they are not linked specifically to present-day technology; i.e., they should not become irrelevant as the result of a change in technology. Furthermore, these should be the variables which have the greatest impact on the market.

In the example given in the following computer print-out, the product consists of light aircraft, seating four passengers and costing about $15,000. The variables of interest which have been chosen are:

(1) Speed
(2) Minimum ceiling for landing
(3) Minimum visibility for landing
(4) Take-off distance

These are variables that remain important over time. Although their settings or values are determined by today's technology, their existence is not. A variable such as "gallons of gasoline per hour" might become irrelevant if breakthroughs in electrical power sources eliminate the need for gasoline engines. Gallons per hour would then be listed as zero, and the fact that certain important characteristics of the aircraft, such as range, had indeed been changed would be obfuscated. "Gallons per hour" is a technology-linked proxy for the important and more basic variable, "range" (or fuel cost/hour). Thus the important variables must be chosen carefully.

The second step in the multiple contingency planning process is to trace the history of the variable in question. (See Figure 5.) This past history is useful in the determination of long-range trends. Basing future predictions on past history has certain drawbacks; new breakthroughs are difficult to anticipate, but they are difficult to anticipate with any prediction method, based on any data available, and when they occur, the trends can be adjusted. In the particular computer program under discussion, previous technological trend data are needed for forecasting. Past trends can be used for long-range planning purposes because their progress is based on effort spent, difficulties encountered, and interest in each technological area. A quadratic curve is fitted to the historical data using the method of minimizing the squared error.[2]

The third step is to establish the envelope of potential progress about the expected mean progress of each variable (see Figure 6); i.e., standard deviation is determined for each of the curves generated in the previous step. This can be done in a number of ways, but in the program Abt has developed, the standard deviation at any point in time has been set as one-third of the distance from the present value of the variable to the expected mean at that point in time. This means that the present state of the art is three standard deviations away from the future mean— a not unreasonable assumption. The quadratic curve indicates the potential mean and the standard deviation of the variable at any point in the

---

[2] In the case where a curve "turns over" at a point in the future, the standard deviation is taken as one-sixth of the difference between the maximum (or minimum) and the present value, and the future mean is the halfway point between the two values. This provides a narrow band for growth, but the data are based on the past history of the variable.

```
TECHNICAL FORECASTING THROUGH SCENARIO GENERATION


TYPE IN THE NUMBER OF VARIABLES OF INTEREST
      N=4
LET'S LOOK AT THE HISTORY OF THESE VARIABLES
DESCRIBE CHANGE OVER THE LAST TWENTY YEARS
    IN 1942 THE VALUE FOR SPEED          WAS*
        VAL=100
    IN 1947 THE VALUE FOR SPEED          WAS*
        VAL=125
    IN 1952 THE VALUE FOR SPEED          WAS*
        VAL=150
    IN 1957 THE VALUE FOR SPEED          WAS*
        VAL=160
    IN 1962 THE VALUE FOR SPEED          WAS*
        VAL=170
    IN 1967 THE VALUE FOR SPEED          WAS*
        VAL=185
    IN 1942 THE VALUE FOR CEILING        WAS*
        VAL=1500
    IN 1947 THE VALUE FOR CEILING        WAS*
        VAL=1200
    IN 1952 THE VALUE FOR CEILING        WAS*
        VAL=1000
    IN 1957 THE VALUE FOR CEILING        WAS*
        VAL=800
    IN 1962 THE VALUE FOR CEILING        WAS*
        VAL=700
    IN 1967 THE VALUE FOR CEILING        WAS*
        VAL=500
    IN 1942 THE VALUE FOR VISIBILITY     WAS*
        VAL=3
    IN 1947 THE VALUE FOR VISIBILITY     WAS*
        VAL=2.5
    IN 1952 THE VALUE FOR VISIBILITY     WAS*
        VAL=2.0
    IN 1957 THE VALUE FOR VISIBILITY     WAS*
        VAL=1.8
    IN 1962 THE VALUE FOR VISIBILITY     WAS*
        VAL=1.5
    IN 1967 THE VALUE FOR VISIBILITY     WAS*
        VAL=1
    IN 1942 THE VALUE FOR T/O-LND DISTANCE WAS*
        VAL=900
    IN 1947 THE VALUE FOR T/O-LND DISTANCE WAS*
        VAL=800
    IN 1952 THE VALUE FOR T/O-LND DISTANCE WAS*
        VAL=775
    IN 1957 THE VALUE FOR T/O-LND DISTANCE WAS*
        VAL=685
    IN 1962 THE VALUE FOR T/O-LND DISTANCE WAS*
        VAL=550
    IN 1967 THE VALUE FOR T/O-LND DISTANCE WAS*
        VAL=500


    NOTE:  The historical progress of each variable of interest is entered
           by the user in response to the question asked by the computer.
```

Figure 5. Historical Data Input.

```
THE COEFFICIENTS OF THE QUADRATIC ARE:
CHARACTERISTIC     AZERO         AONE         ATWO
      1           101.07143     5.22143      -.07857
      2          1482.14286   -54.35714       .64286
      3             2.95714     -.08971       .00057
      4           893.21429   -12.83571      -.13571


A second-order curve is fitted to data for each of the important
characteristics:
```

$$Y = A_0 + A_1 X + A_2 X^2$$

```
ENTER YEAR OF INTEREST
       YR=1980


VARIABLE NUMBER  1   MEAN =   186.409172 SIGMA=      .469724 YR=1980
VARIABLE NUMBER  2   MEAN =   344.857147 SIGMA=    51.714284 YR=1980
VARIABLE NUMBER  3   MEAN =      .373143 SIGMA=      .208952 YR=1980
VARIABLE NUMBER  4   MEAN =   209.485711 SIGMA=    96.838096 YR=1980


HOW MANY SCENARIOS DO YOU WISH GENERATED ?
       SCE=3

NOTE:   When the target year is entered, a mean and standard deviation is determined
        for each variable (important characteristic) in that year.  Scenarios can then
        be generated.
```

Figure 6. Curve Fitting and Extrapolation.

future. These two parameters are all that are needed for probabilistic scenario generation.

The fourth step is the generation of alternative scenarios (combinations of possible setting for the variables). (See Figure 7.) Random numbers are generated, and the settings of each variable are determined, using normal distributions with the means and standard deviations just calculated. This provides settings for speed, minimum ceiling, minimum visibility and take-off distance within the particular target year. These variables also describe the rest of the industry in the target year—the world within which the company has to compete.

The scenario generation method allows an examination of a number of these future worlds and an evaluation of potential strategies in each of them. If a scenario appears to be unreasonable, an explanation can be stated and incorporated in the computer program. Thereafter, the computer will apply the explanation to all further scenarios and will not generate any which are unreasonable because of the same considerations.

The fifth step in using the computer program is to list potential re-

```
                            CHARACTERISTICS


        SCENARIO      SPEED       CEILING       VISIB       T/O-LND
           1         186.345      337.202        .52        330.42
           2         187.350      359.350        .59        205.36
           3         186.595      484.076        .49        230.30

NOTE:  A Scenario is generated by probabilistically determining a value for
       each of the important variables in the target year and combining these values
       to describe a future world.  This process may be repeated as many
       times as the user requests.
```

Figure 7. Scenarios.

```
        ENTER THE NUMBER OF RESEARCH PROGRAMS CONSIDERED
             NPR=4


        FOR EACH PROJECT, ENTER THE VALUE FOR VBLE IN QUESTION
                    SPEED
             XEP [1,1]=205
             XEP [1,2]= N/A
             XEP [1,3]=N/A
             XEP [1,4]=275
                    CEILING
             XEP [2,1]=400
             XEP [2,2]=150
             XEP [2,3]=125
             XEP [2,4]=N/A
                    VISIBILITY
             XEP [3,1]=.85
             XEP [3,2]=.5
             XEP [3,3]=.75
             XEP [3,4]=N/A
                    T/O-LND DISTANCE
             XEP [4,1]=300
             XEP [4,2]=N/A
             XEP [4,3]=N/A
             XEP [4,4]=400


   NOTE:  The expected results (for the target year) of each of the research
          programs are entered into the computer.
```

Figure 8. Research Project Characteristics.

search projects and describe their likely results in terms of the important variables in the target year. (See Figure 8.) Comparisons of the variable settings permit an evaluation of each of the alternative projects in the possible future worlds. Thus, at any point in time (the target year being examined), each research program will have a distinctive pattern of results, indicating both strong and weak points.

```
ENTER VALUES FOR THE VARIOUS POSITIONS
          SPEED
GIVE THE VALUE FOR BEING 10% AHEAD OF THE INDUSTRY
      X10[1]=3
  20% AHEAD ?
      X20[1]=5
  10% BEHIND (PROBABLY A NEGATIVE VALUE)
      EX1[1]=-3
  20% BEHIND
      EX2[1]=-5
          CEILING
GIVE THE VALUE FOR BEING 10% AHEAD OF THE INDUSTRY
      X10[2]=5
  20% AHEAD ?
      X20[2]=20
  10% BEHIND (PROBABLY A NEGATIVE VALUE)
      EX1[2]=-5
  20% BEHIND
      EX2[2]=-7
          VISIBILITY
GIVE THE VALUE FOR BEING 10% AHEAD OF THE INDUSTRY
      X10[3]=5
  20% AHEAD ?
      X20[3]=20
  10% BEHIND (PROBABLY A NEGATIVE VALUE)
      EX1[3]=-5
  20% BEHIND
      EX2[3]=-7
          T/O-LND DISTANCE
GIVE THE VALUE FOR BEING 10% AHEAD OF THE INDUSTRY
      X10[4]=10
  20% AHEAD ?
      X20[4]=25
  10% BEHIND (PROBABLY A NEGATIVE VALUE)
      EX1[4]=-10
  20% BEHIND
      EX2[4]=-25

NOTE:  The expected values (in any desired commensurate units such as
       dollars, market fractions, or utility) for being 10% and 20%
       ahead of or behind the rest of the industry are entered.
       User-defined utility units are shown here.
```

Figure 9. Market Position Utility Input.

The sixth step is that of reducing the important variables to a common measure of value. (See Figure 9.) For each variable, the user of the program is asked to place a value on being 10 per cent and 20 per cent ahead of and behind the market, all other factors being equal. A quadratic is then fitted to the user's preferences, to give a continuous utility function for the company's position as compared to the rest of the industry. This is done for each variable. It is simple to combine the variables once the user's values are stated in common units.

Given a table of R&D project values for several scenarios (Figure 10), there are several strategies for making the final selection of projects. The adoption of a particular strategy is a matter for management policy.

First, the table should be examined to identify any projects which are worse than all others in every scenario. Even though many projects will probably be discarded as a result of this process, the ones that remain will often require more R&D resources than can be made available, and further selections must be made. One possible strategy is to examine each project in turn and note the *smallest* value that it has in any of the scenarios. The projects could then be ranked in order of decreasing value. This procedure represents a conservative policy of minimizing the maximum losses that could occur (the minimax approach). For example, if the minimax method of analysis were used on the data presented in Figure 10, the worst case would yield a value of −90.21 for the first project; 180.32 for the second; 177.95 for the third; and −10.74 for the fourth. Thus the second project would be chosen first, since it has the highest minimum value in all of the scenarios considered.

The option providing the greatest risk is to rank the projects in decreasing order according to the *largest* value that they have in any one scenario, regardless of how small a value they may have in some other scenario—the highest gain in the "best of all possible worlds." In Figure 10 the third project would be selected first, followed by the second project. A project also might be selected because it would yield the highest average value per scenario. In this case, the preferred order would be three, then two.

For choosing several projects from among the numerous candidates which would be generated in a full-scale use of the methodology, the program might be altered somewhat to allow it to consider only marginal contributions of programs added to a previously selected mix. In this case, number three would be selected first if the per-scenario average value criterion were applied. Then other projects and their characteristics would be added to determine which would give the greatest increase in total average value for the total research package. This process would continue until the R&D money ran out, or marginal contributions reached zero.

Numerous other decision criteria could be used which would fall be-

Figure 10. Project Value Matrix.

VALUE MATRIX PROJECTS	1	2	3
1	23.73707	-90.21093	7.57836
2	216.19964	180.32073	245.42719
3	232.59664	177.95098	270.34699
4	55.09250	-10.74989	29.73780

NOTE: As a final result, the program prints a matrix of values, showing the value of each project in each of the postulated possible future worlds. Game theory and other strategy-determining techniques can be applied at this point to determine which projects should be funded.

tween the options listed above, but in any case the result would be a list of R&D projects with relative values assigned to them. Such a list presents an opportunity to obtain a final selection with the aid of mathematical programming. The relative values of the projects could serve as coefficients of an objective function; the costs of the projects, in terms of funds and manpower, could serve as coefficients of constraint equations; and budgets for the resource categories could serve as overall limitations. Additional constraint equations would be needed to make sure that no more than one unit of each project was selected. The final analysis would indicate the best group of R&D projects to support over time, the total "benefit" that the firm could expect from the selection, the cost of selecting any projects that were rejected, and the value to the firm of each of the kinds of resources used by the projects.

SUMMARY

The computer program which has been developed to handle the approach outlined above is only in an early stage. More work is needed to improve techniques for forecasting the envelope of possible futures, to determine the economic values of corporate technological positions relative to the industry as a whole, and to develop a "difference rating" for comparing scenarios.

The evaluation of potential projects through the use of the multiple contingency method gives the user advantages which he cannot derive from other approaches. The number of variables and the number of scenarios in the illustration presented above were limited; however, in actual practice the number would be much greater, and it is in the consideration of many variables and many scenarios that the method is most useful. Through the use of scenarios, the planner can work with a method he can easily understand. He can work with data that are familiar to him, and he will receive outputs in a form which he uses every day. Long-term implications of current R&D decisions can be made explicit. Most important, by studying a relatively small number of scenarios and their associated R&D projects, the planner can develop his intuition concerning the kinds of future worlds he will have to face.

On Mirages

HAROLD A. LINSTONE

Long-range planning in an area characterized by rapidly changing technology and many interrelated functional missions is difficult at best. No single available model or approach can hope to provide a sufficiently sound basis for planning decisions. A combination of methods must be considered, and this chapter explores the use of two need-oriented approaches. It also poses some fundamental questions arising from the central position of "need" as the major determinant of technological forecasts.

Dr. Linstone conceived and directed the first MIRAGE study while he was with Hughes Aircraft Company. He is presently Senior Scientific Adviser, Corporate Development Planning, for Lockheed Aircraft Corporation and Adjunct Professor of Industrial and Systems Engineering at the University of Southern California.

In a recent article which surveys the subject of technological forecasting, James B. Quinn states:

> The various methods of forecasting should be used *in combinations* in order to stimulate imaginative analysis, introduce added objectivity, and make sure that all relevant technological flows are considered.[1]

This chapter discusses a combination approach to need-oriented technological forecasting and examines several fundamental questions raised by

[1] "Technological Forecasting," *Harvard Business Review*, March–April, 1967, p. 89.

such efforts. Essentially, the methodology combines the approaches used in the MIRAGE studies with those of Mission Flow Chart Analysis. Although this work was nurtured in the defense sector of the economy, the methods and questions are applicable to many other areas.

THE MIRAGE STUDY APPROACH

In Quinn's words: "Clearly perceived demand—not excess technological capacity—tends to be the primary force stimulating technological change. In fact, a technology is only utilized if it responds to a need." [2] Sherwin and Isenson also stress need:

> If we identify . . . the events which were motivated by a clearly perceived DoD [Department of Defense] need, we see that they add up to 95% of all events . . . It became clear early in the study that technological innovation was highly correlated with need-recognition.[3]

Agreement with the importance of need as a basic determinant of technological forecasting is seen in the meaning of the acronym, "MIRAGE": "Military *Requirements* Analysis—Generation 19___."

The purpose of the MIRAGE studies is to help R&D planners identify "good risks" for the future in a defense environment characterized by great uncertainty. Three studies have been completed:

	Performed	Subject Period
MIRAGE 70 [4]	1959–60	1965–70
MIRAGE 75	1963–64	1970–75
MIRAGE 80	1965–66	1975–80

Phase 1: Environmental Analysis

Each study begins with an analysis of the projected world environment for the subject period. Figure 1, depicting the regional GNP-population trend, is drawn from such a projection (MIRAGE 80). The figure is titled "The Widening Gap," since it clearly suggests that during the 1970's the per capita GNP gap will widen between the very rich (the United

2 *Ibid.*, p. 91.

3 C. W. Sherwin and R. S. Isenson, *First Interim Report on Project Hindsight (Summary)*, June 30, 1966 (rev. Oct. 13, 1966), Office of the Director of Defense, Research and Engineering, Washington, D.C., p. 8.

4 A summary of this report is available in *Planning and Forecasting in the Defense Industries*, ed. J. Stockfisch (Belmont, Calif.: Wadsworth Publishing Company, 1962).

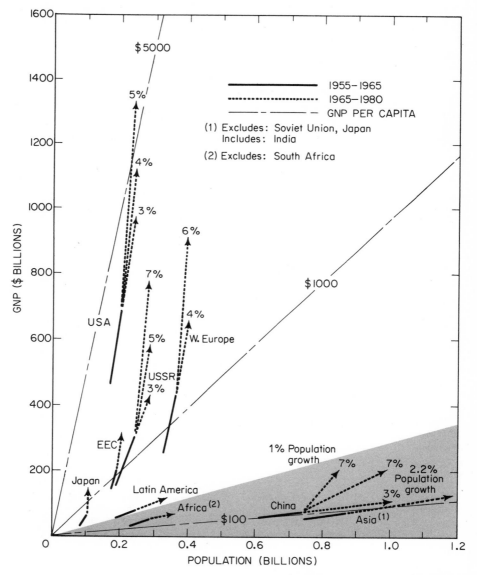

Figure 1. The Widening Gap—A World Dilemma.

States) and the rich (Western Europe and the Soviet Union), and between the rich and the poor.

The widening gap is the most significant "good risk" assumption in the environmental analysis.[5] It portends a few islands of prosperity in a sea of semi-starvation. Largely created by science and technology,[6] the dilemma is continually being exacerbated by further advances. Improved communications are an example. Radio and television have had a shattering effect in breaking through the idyllic isolation of the "happy native" —the individual with low want satisfaction and low want formation (i.e., low frustration index). In other words, technology tends to increase want formation, which, in turn, increases frustration. Analysis clearly shows a strong correlation between frustration and violence.[7] If some assistance is provided (e.g., by AID or the Alliance for Progress), the few satisfactions which are achieved increase the desire for more, thus adding to the sense of systemic frustration. As a result, well-intentioned steps designed to reverse the trend of the widening gap by helping the underdeveloped nations modernize more rapidly are likely to lead to even greater instability and, hence, to more violence.

The widening gap between the very rich and the rich also suggests startling possibilities. Among these is a Soviet–West European economic alliance which could form the basis for future "strategic economic warfare" against the United States.[8] These samples from the analysis suggest that major changes in the world environment of the 1970's are "good risks" (i.e., the probability of change is high). As a result of such environmental changes, new DoD missions would evolve. This is especially evident in relation to the underdeveloped countries. In Secretary of Defense McNamara's words, the widening gap, actually a deep seismic fissure,

> . . . can produce—it *will* produce—thunderous earthquakes of violence, if rich and poor countries alike do not do more to meet the threat . . . The widening economic chasm . . . can be as threatening to our security as the physical emergence of Chinese nuclear weapons.[9]

[5] It is by no means such a "good risk" assumption for the post-1980 period. It seems distinctly possible that a narrowing of the gap will occur in the period 1980–2000 as other nations make their bid for world leadership and as industrialization is achieved in certain underdeveloped countries.

[6] For example, medicine and public health: U.S. medical aid from 1954 to 1961 cut the annual malaria death toll in India from 800,000 to 10,000.

[7] I. K. and R. L. Feierabend, "Aggressive Behaviors Within Polities, 1948–1962: A Cross-National Study," *Journal of Conflict Resolution*, Vol. X, No. 3, Sept. 1966.

[8] It is interesting to note the Kosygin visit to London in which he offered a "rather perplexing proposal for joint, long-range Anglo-Soviet planning for industrial development." (*Wall Street Journal*, Feb. 10, 1967, p. 6).

[9] Robert S. McNamara, Address before Millsaps College convocation, Feb. 24, 1967.

As Algeria showed, a decisive military victory by an advanced country over an underdeveloped opponent may lead to an equally decisive final defeat. The alternatives appear to be a massive attack on the underlying problems in these regions or isolation of the underdeveloped world. A massive attack on the fundamental problems means that manpower must be applied on a scale which dwarfs current efforts. It must work on a time scale of a decade, not a year. Steering a country swiftly toward modernization, past the rapids of turbulence, requires the application not merely of massive but of precisely placed assistance. It requires profound understanding of the complex development process and a "systems approach."

> The problems "are interrelated and interdependent . . . they support each other and cannot be effectively treated separately . . . the government should give fresh thought to dealing with them as an integrated whole." [10]

The need is threefold:

1. Analysis, planning, and systems management;
2. Large-scale financing; and
3. Large numbers of trained personnel.

The 1965 economic aid appropriation for Vietnam, $550 million, was equivalent to about $35 per person. Using a level of $50 per person, such a program for Latin America would require an annual investment of about $14 billion per year, as against the 1965 sum of $0.7 billion. Analysis, planning, and management for a balanced growth of the "system" would require thousands of skilled individuals. Needs range from systems analysts to county agents, from teachers to ombudsmen. The mobilization of manpower for such an effort is a vast job, and the only somewhat analogous precedent is the mobilization of technological manpower in the ICBM and space programs. A search must be made for new joint industry/university/government mechanisms, so that the breadth of the universities can be combined with the skilled specialties of industry in response to the needs of government. The level of effort suggests the need for a large body of personnel organized into *assistance or development forces*. The non-military character of such a body is a striking and essential hallmark. MIRAGE 80 concluded that "creation and employment of these forces for Latin America looms as possibly the most urgent new need for U.S. security in the 1970's."

It must be admitted that this need is not presently—and may never be—clearly perceived. Preventive actions, whether they involve fluorida-

[10] G. C. Lodge, "Revolution in Latin America," *Foreign Affairs*, January, 1966.

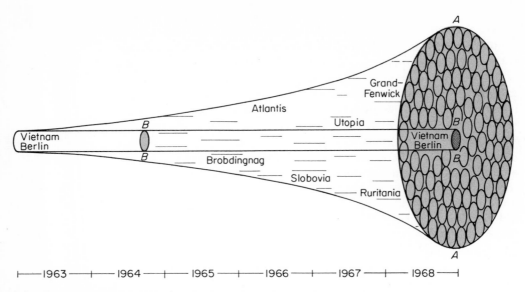

Figure 2. The Danger of Unimaginative Extrapolating (Cross-section BB Hardly Represents Spectrum AA in 1968).

tion of water or costly regional development programs, are always more difficult to "sell" than curative measures, such as individual treatment of cavities or military intervention. This can be observed in recent congressional opposition to the Administration's efforts to expand the very modest U.S. foreign aid program and to obtain a strong resolution for use at the Punta del Este conference.

The alternative of isolating explosive areas raises a very different set of requirements. Protection and extrication of U.S. property and personnel, control of intrusion by other outside powers to exploit the violence, and separation of opposing local forces without the use of U.S. ground forces are some of the potential missions which pose new needs.

A most useful tool for forecasting the missions and needs of the future is the development of scenarios based on the environmental analysis. These are descriptions of possible future situations. Although environmental scenarios are used frequently, all too often they are based on today's environment and today's, or even yesterday's, conflicts. This danger is depicted in Figure 2, a sketch first used in 1962,[11] when Berlin and Vietnam were the crisis spots. Clearly, if only these were used to prepare future scenarios, problems of the Cuban and Dominican Republic type would have been ignored.

[11] H. A. Linstone, *The Weapon Planning Problem for General Purpose Forces: A Functional Approach*, RM-3202, The RAND Corporation, Santa Monica, Calif., 1962. Mythical names are substituted in this version.

The scenarios permit the identification of new needs, and lead to the generation of concepts of operation and missions. The following guidelines are used:

1. A large spectrum of scenarios is essential. For forecasting purposes, safety lies in numbers. Since scenarios are not predictive, only a very wide spectrum can insure adequate coverage of future possibilities.

2. There must be a conscious effort to make sure that the concepts of operation and the missions which are developed are not just conventional responses.[12] To provide the decision maker with more diverse options, the analysis must probe "what if" responses— what if no destructive action is permitted? what if no ground forces may be used?, etc.

3. The need-technology interaction must be stimulated at this early stage. The technologist should take part in the process of formulating concepts of operation from scenarios.

The result of applying these guidelines is a much greater focus on novel or unorthodox missions.

Phase 2: Systems Analysis

Once the environmental analysis is complete, the need-technology interplay is studied in greater depth, using selective systems analyses. "Hypotheses" are formulated, iteratively refined, and then become the basis for study by an analyst or a small team. Each hypothesis embodies a major system innovation which was suggested by the need-technology interaction; e.g., the force separation and neutralization mission may lead to a hypothesis on land barriers.[13] The analysis considers the application of future technological concepts to the problem and makes an initial assessment of the feasibility of selected systems. In this example, permeability of the barrier may serve as one measure of effectiveness. Cost comparisons of alternatives also may be made (Figure 3).

Finally, where needed, the hypotheses are revised and conclusions are developed in terms of "good risks" for R&D planning. Particular emphasis

---

[12] The Cuban missile crisis offers an illustration of this point. According to Theodore Sorensen (*Kennedy*, Harper & Row, New York, 1965, p. 682), President Kennedy was presented not merely with conventional alternatives—do nothing; invade; or strike by air —but with an equal number of unorthodox courses of action—use diplomatic pressure; secretly approach Castro; or employ indirect military action such as a blockade.

[13] Cf. discussion of land barriers as a fresh concept in the *Los Angeles Times*, April 2, 1967, p. G-1.

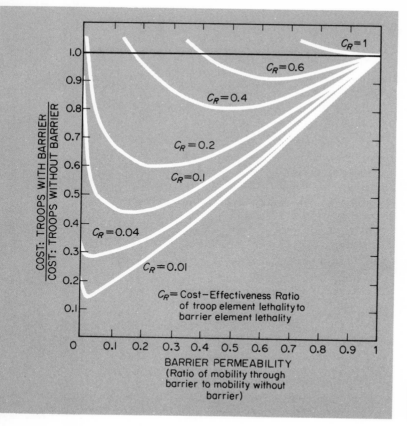

Figure 3. Cost Comparisons: Guerrilla Attack Through Barrier (Defending Troops Using Area Fire).

is placed on the identification of a small number of crucial technological bottlenecks.

Since the first MIRAGE study covered the period from 1965 to 1970, it is now possible to examine its validity. Unfortunately, much of the material is classified; however, an unclassified but highly condensed version was published in 1962.[14]

THE MISSION FLOW CHART ANALYSIS [15]

In addition and parallel to the hypothesis analysis phase described above, a separate and more methodical systems analysis technique is also

[14] See note 4.

[15] The author would like to acknowledge his debt to Messrs. O. Firschein, E. Gavenman, and D. Kyle, of Lockheed Missiles & Space Company in this effort.

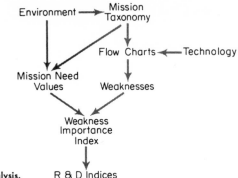

Figure 4. Flow Chart Analysis.

employed. The technique, a Mission Flow Chart Analysis, was originally used to establish R&D priorities for future general purpose forces—an exceedingly difficult problem, since one item may be used for many missions and each mission can be performed in many ways. The original concept [16] has been extended [17] and its development is continuing. The approach, which. is described below, is summarized in Figure 4.

Mission Taxonomy

On the basis of the spectrum of future scenarios and the associated concepts of operation which are derived from the environmental analysis (the MIRAGE approach), strategic or high-level missions are defined. The strategic missions (policy responses) are, in turn, supported by operations missions (operational responses), which are, in turn, supported by service or basic missions (support). This relationship is illustrated in Figure 5.

[16] See note 11.
[17] H. A. Linstone, *MIRAGE 75*, 1965, and a 1966 study supported by the U.S. Army Electronics Command.

Figure 5. The Mission Approach: Relation of the World of the 1970's to Missions.

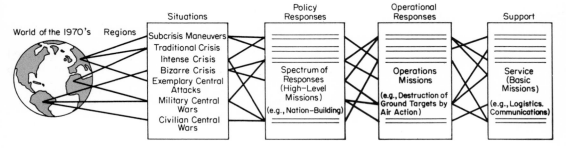

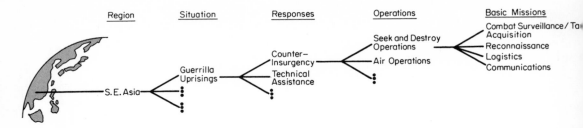

Figure 6. The Mission Approach: Detail of Relation of World of 1970's to Missions.

The overall concept can be thought of as a large network which can be subdivided for analysis and descriptive purposes in many different and equally valid ways. In other words, the classification system is by no means unique. As many as six levels of missions have been considered. Figure 6 shows the detail of one such network.

It should be emphasized that imaginative handling of scenarios and concepts of operation is vital. The use of only familiar missions will adversely affect the technology-need interaction in all subsequent steps.

Figure 7 shows the mission hierarchy approach as applied to private sector air transport. This illustration is presented to suggest that the approach is not restricted to national defense problems.

Figure 7. Interurban Transportation Missions

Policy	Operational	Support
Total system approach	Development of regional master plan	
Subsystem improvements enlarge airports VTOL aircraft	Federal aid to airport construction	Rapid transit to airports
	Procurement program by airlines	VTOL noise reduction research
		Skyscraper parking facilities
	Construction of new central airports	
Reversal of urban growth pattern	Incentives for dispersal of industry	

For each mission, an anatomical chart is developed which shows: the various means or systems for performing the mission, step-by-step; and the location of any major weaknesses in any of the systems. The general structure of a flow chart is shown in Figure 8, and a detailed chart is reproduced in Figure 9.[18] The columns of each chart indicate sequential activities while the rows represent alternative approaches. Problem areas are indicated by comments which are written vertically and are super-imposed on the functional flow lines. Those problem areas considered

[18] Most of the charts involving defense missions (restricted distribution) are far more detailed in terms of subsystems and technological weaknesses.

Figure 8. Peacetime Assistance: Technical.

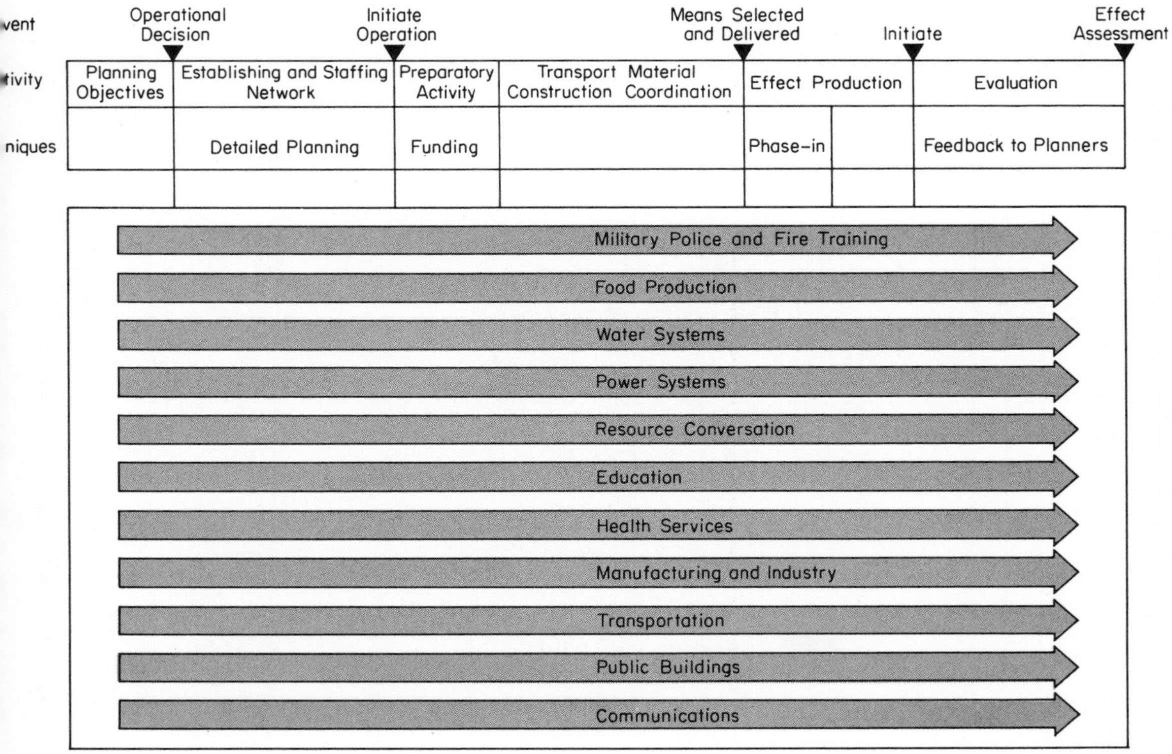

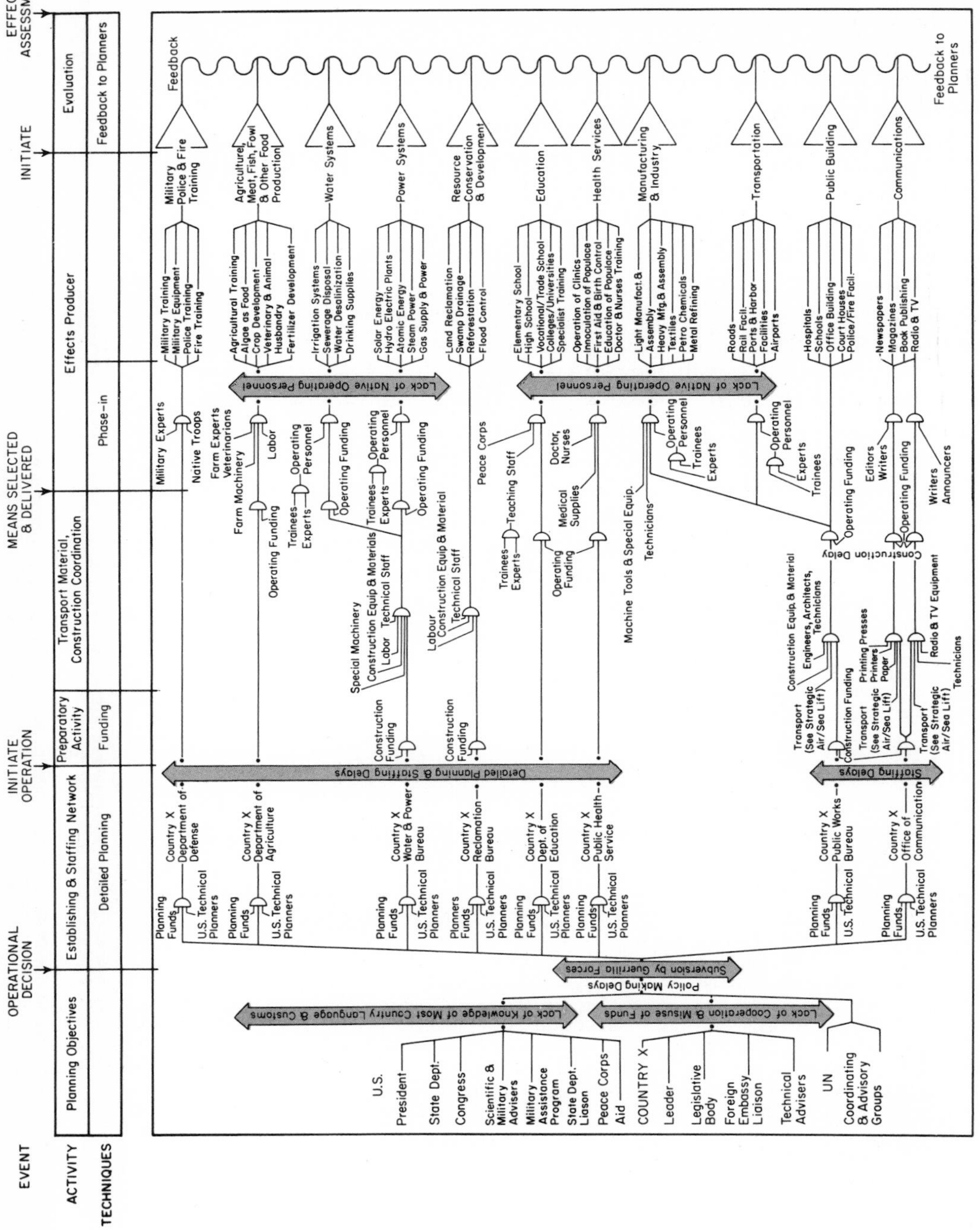

Figure 9. Peacetime Assistance: Technical.

most critical to the mission performance are further emphasized by enclosing the vertical comments with arrows.

The most incisive results are obtained when the analyst prepares the initial version of the chart without extensive external inputs. The analyst can use his intuition to produce rather complex charts, even in fields with which he has not been close, by calling on his general systems experience. After the general outline of the chart has been developed, standard source material is consulted. The chart drawing exercise forces the analyst to think hard about the mission under study, frees him from standardized approaches in a given field, and acts as an organizing tool.[19] Following this step, experts are consulted to pinpoint and rank crucial weaknesses and to indicate new alternatives which have been made possible by technological achievements. At this stage, the weakness rankings within a mission are independent of the importance of the mission.[20] In general, a weakness that cuts across all alternatives for performing a mission will rank high. Weaknesses vary in nature, according to the mission levels with which they are associated. Those at the highest level pertain primarily to policy; those at the lowest levels involve both hardware (e.g., lack of equipment) and software (e.g., obsolete standard operating procedures).

The charts greatly facilitate and stimulate interaction between the technologist and the user or "needs" analyst. They provoke brainstorming sessions, keep discussions focused, and assure that weaknesses are not confined to the "glamor" items. Not infrequently, after several iterations, the final version of a chart and the crucial weaknesses it indicates yield significant surprises.

Computation of Mission Need Values

The relative importance of the various missions at each level must be determined. Relevance or connective values are used to link the missions of one level to the missions of the adjacent levels.

Initially each scenario (S_1 . . . , S_r) is assigned a subjective weight (in accordance with its significance in an assumed national defense posture) and a subset position.[21] Then, starting at the top and working down through the levels via the linkages which have just been established, the

19 It is thus not unlike Helmer's "contextual map" in *Social Technology* (New York: Basic Books, Inc., Publishers, 1966), p. 18.

20 The ranking may depend, however, on which portion of the spectrum the mission is to be used in. Thus weakness w_1 may be crucial for all low-intensity conflict scenarios but not for any high-intensity scenarios. A division of the scenario spectrum into subsets is therefore assumed, and the normalized weakness weights are specified with reference to the applicable scenario subsets.

21 For example, scenarios S_1 . . . , S_k may be grouped into a low-intensity or unsophisticated threat subset.

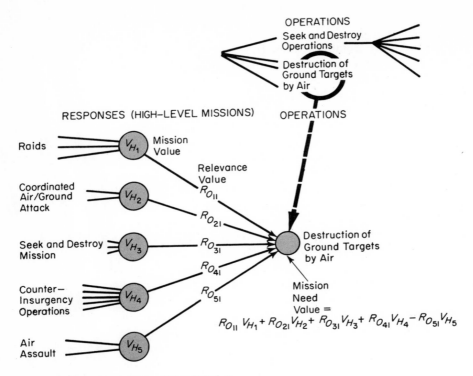

Figure 10. Example of Mission Value Calculation.

need values are computed for all missions at each level. The process is shown in Figures 10 and 11. The process involves repeated multiplication, addition, and normalization. Finally, the missions are ranked at each level.

Sensitivity checks confirm that large overall posture weight differences tend to be dampened by the time lower mission levels are reached. This is most fortunate for the hardware R&D planner. On the other hand, the procedure usually places some of the unorthodox or novel missions among the top-ranking ones at each level.

Combining Need and Weakness Values

Every *mission* now has a need value,[22] and each crucial *weakness* in a mission also has a value. These are combined to produce a Weakness

22 Actually, a set of values, one for each scenario subset (e.g., high, medium, low intensity).

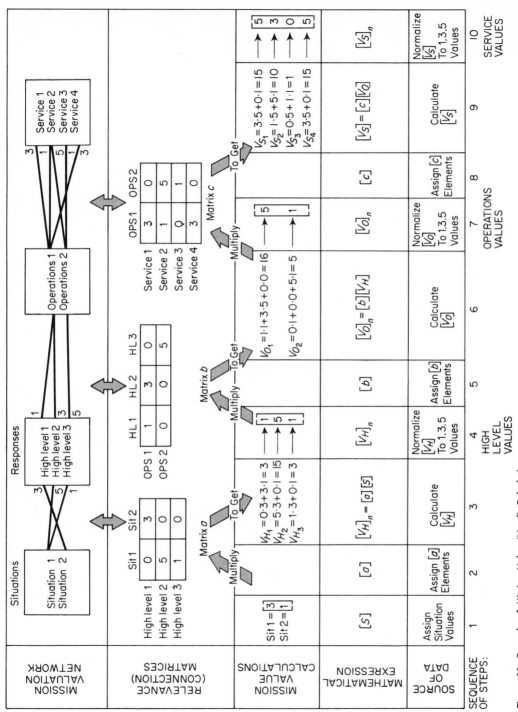

Figure 11. Example of Mission Value (Need) Calculations.

Importance Index (WII) for each weakness. The indices differ significantly from the usual "problem priority lists" for two reasons. First, the early and imaginative interaction of technology and need during the scenario response (first) phase results in a greater focus on unorthodox missions. Second, the anatomical flow chart concept (second phase) tends to prevent the placing of undue emphasis on the glamor items.

R&D Indices

Generally, a weakness can be resolved by one or more systems, which, in turn, require subsystem solutions. The latter pose development problems, and this finally leads to research tasks. A PERT-type structure may be used to display the timing and the relationships. The WII numbers are then translated into research importance values (in a manner similar to the PATTERN approach).

COMMENTS

Just as identification of a fuzzy lunar landscape is facilitated by taking pictures from different angles, so the fuzzy forecast benefits from the use of combinations of analytical approaches. The approach outlined above uses such combinations, although further improvements and other combinations certainly should be considered.

Two fundamental questions are raised by the central position of "need" as a determinant of technological forecasts. (Note that the two quotations which open the first section of this chapter use the phrase "clearly perceived need [or demand]."] [23] The questions are:

1. Who generates the "need"?
2. How is a need "clearly perceived"?

The answers appear, at first glance, to be obvious:

1. The customer or user has a planning staff, supported by operational and technological expertise, for this purpose. In some cases, the manufacturer or supplier undertakes this function.
2. The need is clearly perceived when the customer or user is ready to make a major commitment to satisfy the need. This commitment is not necessarily in terms of dollars. It may be a commitment to focus research and development activities.

[23] Curiously, the concept of "negative need" (i.e., today's needs which can be abandoned in the future) is rarely considered although it is equally important for planning purposes.

The superficial character of these responses hides real dangers. On the first point, it is vital to observe that the statement of need strongly reflects the experience and expertise of those generating it. This is a source of both strength and weakness.

Suppose technologists are not intimately involved in the early stages of the need generating process. One then might expect to find one of two trends:

1. Needs which are expressed may be technologically feasible in the year 2000, but unrealistic within the period of the forecast; e.g., 10–15 years. Example: Near-instant transport of troops to any point on earth.
2. Needs may be expressed in terms of today's technology. A need may be described for 1980 which can be fulfilled much sooner because it only requires technology which is presently available.

In the defense area, the second is far more common than the first. Although there is a tendency toward over-optimism in regard to the short range (1 to 5 years), the long range (10 years and beyond) tends to receive an overly pessimistic treatment.

However, intimately involving the technologist does not necessarily resolve the problem. Interaction between the user (civilian or military defense planner) and the technologist (scientist or engineer) may lead to mutual delusions because these two groups provide a two-sided dialogue where, in fact, a trilateral discussion is vital. This is particularly true in forecasting for an era of widening gaps.

This situation is observable in U S. society today. The poor are not understood. They represent a strange world, and more affluent sectors of society have great difficulty communicating with them. The use of educators and information systems technologists exclusively in forecasting educational needs in such an environment is, therefore, very hazardous. A recent study determined that factors such as classroom size and modern school buildings are of minor significance in improving education for underprivileged children in the United States. The key element was found to be the attitude toward education in the home. Such a conclusion might well elude the two-sided dialogue on needs. Similarly, advanced technology is not the only difference between the "normal" wars of today and the wars between near-equals in the European tradition of 1800 to 1945.

The anticipated widening of the chasm during the next decade is clearly a cause for grave concern in regard to the validity of the dialogue between the user and the technologist in the defense area. This is not the only cause for concern. The dialogue almost invariably assumes that the United States will act in the most rational and logical manner. It is very possible that this will lead, with increasing frequency, to the neglect of crucial factors which are neither military nor technological. One must ask, for example, whether there are sociological (political-psychological) factors operating which invalidate the analysis conclusion that more rapid strategic deployment capability should reduce the total manpower requirements.

Exploration of new alternatives and conceptual innovation urgently require the full involvement of the social sciences or, in Olaf Helmer's words, "social technology." (Significant new hardware needs may also develop from this broader-based, three-sided discussion.)

Turning to the second question, the forecaster must deal effectively with diverse management personnel:

1. The executive who has risen through the ranks and is conservative in any area outside the bread-and-butter line in which all his experience lies;
2. The user who tends to view future needs in the light of his own experience (e.g., past or present conflicts in the case of the military);
3. The research director who is strongly technology-oriented.

Bertrand de Jouvenel observes a characteristic common to all:

> The exercise of power, which is like a great stretching out of the hand, is accompanied by a shrinking of vision. Perhaps the reason is that this hand is not merely muscle for manipulation, but also nerve for the sense of touch, so that immediate pressures the hand encounters or provokes inform the . . . brain and there extinguish the eye's information, vision.[24]

The most common situation is that the need is "clearly perceived" very late. The user recognizes the need clearly when the crisis is upon him; when lack of action becomes patently intolerable; when external pressures are overwhelming. The usual result is solution by improvisation. Neither the needs evolving from the inevitable crisis in airports caused by a tripling of air traffic in the next ten years nor those posed by the critical Latin American situation discussed above are "clearly perceived" today. In a corporation, the benefits of a long-range customer needs analysis may be lost because of an unwillingness to believe the results until a sufficiently loud chorus on the same subject is raised from

---

[24] B. de Jouvenel, *The Art of Conjecture*, trans. Nikita Lang (New York: Basic Books, Inc., Publishers, 1967), p. 151.

the outside. This chorus, of course, is also heard by the competition, and the potential lead time is lost.

One "defense needs analysis," made in 1960, clearly indicated to the company which performed the analysis, the crucial significance of guerrilla warfare for the 1965–70 period. Only after two years, when the problem gained front-page publicity, did the company begin to ponder the advisability of setting up a small laboratory to concentrate on research in this field.

The forecaster must give far greater attention to the problem of "selling" his product. It is his responsibility to communicate effectively, to gain the confidence of the decision maker. A forecaster who is a prophet, except in his own house, is useful only in a nonprofit organization.

The two questions reinforce the feeling that the opening quotations concerning "clearly perceived need" as the key to technological forecasting require very careful interpretation. It is urgent that better bridges be built: (1) between the user/technologist groups and the social scientists; and (2) between the forecaster and the manager/decision maker.

The first is vital to assure the use of both imagination and realism in developing the need. The second is necessary to assure the communications without which there cannot be adequate confidence to pursue implementation.

Four challenging steps may help in building these bridges:

1. Participation of social scientists in the development of long-range needs, in close contact with the users and "hard science" technologists.

2. Inducement of greater empathy on the part of those concerned with development of long-term needs which arise from the "widening gap" dilemma. This can be done by effecting personal and intensive exposure to the appropriate environment.

3. Improved risk analysis to clarify the alternative plans of action and their costs, the R&D decision timetable, and the major uncertainties and their implications.

4. Participation of decision makers in weekend seminars where scenarios, games, and other techniques are used to provide them directly with more vivid insight on the future environment and the "inevitability" of the needs.

Without such steps, without better bridges, technological forecasting will be determined less by needs than by mirages.

Technology, Policy, and Forecasting

THEODORE J. RUBIN

Technological change is a substitution process which is both a product of society and an instrument of societal change. In essence, technological change is the result of policy which flows out of environmental conditions and is society's response to them. An example of environmental conditions as relating to future information technology illustrates the concept and presents methods for organizing effective forecasting activities.

Mr. Rubin, an economist, is a member of the staff of General Electric Company's Center for Advanced Studies, TEMPO. He has been analyzing interactions between technology and the economic, social, and political environment.

The opinions expressed in this chapter are those of the author, and do not necessarily represent the views of TEMPO or of any other component of General Electric Company.

Forecasting has always been a hazardous avocation. As a vocation its hazards are even greater, for the forecasts are taken seriously. Beyond the parlor game and conversational aspects of forecasting is the serious purpose of shaping decisions affecting the allocation of resources. In their simplest form such decisions are economic; in their most complex, they are political. Regardless of form, however, they are the prerogatives of institutions and often turn on factors which are neither evident to the technologist nor in consonance with his goals. Thus, policy, along with technology, becomes an essential part of the forecast.

In essence, technological change is a massive substitution process. The new, the more effective, the more useful, replace the old within the value structure and institutions which make up society. Petroleum and gas are replacing coal, which replaced wood as an energy source. In turn, nuclear fuels are expected to supplant hydrocarbons. Similarly, the supermarket has replaced the corner grocery store as a basic merchandizing technology; the motorized police patrol has replaced the "cop on the beat"; and the Beatles and folk rock have replaced Elvis Presley and rock 'n' roll.

Technological substitution is clearly not limited to the physical or inanimate; it has a social counterpart. Technological change and the evolution of societal organization are closely interwoven. Technology is, at the same time, both a product of society and an instrument of societal change. Its pace and direction are governed by societal institutions, which, in turn, are reshaped by its impacts. The policy decision is the implementing mechanism of change.

A weakness of many forecasting techniques is their preoccupation with the physical, and their treatment of the social as constant, exogenous, or nonexistent. Hence, prognostications are made for what *can* be had and when; i.e., what physical science and technology can provide, *given the green light*. But it is the color of that light—green, red, or amber—which is the key to a useful forecast, and the color is neither constant, exogenous, nor nonexistent. The color indicates what is *likely* to be and when, because it is wanted or it is not, rather than what can be.

The essential components which contribute to the forecast are technology, social needs, and social organization. Social needs are relevant because they stand to be ameliorated or intensified by prospective technological change. Social organization is relevant because the activities and institutions it represents stand to gain or lose through prospective substitutions. The interaction of all three, plus the policy decisions which emerge in the process, dictates the future outcome. This outcome may be termed the future environment. Thus, one of the most challenging fields of modern inquiry is identified: environmental analysis, the systematic forecast of future environmental alternatives.

This chapter examines an example of environmental analysis which relates to information technology. The example is briefly analyzed in terms of (1) its methodological characteristics, and (2) its usefulness for institutional decision making. Then, a methodology currently under development for the analysis of the international political environment is described, along with some of its attributes for decision making. This methodology, termed an "Environmental Information System," is a forerunner of an increasing effort toward the systematic anticipation of the future.

THE CHANGING INFORMATION ENVIRONMENT

This analysis focuses on information technology and its implications for institutional and social change. The organization and institutions of U.S. society are viewed in terms of information processes which are defined as the generation, flow, storage, and utilization of the nonmaterial resources of society to satisfy individual and social needs.

Emphasis is first placed on defining a model within which both information needs and information technology are examined. Matches and mismatches between these elements become evident and provide rationales for the forecast outcomes. The analysis is domestic in its orientation because the United States has advanced further down many of the identified paths than have other nations. Many of the forecast outcomes, however, will have no national boundaries.

Structure of the U.S. Information Environment

SOCIETAL ACTIVITIES

For purposes of this analysis, all activities in the U.S. society are divided into four categories: process activities, connective activities, organizing activities, and consumptive activities. Samples of each appear in Figure 1.

Process activities involve transformations. These may be the transfor-

Figure 1. Societal Activities.

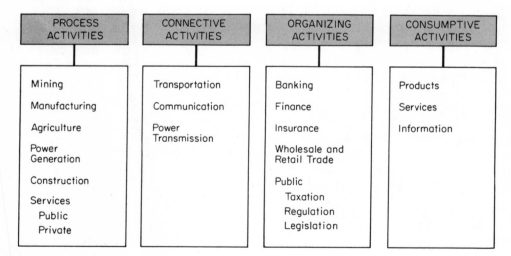

PROCESS ACTIVITIES	CONNECTIVE ACTIVITIES	ORGANIZING ACTIVITIES	CONSUMPTIVE ACTIVITIES
Mining	Transportation	Banking	Products
Manufacturing	Communication	Finance	Services
Agriculture	Power Transmission	Insurance	Information
Power Generation		Wholesale and Retail Trade	
Construction		Public	
Services		Taxation	
Public		Regulation	
Private		Legislation	

mation of materials from one state to another in manufacturing, or the transformation of fertilizer, soil, and seed into agricultural produce, or the transformation of fuels into electric energy. Services are process activities in which people, rather than things, are processed; e.g., sick people are made well in the medical process, people in trouble are punished or exonerated in the legal process, the illiterate and unlearned are taught in the educational process, and dowdy dowagers are transformed into svelte sirens in the cosmetological process.

Connective activities provide linkages among all activities and institutions in U.S. society. Clearly, transportation and communications are of this character, and while power generation is a process activity, power transmission is unquestionably connective.

Organizing activities are the evolved mechanisms for collecting and allocating investment resources, exercising control, providing incentives, and otherwise guiding the arrangement of activities in the society. In the economy, these include the private sector activities of banking, finance, insurance, and distribution, and the public sector activities of taxation, regulation, and legislation.

Consumptive activities are the evolved mechanisms for putting the society's material and nonmaterial outputs to final use. As such, they are basic determinants of the distribution of social energy and attention among the other three classes of activities.

The term "activity," as used, is an abstraction. The fabric of a society may also be portrayed in terms of the institutions evolved for the conduct of activities. Institutions are real and lend themselves to quantitative description; e.g., U.S. transportation institutions include American Airlines, the Pennsylvania Railroad, Allied Van Lines, and so on. The size, economic contribution, work force, income, and myriad other characteristics of such institutions can be measured and expressed quantitatively to serve many purposes. For purposes of this analysis, however, the simple awareness of this relationship between activities and institutions is sufficient. Activities (and the implied institutions) must be structured into a crude model to enhance an understanding of the information transactions which knit society together and are basic to its operation and evolution.

STRUCTURE OF ECONOMIC ACTIVITIES

Figure 2 is a simplified portrayal of activity centers in the U.S. economy and their primary paths of interaction. In the lower portion of the figure are the consumptive and process activities of the economy, along with the organizing activities of retail and wholesale trade. The linkages between pairs of activities depict flow and transaction patterns of goods, services, and information, from supplier and manufacturer, through distribution elements, to the consumer.

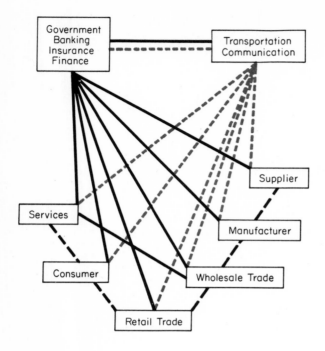

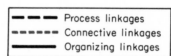

- - - - Process linkages
- - - - Connective linkages
———— Organizing linkages

Figure 2. The Economy.

At the upper left of the figure, the other organizing activities of the economy appear (government, banking, finance, and insurance). These are also linked transactionally to each activity in the supplier-to-consumer chain. Finally, superimposed on the entire milieu, are the connecting activities of transportation and communication.

As the analysis proceeds, this rudimentary model of the economy will be used, or referred to, to illustrate:

1. The nature of the information environment, information flows, and information institutions;
2. The distribution of contemporary usage of computer technology;
3. The likely pattern of development of information technology and its institutional impact.

THE INFORMATION ENVIRONMENT UNDERLYING THE ECONOMY

Normally, the economy is envisioned in terms of a flow of goods and services from producer to consumer, within a context of organizing and connective activities. In fact, the economic structure has evolved and has been organized to expedite such flows and transactions. Suppose, however, the material manifestations of the economy were ignored and an inquiry were made into the nature of the information environment which underlies its operation.

This notion impinges on all activities and institutions in the economy, and not necessarily in proportion to the roles they play in physical flows and transactions. In Figure 3, informational transactions are divided into two classes: those primarily internal to an activity and to its institutions; and those primarily external, i.e., between activities or between institu-

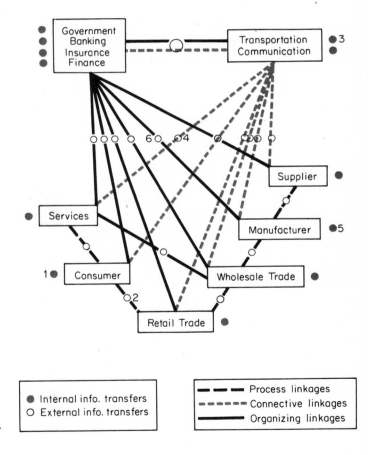

Figure 3. The Information Environment.

1. *Household—Internal*
   Grocery lists
   Appointment lists
   Auto service records
   Personal budget
   Name and address lists
   Financial records

2. *Retail & Consumer*
   Grocery sales
   Auto listings
   Real estate listings
   Entertainment offerings
   Stockmarket reports
   Telephone directories
   Employment opportunities
   Weather reports

3. *Transportation—Internal*
   Freight car locations
   Routes and schedules
   Equipment maintenance
   Operating statistics
      (utilization rates, etc.)
   Plus all business functions
      (see Box 5)

4. *Transportation & Consumer*
   Reservation offices
   Travel agents
   Timetables
   Advertising, mass media

5. *Manufacture—Internal*
   Accounting, inventory control
   Budgeting
   Marketing forecasts
   Scheduling, process control
   Billing, payroll, etc.

6. *Organizing Activities & Manufacture*
   Dun & Bradstreet
   Standard & Poor
   Moody's
   NAM
   Stock brokers
   BLS
   Census Bureau
   Market research services
   Tax accountants

Note: Numbers refer to Figure 3

Figure 4. Sample Transactions and Brokerages

tions. Each of the activities of the economic model is shown as having an internal information environment and as being related to other activities in an external information environment. As will become evident, many of the external transaction patterns have spawned new institutions best labeled "information brokerages."

To convey more fully the meaning and implications of the concept of an information environment, consider some examples (in Figure 4) of information transactions and brokerages common to various activities in the economy (numbers 1 through 6 in Figure 3). On the left of Figure 4 are examples of internal information transactions (boxes 1, 3, and 5). On the right of the figure are examples of external information transactions (boxes 2, 4, and 6).

Familiar samples of information stored and used internally in households appear in box 1 of Figure 4. Despite its value and frequent use, the organization of information such as this varies considerably from household to household. In box 2, a few examples of product and service offerings of the U.S. economy are noted. These represent information flowing from retail activities to consuming households. In part, this information is solicited by the consumer, but to a greater degree it is indiscriminately "broadcast." Because the economic value of this information lies largely with the activities from which it emanates, its cost is borne by such activities. A large number of information brokerage institutions which lie between these activities are used to disseminate such information. The entire advertising industry and the institutional advertising media, ranging from radio and television to newspapers and magazines, direct mail, and door-to-door solicitations, are information brokerages lying between vendor and consumer.

Boxes 3 and 4 relate, respectively, to the internal and external information transactions of the transportation industries. In box 4, the brokerage institutions through which externally oriented information flows to the consumer are listed. The conceptual similarity to boxes 1 and 2 is clearly evident. The pattern is repeated once more in boxes 5 and 6.

These examples barely suggest the magnitude and variability of information transactions and institutions in the economy.[1] Furthermore, these transactions manifest the needs for information transfer and these needs may be documented. Each information transaction may be quantitatively and qualitatively characterized in terms of such criteria as the time sensitivity of the information (perishability), frequency and periodicity, information bits per transaction, economic value, propriety of the information, etc. The concept of an information environment, then, can be documented in terms of institutions, transactions, and needs.

Information Technology

CURRENT TRENDS—THE BASIS FOR TECHNOLOGICAL PROJECTIONS

Current progress in information technology is governed primarily by developments in computer hardware, software, and related communication technology. Although the computer is barely out of its infancy, some notable trends are evident.

1. Computer power. This index of ability to perform a particular mix of operations, reflecting circuit speed and memory size, has increased approximately one order of magnitude every five years.
2. Cost per unit computer power. Improved cost performance over time is an inherent characteristic of young technologies, invariably

---

[1] An information environment is by no means unique to the economy alone. The larger social context, including religion, law, politics, health, education, etc., lends itself to a similar characterization.

leading to more widespread use and increasing applications (substitutions for existing, more costly, technologies). This index has dropped by approximately one order of magnitude in the past five years.

3. Physical limitations. Transistors, printed circuits, micro-miniaturization, integrated circuits, etc., are minimizing physical size, unreliability, and other constraints on computer applications.

4. User accessibility and versatility. With the development of more sophisticated software, simpler access languages, and more effective terminal devices, direct user access to computer power is nearing realization. Originally only a tool of research and something of a military and scientific curiosity, the computer is becoming an accepted and commonplace necessity.

COMPUTERS IN THE INFORMATION ENVIRONMENT

Figure 5 depicts contemporary computer applications in the information environment of the economy. Computer usage is graded as heavy,

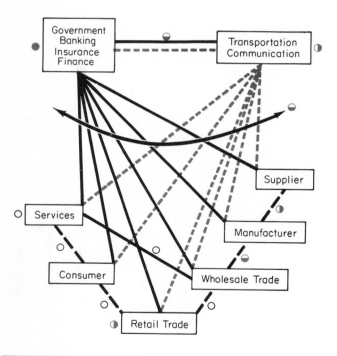

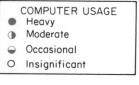

COMPUTER USAGE
- ● Heavy
- ◑ Moderate
- ◔ Occasional
- ○ Insignificant

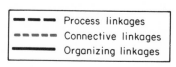

- - - - Process linkages
- - - - Connective linkages
———— Organizing linkages

Figure 5. Current Computer Use.

moderate, occasional, or insignificant. While this is not a fine-grained scale, some meaningful observations are nevertheless possible.

1. The heaviest application of computer technology has occurred in the organizing activities of the economy. These applications have been both internal, within the organizing institutions, and external, between them and other activities of the economy.

2. The connective activities and manufacturing (materials processing) activities also employ considerable computer technology. Most of these applications have been internal.

3. Household, retail, service and wholesale institutional use of computer technology has been insignificant to occasional.

4. The information brokerages which lie between the organizing and connective activities of the economy and all others (the band across Figure 5) exhibit occasional computer applications.

5. In summary, early computer utilization (substitution) in the economy has evolved and centered in large institutions, i.e., those having the most pressing needs and the necessary financial means.

These observations describe a complex technical innovation which is just beginning to permeate the society. But are these observed patterns representative of the future? Will information technology gradually penetrate deeper into the *existing* societal fabric, or will the fabric itself be transformed?

EVOLVING OPERATIONAL CONCEPTS

With modern information technology, it is now possible to think in terms of supplying information *on demand*. This represents a fundamental departure from the currently operational concept of *pre-programming* upon which the activities of most high-information-content institutions are based. Every filing cabinet, library, journal, newspaper, television program, advertising campaign, and timetable stands as evidence of information pre-programming. It is inevitable that, given the option, this operating mode will yield to more efficient and effective means of information transfer. The well-known *New York Times* slogan, "All the news that's fit to print," while journalistically commendable, will be an anachronism in a society geared to obtaining selected information on demand.

One technical and organizational mechanism permissive of this change in orientation is referred to as "the information utility." This concept is based on multiple user, time-shared access (using remote terminals) to very large central processors and memories which offer "real time" responses. The information utility theoretically offers the user continuing access to unlimited computer power at a cost potentially less than that of owning or leasing high-powered information machines.[2]

The implications of this potential innovation for patterns of information transfer, for the structure of information-based institutions, and for the information functions within U.S. institutions at large, are revolutionary. The emergence of new or drastically changed institutions can be anticipated as a result.

Future Impacts and Forecasts

EVOLUTIONARY PATHS FOR INFORMATION UTILITIES

The evolutionary forms that will emerge can best be categorized as intra-institutional utilities and inter-institutional utilities. The intra-institutional utility is already emerging. Its function is the consolidation of the internal information activities of an institution. For example, it has been observed that the more than 150 computers currently in use within the General Electric Company can be replaced (with a resource savings) by a handful of very large machines which offer remote access to users through leased line communications. Similarly, a municipal government, a large banking chain, a retail chain, or any other institutional entity can consolidate internal informational activities through the utility mechanism. *The intra-institutional information utility will have the effect of strengthening and perpetuating existing institutions and will therefore be attractive beyond its economic benefits.*

Some identifiable prerequisites for intra-institutional utilities are:

1. Large size. This implies massive internal information flows and resources for software development.
2. Geographic dispersion. This implies current duplication of information activities at several locations and difficulties of coordination and control.
3. Significant computer usage. This implies existing skills (and staff) for adapting existing internal information systems to the new operational mode.
4. A large common data base. This implies advantages of central data storage with remote retrieval, vis-à-vis redundant decentralized storage.

---

[2] Current literature abounds with references to the information utility. For an elaboration of the concept by its originator, see Martin Greenberger, "The Computer of Tomorrow," *The Atlantic Monthly,* July, 1964.

The inter-institutional utility will emerge to enhance the effectiveness and efficiency of information transfer between institutions. The so-called money and credit utility involving banks, retail institutions, and households already is the subject of much study.

The basic stimulus to the development of the inter-institutional utility will be the inherent economic benefits to the major parties concerned. Initially, the utility will represent little more than the substitution of modern information technology for existing, less efficient, information systems. Information flows among established groups of suppliers, manufacturers, and distributors in respect to orders, shipments, inventories, prices, specifications, etc., will be coordinated and considerable savings will result. *To the extent that new technology can be substituted for old without changing basic institutional relationships, these substitutions will be welcomed by all parties concerned.*

But can multiple institutions retain their autonomy within the context of an information system which binds them together? How will systemic decisions be reached and implemented within a multi-institutional information system? In short, where will operational control lie in an integrated information system? *There is a strong implication that the inter-institutional utility will have the eventual effect of restructuring existing institutional forms and boundaries.* Further, there is a strong implication that the rate of such a significant, technologically induced change in the industrial and commercial power structure will be governed by the degree and success of institutional resistance rather than by the availability of the technology (the light is red).

THE FORECASTS

The foregoing analyses of informational needs and technological trends, when applied to the economy through the utility concept, give rise to the following forecasts.

1. The vertically integrated enterprise, from supplier and manufacturer to retail distributor, will emerge as the basic processing institution in the economy.[3] The control of this institution will center in its organizing elements (distribution and finance) by virtue of their close proximity to ultimate demands. Independent, diversified manufacturing enterprises, however large, will become increasingly dependent on this form of massive, distribution-oriented institution.

---

[3] For example, Sears, Roebuck and Co., with an electronic catalogue.

2. Information brokerages and other high-information-content institutions will lose much of their autonomy and come under the control of nationwide utilities operated under close federal government scrutiny. Current-events publishing institutions (e.g., newspapers and news magazines) will diminish in importance as substitute functions in utilities become prime recipients of advertising revenues.

3. The organizing activities (government, banking, finance, and distribution) will become ever more dominant in the economy as their access to information increases through direct utility linkages to ultimate consumers (households) and to other utility systems.

4. The relative importance of transportation to communication as an information linkage in the economy will drop. Business travel, whether from home to work for the employee, from business to market for the salesman, or from field to home office for the agent, will diminish as information technology advances. In air transport, freight will increase in importance as a determinant of the rate of growth of the industry and of its equipment requirements.

5. Overall, consolidation and centralization will continue as trends in economic organization. The economy will be composed of fewer large institutions. A small number of these, in company with government, will regulate and control the behavior of the economy.

Review of the Example

METHODOLOGICAL CHARACTERISTICS

The three components that are essential to an environmental analysis (technology, social needs, and social organization) are all present in the example. However, because of the limited scope of the analysis, what emerged might better be characterized as a "structured environmental overview" than an analysis. This description does not imply superficiality, however, because: (1) within the structure, the requirements for a more objective, more highly quantified, more detailed analysis have been set forth; and (2) the structure provides more analytic sophistication than would an "intuitive estimate" of the future.

The main subject areas treated in the example are outlined in Figure 6. Opposite the outline are the outputs which derived from each subject area. These outputs are further differentiated in terms of whether they constitute part of the historical data base for the forecast or whether they represent a projection. In keeping with the introductory distinction made in this paper, the column entitled "non-policy oriented projections" corresponds to the technological forecast and the column entitled "policy-oriented projections" corresponds to the environmental forecast.

OUTLINE	METHODOLOGICAL COMPONENTS AND OUTPUTS		
	Historical Data Base	Non-Policy Oriented Projections	Policy Oriented Projections

Structure of the U.S. Information Environment
  Activities and Institutions
  Structure of the Economy
  The Information Environment
    of the Economy
	Units of Analysis
	Theoretical Relationships		

Information Transactions	Current Needs		

Information Technology
  Current Trends
 	
Computers in the Information
  Environment
 	
Evolving Operational Concepts
	Current Technology
	
	Current Environment
		Future Physical Technology	

Future Impacts and Forecasts
  Intra-Institutional Utilities
  Inter-Institutional Utilities
		Future Social Technology	

Forecasts			Future Environment

Figure 6. Analysis of the Example.

To illustrate the difference in scope between the technological forecast and the environmental analysis, those portions of the outline (which is a scope statement) which are generally included in the technological forecast are heavily shaded in Figure 6. Those portions of the outline sometimes included are less heavily shaded. The environmental analysis, however, is committed by definition to full coverage of all the components represented in the outline.

USEFULNESS FOR INSTITUTIONAL DECISION MAKING

The usefulness of the environmental forecast is high, since, in theory, it reveals not only the potential of a technology, but the societal decision as to its acceptability and rate of implementation. However, the individual decision maker must assess the forecast for the implicit gain or loss it portends for the institution he represents, and from this he must determine a future strategy for his institution.

The shortcomings of the structured environmental overview as such a decision aid are:

1. It is often not specific enough as to the time of impact of the changes it forecasts.
2. Because its assumptions and data are, for the most part, implicit or intuitive, the sensitivity of the forecasts to variations in these factors cannot be determined.
3. Similarly, the forecast is not reproducible, either (1) to enable a determination of why it was right or wrong, or (2) to facilitate a recycling, as new events occur and new data become available.

On the other hand, the example presents several positive attributes of the structured overview:

1. It provides future insights for the decision maker which are neither inherent in technological forecasting nor available from intuitive estimates.
2. It offers guidelines for detailed analysis of any or all those components which are insufficiently developed in the overview for decision-making purposes.

THE ENVIRONMENTAL INFORMATION SYSTEM

In order to develop the positive attributes of the environmental forecast and to minimize the shortcomings of the structured overview, the notion of the environmental information system (EIS) has emerged. In essence, an EIS is identical in concept and intent to a structured overview, but instead of being implicit, intuitive, and nonreproducible, it is designed to be explicit and objective in data and assumptions, and continuous or repetitive in operation.

An EIS is currently under development for forecasting the characteristics of the international political environment ten to fifteen years in the future. Whether successful or not, this development will be the forerunner of a growing series of attempts to systematically appraise the future on a continuing basis in order to offer relevant guidance to decision makers. This final section of the chapter is devoted to a description of the components of the environmental forecast as they are incorporated in the international EIS.

User Requirements and EIS Outputs

The potential users of the international political EIS are U.S. government decision makers who are concerned with current resource allocation decisions which will have an impact ten to fifteen years in the future.

Their decisions require foreknowledge of the alternative future international political outcomes which may:

1. Perpetuate or change the current roles and missions of the institutions the decision makers represent;
2. Increase or decrease the international importance of each of these institutions;
3. Change the geographic postures of the institutions, or their force mixes (the systems and programs they develop to implement U.S. foreign policy); or
4. Affect the strategy and policy of the institutions as a result of the above contingencies, and thereby
5. Influence the resource allocation decisions to be made.

For these reasons the primary focus of the EIS has been placed on the forecast of international political changes or discontinuities. Specifically, the outputs selected as most relevant to the decision-making needs are:

1. Discontinuities in the form of the inter-nation system, or likely changes in the group of major nations which are separate foci of power and policy;
2. Discontinuities in political alignment patterns among major nations and between major and minor nations;
3. Likely changes in the levels of internal political instability of minor nations;
4. Likely changes in the levels of instability of local conflict issues existing between two or more minor nations;
5. Likely changes in the inherent power of nations, in their capacity to influence other nations, and in the patterns of influence attempts likely to be employed.

These outputs are sythesized to identify alternative future international political patterns which may precede, necessitate, or de-emphasize U.S. government commitments of resources to foreign policy implementation. The means for operational attainment of these outputs constitute the design of the EIS.

International Activities and Institutions— the Units of Analysis

Early in the design of the EIS it was evident that its coverage had to be limited to some discrete set of actors which were more important

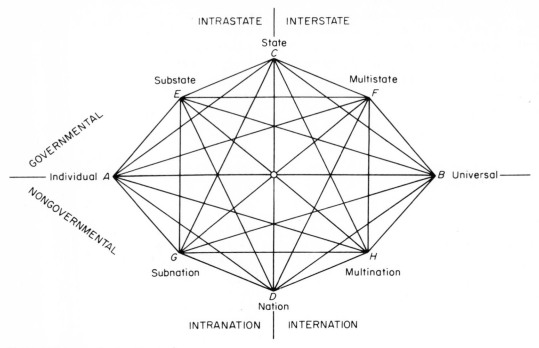

Figure 7. Actors and Interaction Paths.

than any others to the evolution of the stated future outcomes. Instead of arbitrarily delimiting the focus of the system to a few "important" nations, a structural context of international actors and interactions was examined in detail.

Figure 7 illustrates this contextual model. In its two dimensions, the level of organizational hierarchy increases from left to right—from the individual (*A*) to the universal organization (*B*)—and the axis *A-B* separates the hierarchy into governmental and nongovernmental components. All organizational strata shown in the hierarchy, both governmental and nongovernmental, have a capacity for interaction (illustrated by the connecting paths), both within traditional nation-state boundaries and among nation-states.

The insights and ramifications suggested by this model of international organization and interaction are too numerous to discuss here. It is sufficient to say that any EIS composed of but a small fraction of the total actors of this international context runs the risk of potentially serious omissions. Yet the need to constrain the selection of units of analysis for the practical reasons of theoretical, data, computer, and resource limitations is obvious. This dilemma is ever present in environmental analysis.

In the present EIS design, the organizational units of analysis selected are the nation-states and their multinational political groupings. These groupings include formal military, economic, and political treaty organizations, and informal behavioral groupings reflecting compatibility among the policies of individual nations. All the units of analysis may be treated simultaneously in a global version of the system, or units may be treated selectively, as in a geographically limited regional version.

Needs and Technology

In the EIS, the basic needs or interests of the participating nations are assumed to be the maintenance of internal political stability, territorial sovereignty, and international security and influences. Conflicting views among nations in the interpretation of their respective interests are assumed to give rise to a second set of needs—those for technologies capable of promoting such international interests. These latter requirements include the technology of war or deterrence (military), the technology of economic and social development, the technology of communication (diplomacy), and so on. In the EIS, each nation is characterized in terms of its apparent national interests and the status of development of its internationally oriented technologies.

Basic Theoretical Assumptions

Unlike the structured environmental overview, the linkage in the EIS between the units of analysis, their needs, their technologies, and the environmental forecasts, is a set of explicit rather than implicit or intuitive theoretical assumptions. The major forecasting assumptions employed in the EIS design are the following:

1. The relative importance of nations in international politics is related to their inherent power and the rate of change of such power.
2. Changes in political alignment among nations result from:
   a. Changes in the relative inherent power among nations,
   b. Changes in the patterns of influence attempts among nations,
   c. Changes in the levels of internal political instability of minor nations, and
   d. Changes in the levels of instability of local conflict issues to which minor nations are party.

3. The importance to the leading major nations (focal nations) of potential political alignment changes by minor nations is related to:

  a. The prior alignment status of the minor nations, and
  b. The patterns of influence attempts made by focal nations to maintain or alter alignments.

EIS Analytic Components and Flow

When the EIS units of analysis, needs, technologies, and assumptions were synthesized, a model emerged which appeared to best identify and interrelate the components whose analysis might be expected to yield the specified forecast outputs. This model is shown in Figure 8. The conceptual definitions of its components are presented in Figure 9.

It is not the purpose of the paper to describe this particular EIS in detail. It should be noted, however, that each of the components of the EIS model has been brought to some degree of quantitative operationalization by (1) stipulation of relevant political science theories; (2) identification of input variables; and (3) identification of analytic procedures for manipulating the variables within the theories, to attain the component output. As presently conceived, the EIS will operate with a total of approximately fifty variables for each nation.

Figure 8. EIS Components and Flow.

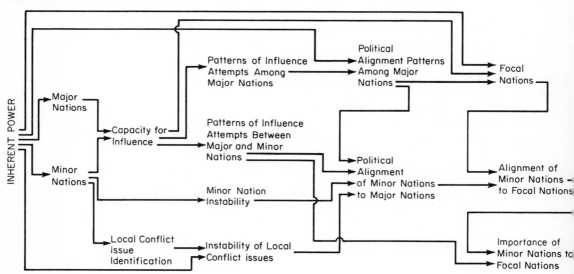

Inherent power—the underlying military, political, and economic strengths of a nation which provide a base for its participation in international politics.

Major nations—those nations whose level of inherent power identifies them as actual or latent competitors for international influence.

Minor nations—those nations which have not or cannot achieve the status of major nations.

Capacity for influence—the policy resources available to nations for attempting to influence the behavior of other nations.

Patterns of influence attempts—the allocation pattern at time T of the policy resources of a given nation among other nations.

Minor nation instability—the status at time T of those internal conditions in a minor nation which are related to unprogrammed changes in governmental leadership.

Local conflict issues—unresolved political and legal disputes, often of long-standing duration, which exist between two or more collocated minor nations.

Instability of local issues—the status at time T of the causes of local conflict issues in those nations which are party to the issues.

Alignments—groups of nations which usually act in concert in international politics.

Focal nations—the dominant policy setting nations within an alignment.

Importance of minor nations to focal nations—the perceived value to focal nations of the political alignment of minor nations.

Figure 9. Conceptual Definitions of EIS Components

The Data Bank, Projection, and the Environmental Forecasts

To complete the description of the EIS, it is necessary to distinguish its operations in the same terms employed in the review of the information environmental analysis (see Figure 6). The EIS also consists of the construction of a data bank and employs both non-policy-oriented and policy-oriented projections.

In the EIS, the data bank provides bench-mark data against which projections can be compared to identify the specified change outputs. The policy-oriented components of the EIS are those relating to a nation's capacity for influence and to the allocation of this influence among other nations. In the non-policy-oriented projections, therefore, the current policies of each nation in respect to such allocations of influence are held constant. In the policy-oriented projections, these allocations are selectively varied. The final output of the EIS, then, is an array of alternative environmental forecasts, each linked to a particular and unique set of explicit policy assumptions.

Finally, it should be noted that the EIS is designed for continuity of performance. It is intended to be operated repetitively over time, and herein lies one of its greatest strengths. Of the fifty or so variables in the system, only about half are separately projected. The rest are to be monitored over time, to independently measure outcomes and compare them with the forecasts as original projection points approach and pass.

Attributes of the EIS

The EIS described has, as its point of departure, the same attributes for environmental forecasting as has the "structured overview." Specifically, it reflects a particular set of institutions and activities (in this case, the nations and their international political behavior), and the structure of their needs and interactions.

Beyond this, however, the EIS is designed to be fully and explicitly documented in assumption, data, and theory so that the sensitivity of its forecasts may be ascertained. Further, through the notion of continuity, its reproducibility over time is assured. And most importantly, its design has been based on the provision of a set of outputs which meet the specific needs of identifiable decision makers.

APPLYING TECHNOLOGICAL FORECASTING

PART FOUR

The two preceding sections described methodology; in this section practitioners show how technological forecasts can be applied in various functions such as research, product planning, and corporate long-range planning.

These suggestions for application are not limited to the foregoing techniques. Each author has his own definitions and adaptations and adds to concepts of methodology. One chapter, for instance, shows how the forecast can be applied to planning development programs for extremely complex engineering projects. Another describes a procedure useful in systems development. A third chapter introduces the notion of economic evaluation of potential products.

How can the manager use the technological forecast for business purposes? Various types of corporate uses are described. A number of research findings on technological innovation and suggestions as to how these findings can help the manager use the technological forecast are included. Given a good forecast, what factors will influence its materialization?

The two closing discussions describe applications to specific industries. Each contains a concept not proposed in prior chapters, and each shows how industry guidance can be obtained by some form of technological anticipation.

The Use of Technological Forecasts for Planning Research

JOSEPH P. MARTINO

An extremely valuable tool for research planning is the technological forecast. The ultimate aim of research activities—useful products, processes, or systems—can be viewed as sets of performance characteristics. By combining estimates of future needs with technological forecasts of these performance characteristics, the research manager is in the best position to evaluate the feasibility of his goals, examine competitive technologies and their cost and performance implications, and select the best research avenues for reaching his objectives.

Major Martino is Assistant Executive Director for Research Communication within the Air Force Office of Scientific Research. He has had a great deal of experience with the development of techniques to identify research opportunities and establish research plans for the Air Force.

The opinions presented in this chapter are those of the author, and do not necessarily represent the views of the U.S. Air Force.

The planning of research is a broad field and many articles have already been written on the subject,[1] but little has been written about the influence of technological forecasting on research planning. Air Force experience has shown that technological forecasts are useful for planning

[1] J. B. Quinn, and R. M. Cavanaugh, "Fundamental Research Can Be Planned," *Harvard Business Review*, January–February, 1964; W. L. Swager, "Improving the Management of Research," *Business Horizons*, Vol. 2, No. 4, Winter, 1959, and E. D. Reeves, "Industrial Research: A Kind of Business Strategy," *Chemical and Engineering News*, Vol. 43, No. 43 (Oct. 25, 1965), 92–97.

research, including choosing research areas, selecting projects within these areas, and formulating sound personnel policies. However, to do this effectively one must have a clear understanding of categories of technical effort.

DEFINITIONS

The term "research" is defined here as an attempt to acquire new knowledge about some phenomenon in the universe, or about some phenomenon in an abstract model of a portion of the universe, which is not necessarily made with an application in mind. The definition makes no distinction between basic and applied research, since the difference between the two terms is usually in the motivation of the researcher, and this is not an objectively measurable quantity. Although an application may well be in the researcher's thoughts, no inference is made here about what is going on in his mind while he is doing his research.

There is, however, a meaningful distinction between research and development: development is an attempt to construct, assemble, or prepare for the first time, a device, material, technique, or procedure, meeting a prescribed set of specifications or desired characteristics and intended to solve a specific problem. This definition includes not only mechanical devices and hardware, but such things as computer programs, chemicals, and other materials. The essence of this definition is that development is intended to meet some set of specifications in order to solve a specific problem.

Figure 1. A Common "Research-to-Product" Model.

The interaction between research and development is shown in Figure 1, which depicts a common model of the way research progresses into products. This is usually phrased in such terms as "getting an idea out of the laboratory and into production." The kindest thing one can say for this model is that it is erroneous. Research and development are two entirely different categories of activity, and there is no neat linear progression from one into the other, as this model would imply.

Figure 2 shows a more nearly correct model in which research feeds a pool of knowledge which is drawn upon for exploratory and advanced

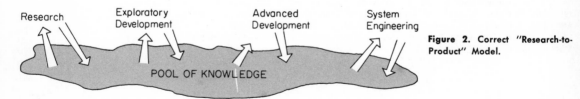

Figure 2. Correct "Research-to-Product" Model.

development, and for systems engineering. This model recognizes that additional knowledge is added to the pool at each of these stages. It was originated by Al Shapero [2] and has received support from the recent report of the Materials Advisory Board. [3]

Companies perform research for the following reasons:

1. To stay competitive in present areas of business;
2. To produce new products to enter new areas of business;
3. To maintain a pool of talent which can be used for problem solving or advising management;
4. To exploit outside discoveries which occur elsewhere in the field of science;
5. To anticipate outside threats to present markets from discoveries elsewhere in science;
6. To avoid an adverse patent or know-how situation which might erode present business or freeze a company out of a new area of business;
7. To give a firm an image of progressiveness.

Research can be divided into three main categories—connecting, supporting, and pioneering.

Connecting Research is the research an organization does for the purpose of remaining in touch with the world of science—to see what is going on. In order to keep up with the latest activities in any field of science a company has to have a ticket to the club. The ticket is being able to say something which is of interest to the other researchers in the field. In short, if an organization is to keep in touch with the latest activities in any field of science, it must have at least one man who is doing high-quality research in that field of science.

Supporting Research is the research a company does to support its present products and markets. This, too, must be high-quality research, on the frontiers of the area of science in which it is done. However, the purpose of this research is to find answers to problems encountered while improving products in order to keep abreast of competition. It should not be confused with "quick-fix" efforts to cure some immediate production or application problem. The problem which provides the initial motivation for a piece of supporting research must be one which is going

[2] A. Shapero, *Diffusion of Innovations Resulting from Research,* Stanford Research Institute, 1965.
[3] *Report of the Ad-Hoc Committee on Principles of Research Engineering Interaction,* National Research Council, Washington, D.C., July, 1966.

to be around for some time, because there will be a considerable time lag, of the order of years, between initiation of the research and incorporation of the results into products. The problems must be chosen so that they will still be of interest when the answer is found.

Pioneering Research is undertaken in order to enter new fields and create new products and markets. Like the other two types of research, it must be of high quality, and it must be on the frontiers of the area of science in which it is done. Choices of research areas and projects for pioneering research will be discussed later.

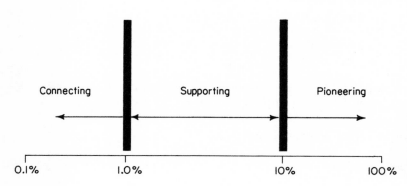

Figure 3. Research Efforts Required for a Company to Perform Each of the Three Categories of Research (As a Percentage of Industry-wide Activity).

	Connecting	Supporting	Pioneering
Stay Competitive		★	
New Products			★
Pool of Talent		★	☆
Exploit Outside Discoveries	★		
Anticipate Outside Threats	★		
Patents and Knowhow		☆	★
Image			★

Figure 4. Relationship Between Goals of Research and Types of Research.

Figure 3 shows the requirements for performing each of these categories of research. Connecting research requires approximately one full-time man who will do 1 per cent or less of the research being done in that field. Research to support present markets requires the performance of 1 per cent to 10 per cent of all the research in the pertinent field. To pioneer in some field, a company must plan to do over 10 per cent of all the research in that area. These percentages tend to vary with the field of science, and with the number and activity of competitors.

Figure 4 shows the relationship between the goals of research and the kinds of research. In order to stay competitive, a company clearly has to do supporting research. To get new products, it needs to do pioneering research. A pool of talent is provided primarily by supporting research although pioneering research also accomplishes this objective. Exploiting outside discoveries and anticipating outside threats are facilitated by connecting research. Protecting and generating a patents and know-how position are aided somewhat by supporting research but are achieved primarily through pioneering research. Finally, producing a company image for progressiveness requires pioneering research.

RESEARCH PLANNING

If a company is going to plan for research, it must plan:

1. The goals and strategy of the research organization;
2. The choice of research areas;
3. The choice of projects within research areas;
4. The research personnel (their recruitment, career development, and purging);
5. The organization of the research program (discipline vs. project research, and organizational and physical barriers between the research group and the rest of the organization);
6. The communication patterns with the rest of the organization (the researcher with his peers, with the users of his research, and with the executives who make decisions about his research);
7. The motivation and incentives for the researchers; and
8. The research facilities.

APPLICATION OF TECHNOLOGICAL FORECASTING

Figure 5 shows a schematic of a manufacturing process. From suppliers, companies receive raw material, intermediate products, and components.

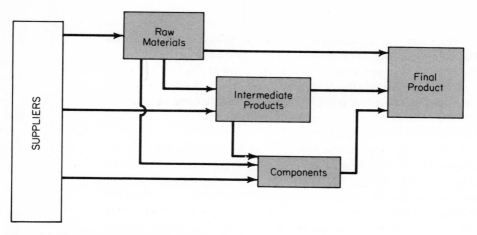

Figure 5. Schematic of Manufacturing Process.

These are processed into a final product. From the standpoint of research planning it is necessary to consider each of the four items as sets of performance characteristics, not just as physical items. Similarly, the processes by which this transformation takes place must be considered as generalized rather than detailed assembly processes. This approach makes it possible to inquire how research can lead to improvements in both the materials and the processes involved in the manufacture of products.

Performance characteristics include such things as:

1. The function(s) performed by the product;
2. Factors (such as time, distance, etc.) of function performance;
3. Size and weight;
4. Dollar cost;
5. Other problems relating to handling, storage, manufacturing operations, lifetime, etc.

The idea of viewing a product as a set of performance characteristics may be clarified by some examples. The performance characteristics of the whale oil lamp were also satisfied by both the kerosene lamp and the electric light. The performance characteristics of vacuum tubes in portable radios were also satisfied by transistors. The performance characteristics of plant-derived dyes, such as indigo, were also satisfied by synthetically produced chemical dyes. The key point is to avoid getting bogged down in detailed questions of a product's composition and how it is made, and, instead, to look at what it does and how well it does it.

Similarly, the transformation processes involved in converting raw materials, intermediate products, and components into final products must be viewed from a more generalized aspect. Are they chemical concentration processes? Are they heat transfer or mechanical assembly processes? If an open-hearth steel furnace is viewed only as an assemblage of bricks, pipes and so forth, it is easy to overlook the fact that steel making involves a heat transfer process which can also be performed by an electric arc furnace, or, perhaps in the future, by a solar furnace operating in space or on the moon. As another example, the assembly of electronic components into a radio set, either manually or mechanically, is a mechanical assembly process which can also be performed by methods which produce printed circuits.

The reason for looking at a manufacturing process in terms of the performance characteristics of the intermediate and final products, and the transformation processes used, is to make it clear that a product may be replaced by another product which has the same performance characteristics, but is based on an entirely different field of science. The indigo industry was overturned, not by a better species of indigo-producing plant, but by developments in the field of chemistry. The kerosene lamp industry was overturned, not by better petroleum-refining methods, but by developments in the field of electromagnetics. The radio manufacturing industry is undergoing a revolution brought about by advances in solid state physics which have nothing to do with vacuum tubes.

One of the major functions which a research organization performs is to warn a firm of the possibility that a field of science which is unrelated to its product or the processes by which it manufactures can provide performance characteristics which would permit substitution for the company's components or intermediate products, transformation processes, or worse yet, final products. Another function, of course, is to permit the firm to take advantage of these advances before competitors do.

Here, then, is a very important role for technological forecasting. Research planning staffs must evaluate the possibility that any given area of science could provide a threat or an area which might be exploited. In those areas where such a possibility exists, a technological forecast is needed. Such a forecast should estimate the performance level to be expected and the probability that this performance level will be achieved by a certain time. Figure 6 illustrates the type of forecast which should be used.

Companies then have to decide whether they want to ignore that field of science completely, connect with it, or do supporting research in that field. If the probability of the field's development is extremely low, the company may decide it can ignore the field. If the likelihood of an advance is small, but still too big to ignore, the company may want to hire a man to do nothing but keep in touch with the field and warn the firm of any pertinent developments. Finally, if the likelihood of an advance

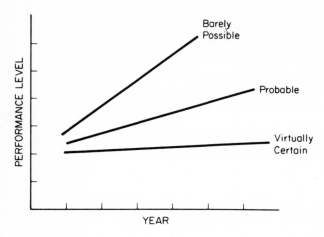

Figure 6. Forecast of Performance Obtained from a Field of Science.

is sufficiently high, a company may wish to do supporting research in that field rather than become boxed in by competitors who may gain a patent or know-how position.

PIONEERING RESEARCH

Most important is the field of pioneering research. The primary purpose of pioneering research is to give a company new products. The industrial function consists of three parts: a set of manufacturing processes and skills; a distribution system geared to reach a certain set of users; and a set of users with a common demand. These users are not really a part of the organization and, in fact, a company and its competitors are competing for them, but they are essential to operations.

If a company is to manufacture a new product, it should take advantage of at least one of these three areas. It might decide to manufacture a new product which uses current manufacturing processes and skills, but is aimed at a different market; e.g., if it manufactures automobile radios, it might decide to go into the business of making portable radios. Or it might wish to capitalize on a distribution system which is set up to reach a certain set of users. If a company currently makes one type of kitchen appliance, it might decide to manufacture a different kind, even though this called for a different set of manufacturing processes and skills, because the firm could capitalize on its present distribution system.

Finally, there are sets of users with common demands—demands which a company is satisfying only in part. Such a company might decide to go to a new product which satisfies another portion of the same demand;

e.g., nylon stockings satisfy the same demand as silk stockings although in a different fashion. These three factors, then, are the major constraints on a firm's decision on whether to go into manufacturing a specific new product.

Pioneering research can be divided into two categories: science push and demand pull. *Science push* research is that which is based on developments within a field of science. *Demand pull,* conversely, is based on the discovery or realization that there is a demand for a certain product or service but that pioneering research will be needed in order to make that product or service possible.

In science push research, the major role of technological forecasting is that of forecasting instrumentation technology. New instrumentation almost always makes possible advances in various fields of science. By way of examples from the past, the computer has tremendously speeded up old fields such as differential equations and statistics, and has even created new fields of science, such as computational linguistics. Two new techniques, nuclear magnetic resonance and electron spin resonance, both originally developed out of research in physics, have had a tremendous impact upon the field of chemistry. In some cases they make it possible to cut chemical analysis time to one-tenth or one-twentieth of that required by previous methods. A new device—the laser—is currently having a major impact on the field of aerodynamics by making it possible to examine transient flow fields and shock waves in much more detail than was previously possible.

All of these developments have had and are having tremendous impact upon many fields of science. Other devices can be foreseen which will have similar impact in the future. For instance, within the next few years, the improvements in clocks for scientific research should permit time measurements which are accurate to a resolution of one picosecond (i.e., it will be possible to divide one second into a million parts and then divide each one of those parts into a million parts). Clocks with this resolution will make it possible to test the general theory of relativity for the first time.

Another upcoming development is that of an electron microscope with a beam of energy of ten million electron volts and a resolution of about half an Angstrom unit. Since atoms have a diameter of about one to two Angstrom units, this new electron microscope will literally make it possible to take a snapshot of a molecule, showing the position of all the atoms in that molecule. The impact of this capability on the field of chemistry will be tremendous.

In a similar way, forecasts of the technology of scientific instrumentation will show which fields of science can be expected to advance most rapidly. It then becomes necessary to estimate what new products can be derived from advances in these fields. If the potential new products are of interest to an organization, then it would be desirable for the firm to do pioneering research in these fields.

Demand pull research starts at the other end. Through such things as demographic and economic analyses, demands are derived which would be difficult or impossible to satisfy without technological and scientific advances. The need for such advances may result from shortages of certain required materials, side effects of current technology, or deficiencies in current technology.

An example of a clearly predictable shortage which will call for substitutes is animal protein. It is reasonably clear that, before the end of this century, there simply will not be enough animal protein available to provide an adequate diet for all the people of the world. Some substitute is going to be necessary.

To cite another example, by the mid-1980's there will not be enough animals slaughtered to provide sufficient leather for shoes for all the people who are going to be living at that time. Some substitute for shoe leather is going to be required.

Also, as the population increases and as the literacy rate increases, within a few years there will not be enough newsprint available to print all the books and newspapers which will be required. Some substitute for newsprint will be needed.

A side effect of current technology which is clearly going to demand alternative technologies is environmental pollution. The combustion process in the automobile engine is so inefficient that we simply cannot live in an environment containing large numbers of automobiles. Some changes in the technology of automobile engines are going to be required.

Probably the classic example of inefficiency in technology is that of the manually operated telephone system. If the telephone system that we have in the United States today, handling as many calls as it now handles, had to be run with the manual operation of the 1920's, there simply would not be enough women in the United States to supply all the operators needed. Clearly, here was a demand which, in fact, was foreseen by the telephone system and the demand was met by improved technologies.

Once demands have been identified, they must be reduced to research opportunities. Figure 7 shows how this is done. First, it is necessary to lay out broad alternative approaches. For instance, if the demand to be filled is the supply of adequate protein, direct synthesis of protein, improved fishing, or breeding of plants which have adequate quantities of the necessary proteins in them might be considered.

For each of these broad alternative approaches it is necessary to define one or more processes and methods by which the approach might be realized. For instance, if it were decided that "improved methods of fishing" was a worthwhile approach to a solution for the protein prob-

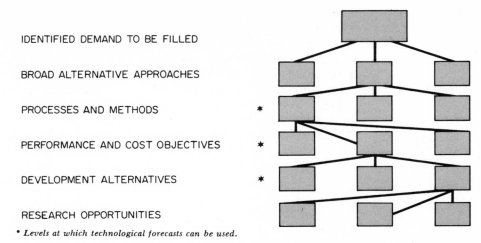

IDENTIFIED DEMAND TO BE FILLED

BROAD ALTERNATIVE APPROACHES

PROCESSES AND METHODS   *

PERFORMANCE AND COST OBJECTIVES   *

DEVELOPMENT ALTERNATIVES   *

RESEARCH OPPORTUNITIES

* *Levels at which technological forecasts can be used.*

Figure 7. Reduction of Demands to Research Opportunities.

lem, then possible processes and methods might include deliberate fish farming, new ways of catching fish in the open sea, or methods for attracting fish to a place where they could be caught.

The performance and cost objectives would have to be determined for each of these processes and methods. Clearly, high cost can be tolerated only if it is accompanied by high performance. Low performance may be tolerated if it can be obtained at low cost.

The next step is the determination of development alternatives for each of the performance and cost objectives. For instance, it might be decided to develop an electronic fish locator which would make it possible to locate fish on the open sea. In order to provide adequate performance characteristics at acceptable cost, certain technological barriers may have to be removed. This will, in turn, give rise to further research opportunities. The role of technological forecasts in this process is to forecast: (1) the cost and performance of various processes and methods, and (2) the performance of the components and materials which can be considered in development alternatives for these performance and cost objectives.

SUMMARY

The use of technological forecasts in the planning of research has a very definite concrete objective. That objective is to determine what research a firm should be doing this year, next year, and perhaps the year after, based on the products, markets, needs, and possibilities for five, ten or more years in the future. For most institutions, there is no point in forecasting the research that might be done at the end of the century or what the technology of the year 2050 will be. Primary concern is with making decisions today, for immediate research goals. These, however, must be based on a reasonable forecast of the technology that will be available or required at the time a company is interested in going into a market.

Generation and Application of Technological Forecasts for R & D Programming

A. W. SCHMIDT

D. F. SMITH

The U.S. Navy at the Marine Engineering Laboratory has developed a comprehensive program for identifying future needs and channeling the research and development activities into areas which will fulfill these requirements. The program employs projections of both capabilities and techniques. It also identifies and focuses efforts on the particular design functions of techniques which offer the most promise for future progress of that technique.

Mr. Schmidt is in charge of the Long Range Planning and Appraisal Branch of the U.S. Naval Ships System Command. His organization provides the overall requirements and missions for the system described in this chapter. Mr. Smith, head of the U.S. Navy Marine Engineering Laboratory planning function, has been instrumental in applying technological forecasts to engineering and development activities.

APPLICATION OF TECHNOLOGICAL FORECASTING

Navy Research and Development is divided into four distinct categories, to facilitate the varied handling procedures deemed appropriate for each stage of development:

RESEARCH encompasses effort directed toward increasing knowledge of natural phenomena and environment and the solution of problems in the classical sciences.

EXPLORATORY effort is directed toward expanding technological knowledge and developing materials, components, devices, and subsystems which may have military relevance.

ADVANCED projects are directed toward the solution of existing or anticipated military problems. They carry technology, components, and subsystem feasibility demonstrations into experimental and operational suitability models.

ENGINEERING EFFORT is directed toward development of systems and end items, for service inventory and use, prior to approval for procurement or operational deployment.

The primary role of exploratory development is to prove the feasibility of ideas or theories. Specific military problems, of historical naval interest or indicated in requirements documents, demand study. Possible solutions are sought through the adaptation of advanced versions of current devices or the application of new research knowledge to the particular tasks. In addition, new technological concepts which have shown practical value are continually examined for possible military applications.

Potential military values can be predicted as soon as ideas are conceived, both as the result of purpose-oriented studies and as by-products of other efforts. Typically, funds and manpower are allocated to projects on the basis of intuitive judgments of the most qualified technical managers. Progress is measured by the number of alternatives generated, the resultant increase in capabilities, or the economic aspects of the new concepts (e.g., lower cost substitutes).

Exploratory development encompasses a large number of diverse developmental efforts. Decisions must be made at middle management levels with only cursory review by higher authority. This field in the R&D spectrum needs a technique to guide these comparisons and selections. The Functional Planning Matrices (FPM) system described here is a proposed approach.

Functional Planning Matrices System (FPM)

The Navy exploratory process is continuous and has relatively stable overall resource allocations. Its end products are only categorically specified before development begins, and many are conceived during the process. The current equipments and activities of the naval forces exert strong influences on the direction of future applications. Recognition of the historical emergence of new concepts or new applications of old concepts is an inherent driving force in the management of the exploratory program.

The technical leadership in exploring applications of new scientific knowledge and techniques revolves about a primary set of philosophical concepts. Basically, some form of guidance is necessary for the developer in forming his own definition of utility and progress. This future-oriented display of needs must reflect both the possibilities offered by the advance of science and technology and the needs of transient economic and political environments. The timeliness and impact of these ideas influence the choice which must be made in expending the limited resources available.

As the development of an idea progresses, the work that is underway is reported and detailed plans for excursions from the basic idea are presented. Thus, progress is kept under scrutiny, and new decisions are made in accordance with the promise and rate of advance of supported work. A set of concepts—guidance, forecasts, proposals, priority, and progress—form the ingredients of a management tool which will improve communication among R&D directors.

Forecasts

When talking about the future, it is assumed that the present situation is understood and used as a base for the prediction. The ability to achieve a change depends not only upon the amount of allocated resources and the effective direction of efforts, but also upon the maturation of contributing technologies (i.e., the fulfillment of their promises). Awareness of these contributory promises, with some measure of their confidence (depending upon the source or consensus), is just as important to the predictor as it is to the planners who will use his forecasts. The probability distributions of forecast items are, thus, paramount to the utility of the forecast. The level of achievement possible and the time required to realize it are essential to planning future capabilities and guiding progress with confidence.

These considerations lead directly to the formulation of a communications structure which reduces the intuitiveness of decision making in exploratory development. Where intuition cannot be eliminated, it must be channeled into spotlighted steps which can then be analyzed independently to provide better understanding and guidance. A summary of the requirements for such a structure is as follows:

1. Recognize the dependence relationships between technological interests;
2. Separate short-term needs from those which need continuous or future attention;
3. Distribute all necessary information (and only that information) to groups that have a primary interest in the particular subject or need;
4. Make full use of the accepted terminology of each area;

5. Narrow the necessary depth of consideration when seeking to fulfill needs;

6. Maintain awareness of the history and potential future of an area;

7. Recognize the sphere of influence of a bit of information;

8. Advertise the interest areas of organizational groups;

9. Realize the relative importance of the various efforts undertaken;

10. Be able to measure values;

11. Record the alternatives available to a decision maker;

12. Provide a practical link for coordination of diverse efforts;

13. Be specific about the objectives of each interest;

14. Make required communications comprehensible;

15. Establish progressive continuity in the justification of programs;

16. Balance the advance of technology.

Any attempt to improve the conditions of the management process must take these many requirements into account. A system that is flexible enough to meet many of the foregoing criteria must recognize the similarity of features among the subordinate processes and satisfy their requirements in an integral manner. Such considerations have led to the formulation of the following set of functional planning matrices, which supply a unifying systematic treatment.

PARAMETERS AND DISPLAYS

Figures 1 through 9 display the planning parameters (PAR) which are employed, in the form considered to be most useful for communications purposes. (They are consolidated and tabulated in Figure 10.) The operational needs of the Navy must be recognized, studied, and displayed in such a manner that the consumer can be assured of the producer's awareness of them and, in turn, the producer can respond in an orderly fashion with an identifiable purpose.

Figure 1 portrays the primary purposes of a particular R&D effort which is being sponsored. This display can be specifically oriented to provide the basic guidance desired by OPNAV. The intents of Naval Missions, PAR (2), are combined with Strategic Concepts, PAR (1). These are both predetermined philosophies for which each combination can be assigned a "relative importance" rating. These intersections then, each with its own priority, form the elemental, qualitative operational objectives which require a search for means to fulfill.

Figure 2 displays the situations under which the preceding objectives

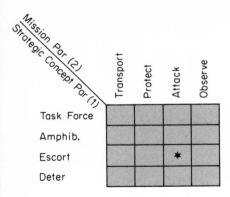

Figure 1. Objectives.

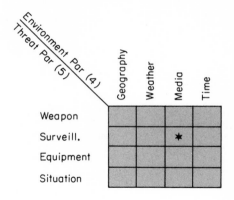

Figure 2. Situations.

must be carried out. These conditions are beyond the control of the Navy. The environmental conditions presented by nature, PAR (4), occur in combinations and at times that are independent of the needs or desires of naval forces or of enemy actions. The man-made obstacles or Threats, PAR (5), are just as random as nature but can be influenced by history, philosophy, time, and technology. These constraints determine the degree to which a primary objective can be carried out. They must be considered in evaluating the effectiveness of efforts and, in fact, are conditional units for judging utility. Estimates of probable occurrence identify their importance.

As with the primary objectives of Figure 1, the situations depicted in Figure 2 are fairly well established and change only slowly. Both can be considered as constant inputs for one cycle of the planning process. They provide the basis for all subsequent R&D efforts and the *forecast* of technological need. The value of subsequent forecasts must be related to these naval purposes.

In the real world, the action that takes place between warring nations occurs via the use of hardware. Installations or mobile forces are combinations of equipments or Units, PAR (7). Units may be fixed, transportable, or self-propelled. They are distinguishable by their ability to perform their functions independent of other Units. Figure 3 lists the concepts of Units existing, planned or proposed. This represents a *forecast* of the system entities which could be available at some time in the future.

For describing the operational needs of the Navy, the Capabilities, PAR (6), of these Units are more important than a description of the techniques used or the arrangement of Units. A simple designator, such as CVA, is sufficient to identify the Unit, but, in addition, each capability must be displayed. By definition, the Units are combinations of equip-

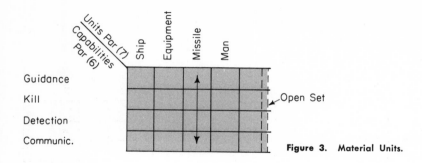

Figure 3. Material Units.

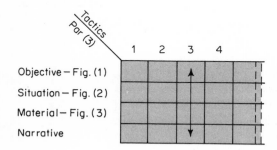

Figure 4. Op-Tasks.

ments, or systems, each of which has its own component abilities. The description for this display must exclude intrafunctional abilities and include only capabilities which directly affect the Unit's ability to perform an operational task.

Figure 4 lists Tactics, PAR (3), which are specifically formulated, in narrative form, to employ the Units of Figure 3 in the situations of Figure 2 for the purpose of attaining the objectives of Figure 1. The infinite number of combinations possible are not amenable to predetermination, but PAR (3) is designed as a cumulative listing. War games provide the most appropriate means of handling situations which are constrained by limits on available resources, capabilities, etc. Since alternative solutions to each operational problem are presented before an analysis of cost or availability is performed, these combinations of capabilities are considered to be proposals, not requirements. Each combination is called an OP-TASK, and it constitutes the basic guidance for elicitation of R&D programs. Because of the time-varying situation for each war game, one of the OP-TASKS will be the current practice or point of departure.

Each OP-TASK is a column in Figure 5. It is combined with the capabilities of the various Units needed to make this method operationally attractive. The optimization of the dispersion of the necessary capabilities not only determines the choice of vehicles, but also (where vehicles are not available) suggests new "combinations of capabilities" which must be technically analyzed as vehicle/installation systems to supplement the list of Units in Figure 3. The intersections of Figure 5 therefore constitute a set of Objectives for Technology, PAR (11).

The OP-TASK is a potential solution to a problem and does not constitute a requirement which demands the scheduled allocation of resources. Of the alternatives offered in Figure 5, the best, cheapest, or otherwise preferred choice will become known as the primary target for direction of effort, but only as emerging advances in technology permit major improvements over current OP-TASKS. By this method, an orderly progress into new systems can be attained.

The early identification of these alternatives presents a long-range plan to justify the execution of program tasks. In the terminology of current Navy R&D, the competitive set of OP-TASKS or subservient capabilities remaining after, or generated by, the prosecution of exploratory R&D provides the basis for Proposed Technical Approaches (PTA).

The approaches, after reaching, in the developer's opinion, a stage that apparently assures fulfillment of one or more Objectives for Technology, are presented for selection. The approval of a particular alternative initiates the development of a new system in the Engineering Development category of R&D.

On the other hand, indecision concerning the best choice returns the ball to the developer. If there is a valid basis for the proposal in the first place, Advanced Development Objectives (ADO) encourage concentrated effort to further definitize the existing alternatives, as well as any additional alternatives which are incited by the aroused interest. The ADO provide a revised set of ground rules which supplement those previously supplied to the developer.

As a result of this procedure, the organization responsible for the provision of a particular capability for the Navy has available to it the particular sets of conditions and levels of achievement that are deter-

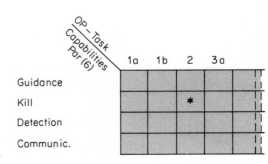

Figure 5. Objectives for Technology.

mined to have the most utility for primary naval objectives. The technological input (feedback) has been combined with operational needs and experience, and the resulting goals are specific, although not restrictive.

The primary task in generating Figures 1 through 5 is rearranging existing documentation. Two problems arise: finding the appropriate material and arranging the information on the axes of the displays so that physical handling and mental comprehension are both attained. A second major task is prescription of the responsibility assignment and procedural efforts for implementation. A third task is that of describing the complementary material-command-oriented program which uses this guidance and, in fact, prescribes the character of the guidance.

There are two responsibilities associated with an assignment of providing a capability for the Navy: (a) to maintain awareness of, familiarity with, and advancement programs for, the possible technological alternatives; and (b) to ascertain the optimum set of components which will fulfill each need. In practical exploratory development execution, each alternative solution is often a complex system containing subchoices of components. The alternatives themselves present an open set and are here called "technique sets," whereas the components of one alternative constituting a closed set are called "functions," PAR (8). Functions are the primary categories of the R&D effort.

Figure 6 displays the function and technique scope for one capability. This determination is independent of the OP-TASKS and can be thought of as a look along a row of Figure 5. Any point along this row presents two requirements for information. One is knowledge of the needs for that particular OP-TASK, PAR (11), and the other is knowledge of the status of fulfilling those needs.

The status is a combination of the current practices, the development tasks programmed, and the forecast of possibilities. Figure 7 displays the status for each component capability of one OP-TASK. The analysis of the OP-TASK establishes a compatible set of Objectives for Technology, PAR (11), which are represented as 100 per cent of the need. The status

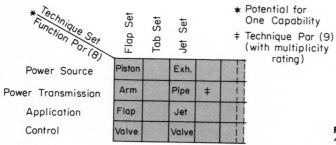

Figure 6. Function and Technique. Set for "Maneuver."

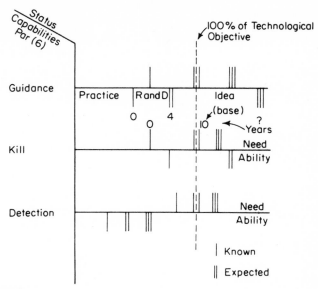

Figure 7. Status for One Op-Task.

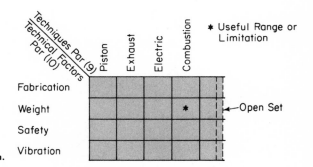

Figure 8. State of Art for One Function.

is presented relative to this need. Since the need is influenced by the time period, the effect of time is noted. The development manager decides which set of functional techniques (from Figure 6) will most likely match the requirement, and his decision is presented as an achievable level.

Since these are only potential solutions to projected needs, Figure 7 becomes the means of justifying R&D efforts. The multiplicity of applications resulting from consideration of all OP-TASKS is indicated as an indication of importance for each alternative shown in Figure 6.

The states of the arts are exhibited in Figure 8. For each function, PAR (8), which is considered necessary in Figure 6, Technical Factors,

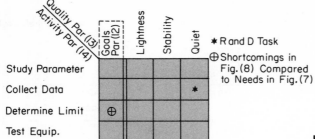

Figure 9. Program for One Function.

Figure 10. Schematic of Parameters.

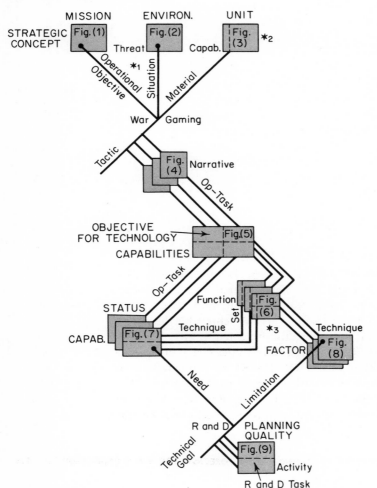

Parameters and Displays

a. Planning (PAR)ameters

    (1) Strategic Concepts (Doctrine)
    (2) Missions (Intent)
    (3) Tactics (Situation Strategy)
        (OP-TASK)
    (4) Environment (Nature)
    (5) Threat (Targets, Obstacles)
    (6) Capabilities (Tactical Concepts)
        (Technique Sets)
    (7) Units (Systems)
    (8) Functions (Capability
        Components)
    (9) Techniques (Functional
        Applications)
    (10) Factors (Technical Parameters)
    (11) Objectives for Technology
        (Utility)
    (12) Technical Goals (Advancement)
    (13) Qualities (Value)
    (14) Activities (Types of Effort)

b. Display Figures

    (1) Primary Objectives
    (2) Situation
    (3) Material Unit
    (4) OP-TASK
    (5) Objective for Technology
    (6) Potential
    (7) Status
    (8) State-of-Art
    (9) Program
    (10) FPM Structure

* Necessary Forecasts

PAR (10), are matched with the various required Techniques, PAR (9). Three benefits are derived from Figure 8: (a) functional concepts are presented in a manner independent of the capabilities which they support; (b) the intersections provide the limitations which must be overcome to obtain an advanced capability by a particular technique; and (c) the basis for judgment which helped determine the feedback of Unit capabilities of Figure 3 and the status in Figure 7 is recorded.

When the manager selects a set of functional techniques to provide a particular OP-TASK capability, he also determines the existence of possible "critical limitations which must be overcome." These Technical Goals, PAR (12), are stated in a "response."

The response takes the form of R&D tasks. These tasks do not just say "meet the objective." Instead, they are couched in terms of improving some Quality, PAR (13). The description of the effort which is necessary to accomplish the task provides a means of classifying the effort by type of Activity, PAR (14). These qualities and types of effort, which are displayed in Figure 9, are amenable to predetermined definition. The qualities provide criteria for judging the value of particular proposed R&D tasks. The activity listing provides a gradient of exploratory development, ranging from research to test and evaluation.

Management has the right, and the need, to know both the reasons for which a response is being offered and the alternatives from which the specific response was chosen. The former allows the manager to identify the significance of proposed efforts, and the latter provides managerial confidence in the supporting judgment of the developer. This information has been available in the past but has not been used in its utilitarian role. The formalized presentation of current thinking provides this link. A schematic representation of this procedure is presented in Figure 10.

Groups

The validity of various parameters can only be ascertained with the cooperation of the groups using the structure. Four types of groups share the responsibility for managing exploratory development and, consequently, for generating parameter elements (see Figure 11).

The *Operational Managers* have unique competence for establishing PAR (1), (2), (4), and (5). Their field encompasses intelligence collection, military policy establishment, strategic analysis and importance classification. Because the primary responsibility for parameter generation is theirs, they determine the terminology and the format to be used.

The *Operators* are the most fleet-oriented. Their interests lie in the utilization of available resources for assigned missions. They design tactics

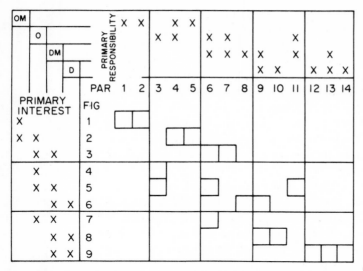

OM — Operational manager   DM — Development manager

O — Operator   D — Developer

Figure 11. Summary of Management Groups' Relationships with Parameters and Displays.

to carry out strategic concepts and are aware of the capabilities necessary to carry them out. They optimize the application of resources and evaluate the sufficiency of equipments and procedures. Therefore, they are best qualified to describe PAR (3), (4), (6), (7), and (11).

A cooperative effort is achieved by assigning PAR (4) to both Operational Managers and Operators. The overlapping of organization responsibilities allows this imprecise delegation. Another rationale for this duplication of primary interests is exemplified by PAR (7). The Operators, as users, are initially unaware of the next generation of Units emerging from advances in technology, since these are known only by the Development Managers.

The *Development Managers* generate PAR (6), (7), (8), (9), (11), and (13). They are responsible for the allocation of development resources to advance the material products available to the Operators. They are aware of the broad technological requirement spectrum and the progress in integration of the many technical details. They must choose the most timely and progressive directions from among the best programs conceived by the Developers.

The *Developers* are concerned primarily with PAR (9), (10), (12), (13), and (14). Their forte is familiarity with the state of their particular arts and familiarity with the location of technical authorities, both in-house and out. They must initiate the program offered to the Development Managers and must manage the execution of the accepted tasks. Their success enhances the material readiness of the fleet, provides the operators with better tools for their mission, justifies the decisions of the managers on allocation, and advances the state of the art involved.

The foresight of individuals in expressing and applying their ideas influences remote areas and stimulates others through revelation of possibilities. The germ of an idea can infect large surrounding areas if properly nourished. In the *forecasting* sense, this nourishment is the means of communicating possibilities to those responsible for considering such alternatives.

GENERATION OF THE TECHNOLOGICAL FORECAST

The FPM procedure is recast in flow chart form in Figures 12 and 13. It uses a combination of simulation and analysis to get from the mission requirement to the mission technical objectives. The simulation

Figure 12. USN Marine Engineering Laboratory Long-Range Planning.

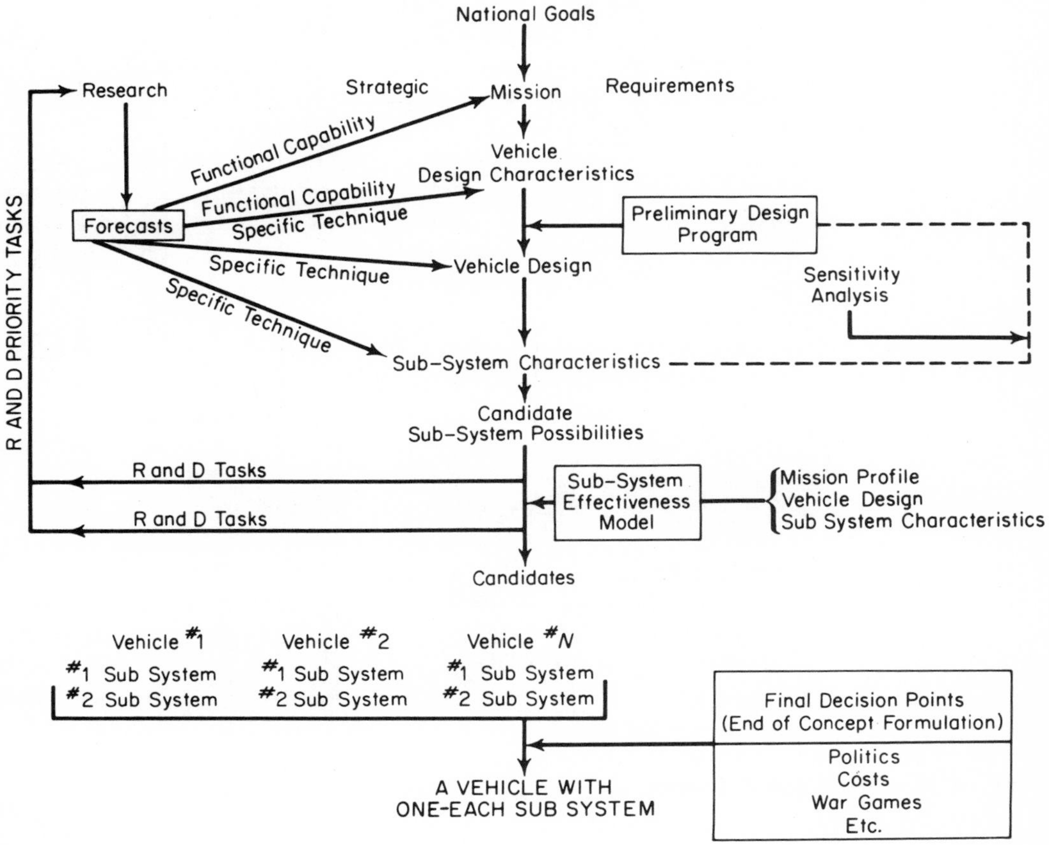

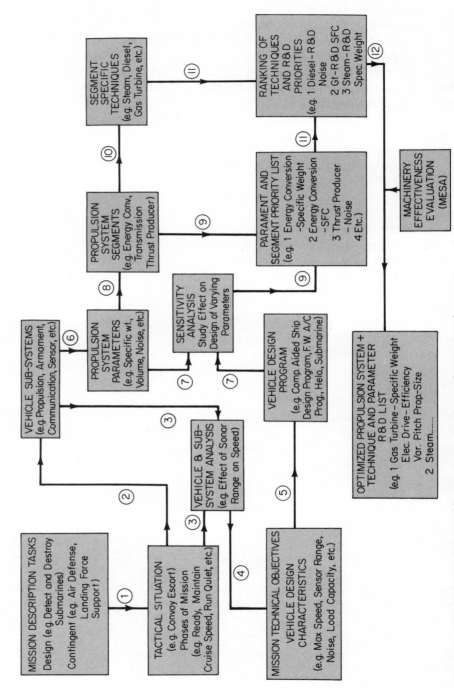

Figure 13. USN Marine Engineering Laboratory Navy Long-Range Planning Procedure.

model examines various tactical situations which combine to define each mission task. These tactical situations are broken into discrete phases. Various types of parametric vehicles are simulated for the anticipated environments. Only those operational characteristics (e.g., speed, sonar range, etc.) clearly needed to perform each phase are examined. The optimum vehicle design characteristics are selected by varying trial values within the phases of each mission. This procedure is repeated for every tactical situation which defines the mission task. For any given set of mission tasks, only those vehicle types which are common to all phases are carried through the total program procedure.

The analytic model examines the effects of hardware (subsystems) on the particular vehicle and establishes the remaining vehicle design characteristics. To accomplish this, lists of the types of subsystems required to perform each mission task are assembled in a matrix format. The significant performance parameters of the subsystems are established, and forecasts for each of their parameters are obtained. Some of the subsystems impose severe restrictions on the vehicle characteristics. For example, the performance of sonar is dependent upon the speed and noise of the vehicle on which it is mounted. Other equipments could limit the operating depth or altitude of the vehicle.

Some of the vehicle design characteristics which have already been established through simulation are now modified, to include both rigid constraints and parameter trade-offs. Finally, the vehicle's capability to perform the mission is again determined by exercising the simulation model. The physical vehicle design characteristics are determined from the forecasts. Typical forecasts required are: specific weight, volume, deck area, manning levels, and power requirements. Forecasts of support functions for men and equipment are also needed. From this forecast information and the list of subsystems, it is possible to approximate the size and physical layout of the vehicle. (Figure 14 presents a schematic of the terminology which is involved.)

The mission analysis procedure can be presented best by example. Assume a mission task to be, "detect enemy submarines." Under some conditions, "many small ships" would be more effective than "one large ship," and "many aircraft plus many small ships" would be still more effective. To use a simulation model to determine what ship, ships, or mix should be used, some constraints are required. Either a total cost, a mission effectiveness, or some other criteria must be specified. Cost would restrict the number and size of ships that could be built and employed to perform the task. Mission effectiveness criteria should define the objectives in such a manner that they might be achieved by one vehicle or possibly a combination of two types of vehicles. A typical mission effectiveness criterion would be to achieve a probability of detection of Y within an X-radius range.

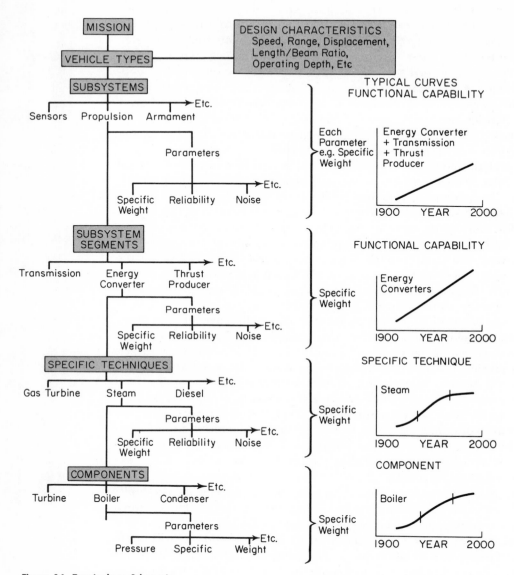

Figure 14. Terminology Schematic.

The constraints that must be imposed depend on the answers to such questions as whether the vehicle is to operate as part of a task force, to defend a convoy, or singly to defend the coastline. In other words, unless the statement of mission tasks is sufficiently detailed, many different answers will result. Furthermore, because most vehicles are multi-purpose and generally are required to perform more than one task, many varied simulation runs must be made to determine the effect of the varied conditions on the vehicle characteristics. From initial work in this area, it appears that, although many different mission tasks can be ascribed to a vehicle, there are many phases of all of those missions which are common. Consequently, several types of missions might be achieved by incorporating a few additional design characteristics. This planning procedure should display the operational flexibilities that can be gained in terms of the additional cost and complexity.

The time period during which any given vehicle characteristic is utilized may be the entire mission or only some part of it. A mission can then be described in terms of the uses which will be made of the characteristic resources. These actions form a few basic categories which are repeated, in various combinations, until the mission goal is achieved. The characteristics are the catalogued set of general actions required to accomplish any mission. These categories are also expressions of the stress levels placed upon the vehicles subsystem characteristics during that time period. As an example, the activity phase "Vehicle Delivery" refers to the activity period commencing when the vehicle leaves port and ending when it reaches the mission destination. This activity phase places various requirements upon such characteristics as: cruising speed, top speed, defensive surveillance capability, and others.

The order and timing of these actions are specified by the tactics. The FPM analysis is order-free and thus independent of any tactics the military may want to use. It is necessary only to know the relative frequency with which the different activity categories are used, and this should be obtainable from record histories. The mission and vehicle characteristics are then analyzed in terms of the stress levels imposed by the various mission phases. A combined matching and elimination procedure locates feasible matches of vehicle hardware characteristic possibilities to mission needs. Different missions require different degrees of vehicle characteristics, and this leads to a desire for specialized vehicles. On the other hand, when a group of missions requires similar vehicle characteristics, a standardized multimission vehicle could be envisioned.

While the total mission analysis is complex, the basic inputs are simple and easily understood. For example, the mission phase "Ready" (fueling, supplies, engine start) is common in some way to all vehicles. The operating characteristics (e.g., cruising speed or burst speed) are understood and can be related to the mission phases in a very reasonable way.

The analysis and mathematical programming of the matrix model results in several vehicle types or combinations of types, a measure of the capability of each to perform the mission, and a statement of the vehicle design characteristics. The vehicle design characteristics are the input to the preliminary design program which will be described below. The result of this work can then be tentatively verified by simulation and war gaming under the impact of whatever tactics the military participants may wish to devise.

Trend Extrapolation

The FPM procedure employs forecasting as a primary tool. Technological forecasting extrapolates data from a set of curves which summarize the history of any given technology over its life span. It produces justifiable predictions as to where the future state of the art will be for any given technology. To establish the potential benefits of this form of forecasting, a procedure was developed for ship propulsion systems that would be applicable to other Navy vehicle subsystems. At this stage of evolution, it appears that a valid procedure, providing a high confidence level, has been developed.

Two types of forecasting curves are used in the procedure: "specific technique" and "functional capability." A specific technique curve presents the level of development of the technique at any particular point in time. Thus far, the following propulsion system techniques have been investigated: steam, diesel, simple and regenerative cycle gas turbine energy converters, and mechanical and electric drive transmissions.

A functional capability curve presents the maximum capability (over the years) of any subsystem which can perform the desired function. The capability is independent of any particular specific technique. The functional capability curve is the envelope of the maximum development levels taken from all of the specific techniques that can perform the function. Historically, it plots as a straight line on a semilog graph and is simple to extrapolate.

SPECIFIC TECHNIQUE FORECAST CURVES

First, historical data were collected for each technique. This was done initially for three representative parameters: specific weight, volume, and fuel consumption. These data were obtained from a thorough survey of the literature and discussions with manufacturers, other Navy installations, government agencies and the Maritime Commission. The data were recorded, and an envelope curve which connected the maximum points over the years was plotted for each parameter and for each technique.

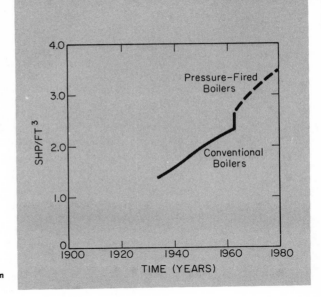

Figure 15. Specific Technique Marine Steam System (Shaft Horsepower Per Unit Volume—SHP/FT³).

The curves generally exhibit three distinct phases. The first occurs at the basic research or laboratory level, where the concept is proved. The rate of improvement at the beginning is slight. Once a technique has been proved feasible, there is generally a significant increase in the funding and manpower level, resulting in a rapid rise in the parameter capability. Finally, as physical or material limits are approached, the improvement levels off.

When the plotted historical data indicated that a parameter had reached a plateau, it was necessary to ascertain that these limits were, in fact, physical or material and not caused by a shortage of funds or investigators. The specific technique curve for steam (Figure 15) is a case in point. The specific volume had apparently reached a plateau when suddenly the pressure-fired boiler was developed, became operational, and significantly changed the parameter values. The plateau, in this case, was not due to physical or material limits. Because this pressure-fired boiler represented a breakthrough, the curve was broken by a major step to show this significant change in capability. If the future extrapolation of the parameters had been based on historical data alone, they would have shown a significant discrepancy from what is now available. Accordingly, the parameters of significant components of such techniques were investigated to separate true plateaus from potentially high payoff areas.

Technical developments of these items at the basic research and development level were investigated. From these, an extrapolation or forecast was made for each of the pertinent parameters of these components. By correlating component data with the historical specific weight, volume, and fuel consumption curves of the technique, it was possible to make a valid forecast at the technique level.

FUNCTIONAL CAPABILITY FORECAST CURVES

After establishing forecasts of techniques, a functional capability forecast was made for subsystems in general. This was accomplished by assembling the technique curves for each parameter and drawing envelope curves (as in Figure 16). Since application and natural environment are influencing factors on technology, both aircraft and marine applications were considered in the forecasts. The envelope curve for these examples did turn out to be an exponential curve (which plots as a straight line on a semilog graph) as expected.

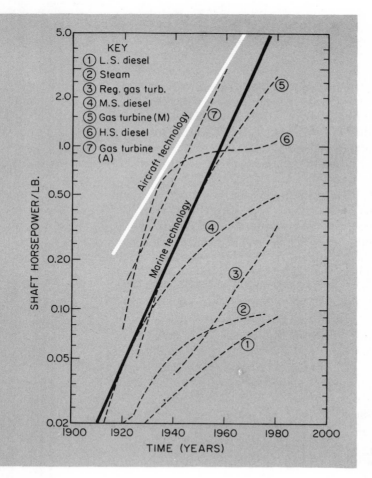

KEY
① L.S. diesel
② Steam
③ Reg. gas turb.
④ M.S. diesel
⑤ Gas turbine (M)
⑥ H.S. diesel
⑦ Gas turbine (A)

Figure 16. Functional Capability Energy Converters (Specific Weight).

To perform a complete forecast, the following additional parameters must be considered: reliability, maintainability, ease of automation, noise, costs, manning requirements, maneuverability, and availability. Present plans provide for the forecasting of only two of these additional parameters. The two selected, noise and reliability, are difficult to assess, and their inclusion will subject the program to a more severe test of creditability. The reliability study is a contractor-assisted effort, while the noise study is being conducted as an in-house effort.

The *vehicle design program* will accept the vehicle design characteristics as goals. It will produce a preliminary vehicle sufficiently detailed to enable analysis of the effects of changes in the various subsystem parameters. Vehicles, as used in this program, may be surface ships (combatant, cargo, support), fixed-wing aircraft, helicopters, submarines, foil or air-cushion-borne craft, or some new type not yet categorized.

A computerized vehicle design program will be the final output of this phase. This program will be made up of individual subprograms, one for each category of vehicle. The subprograms will be modifications of existing programs, such as the destroyer computer-aided ship design program. A Marine Engineering Laboratory (MEL) submarine program is available in-house, and it can be adapted for this purpose. Aircraft companies have been contacted, and it appears that both fixed-wing and helicopter programs, suitable for adaptation, will be available when required.

The destroyer program, modified to satisfy the requirements of the FPM procedure, will serve as a model for the other vehicle design programs. The modification will include: programming for the MEL computer (IBM 360), changing the propulsion section to accept the functional capability curves, and adding an optimization procedure to permit the incorporation of a sensitivity analysis.

The absence of a vehicle-measuring standard in the present destroyer program precludes the addition of an optimization procedure. Ship displacement is one possible criterion, when only the propulsion system specific weight, volume, and fuel consumption are used. However, the standard is inadequate when reliability, maintainability, and noise level parameters are added. Therefore, the major requirement for this portion of the FPM procedure will be to obtain vehicle-measuring standards, in the form of effectiveness criteria, which reflect the mission requirements and will apply to all the various subsystem parameters.

Subsystem Sensitivity and Optimization

The interaction of the subsystems, the effect of their parameters on the vehicle, the subsystem optimization, and the determination of R&D tasks are established by the analytical program shown in Figure 17.

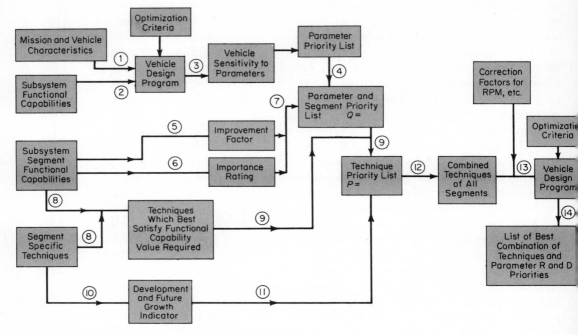

Figure 17. Subsystem Sensitivity and Optimization Analysis.

To perform the sensitivity analysis, vehicle-measuring standards are required. Since these are lacking at present, this portion of the program has been deferred. Once the criteria are established, the values of subsystem parameters that are used in the computerized vehicle design program will be varied. The range of values will be taken from the subsystem functional capability curves. This will result in a parameter priority list determined by the relative effects of the subsystem parameters on the vehicle.

Starting with this priority list as one input and the functional capability forecasts as another, the program calculates an improvement factor (I_f) and an importance rating for each of the subsystem segments.

$$I_f = \frac{V_f - V_p}{V_p}$$

where V_f is the value of the segment parameter in the required year [1] and V_p is its present value. The improvement factor is a measure of growth

---

[1] Required year means the year when the design is frozen.

potential, and as such, it indicates where future R&D funding should be applied. This will assure that scarce R&D funds are not expended in areas that have little or no growth potential.

The importance rating is derived by determining which of the segments of the subsystem has the greatest effect on the parameter. For example, in a propulsion system, if the parameter being examined is weight, an importance rating is given to the segments (the energy converter, the transmission, or the thrust producer) according to which is the heaviest. This comparison is made from the forecast curves of the parameter corresponding to the present year.

For each parameter at the subsystem segment level, the improvement factor and importance rating are normalized and multiplied together. These values are combined [2] with the normalized subsystem level parameter priority list (from the sensitivity analysis). The combination yields the subsystem segment—parameter priority list, Q, which is the R&D priority list. Thus, the initial sensitivity analysis rating of the parameters is modified to include the effects of the improvement factor and importance rating. Q is normalized to rank proposed R&D tasks.

The type of subsystem to be employed is established by determining which specific techniques best satisfy the requirements set by the segment parameter priority list, Q. To do this, the forecast parameter values in the required year are compared with the values from the subsystem segment functional capability curves. For this comparison, an acceptable lower limit is selected for the functional capability values. The specific techniques which show values falling above this limit are rated on the basis of their potential. Segments made up of combinations of techniques are also rated by this method. All the techniques (including combinations) are then ranked for a particular parameter. This rating is designated P^1.

In calculating combinations of techniques for subsystem segments, both "or" and "and" systems are considered. Typical combinations for propulsion system segments would be combination diesel *or* gas turbine (CODOG) and combination diesel *and* gas turbine (CODAG).

Since two or more techniques may have equal potential for a particular parameter in the required year, the program will calculate a development and future growth indicator to assist in the final selection. The development indicator is the ratio of the value in the required year to that in the present year. Such an indicator is useful if two techniques provide the same capability in the required year. On the basis of R&D expenditures, the one that requires the least development would appear to be the most

---

[2] The method of combination has not been determined yet. At this time, addition appears to be the best approach.

desirable, not only because the least cost is involved, but also because the chances of reaching the capability are greater. However, a further consideration which influences the choice is growth factor. To obtain a measure of this, the value of the parameter in the required-year-plus-five years (arbitrary choice) is divided by the value in the required year, to give an indication of the future growth potential of the technique.

The criteria employed for the consideration of development indicators and growth potential depend on the economic, military, or political climate existing at the time such consideration is required. The answers may be vastly different in times of peace, cold war, or imminence of war.

For every subsystem segment and parameter combination, a ranking is calculated for the techniques still being considered, and their parameters. To accomplish this, the P^1's for each parameter of a technique are multiplied together, and the result is designated as P. This ranking (P) reflects the capability of the technique to satisfy the vehicle requirements. A list of the P's represents the end of the optimization procedure for each subsystem segment. What remains to be done is to combine the various P's to achieve a set of complete subsystems that can be fed back into the vehicle optimization criteria.

Ship propulsion subsystems using gas turbines of simple and regenerative cycles have been chosen to illustrate how this method of forecasting can be applied. Forecasts of specific weight (shaft horsepower per pound), volume (shaft horsepower per cubic foot), and fuel consumption (pounds of fuel per shaft horsepower per hour) for the subsystem segments are presented. The forecasts present a history and prediction of the maximum capability of the parameters under consideration. The maximum capability at any particular time has several constraints, the primary one being the funding level. Certainly, if cost had been no object, significant changes would have occurred in the development of certain techniques.

Some areas, particularly the specific weight and volume of transmission systems, have received little impetus for improvement, as evidenced by a history of little R&D funding. Consequently, the specific technique curves so far developed for transmissions (but not included here) have flattened out, indicating that a limit has been approached. Investigation of subparameters and the technical approaches involved reveals that, in this case, the limit has been a combination of funding and acceptable noise output. Studies are currently under way to determine what an extrapolation of the curve could look like if funding and noise constraints were liberalized. The result will be additional forecasts for these systems. These new forecasts will then be used as inputs to the subsystem sensitivity analysis program, to determine if the easing of these constraints is worthwhile. This application of forecasting illustrates one way the procedure can be used in system formulation.

FORECAST OF THE FUTURE STATE OF THE ART

Marine gas turbines have a tremendous potential for development, and the possibilities for high-power, lightweight, compact power plants are unmatched in any other type of plant. These characteristics are particularly vital for powering the "new concept vessels" (hydrofoils, air cushion craft, etc.) now under development.

A rapid growth in the horsepower capacity of gas turbine units has occurred (Figure 18). Engines as large as 43,000 hp have been built, and units exceeding 50,000 hp are projected. This growth trend will probably continue but at a lesser rate as limitations of mechanical, thermal, and ducting size factors apply. However, much larger power outputs will be obtained by using multiple gas generators to drive a single power turbine. Power outputs as high as 150,000 hp have already been attained by this method.

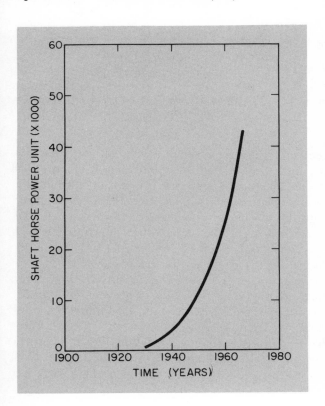

Figure 18. Gas Turbine Maximum Power Capacity.

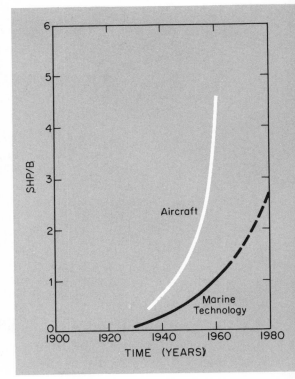

Figure 19. Specific Technique Simple Cycle Gas Turbine (Shaft Horsepower per Unit Weight).

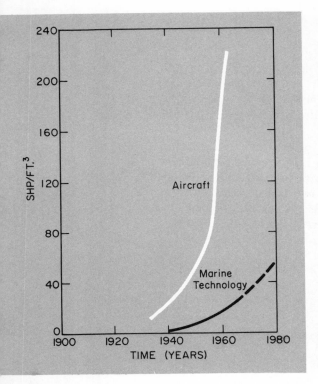

Figure 20. Specific Technique Simple Cycle Gas Turbine (Shaft Horsepower per Unit Volume).

Figure 21. Specific Technique Simple Cycle Gas Turbine (Specific Fuel Consumption).

The development trends for the specific weight, volume, and fuel consumption for the simple cycle gas turbine are presented in Figures 19 through 21. The engine components, namely, the compressor, combustion chamber, and turbine, were investigated to determine their development trends. As shown in Figure 22, the compressor, combustion chamber, and turbine efficiencies have reached a plateau. Any future improvement will be limited; consequently, these component efficiencies will have an insignificant effect on the future engine characteristic parameters.

The compressor pressure ratio has increased significantly during recent years, but any further increase will be small. This is because compressors are now designed (because of improvements in blade loading) to an optimum pressure ratio which is determined by turbine inlet temperature. Blade loading, which has enabled the engines to obtain higher pressures with fewer stages, appears to be approaching a practical limit. The addition of more heat energy within the same basic engine configuration has been the major contributing factor to the recent and future improvement in the engine characteristic parameters. Therefore, the parameter that will have a significant effect on the engine is the turbine inlet temperature. The increase of inlet temperature is presented in Figure 23. The extrapolation of the curve to temperatures in excess of 3000°F. is based on laboratory tests in which operating temperatures as high as 4000°F. have been achieved. The specific weight, volume, and fuel consumption improvement parallels that of the turbine inlet temperature.

Additional savings in the weight and volume of the gas turbines can be expected by utilizing improved materials and better structural designs and blade-cooling techniques. These techniques have, of course, been employed to increase inlet temperature to today's figures, but major improvement in these areas is still possible.

Another by-product of the better materials and design criteria has been the reduction of the hub-tip ratios of the compressors achieved by lengthening the blades and increasing the blade tip speeds. The result

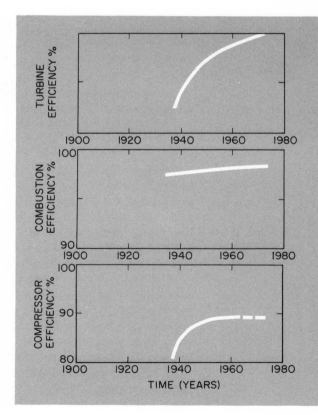

Figure 22. Gas Turbine Component Characteristics.

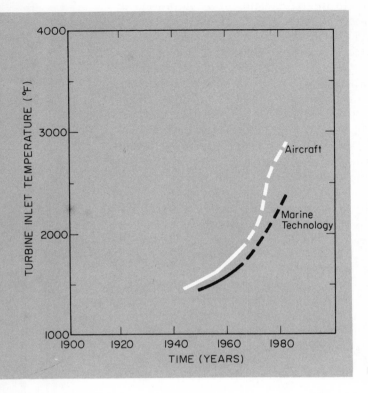

Figure 23. Gas Turbine Inlet Temperature.

of this is the small frontal area and reduced volume associated with axial flow gas turbines.

Regenerative Gas Turbine

The forecast curves of the specific weight, volume, and fuel consumption for the regenerative gas turbine are presented in Figures 24 through 26. Excluding the regenerator, the other components of the regenerative cycle gas turbine are identical to the simple cycle. Accordingly, the discussion already presented for the simple cycle is applicable to the regenerative cycle.

As demonstrated by the figures, the regenerator is the major contributor to the weight and volume of the system. It is for this reason that present regenerators are designed for approximately 80 per cent recovery. An increase in the recovery to 90 per cent would result in a weight increase of approximately 2.5 times the present value. Improvements in weight and volume of the regenerator through improved structural and

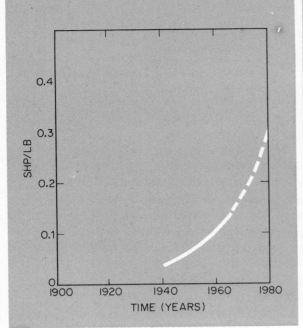

Figure 24. Specific Technique Regenerative Cycle
Gas Turbine (Shaft Horsepower per Unit Weight).

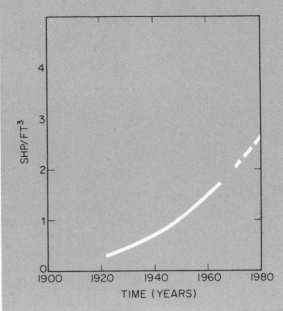

Figure 25. Specific Technique Regenerative Cycle
Gas Turbine (Shaft Horsepower per Unit Volume).

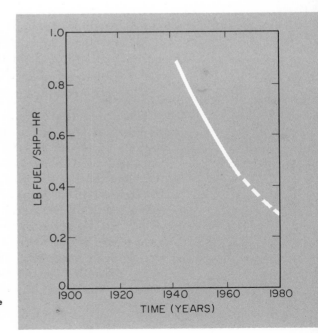

Figure 26. Specific Technique Regenerative Cycle
Gas Turbine (Specific Fuel Consumption).

thermodynamic design, which are expected, should result in higher recovery and improved specific fuel consumptions (SFCs).

HIGH PAYOFF AREAS

Research and development effort should be concentrated in the following areas on the basis of the high payoff possibilities of the potential improvements:

1. Cooling of turbine blades and other hot components. This will allow higher turbine inlet temperatures, which will, in turn, lead to significantly improved performance levels.
2. New materials and protective coatings for turbine blades and other hot components. This will increase high-temperature capabilities by increasing resistance to high-temperature oxidation and sulfidation. An increased resistance to thermal fatigue and creep is also required.
3. Improved materials, designs, and fabrication techniques for regenerators, to reduce their cost, weight, and bulk.
4. Further application and adaptation of aircraft gas turbines and technologies to marine service.

LOW PAYOFF AREAS

Technical areas wherein relatively low payoff for the expended effort could be expected, include:

1. Attempts to improve efficiency of combustion, compressor, and turbine. These efficiencies in the best existing units are about as high as can reasonably be obtained.
2. Attempts to significantly increase blade loading or compressor pressure ratio unless accompanied by major design changes.

Once the technique for technological forecasting has been determined, the practical problems of implementation have to be overcome. These are basically of two categories. The first can be considered technical, and is comprised of such items as parameter and function definitions, analysis of factors contributing to functional performance, origin and span of the life cycle of the functions, and breakdowns of the subsystems and subsystem segments into their proper elements, in addition to the problem of locating the necessary technical data. The second category of problems is concerned with people. These problems are of major importance to the success of the forecasting effort and are the most difficult to resolve. The major difficulties are the usual ones which arise when people become involved in the "loop" of technology; e.g., subjectivity, pre-formed opinions, bias, etc.

The selection of the parameters is the first step in preparing a technological forecast for any area of interest. Experience indicates the desirability of selecting parameters that can be considered independent of any specific technology or constraint which derives from man-generated rules or regulations. Selecting such parameters is not a simple task, as subjective interpretation could include, or rule out, almost any suggested capability. The approach used at the Marine Engineering Laboratory was to seek out individuals who were considered experts in their fields and ask them to choose the parameters. As an example, to establish the future possibilities of an energy converter for the propulsion system of a ship, one must have forecasts of at least the following parameters: specific weight, specific volume, efficiency, and total power capacity per unit. These predictions, or forecasts, are associated with marine energy converters in general, and the optimums of each capability represent, in summation, an idealized energy converter. A unit incorporating the optimum value of each of the forecast capabilities will probably never be achieved because some of the capabilities are, in a sense, contradictory. The lightest system generally does not give the highest power per unit, etc. However, these functional capabilities do represent a set of potentially achievable goals for development programs.

The same considerations arose in selecting the parameters to be forecast for specific techniques. To continue the example of energy converters for a ship propulsion system, if a selection is to be made on other than a subjective basis, forecasts of the following parameters must be available: specific weight, specific volume, efficiency, reliability, maintainability, ease of automation, noise, and cost. Furthermore, these parameters must be related to each other for each technique under consideration. It would certainly be fallacious to select the diesel engine as the best technique, solely on the basis of efficiency and ease of automation, without, at the same time, accepting the fact that diesels are not the lightest or quietest, etc.

Once the problems of parameter selection have been solved and the areas of data gathering have been delineated, the problem of "what constitutes valid data" must be faced. The researcher gathering the data must be sufficiently knowledgeable in the technical area to reject "fluke" data points but open-minded enough to accept valid points beyond his personal expectations. The U.S. Navy Marine Engineering Laboratory (MEL) utilized engineers who were trained in the technical area (i.e., electrical engineers for electric drives, mechanical engineers for steam and diesel, etc.), but were not considered "expert," to do the literature research and to plot the historical data.

For functional capability curves, "record setters" and experimental units were investigated to insure that peak values were used. Only data from operational equipment were used for the specific technique curves so that the curves reflected only practical capabilities. Each data point was thoroughly documented and filed. These files proved extremely valuable when the curves were being reviewed by the "experts," since many arguments occurred when data points did not agree with subjective opinions.

In searching for data, the technical library was invariably the starting point. The early data were obtained from classical texts and the life span of the technology established. Technical reports generally provided recent data, particularly reports of ships trials. In the case of ship propulsion, the files of NAVSHIPS were a prime source, although industry was most helpful.

Data gathering is the most time-consuming portion of forecast generation, and the cost, in time, is not insignificant. In some cases (e.g., reliability) no good data exist in recognizable form and any which are collected must be accumulated at the source (i.e., ship records, shipyards, manufacturers, etc.) and reduced before they are useful in forecasting.

For the extrapolated portions of the specific technique curves, which are, in fact, the forecasts, several constraints were imposed. First, wherever possible, a theoretical limit was established, and this indicated a capability that could not be exceeded, or even approached too closely. Second, the functional capability curves were monitored because, without a scientific breakthrough, these would not be exceeded by any specific technique. Third, and of most significance, the design functions of the specific techniques were examined for those components and/or subparameters which had the most influence on the performance of the equipment. Once the most important contributors were identified, forecasts were made to show how much improvement could be expected as a result of anticipated improvement in the component or design limits. When forecasting at the subparameter level, experimental units, laboratory tests, and basic research results were used to estimate likely advances in the state of the art.

Finally, related technical fields were examined to learn of technological advances in other areas which might have been ahead of the area being investigated. An example of this is shown in Figure 16, where the curves of aircraft propulsion technology lead those of marine propulsion.

In forecasting marine propulsion, ease of automation has been listed as an essential parameter. Since this parameter is not forecastable, at least by the same technique as used for other parameters, it was treated on a per-case basis and a ranking technique was used, based on complexity. This complexity number reflected the amount of automation which was possible, its desirability from a cost-effectiveness viewpoint, the state of the art for the technique under consideration, and, therefore, the amount of development which had to be undertaken and the effect the degree of automation might have on the missions for which the equipment would be used.

Probably the first reaction to technological forecasting is one of skepticism. Admittedly, the procedures described here are no crystal ball, providing a clear look into the future. However, the lack of certainty regarding the future does not materially depreciate the value of forecasting for long-range planning purposes. If one can delineate factors that have contributed to the state-of-the-art advancement and plot their progress over the years to establish trends, these trends will continue unless stopped by external constraints such as the reaching of a theoretical limit or the displacement by a new technique with clearly superior capabilities. Surely the inability to predict the future exactly should not negate the value of the indications these projections provide. Another argument against skepticism might well be that the accuracy of the forecast (i.e., quantitative predictions) is relatively unimportant, and it is only the trend that is of interest. Accepting this, errors, even on the order of 50 per cent, would have little effect on the usefulness of the forecast.

Another "people" problem is the tendency to reject as exceptions any data which do not agree with preconceived ideas. This is especially prevalent among the "experts," and is evidenced by claims that the data are "obviously in error," are the result of artificial conditions, or are not usable because the facts come from nonconventional sources. In the MEL, the validity was judged by how well the data plotted in relation to other data and agreed with functional capability curves and theoretical limits. In general, the MEL curves were generated by drawing envelope curves. Unexplained high capability points were not included.

Another problem related to whether or not the levels of effort which had been applied in the past to some techniques would continue to be applied in the future. Some individuals believed that a certain technique had come into disfavor with higher levels of Navy management and that support for that technique could be expected to be withdrawn, thereby implying an artifically generated change in the slope of the progress curve. On the assumption that these periods of favor and disfavor generally alternate during the life span of any technology and, therefore, have been present throughout the historical parts of the curve, the MEL philosophy ignored such implications and assumed that the combined effects which produced the history would continue relatively unchanged in the future.

All subjectivity should be eliminated both in gathering historical data and in preparing forecasts. However, this is an impossible thing to do.

The only solution to this problem is to constantly emphasize the necessity of complete objectivity and hope for the best. This is not to imply that good forecasts cannot be made on a subjective basis; in fact, some of the most accurate predictions have been made completely subjectively. The big difficulty in broadly applying such a technique is that there is no way that the engineering community can assign a confidence level to subjective forecasts. The MEL forecasts might well be questioned regarding confidence levels; however, the rationale is visible and can be universally applied at the same confidence level, whatever that may be. If a statistical regression analysis were used to generate the forecasts, the curves would exhibit a much higher confidence level, but the forecasts would be extremely conservative and of no value in the long-range planning of R&D. In summation it may be said that the MEL forecasts attempted to pick a middle ground between subjectivity and statistical extrapolation by injecting a substantial dose of logic.

Technological Forecasting in Product Planning, with Emphasis on Systems Development

HOWARD A. WELLS

The objective of all product planning groups is to select the most desirable products from among current or future alternatives. Product planning guides assist managers with such decisions. They identify future environments (scenarios) and product lines. Then, by forcing managements to quantify their objectives and relate individual product contributions to the attainment of these objectives for each scenario, these guides assist in identifying the most advantageous product development activities for firms.

Dr. Wells is presently Associate Director for Operations Research in the Future Systems Research Department of Bell Aerosystems Company. Previously, he had been Chief of the Planning Activities Control Office for the U.S. Air Force Systems Command. Since 1957, he has been engaged in technological forecasting, starting with resource allocation models used to prepare R&D budgets. Some of his early work has grown into the Air Force "Systems Planning Guide" for selecting from among various systems alternatives.

If companies wish to exert technological product leadership, they must forecast the feasibility of attaining various levels of technology, or states of the art. Usually, forecasts are required for a large number of seemingly unrelated technologies. This is obvious in the case of a complex product such as a major military weapon system. Even for a fairly simple product, forecasts must be made concerning technologies that could produce competing products. Many nontechnical forecasts are also required to establish the environmental assumptions concerning the future characteristics of the market and of the individual company.

During the past ten years, the U.S. Air Force has conducted several massive technological forecasting exercises. These exercises were intended to provide the basis for planning decisions concerning the advancement of broad technologies through exploratory development; advanced development demonstrations to establish feasibility of some specific technique; and the engineering development of major weapon systems. Two of the problems observed in most of these exercises were the very human tendencies (1) to forecast those fields of greatest familiarity, and (2) to emphasize the criteria most favorable to the preconceived notions of the participants. These problems were minimized in those instances where a planning guide of some type had been established at the beginning of the exercise. This provided a checklist to assure that all relevant criteria were considered thoroughly and objectively. This chapter describes some of the principles used in these planning guides and shows how the concept can be applied to industrial product planning.

PRODUCT PLANNING GUIDE

The objective of all product planning groups, in industry or in government, is to select the most desirable products from among the current and future alternatives. A product is relatively more desirable when it has greater utility, greater feasibility (or lower risk), and lower cost.

$$\frac{\text{PRODUCT}}{\text{DESIRABILITY}} = \frac{\text{UTILITY} \times \text{FEASIBILITY}}{\text{COST}}$$

It is sometimes argued that in certain monopolistic markets or in certain cost-plus-fixed-fee contractual arrangements, cost should appear in the numerator of this equation. However, this argument confuses price with cost. In any event, these are rare situations today and should not be allowed to detract from the general principle.

If these three factors—utility, feasibility, and cost—could be expressed as single-valued quantities, the product desirability could be estimated easily. However, this is not the case. Each factor is composed of a great many subfactors, and each varies considerably over time (often in an unexpected manner) as forecasts are projected further and further into the future. (See Figure 1.) The problem facing the product planner at this point, then, is how to consider explicitly all of the subfactors involved in the decision and how to express their relative importance. Most of these factors and subfactors depend quite heavily on technical estimates and military and/or management judgments. The most productive approach to this situation is to break the problem into segments which can be supported by measurements or quantitative data and segments which must be handled by using the judgment of groups of experts.

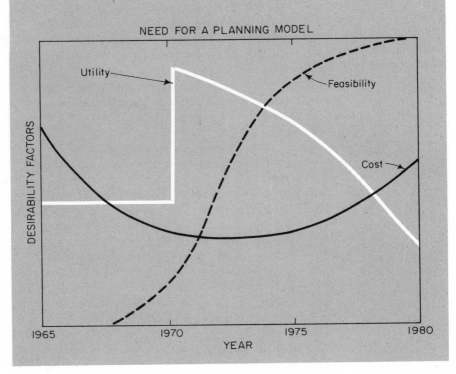

Figure 1. Example of Variation of Utility, Feasibility, and Cost.

A computer is most useful for storing, tracking, and relating the many judgments, once these relationships have been identified. Even though the computations are usually quite simple, it is also useful to have a computer provide an immediate calculation of the impact of new data or changes in judgments whenever it is feasible to establish such man-machine interfaces. Such real-time iterations of the planning problem permit the person who is making a judgment to adjust his thinking if the problem is more sensitive to a particular factor than he expected. This also helps to minimize over-reaction to dramatic pieces of information or emotional elements of the problem. It should be emphasized that the computer, and the entire planning guide for that matter, is only an aid to the planner's judgment, not a substitute for it.

There are four major steps in the approach to the development and use of a product planning guide: (1) to identify the product lines, planing periods, and scenarios [1] of interest; (2) to evaluate the utility, feasibil-

_____

[1] Scenarios are descriptions of future environments which are pertinent to the characteristics of the product and the time periods of the forecast.

ity, and cost of each product; (3) to calculate the desirability of each product using these evaluations; and (4) to select products until some constraint is encountered.

The product mix to be evaluated should normally include all of the current product lines as well as potential new products. Usually, it is possible to forecast future periods when some of the present products are likely to become so undesirable that they should be replaced by new ones. This option should always be considered, even for the shiny new product just introduced. A preliminary estimate of expected availability dates should be made for each of the new products. (This estimate will be refined during the course of the planning exercise.) The planning period should be long enough to encompass the expected lifetime of most of the potential new products as well as the current product lines. This permits consideration of total lifetime utility of each product. A shorter planning period penalizes new products in favor of established lines.

The scenarios selected for the planning guide should be based on the most realistic forecasts available for each of the environmental factors which are expected to influence the products of interest. Economic forecasting is important and should be included explicitly in every scenario. Other market factors must also be included; for example, if the organization is involved with military products, it will be important to obtain forecasts of the intensities of violence expected in military operations during the planning period. All of the relevant forecasts should be combined into at least three complete scenarios—a most likely, an optimistic, and a pessimistic, with respect to the expected impact on the overall operations and welfare of the organization.

The next step requires value judgments at the highest level of abstraction in the entire model. The significance of these judgments are such that they probably should be made by the highest level of responsibility in the organization. An estimate must be made of (1) the likelihood of occurrence of each scenario (or of a real situation sufficiently similar to it for planning purposes), and (2) the consequences to the organization if each occurs. A multiplication of these value judgments for each scenario will provide an index of the relative emphasis that should be placed on planning for that type of situation. Multiplication is the method selected for this combination because the emphasis should go to zero if either the likelihood or the consequences were to be judged as zero. (See Figure 2.)

Each major company objective and policy should then be evaluated to determine its relative importance in the context of each scenario. For purposes of illustration, Figure 3 uses profitability, gross sales, product balance, and company image as the objectives to be evaluated. These are aggregate objectives and are composites of a great many components. Although most people in a particular company are concerned with the com-

Type of Environment	Likelihood of Occurrence		Consequences if it Does Occur		Relative Emphasis
I	0.4	×	8	=	3.2
II	0.4	×	5	=	2.0
III	0.2	×	10	=	2.0

Figure 2. Emphasis on Preparation for Various Environments (hypothetical example)

Company Objectives and Policies	Environmental Projection		
	Environment I	Environment II	Environment III
Profitability	8	10	8
Gross sales	10	5	2
Product balance	2	8	10
Corporate image	5	10	8

Figure 3. Environment/Objective Table (hypothetical).

ponents, someone in the top echelon must think in terms of the aggregates.

All of the components of the first two objectives are easily quantifiable, using measures such as dollars of sales, percentage increase in sales, return on investment, or pretax return on sales. On the other hand, the last two objectives are highly dependent on management judgment. For this example, "product balance" is defined as that mix of product lines which assures the company the greatest degree of corporate stability in the face of a changing environment while it exploits current and projected competence, equipment, and facilities. "Corporate image" is even more subjective because it depends on a second-order judgment—management's judgment of how others view the company. It relates, however, to a few quantifiable factors such as product quality, contract performance, and degree of technological leadership, as well as intangibles such as the effectiveness of advertising and public relations.

Under normal conditions, profitability or image may be very important, but they may give way to the security provided by product balance if a period of economic recession is expected. Explicit judgments should be made concerning the relative importance of each objective under the conditions postulated for each environmental scenario. The overall relative importance of each company objective can then be calculated by multiplying its value in each environment by the emphasis placed on that environment, and summing these products for all three environments. This is a very useful assessment for dissemination throughout the company because management is daily confronted with decisions that can contribute to the attainment of one company objective at the expense of other objectives. However, the overall importance of each objective is not used in this planning guide or model because it is desirable to retain environmental sensitivity throughout the process, to assist in making the judgments required later in the process.

The planning structure is now complete enough to permit the estimation of the utility of each product at a given point in time (e.g., for a selected fiscal year). This is accomplished most easily through the use of a table which indicates the contribution for a particular year that each product makes to each of the company objectives in each environment. (See Figure 4.) With respect to a particular objective and environment, these judgments are usually made at one time for all products. The product with the greatest contribution is assigned some arbitrary value, such as ten on a scale of zero to ten. Every other product is then related to it. A product which contributes half as much is assigned a "five"; one

Figure 4. Format for Estimation of Product Utility.

PRODUCT CONTRIBUTION TABLE FOR FISCAL YEAR _____

| | PRODUCT NUMBER | | | | | |
	1	2	3	4	5	6
ENVIRONMENT I						
Profitability						
Gross Sales						
Product Balance						
Image						
ENVIRONMENT II						
Profitability						
Gross Sales						
Product Balance						
Image						
ENVIRONMENT III						
Profitability						
Gross Sales						
Product Balance						
Image						

tenth as much, a "one," etc. This is strictly a weighting process rather than a ranking, and "ten" can be assigned to all products if there is no difference in their contributions.

The next step is the assessment of the marginal contribution of each product to each objective and environment, using the values assigned in the previous step as a rough guide. The marginal contribution is very sensitive to the product mix in which a specific product is being evaluated. It would be very helpful at this point if the product planning group already knew the mix selected by the model as an input. However, in the absence of that data an assumption must be made. It may be assumed, as a point of departure, that all products under consideration constitute the product mix. With this given product mix, a judgment should be made concerning the degree to which the corporate goals for each objective and environment would be met, and this should be expressed as the percentage of attainment. One product at a time is then removed from the product mix; new judgments of percentage attainment are made for each goal; and the decrease in percentage attainment is taken as the marginal contribution of that product to the particular objective in the environment considered. It should be noted that any increase in attainment that may occur when a product is removed from the mix should be expressed as a negative marginal contribution. When all marginal contributions have been assessed, the utility of each product in the specified fiscal year is calculated by summing the products of its marginal contribution to each objective in each environment and multiplying the sum by the value of that objective in that environment.

This computation of utility at one point in time can be very misleading if it is used as an estimate of the total utility of each product. Ideally, the marginal utility of each product should be computed for each year of its lifetime and summed over its lifetime. Since the number of discrete judgments required for such a process rules out this approach, the total lifetime utility of each product can be estimated by using standard value profiles. The most useful profile probably looks something like a child's drawing of a rooftop. (See Figure 5.) Utility normally increases as a step function in the year that the product is introduced, and it continues to grow until the point of maximum utility is reached. This can be the point of maximum market penetration or the point at which some competitive product begins to replace the old one. Then a steady decline occurs until the product is phased-out or removed from the market. This phase-out point is often not as sharp a drop as the initial rise in utility because of a tendency to hang on to old familiar products long after they actually should be phased out.

Such a simplified product value profile can be completely defined if its height at any point of the product lifetime is computed by the mar-

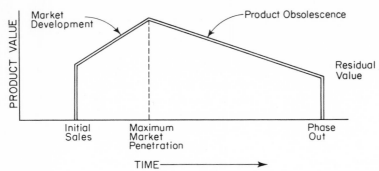

Figure 5. Product Value Profile.

ginal utility calculations described earlier and if estimates are made for the following: date of initial sales, date of maximum utility, date of product phase-out, rate of increase in utility (slope) during market development, and rate of decrease in utility (slope) during product obsolescence. Thus, the area under the product value profile curve (or the summation of the utility of the product each year over all of the years in the product lifetime) represents the total marginal utility of the product. These marginal utilities can be added for all products available (on the market) in any given year to obtain the total value of the product mix for that year. Discussion of the absolute utility of a single product is meaningless and dangerous, except for the case of the single-product company.

Product utilities or values are usually discussed without explicit provision for the fact that it may not be feasible to market a product with the technological attributes described during the planning period or to meet the delivery time specified in the plan. Since a delivery schedule had to be assumed for each new product in the early phases of this planning guide, the most useful expression of feasibility may well be the probability that the assumed schedule can be met. The estimate of this schedule feasibility usually requires a technological forecast for each identified problem area and a method of estimating the time required for all of the many activities which can be grouped under the heading of "Acquisition Phase" (e.g. engineering, tooling, and manufacturing).[2] Methods of planning the Acquisition Phase are fairly well known and in common use. Therefore, it is sufficient to say here that three time estimates will be obtained from the responsible personnel concerning this phase—optimistic, most likely, and pessimistic.

Taking one problem area at a time, the pacing technological parameter first must be selected. Then, historical progress data on this parameter

---

[2] The development of a new product can be divided into three phases: Concept Formulation, Acquisition, and Product Delivery.

must be accumulated, including the costs of achieving that progress. Forecasts of future progress, using the current rate, must be made, and the factor by which progress must be accelerated if the goal is to be met must be identified. The probability of successfully attaining the goal without encountering some physical limitation and the operational value of attaining the goal must also be estimated. All of these factors have a direct bearing on the allocation of resources to technical areas and determine to a large degree the time that will be required to solve each technical problem which will confront the introduction of the new product.

Using the method of technological forecasting just described, along with an estimate of the total resources available for the advancement of technology in the relevant fields, the product planners can make estimates of the most likely, the longest, and the shortest time that will be required to solve each problem. By the use of PERT-type procedures, the expected time to complete each problem can then be calculated. The problems are usually grouped in such a manner that they are not sequentially linked. The longest expected time to solve any one problem can then be taken as the time to complete the Concept Formulation Phase. This expected time, added to the expected time required to complete the Acquisition Phase, gives the expected time to the first Product Delivery. The feasibility can then be expressed as the probability that delivery can be made during or before each future year.

When the product characteristics and time estimates have been described in sufficient detail and the utility and feasibility judgments have been made, it should be possible to estimate the cost of delivering the product in the quantities predicted by the market forecasts which provided the basis for the utility estimates. This cost estimate should include total costs from the present time until product phase-out. For new products, this will include research and development costs, market development costs, product acquisition costs, and field service costs.

If it appears impractical to project year-by-year costs for products which will be developed several years in the future, it should be possible to use standard cost curves associated with classes of products so that product costs are at least treated with a consistent level of ignorance. It would be unfortunate if one future product were favored over another purely on the basis of cost estimates when the costs of both were equally unknown. This can happen, however, if different groups make independent cost estimates, without the use of standard costing methods.

The product planning group is now in position to calculate the value (total marginal utility), the expected value (total marginal utility multiplied by feasibility), and the desirability (expected value divided by cost) of each product. Products can now be selected in the order of decreasing desirability, intermixing current products with potential new ones, until a limit is reached (e.g., funds, manpower, equipment, or facilities available in a specific year).

Up to this point the model can be handled manually unless a large number of products are included. However, even with a small number of products it will be very useful to have a computerized linear programming model available to test whether a truly optimum product mix has been selected. Such a model can test every possible product mix, in groups of nine or ten, without excessive computer running time. A situation is occasionally found in which the most desirable product consumes such a large portion of some critical resource that it displaces several others, the sum of whose desirabilities is greater than the more expensive product. Thus, the concept of marginal desirability is shown to be very useful, even though it is usually too complex to implement manually.

Once a product mix has been selected within the appropriate resource constraints, the total contribution of all selected products to each objective can be calculated for each future year. This analysis will usually indicate that certain objectives are not completely satisfied while others are exceeded. An additional feature can be added to the model to halt the addition of products to the mix once preselected levels of attainment are reached for any or all company objectives. However, this usually makes the procedure so complicated that it becomes too difficult for the users to follow manually. It has been found that product planning guides will not be used at all unless they are so simple that the least sophisticated member of the product planning group can reproduce its essential features with pencil and paper. Even without this extra sophistication, however, the product planning guide permits the selection of "optimum" product mixes. Also, it provides management with a device which can assess the value of the selected product mix with respect to each company objective and policy, and determine the overall value to the company. It can also serve an important role by indicating the impact of various policy decisions and the effect which variations of each type of resource constraint have on the value of the product mix.

Technological Projection and Advanced Product Planning

FREDERICK S. PARDEE

In the planning of future products it is important that the assumptions of technological forecasting be clearly identified, that interdependencies be clearly stated and that uncertainties be treated in an explicit fashion. The evolution of a product into final marketability involves a series of steps. To be sure of pursuing worthwhile paths, companies must link their technological projections with techniques of capital investment analysis and new product planning.

Mr. Pardee, head of the Management Research Group of the Cost Analysis Department, The RAND Corporation, has had extensive experience in the development of methodology and in the application of technological forecasting to government and industry. He has participated in early defense system studies of weapons, force structure and posture, and in current studies to determine criteria for allocating support to technology and potential system development projects.

Any views expressed in this chapter are those of the author. They should not be interpreted as reflecting the views of the RAND Corporation or the official opinion or policy of any of its governmental or private research sponsors.

It makes sense in the defense environment to limit the scope of technological forecasting to projecting technical potential or research *opportunities,* and to treat techniques for analysis of requirements or *needs* as a separate body of methodology. This distinction can be retained in the commercial realm only up to the stage where potential profitability must be assessed, at which point need or *demand* must be taken into account. This chapter delimits the subject matter by treating only certain contextual considerations associated with distribution of the product. It then moves directly to techniques for measuring return on investment. Detailed discussion of the wide range of methods and procedures for economic and market analysis is avoided. Much of this—but probably not all—can be viewed as subsidiary to a comprehensive methodology for analysis of return on investment in projected new technology.

Technological projection is based on the assumption that the overwhelming majority of technological improvements are evolutionary in nature. These build, in a more or less orderly fashion, on earlier technology, and those technological achievements genuinely deserving the label "break-through" are rare. There exists, therefore, an underlying rationale to systematic forecasting.

REFINEMENTS IN BASIC METHODOLOGY

It is necessary at the outset to identify those features that are inherent in the basic methodology.[1] This background is a prerequisite to an understanding of the ways in which the utility of information generated by technological forecasting can be increased.

Basic Framework and Criteria for Selection of Performance Characteristics

To develop a quantitative projection of potential advance in the state of the art, one first selects a performance characteristic or combination of characteristics which provides a satisfactorily comprehensive measure of the state of the art in a given technical area. This presupposes that actions such as the following have been taken:

1. The breadth or scope of each technical area has been defined clearly. Guidelines must be established to determine the appropriate breadth to be used for each of several planning contexts or durations.

2. A comprehensive and non-overlapping structure of all major technical areas has been developed which details the content of each individual area. For most purposes, especially those associated with militarily sponsored research, the technical areas, as well as the major projects within technical areas, should be linked to major defense or corporate objectives and perhaps to classes of weaponry

[1] These are described more fully in reference 26 of the bibliography to this chapter.

which are proposed to meet the more important types of anticipated threats, or to product lines designed to capture potential types of markets.

3. A system has been formulated for maintaining continuity in the overall technical area structure so that any narrowing, branching, or other change can be identified easily on a historical basis. This could take the form of a system for maintaining a running record of the original plan and its changes and a method for tracking progress against the projection.

Assuming that such an overall technical area structure has been adequately formulated, the search for characteristics suitable for quantification can then begin in earnest. The following is an illustrative list of the types of guidelines or criteria which, with further study, might be developed in more precise—hopefully quantitative—form to serve as an aid in the selection of acceptable measures of performance capability:

(1) Comprehensiveness
(2) Operational significance
(3) Ease of measurement
(4) Probable accuracy
(5) Identification and measurability of interdependencies
    (a) with other characteristics
    (b) with other technical areas

COMPREHENSIVENESS

The selected characteristic or combination of characteristics should incorporate a high portion—perhaps some explicit percentage—of the technical approaches, and quantitatively identifiable objectives within these approaches, which are likely to be derived from research in the technical area during the time period covered by the forecast. A single variable is preferable if it can be made to adequately represent progress in the area. As a practical matter, the number of variables selected usually should not exceed three or four.

OPERATIONAL SIGNIFICANCE

Preferably, the characteristic or characteristics selected should bear a direct relationship to a specified need (in military context, to a major design specification such as those which might appear in future System Operational Requirements-SORs). Examples of these are measurements such as range, speed, accuracy, and payload capability.

EASE OF MEASUREMENT

Consideration should be given to the ease with which values can be measured. Likely sources for such data include research activities which involve the use of mathematical simulation of the operating characteristics of future hardware; partial scale or partial duration tests, including breadboards and mockups; or full-scale and full-duration testing.

PROBABLE ACCURACY

Evaluation of probable accuracy can be performed using informal checks for reasonableness, formal tests of statistical validity, or similar means.

IDENTIFICATION AND MEASURABILITY OF INTERDEPENDENCIES

In some instances, a *pacing* characteristic can be identified, and other variables can be related to it. This often is difficult, however, since the pacing item may change as performance levels move from one portion of a range to another. For example, in aircraft design, propulsion developments—measured by acceleration or thrust levels—may be the pacing item at one part of the speed range, whereas at higher levels, heat-resistant material—measured by temperature—may be the pacing element. This type of interdependent relationship is also identifiable at lower subsystem levels.

In addition to selecting the characteristic or characteristics which will be quantified in the projection, it also may prove useful to provide a brief statement or list of other important characteristics or considerations which should be evaluated qualitatively when assessing a given technical area. This will insure that they are not overlooked.

Figure 1 presents two examples from the *hard* sciences which use a single performance measure to represent technical advance. These are taken from impressive work performed several years ago at Wright Field.[2]

There are certain additional difficulties in attempting to select characteristics which can be used for quantitative projection in the "soft" sciences. Some soft science fields cannot be handled in this fashion. With a little ingenuity, however, a great deal can be done in attempting to quantify research in many of these areas.[3] For a project in the life sciences, for example, some quantitative measure of knowledge attained might be developed, or a measure of success in training a living creature to adapt to successively increasing exposure to a zero gravity might be formulated.

---

[2] See references 17, 18, and 40 in the bibliography for this chapter.

[3] Such an attempt also may have the advantage of improving the focus of research within the area; i.e., make it a bit "harder" or more firm and hence more clearly worthy of additional support.

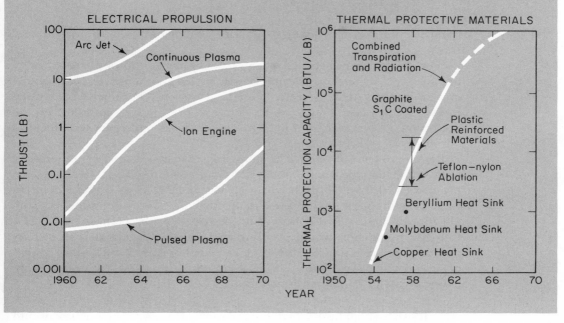

Figure 1. First-Order Technological Projections in the "Hard" Sciences.

Perhaps relaxation of conditions of confinement could be demonstrated, starting with no allowance for change in posture, then moving to limited motion, and then to limitations of pressurized chambers of increasing dimensions—10, 20, or 50 feet in diameter. Comprehensive measures of improvements in the specifications of successfully constructed space suits could be plotted.

Admittedly, each of these possibilities depends, to some extent, upon identification of the "soft" science research involved with the eventual hardware required. This need not always be the case. In the mathematical sciences for example, measures might include the size and/or complexity of the programming problem for which a general solution may be obtained, a measure of the number of levels, the flexibility of functional forms, or the number and extent of the interdependencies which can be handled in projected extensions of decomposition techniques.

Uniformity in Time Frames and Research Status Points

In forecasting development of performance characteristics within each technical area, it is important that uniformity be obtained, both in the time period covered and in the phase of development which is plotted. A standard time period should be selected and maintained throughout the study.

For short-term projections it may be desirable to plot anticipated progress for short increments of time (a year or less), although this may imply greater accuracy than is really possible. However, the objective of using short time periods should be to ensure clarity in the meaning of the projection rather than to imply precision about uncertain technological advances.

In the absence of explicit assumptions, a second source of unnecessary imprecision derives from a misunderstanding of the actual level of performance which will have been developed and tested by a given point in time. A plot point may represent an analytic effort indicating that no violation of basic physical law would be required; the point at which first full-scale production would be completed; or any of several intermediary points. In many instances, such a series of points can extend over a period of several years. An illustrative list from which to select the one or more major events to be plotted is as follows:

1. Analysis indicates that no violation of known physical law would be required.
2. The technical feasibility of a new approach is proven
   (a) by paper studies (mathematical analyses, optimization studies, etc.);
   (b) by small-scale and/or short-duration test;
   (c) by full-scale, full-duration test;
   (d) by enough full-scale, full-duration tests to insure an adequate size sample.
3. The engineering design of the full major subsystem is complete.
4. A prototype of the complete major subsystems is thoroughly tested.
5. The improvement is integrated into the total system
   (a) on paper;
   (b) the first test is completed successfully;
   (c) the total test series is completed successfully.
6. The production redesign is completed.
7. The production facility is completed.
8. The first production units are produced in quantity and are ready for delivery.

And as will be discussed subsequently:

9. Conversion from technical feasibility to commercial profitability (as either a good or service) is achieved.

This list may be more lengthy than required for a set of guidelines for preparation of technical projections. Its full detail is included here to emphasize the extent of the phases in the development process. In many instances it would be most logical to plot event 2d in the list—the technical feasibility of the approach has been demonstrated through a statistically adequate program of full-scale tests. At this point the technology is available to the systems engineer for inclusion in new overall system developments. If event 2d is used as the standard in a forecasting exercise, any exceptions to this practice must be clearly identified in order that the various projections in an overall package can be meaningful.

Explicit Treatment of Uncertainties

Attempts to deal with uncertainty are handled in an explicit fashion only infrequently. Forecasters are not unmindful that their function is an uncertain one, but preparing forecasts is not a very widespread activity and specifying estimates in terms of high, mid, and low points, or confidence limits, or including qualitative commentary on the probable range accompanying such estimates, is a refinement yet to be accomplished. However, it is often easier for an expert in a given field to prepare such a range than to identify a specific single value, and, as a result, confidence in the projection may be considerably enhanced. Figures 2 through 4

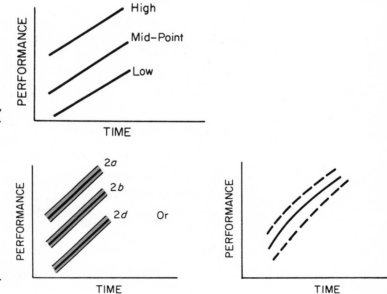

Figure 2. Incorporation of High, Mid and Low Estimates of Progress.

Figure 3. The Use of Bands or Informal Confidence Limits.

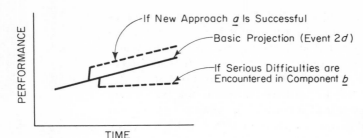

Figure 4. Identification of Anticipated Results if Selected Special Circumstances Occur.

present several methods for graphically presenting such information on uncertainty.

Such projections may be accompanied by information which provides an approximation of the sensitivity of the estimates (see Figure 5). Far more formal probabilistic tools also are available to the forecaster who is not fearful of the spuriousness in accuracy which they may imply. At present, in the majority of instances, it probably makes more sense to place major emphasis on developing additional sensitivity ("what if") information than to introduce more elaborate probabilistic refinements.

Figure 5. Sensitivity of Estimates.

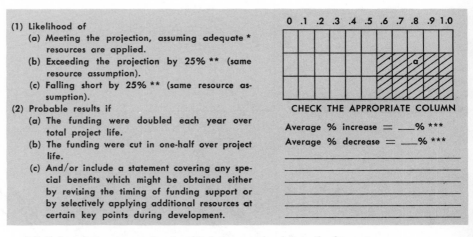

(1) Likelihood of
   (a) Meeting the projection, assuming adequate * resources are applied.
   (b) Exceeding the projection by 25% ** (same resource assumption).
   (c) Falling short by 25% ** (same resource assumption).
(2) Probable results if
   (a) The funding were doubled each year over total project life.
   (b) The funding were cut in one-half over project life.
   (c) And/or include a statement covering any special benefits which might be obtained either by revising the timing of funding support or by selectively applying additional resources at certain key points during development.

0 .1 .2 .3 .4 .5 .6 .7 .8 .9 1.0

CHECK THE APPROPRIATE COLUMN

Average % increase = ___% ***
Average % decrease = ___% ***

    * Sufficient, but not excessive. Specific interpretation left to the forecaster.
   ** A substitute percentage may be inserted in cases where 25% is clearly unreasonable.
  *** Or use a curve, plotting percentage increase by year, if an average value would be misleading.
    a Values above .5 would indicate either that the basic projection was in error or that an "inadequate" resource application was assumed.

Of all the methodological issues facing the technological forecaster, the problem of interdependencies is probably the most vexing. The nature of the interdependency problem can be illustrated in simplified form by the following example from the propulsion field. Propulsion systems can be designed for long life or for high acceleration. To some extent these two objectives are contradictory; yet in attempting to quantify state-of-the-art advance, it probably is necessary to incorporate both of these variables in the projection. Assume, for purposes of illustration, that the combination of these two characteristics provides a comprehensive measure of the overall potential of the mode of propulsion being examined. It then is necessary to make an assumption similar to one of the following concerning interdependency:

1. That time to failure—as a measure of design life—will remain at current maximum levels and all improvement will take the form of increased acceleration capability, or vice versa;
2. That design life and acceleration will increase in (a) a constant ratio or (b) other prespecified relationship; or
3. That since the need for increased acceleration (or design life) can be justified more substantively than the need for the other capability, performance improvements will be dictated by demand. Thus, required increases in acceleration will be plotted as the dominating characteristic, perhaps including a maximum or plateau at some point. Then, assuming this pattern of development of acceleration capability, possibilities for improvement in design life will be estimated.

It is important to recognize both: (1) that such projections probably can be meaningful only within the basic mode of propulsion—changes in mode may place the projection in a new flight category [4]—and, (2) that no provision has been made for the possibility of a genuine breakthrough (i.e., very special scientific advances). In addition, any such time-phased projections are dependent upon the priority and consequent resource support which is assigned. Probably the most feasible way to deal with this interdependency problem is to search out *dominant* relationships which can be expressed simply and to ignore lesser interdependencies.

The following are a series of alternate approaches to incorporate in-

---

[4] However, it should be noted that, frequently, more aggregative projections can be prepared which summarize individual projections and encompass a series of successive modes. Obviously, definitional and classification considerations also are involved in the question of how great the design change must be to constitute a change in mode.

terdependencies in projections, each representing an increasing level of sophistication:

1. Using narrative, indicating that the major performance characteristics are related but not specifying the precise nature of the relationship;
2. Separately plotting each of the three or four major characteristics which are interrelated, but juxtaposing the charts and accompanying them with a set of common underlying assumptions;
3. Selecting from a small series of perhaps three to ten pre-specified forms ("black box" or "plug-in" relationships) which most closely approximate the estimate of the potential real world situation;
4. Plotting the specific relationships among each set of characteristics to the extent that they can be determined.

The third approach might be partially accomplished through the use of a simple weighting scheme. As an example, if three major variables are involved, reasonable combinations of weights might be as indicated in Figure 6. This assumes that, if any one characteristic is more than three times as important as the others, it probably should be considered as dominant and thus might be used alone to project potential progress. A complicating, but not insurmountable, consideration would be the circumstance requiring that different weights be plotted for various portions of the range of technical progress.[5]

Weight	Characteristic		
	1	2	3
	1	1	1
	1	1	2
	1	1	3
	1	2	2
	1	2	3
	1	3	3
	2	3	3

Figure 6. Weighting Variables.

[5] In an earlier paper (bibliography reference 26), the author included a brief discussion referencing possible methods for coordinating the estimates of a group of experts. Since that time, consensus techniques have been the subject of considerable intellectual activity, and a number of interesting papers have appeared or are about to appear. These probably will soon offer substantial refinement in query methodology and such refinements should prove adaptable to the technological forecasting environment. At the moment, however, the "Effort Allocation Guide" work at Wright Field (reference 40) and the efforts of Helmer et al. (references 6, 9, and 10) are as directly addressed to the problem at hand as any of which the author is aware. Portions of three forthcoming RAND Memoranda (references 34, 20, 27) also deal with this subject. See also chapters by North, Helmer, and Gordon in this book.

This section attempts to establish the linkage between the tools for projection of technological opportunities and techniques for analyzing potential return on investment so that the value of each is enhanced. Accomplishment of such an objective is no easy task because of the almost unlimited number of factors which can influence the success or failure of a new product.

In a sense, analysis of the market environment would seem to be less difficult than analysis of future international conditions and their impact on defense requirements. One might argue that economic trends, by comparison, are more stable and predictable, and that in many, if not most, business circumstances the time horizon under intensive analysis is significantly shorter. On the other hand, new commercial products are frequently at the mercy of a fickle or lethargic mass market, while, at the same time, the resources available to develop and merchandise the product may, by comparison with defense resources, be extremely limited. Hence, at least from the standpoint of the individual firm, in many respects new product ventures may be far more uncertain and risky than analyses of defense requirements.

A Context for Analysis

It is necessary to delimit the field of technological forecasting for defense purposes; however, a conceptually comprehensive methodology for that field is still rather complex. In the commercial environment it is also imperative to spend adequate time at the outset to establish a *context* for analysis.

Specific Technological Attribute
or General Environment Trend

First, it is important to clarify whether the information being sought deals with the commercial implications of a specific technological attribute or set of attributes, or whether initially, at least, it is more concerned with the environmental trend implications of a new technology. Both are important and both are appropriate subject matter for the field of technological forecasting. However, tools for the analysis of each may differ significantly. The former is concerned with the specific profit possibilities of, for example, the increased resistance to heat of a new material, or the capability of microminiaturizing an electronic circuit, or somewhat more specifically, an increase in acceleration made possible by an improved gear ratio.

Environmental trend forecasting, on the other hand, is more concerned with the extent and implications of such things as growth of accessible world-wide communications networks; the effect of supersonic transportation on international relations; or the impact of improved contraceptive techniques on population, morals and mores. Such trends may have important economic, social, or even political consequences, but the subject matter is delimited somewhat by the fact that technological forecasting should logically be concerned only with trends that are technologically induced. Environmental trend analysis is a fascinating topic; however, primary attention here is on a methodology for determining more direct implications concerning potential profit which stems from specific technical attributes.

Extent of the Technological Advance

A second factor in establishing the context for analysis of potential profitability is the extent of the technological advance involved. The impacts of technological changes can range from very modest improvement in a single physical or performance characteristic to dramatic increases in capability, or completely new types of capability. The advance may extend to a single use, or it may exhibit a potential for thousands of current and future products. Bracketing the extent of the improvement in some preliminary fashion—hopefully quantitative—is therefore exceptionally important before proceeding with subsequent phases of the analysis; however, a small improvement in capability does not necessarily offer less potential for profit than does larger technical growth. Many commercial products can absorb only modest improvements. But such improvements can often convert unprofitable articles into highly successful ones. Furthermore, dramatic increases in capability may also require sizable increases in both investments and selling prices.

Magnitude of the Impact on the Company

A technical advance, even within a firm's general field of activity, may have little or no effect on the company if the firm fails to see or deliberately chooses to ignore the potential. It is important at the outset to develop some preliminary assessment of the magnitude of this impact on the company. Will the advance be a modest modification of a single product, or will it introduce a new product line which may grow to the point of establishing a new division or an entire company? In preparing such an evaluation, it is obvious that, in many instances, the size of impact is largely a reflection of the extent to which company management chooses to capitalize on the advance, either in an effort to lead the industry or in self-defense to protect itself against competition.

Technical Market or the General Public

Even before considering whether "the product is right for us," the nature of the market must be determined. Will the advance result in products which are salable in a highly technical market in which major customers are few and readily identified, or will it be salable primarily in the mass market?

Distribution as Product or Service

In many cases, high cost, the necessity for special skills or handling, or other reasons make it clear that the new advance stands its greatest chance of achieving profitability as a contributor to a service function. In such situations, an innovator may have the option of selling a resultant high-cost product to a limited market, which will then convert it to a service—as is done, for example, in jet transport sales. A company may choose to market the services of the equipment it manufactures; e.g., computer and copying machine companies renting their equipment; automobile manufacturers running their own car rental agency; appliance manufacturers operating coin laundry chains; or car wash manufacturers operating their own equipment.

Lead Time and Timing in the Innovation Process

Another important factor to be determined at the outset is the time period in which the product might be introduced. When will it be technically feasible? Once such information is estimated or established, then other appropriate lead time allowances can be estimated for obtaining administrative approval, contracting for and constructing manufacturing facilities, building inventory and distribution channels, and obtaining market acceptance. The date when the market might be ready for such a product or service should also be considered at this point. Experience has shown that introduction too soon can be just as devastating as an arrival after the competition has already captured the market or the demand for the product or service has been exhausted.

Producibility Implications

During the analytic process it is necessary to conduct an intensive engineering and economic evaluation of the conversion of technically feasible accomplishments to a product which can be "produced at a price." Design simplification without excessive loss of technical performance, analysis of production methods and rates, and capital and manufacturing costs must be assessed. Such factors, frequently only of tangential interest during development, become of primary importance during market evaluation. Technological forecasting methodology probably has little, if anything, unique to contribute to the analysis at this point. In general, time-honored methods will do very well.[6]

Size of Firm and Capital Requirements

It is important to determine during the initial analysis whether the magnitude of the investment involved in developing the products, building the manufacturing capability, and waiting for customer acceptance is appropriate to the size of the firm considering the innovation. The failure rate of new enterprises attests to the significance of this factor.

Once a preliminary assessment of this series of considerations has been made, a full-scale analysis can be performed to show how potential new products relate to the capabilities of the firm—its long-term objectives, engineering organization, capital, plant, and equipment, available cash reserves, management and human resources, marketing and distribution channels, existing product lines, etc. A checklist summarizing some of these factors, attributed to T. V. Miller of Dewey and Almy Chemical Company, is included as an appendix. A similar list has been prepared and annotated by John T. O'Meara, Jr., and discussions of similar content are available in a wide variety of texts and articles on market analysis.[7] In addition, several recent developments in quantitative analysis which have been applied to aerospace problems (e.g., "probability of capture" models) could serve to make this analytic process more systematic.

Linking with Capital Investment Analysis
Methodology—Current and Potential

The final phase of the analysis is measuring return on investment. Ideally, in assessing the profitability of a new potential value for a technical attribute, one would like to be able to plot a curve which relates technical performance to return on investment (see Figure 7). Such curves would be marvelous if they could be made credible. In theory, this can be accomplished by systematic specification of an enormous number of underlying assumptions. And if enough families of curves are presented,

[6] These techniques frequently are exercised in a cumbersome and time-consuming manual fashion, whereas appropriate use of the computer to perform the extensive routine aspects of this process not only make it much faster, but also permit examination of alternative production methods. In addition, in the future, automation of many basic design functions should increase the breadth and depth of such simulations and sensitivity testing capabilities.

[7] See reference 24 in the bibliography.

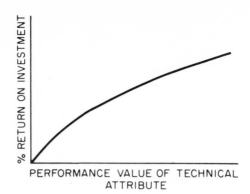

Figure 7. Technical Performance vs. Return on Investment.

PERFORMANCE VALUE OF TECHNICAL ATTRIBUTE

sufficient sensitivity information should be available to suggest the implications of many of the more important uncertainties involved. At the moment, the underlying methodology is not sufficiently developed to make this feasible. A discussion follows on several of the more important features of such an underlying capital investment methodology. There are, however, capital investment methodologies, both current and proposed, which offer considerable potential for meaningful linkage with technological projection techniques, and hence for provision of an integrated and comprehensive advanced product analysis methodology.

At present, a variety of simple formulas for assessing new products exist, of which the following is an example: [8]

$$\frac{\begin{array}{c}\text{Chances of} \\ \text{Technical} \\ \text{Success}\end{array} \times \begin{array}{c}\text{Chances of} \\ \text{Commercial} \\ \text{Success}\end{array} \times \begin{array}{c}\text{Annual} \\ \text{Volume}\end{array} \times \begin{array}{c}\text{Price} \\ \text{less} \\ \text{Cost}\end{array} \times \text{Life}}{\text{Total Costs}} = \begin{array}{c}\text{Product} \\ \text{Value} \\ \text{Index}\end{array}$$

Payout, average return on average investment, and discounted cash flow or present worth methods are described in numerous references, although the extent of their utilization varies considerably, particularly the discounted cash flow method.[9] Each of these methods has its usefulness and certainly is preferable to no attempt at analyzing the financial implications of a new product. On the other hand, all need improvement before they can provide decision makers with the full information required. Building upon the most sophisticated—the cash flow method—such extensions or refinements are of at least four types.

[8] See reference 11 in the bibliography.
[9] For one good description of these techniques, see reference 4 in the bibliography.

The first of these relates to the necessity for specification of major underlying assumptions. Widely differing results can be obtained, depending upon the types of direct manufacturing and overhead costs included; the depreciation methods employed; and, especially relevant in this application, the method of write-off used for initial research and development costs. Assuming that methods are comprehensive and are applied consistently, problems in this area can be minimized, but most managers would probably feel more comfortable if major assumptions were identified in analyses of new products. Basic assumptions regarding quantity, price, production rate, time-phasing, etc., also should be identified.

The second improvement is easy to describe but frequently more difficult to handle. The analysis should deal with the total life-cycle of the product. Since both product and capital equipment life are usually unknown, it is necessary to incorporate an estimate that is often really quite arbitrary. Methods utilized by many firms employ a standard, often arbitrarily short, time period, e.g., three to five years. Such methods implicitly assume equal residual product lifetimes in situations where such assumptions are patently unrealistic. This would cause no particular problem if all potential products which met the minimum criterion were to be funded. But capital resources generally are limited and the assumption of equal product lifetime, in effect, causes the decision to be resolved on the basis of other criteria which may or may not be equally important or as directly relevant.

Only after these two refinements have been made is it meaningful to consider depicting the financial implications of product life in graphic form similar to that illustrated in Figure 8.

Figure 9 summarizes some of the major types of subsidiary financial information necessary to construct a meaningful analysis of product cash flow considerations. Significant underlying assumptions identified in this figure include: before- and after-tax comparisons, of which the after-

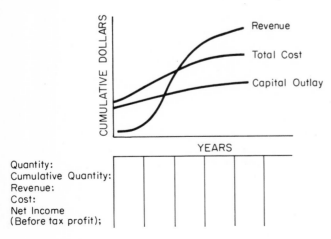

Figure 8. Product Life Cycle.

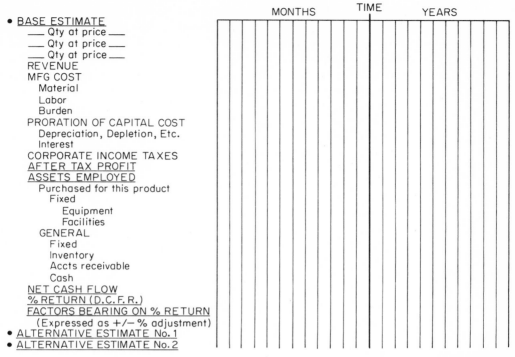

- BASE ESTIMATE
  ___ Qty at price ___
  ___ Qty at price ___
  ___ Qty at price ___
  REVENUE
  MFG COST
    Material
    Labor
    Burden
  PRORATION OF CAPITAL COST
    Depreciation, Depletion, Etc.
    Interest
  CORPORATE INCOME TAXES
  AFTER TAX PROFIT
  ASSETS EMPLOYED
    Purchased for this product
    Fixed
      Equipment
      Facilities
    GENERAL
    Fixed
    Inventory
    Accts receivable
    Cash
  NET CASH FLOW
  % RETURN (D.C.F.R.)
  FACTORS BEARING ON % RETURN
  (Expressed as +/− % adjustment)
- ALTERNATIVE ESTIMATE No. 1
- ALTERNATIVE ESTIMATE No. 2

Figure 9. Analysis of Product Cash Flow (including Sensitivity Testing).

corporate income tax is usually the more important; [10] and segregation of the assets purchased for (and peculiar to) the new product from those otherwise idle assets, already purchased by the firm for other special or general purposes, but now available for use on the new product.

This figure also illustrates, albeit crudely, the third and in many respects most interesting potential improvement in capital investment methodology—the importance of introducing sensitivity information to the basic estimates. This is of considerable use in assessing the profitability implications of growth values for specific technical attributes. This is illustrated in Figure 9 by the reference to percentage point adjustments in the discounted cash flow rate. These figures explicitly identify the impact

[10] Frequently, profit is also expressed in terms of earnings per share. For new products, in which the major return on investment is expected in future years, average annual rather than first-year earnings per share is the more relevant statistic. New products must be carefully phased into a company's overall product mix to ensure that an adequate earnings level is maintained each year. (See Figure 10.)

on profitability of various accounting methods and other factors of special interest, for example, major contributions to community relations activities, etc. Sensitivity is also illustrated by the provision for alternative estimates in which broader types of variations (e.g., changes in the performance value of the new technical attributes) can be shown. Development of a capital investment simulation capability should make it possible to provide sensitivity information for several of the more important characteristics or assumptions which underlie estimates of percentage return and are responsible for uncertainties in the results. With judicious selection of the characteristics or assumptions of most interest, such a package of information could prove of immense value to decision makers, both in assessing potential profitability and in bracketing the range of risk their companies should assume.

The fourth and final improvement in investment analysis techniques is associated with the impact of a new product on product mix and division or corporate profitability. Figure 10 is of assistance in illustrating this important consideration. In recent years it has been fashionable to analyze new projects or products in terms of their marginal contribution

Figure 10. Impact on Product Mix.

	BASELINE MIX						MIX CHANGE No.1		MIX CHANGE No. 2		ETC.
	P_1	P_2	P_3	P_4	Etc	Total	Change	Revised Total	Change	Revised Total	
REVENUE (Based on __ qty at price __)											
COST											
Manufacturing											
Proration of capital cost											
PROFIT											
Before taxes											
After taxes											
ASSETS EMPLOYED											
Product peculiar											
General											
NET CASH FLOW											
% RETURN (D.C.F.R.)											
FACTORS BEARING ON % RETURN											
___											
___											
___											

Extend over a → series of time frames

to the firm. This type of analysis is useful, but analyzing successive marginal investments without maintaining a running record of their cumulative impact on total profitability has led many a firm into serious trouble. Obviously, sensitivity information on a series of alternative changes to product mix could prove to be of tremendous value.

SUMMARY

The methodology suggested above includes several extensions of basic technological projection techniques, the identification of context in the analysis of the transition from technical feasibility to commercial profitability, and refinements in capital investment methodology. If a comprehensive methodology incorporating these features can be developed and implemented, the validity of summary projections directly relating growth in technical attributes to percentage return on investment will be greatly enhanced.

APPENDIX: NEW PRODUCT PLANNING PROFILE

	Very Good	Good	Fair	Poor	Very Poor
I. Stability Factors					
a. Permanence of market					
b. Possibility of captive market					
c. Stability in depression					
d. Stability in war					
e. Size of market					
f. How difficult to substitute or copy					
II. Growth Factors					
a. Chance of substantial future growth					
b. Demand situation or need for additional suppliers					
c. Export possibilities					
d. Unique character of product or process					
e. Is a change going on in this industry which this product can ride?					
III. Marketability Factors					
a. Product does not compete with, imitate or injure present customers					
b. Company's reputation in similar fields					
c. Relation to markets we now sell					
d. Customer's service requirements compared with company's ability					
e. Standing in relation to probable competition					
f. Few variations or styles required					
g. Large volume with individual customers					

Very Good | Good | Fair | Poor | Very Poor

IV. *Financial Factors*
a. Return on investment
   1. Fixed capital
   2. Fixed and working capital
   3. Fixed, working and initial R&D cost
b. Investment required relative to competitive product
c. Investment required per dollar of sales

V. *Position Factors*
a. Time required to become established and accepted
b. Effect on sales of other product lines
c. Value added by our processing
d. Chance of exclusive or favored purchasing position
e. Raw materials improve vertical integration
f. Raw materials improve position in other purchases

SOURCE: Adapted from Carl Heyel (Ed.), The Encyclopedia of Management, *Reinhold Publishing Corporation, New York, 1963, pp. 580–581; and attributed to T. V. Miller, New Product Planning Committee, Dewey and Almy Chemical Company.*

BIBLIOGRAPHY

1. Adler, Lee, "Systems Approach to Marketing," *Harvard Business Review,* May–June, 1967, pp. 105–18.
2. American Management Association, *Developing A Product Strategy.* New York, N.Y., 1959.
3. Bagby, F. L., D. L. Farrar, G. W. James, et al., *A Feasibility Study of Techniques for Measuring and Predicting the State of the Art.* Battelle Memorial Institute, Columbus, Ohio, 1959.
4. Bierman, Harold, Jr., and Seymour Smidt, *The Capital Budgeting Decision —Economic Analysis and the Financing of Investment Decisions* (2nd ed.). New York: The MacMillan Company, 1966, Chap. 13.
5. Churchman, C. West, Russell L. Ackoff and Leonard E. Arnoff, *Introduction to Operations Research.* New York: John Wiley & Sons, Inc., 1957.
6. Dalkey, Norman, and Olaf Helmer, "An Experimental Application of the Delphi Method to the Use of Experts," *Management Science,* Vol. 9, No. 3 (April, 1963), 458–67.
7. Day, Ralph L., *Marketing Models—Quantitative and Behavioral.* Scranton, Pa.: International Textbook Company, 1964, Section E.
8. Dimsdale, B., and H. P. Flatt, "Project Evaluation and Selection," *IBM Systems Journal,* Vol. 2 (September–December, 1963).
9. Gordon, T. J., and Olaf Helmer, *Report on a Long-Range Forecasting Study,* P-2982. The RAND Corporation, Santa Monica, Calif., 1964.

10. Helmer, Olaf, *Social Technology,* P-3063. The RAND Corporation, Santa Monica, Calif., 1965.

11. Heyel, Carl, ed., *The Encyclopedia of Management.* New York: Reinhold Publishing Corporation, 1963, pp. 576–83.

12. Hill, Lawrence S., *Management Planning and Control of Research and Technology Projects,* RM-4921-PR. The RAND Corporation, Santa Monica, Calif., 1966.

13. Holtz, James N., *The Technology Utilization Process: An Overview,* NASA Research Paper No. 19. University of California, Los Angeles, Graduate School of Business Administration, 1966.

14. Jantsch, Erich, *Technological Forecasting in Perspective,* Working Document, DAS/SPR/66.12. Organization for Economic Cooperation and Development, Paris, France, October, 1966.

15. Jewkes, John, David Sawers, and Richard Stillerman, *The Sources of Invention.* London: Macmillan & Co., Ltd., 1958.

16. Knight, Kerneth E., *A Study of Technological Innovation—The Evolution of Digital Computers.* Doctoral Dissertation, Graduate School of Industrial Administration, Carnegie Institute of Technology, November, 1963.

17. Lenz, Ralph C., Jr., *A Development of Explicit Methods in Technological Forecasting.* Master's Thesis, Massachusetts Institute of Technology, Cambridge, Mass., 1959.

18. ———, *Methods of Technological Forecasting,* WADD Technical Report 61-46. Air Force Systems Command, Wright-Patterson Air Force Base, Ohio, 1961.

19. Lindsay, J. Robert, and Arnold W. Sametz, *Financial Management—An Analytical Approach.* Homewood, Ill.: Richard D. Irwin, Inc., 1967, Chaps. 11–12.

20. MacCrimmon, Kenneth R., *Decision Making Among Multi-Attribute Alternatives.* The RAND Corporation, Santa Monica, Calif. (forthcoming).

21. Marples, David L., "The Decisions of Engineering Design," *IRE Transactions on Engineering Management,* June, 1961.

22. Masse, Pierre, *Optimal Investment Decisions—Rules for Action and Criteria for Choice.* Englewood Cliffs, N.J.: Prentice-Hall, Inc., 1962.

23. Mumford, Lewis, *The Myth of the Machine—Techniques and Human Development.* New York: Harcourt, Brace & World, Inc., 1966.

24. O'Meara, John T., Jr., "Selecting Profitable Products," *Harvard Business Review,* Vol. 39 (January–February, 1961), 83–89.

25. Pardee, F. S., *Scheduling State of the Art—Anathema or Necessity?* P-2511. The RAND Corporation, Santa Monica, Calif., 1961.

26. ———, *State-of-the-Art Projection and Long-Range Planning of Applied Research,* P-3181. The RAND Corporation, Santa Monica, Calif., 1965.

27. Pardee, F. S., C. P. Bonini, H. B. Eyring, N. H. Hakansson, K. R. MacCrimmon, and E. V. W. Zschau, *Techniques of Technology Analysis—With Special Emphasis on Basic and Applied Research Allocation.* The RAND Corporation, Santa Monica, Calif. (forthcoming).

28. Pessemier, Edgar A., *New-Product Decisions—An Analytical Approach.* New York: McGraw-Hill Book Company, 1966.

29. Quinn, James Brian, and James A. Mueller, "Transferring Research Results to Operations," *Harvard Business Review,* Vol. XLI (January–February, 1963).

30. Secrest, Fred, "The Process of Long-Range Planning at Ford Motor Company," *Managerial Long-Range Planning,* ed. George Steiner. New York: McGraw-Hill Book Company, 1963.

31. Shaller, Herman I., *An Exploratory Study in Research Planning Methodology*, ONR Report ACR/NAR-27. Department of the Navy, Washington, D.C., 1963.

32. Spangler, Miller B., *A Conceptual Model for the Treatment of Conflicting Planning Objectives*. Paper presented at 1963 American International Meeting of the Institute of Management Sciences, New York, September 12, 1963.

33. Summitt, Roger K., *Aerospace Business Environment Simulator*. Lockheed Aircraft Corporation, Missiles and Space Division, Sunnyvale, Calif., 1961.

34. Timson, Frederick S., *Measurement of Technical Performance in Weapon System Development Programs: A Subjective Probability Approach*. The RAND Corporation, Santa Monica, Calif. (forthcoming).

35. U.S. Department of Commerce, *Technological Innovation: Its Environment and Management* (Report of the Panel on Invention and Innovation), 1967.

36. ———, Bureau of the Census, *Long Term Economic Growth—1860–1965*, 1966.

37. ———, Business and Defense Services Administration, *Measuring Markets —A Guide to the Use of Federal and State Statistical Data*, 1966.

38. University of California, Los Angeles, *UCLA Engineering Executive Program, A Systems Engineering Approach to Corporate Long-Range Planning*, Report No. EEP 62-1, June, 1962.

39. ———, *UCLA Engineering Executive Program, A Theory of Planning for Research and Development*, Report No. EEP 63-3, June, 1963.

40. Wells, Howard, *The Allocation of Research and Development Resources*, WADC Technical Note 58–119. Air Research and Development Command, Wright-Patterson Air Force Base, Ohio, 1959.

41. Zschau, E. V. W., *Project Modeling: A Technique for Measuring Time-Cost-Performance Trade-offs in System Development Projects*. The RAND Corporation, Santa Monica, Calif. (forthcoming).

The Manager and
Technological Forecasting

JAMES R. BRIGHT

The principal management uses of forecasts are to help set product line performance goals, establish research goals and budgets, to identify areas of promise,
as well as technological opportunities and threats, to aid in long-range corporate
planning, and for communications between technologists and managers. The purpose of this chapter is to assist the manager to evaluate the output of any
technological forecast. Before using forecasts, the manager should understand the
rationale underlying the basic types of forecasts since the resulting predictions
may have quite different implications for the firm.

Patterns of experience with technological innovation are included. They can help
the manager to be more effective in dealing with the possible materialization of a
technological forecast.

Professor Bright has spent the past fourteen years at the Harvard Business School,
specializing in the interaction between technology and business. He launched
Harvard's course on Technological Innovation and planned and conducted the
first conference for industry on technological forecasting (which led to this book).
His major publications include *Automation and Management,* Division of Research, Harvard Business School, (1958) and *Research, Development and Technological Innovation,* Richard D. Irwin, Inc. (1964).

Since about 1940 and as a result of World War II, technology has become noticeably more dynamic. Products have changed more frequently,
and capabilities of many new devices vis-à-vis their predecessors have accelerated, not by percentage points, but by orders of magnitude (as in
aerospace speed, the computational power of the computer, explosive force,

miniaturization of electronic components, etc.). New technology has created literally millions of new jobs and thousands of new firms. Conversely, thousands of existing businesses have been adversely affected by technological progress. It is becoming clearer that technology deserves the same systematic evaluation and consideration that is given to other environmental forces affecting the manager and his institution. Technological forecasting is a relatively new and promising management tool for this purpose. However, the manager should understand certain principles, concepts, and experiences related to technological innovation, as well as application problems of technological forecasting, before he adopts any forecasting method.

IS TECHNOLOGICAL FORECASTING NECESSARY FOR MANAGEMENT?

The introduction to this book points out that a common approach to managerial planning—sometimes deliberate, sometimes unconscious—is to ignore future technological change—in other words, to hold technology constant. This assumption is quite realistic and useful in some stable activities, for perhaps one to three years, because new technology apparently requires five to fifteen years to diffuse throughout society to a significant degree. Thus, a company may have time to recognize and adjust to technical progress.

On the other hand, the assumption is not satisfactory for advanced technology activities such as electronics, drugs, plastics, computers, aerospace or energy conversion. It is also unrealistic at those times when relatively stable industries are being inundated with new technology. This is currently the situation in the traditional materials field—steel, paper, glass, and textiles—and in the machine tool industry, which at present must develop numerical control equipment and simultaneously consider new methods of material forming and joining, such as spark erosion, electrodeposition, chemical milling, and electron beam welding.

The manager should appreciate that this assumption of constancy *is not the omission of a technological forecast* but only the projection of a negligible rate of change. There are many times when this is a perfectly valid and useful conclusion. The issue for the manager is whether he should arrive at it through ignorance, wishful thinking, or deliberate omission, or should reach this conclusion through explicit analysis.

A variation of this approach is the assumption *that anything of technological significance can be dealt with after it has materialized and has proven itself in practice.* In some cases, this may be a satisfactory approach; and it has the advantage of certainty, and of not leading the firm down false trails. One dangerous aspect of such a policy is that the technological lead time gained by others may leave the firm hopelessly behind. Vital patent positions may be lost. Another possibly serious result is that the firm may commit itself to products, processes, capital expenditures, research programs, or even personnel that ultimately reduce its ability to respond to the new technology.

Waiting until the technology appears also carries psychological hazards, with a potential for horrendous economic errors. First is the "crash" program fiasco. When management believes it is behind, there is a tendency to spend any sum, and to go to any extreme, to "buy" its way into a competitive position. But by this time others also have seen the merit of the new technology, and a seller's market is likely to exist. The high cost of haste and the "bandwagon effect" which pervade this atmosphere distort judgment and lead to overenthusiastic or overfearful attitudes and to painfully expensive actions.

The very real hazards in this wait-till-it's-here method of keeping up with technology can be seen in the experiences of Douglas and Convair with the jet transport, of xerography and the copying machine industry, and of the computer and many firms in the business machine industry. The policy of insisting on materialization as the *only* guide to technological progress is dangerous and unsatisfactory.

RATIONALES FOR ASSERTIONS ABOUT THE FUTURE: THE MEANING OF FORECASTS

Assuming that the manager is persuaded that technological forecasting is desirable, just what is a technological forecast? The answer cannot be too rigorous or immutable at this time since the field is in its infancy, as indicated by some disagreement among authors in this book. But there are basic philosophical positions that underlie assertions about the future, and it is most important for the manager to realize what types of assertions he is dealing with. In a classic paper, Irving Siegel establishes the different rationales underlying the assertions loosely regarded as "forecasts." This can be modified and adapted to technological forecasting as follows: [1]

1. PROPHECY

The most common kind of anticipation is an *opinion* about future conditions based on a personal belief, "hunch," speculation, wishful thought

[1] Irving H. Siegel, "Technological Change and Long Run Forecasting," *Journal of Business of the University of Chicago*, Vol. XXVI (July, 1953), 141–56. While my adaption is quite different from Dr. Siegel's descriptions, I am completely in his debt for the idea of such categorizations and for stressing the importance of understanding them.

or fear. The result is not reproducible by systematic logic. Generally, timing and degree are unquantified or unsupported by analysis. Therefore, it is not a technological forecast by the definition used here. However, a *prophecy is not necessarily wrong.* It may be the product of the wisest sort of intuitive selection of relevant factors and judgment; and it may prove to be more nearly correct than any rigorous forecast.

When the businessman turns to the brilliant scientist or engineer for his opinion (prophecy) on future developments, he hopes to obtain a sound forecast through this happy blend of wisdom and experience. He may or may not be successful. Unfortunately, as noted in the Preface, history shows that the technical forecasts of brilliant technologists are often wrong. The manager, and the technologist himself, should appreciate *why* these errors can happen. They seem to be traceable to several causes. For one thing, technologists are human, and thus may be biased, perhaps unconsciously, toward their own accomplishments, academic disciplines, and vested intellectual and financial interests. They find it hard to visualize or accept approaches that invalidate their own knowledge and a lifetime of solid accomplishment.

Second, technologists appreciate physical limitations and technical difficulties, their experience and training having taught them to be conservative in certain areas of their own knowledge and fields of work. They find it difficult to believe that obstacles which delayed them so long can be readily overcome.

Third, the scientifically inclined naturally judge from known scientific laws and principles; and what is known about science apparently is still much less than what is to be learned. The engineer may make similar errors because he uses textbook statements about design principles or the standard practice of the day. Kettering, General Motors' great Director of Research, told how his development engineers assured him that a proposed new approach to diesel engine piston ring design could not possibly work as it violated all known and proven principles. Kettering replied to the effect that they were "butting in too early. Let's let the engine tell us." [2] Anyone can satisfy himself as to the inherent conservatism of competent technologists by browsing through the technical society papers of ten, twenty or thirty years ago. For typical examples, read engine performance predictions, airplane projections, or the Atomic Energy Commission and power plant engineering publications for projections about nuclear power. While the technologist often sees *possibilities* far ahead of others, the record suggests that very often he is too conservative on the timing of the

[2] Kettering's speeches and papers are filled with the philosophy of disbelieving theory and past empirical rules, and putting more faith on experiment. See T. A. Boyd, *Prophet of Progress, Selections from the Speeches of Charles F. Kettering.* New York: E. P. Dutton and Co., Inc., 1961.

materialization of a technological capability (and too optimistic about the timing of its economic benefits). For an extremely disturbing example of this phenomenon consider how the Department of Defense, presumably sparing no brains and money anywhere in the U.S. technical and military society, has frequently underestimated Russian and Chinese progress with nuclear weapons.

Fourth, with rare exceptions, the technologist is *not* a student of technological progress, any more than most of us. Like the economist, he has not had courses on how technological progress evolves; what encourages and impedes it; or how social and political factors, personalities, and the interaction of other technologies speed or delay the progress of a given technological device. Neither science nor engineering curriculums have included courses in technological innovation; these are only now beginning to be offered.[3] Furthermore, the technologist does not always appreciate the characteristics of the diffusion of technological innovations (which will be mentioned later). He too has his mythologies about technological progress. The brilliant Dr. Norbert Wiener stated that it took radar only two years to get on the battlefield with a high degree of effectiveness,[4] and a vice-president of research at Bell Laboratories recently claimed that radar was developed in five years.[5] Yet radio detection of obstacles was suggested by Tesla in 1900, was resuggested by Marconi in 1922, was demonstrated by the Navy Research Laboratory in vessel detection on the Potomac River

---

[3] Since perhaps 1950 or so, many business schools and some liberal arts and engineering schools have offered courses on Research and Development. These courses serve the very useful purpose of improving knowledge and skill in managing this activity in industry and government. Notice, however, that these courses are directed, quite properly, to the function implied in their title; and this function is only a *part* of the process of technological innovation. Harvard Business School's course on technological innovation was proposed in 1959, conducted as a seminar in 1960, and accepted as a course in 1962. About twenty business schools and a few engineering schools are now conducting courses in this area. All of us teaching in this field agree that definitive, systematic knowledge of the topics is still very limited.

[4] Norbert Wiener, *The Human Use of Human Beings* (Boston: Houghton Mifflin Company, 1950). Dr. Wiener was also very wrong on the automatic factory which he stated would appear in widespread form in ten years if we had a war, and twenty years if we did not. Despite two wars in the past twenty years, there are still only a handful of highly automatic processing plants. This is not to deny that the growth of automatic control, processing and materials handling is evident in much manufacturing in 1967. However, it is another proof that great scientists, philosophers, and mathematicians are not necessarily skilled in projecting the economic realities of technical progress.

[5] Dr. William O. Baker, writing in Eli Ginzberg, *Technology and Social Change* (New York: Columbia University Press, 1964), gives this example (Fig. 5, p. 87). This chart typifies the errors that exist about technological innovations. It shows that the electric motor was "discovered" in 1821 and "applied" in 1886. The latter date is grossly in error if "application" means "first operational use." However, these facts do not deny the possible validity of Dr. Baker's point that the time from *laboratory demonstration* to *commercial introduction* of new technology is generally shortening.

in 1922, and was the subject of military research and development programs for at least fifteen years in the United States alone.[6]

Fifth, the technologist and the manager may confuse and compound the forecasting problem by asking such questions as: "How soon will technology X be in use?" or "Is technology X going to replace existing technology Y?" Such questions imply three predictions: (1) that the new technology will be reduced to practice; (2) that it will be adopted by society to a significant degree; and (3) that no superior technological economic competitor will emerge meanwhile. The technologist often is no wiser than anyone else on all the many factors that will influence the diffusion of the new technology.

Prophecy or opinion, therefore, may be the most common means of technical anticipation, and it may be very useful, but it does not meet the definition of a forecast. It lacks rigor and logic. The Delphi method, discussed on pages 116–143, is an important attempt to gain validity by obtaining the consensus of a number of experts who are successively reacting to and refining the reasons for their opinions in a climate that eliminates the influence of personalities. Provided the questions are well chosen (and similarly the experts), the method promises to be a distinct improvement for using opinion to make predictions. Strictly speaking, it is not a forecasting technique, but a means for obtaining a consensus.

2. PROJECTION OR EXTRAPOLATION

This is the most common type of forecasting based on a system of logic, namely, various types of relationships of significant parameters to a historical record. It assumes that there is a past trend, that this trend will continue with some variation, perhaps, and that great discontinuities are not common to most technological progress. It has substantial historical and logical support because examination of technological evolution shows that most devices change through gradual accretion of greater capabilities.

Notice that the forecaster is not necessarily asserting that his forecast will come to pass. A projection implies that *if* certain specified conditions exist, the given parameter, etc., will continue to progress in accordance with its historical pattern, although suitably modified. The manager must ask the question when dealing with projections: "What conditions are assumed in this projection?" Often, past projections have produced poor predictions, but one should be careful not to misjudge such efforts. It is the assumptions, not the concept of projection, that deserve criticism.

[6] John H. McKinney, "Radar, The Reluctant Miracle," *Signal,* October and November, 1966.

Another question is the kind of trend line relationship to be used. Economists commonly use the following in their statistical work:

Arithmetic trend—change of an absolute *constant* amount each period.

Logarithmic trend—change by a *constant percentage* each period. When plotted on semilogarithmic graph paper with time on the horizontal (arithmetic) axis, a straight line results.

Modified exponential trend—change proceeds by a *constant per cent of the previous change.* Thus the curve approaches an upper limit, or asymptote.

Logistic trend—growth curves that have upper and lower asymptotes. The parameter plotted is assumed to grow at one rate in its early stages, to accelerate, and then to gradually decline. This leads to the familiar *S*-curve, such as a Gompertz curve or Pearl's curve of population growth.

Very little has been done to determine what kind of technologies follow these different curves, if indeed they do. Crude trials seem to suggest that the last three curves are appropriate to many technological advances. Overall exponential progress will be seen in the envelope curves suggested by Ayres on pages 77–94. Cetron, pages 144–179, discusses these curves further.

However, mathematical precision may be quite secondary for most *management uses* of trend projections. Whether the phenomenon is exponential or logistic in progress may not matter, at times, because all a manager may need to know is that the capability, etc., is apparently going to increase substantially in the next five or ten years or so; or that it is relatively constant; or that progress seems to be approaching a limit.

3. PROGRAM

Programs can lead to good forecasts, for here the forecaster is part of a purposeful act. A government official, corporate officer, or a technical director specifies a technical goal such as "Man on the moon by 1970" or "Build a Mach 3 transport by 1973." If the program is successfully conducted, announcements about goals and progress are indeed good forecasts. Of course, the manager may want to question whether the goal is realistic and whether the organization is capable of executing it. Programs also identify goals that must be met by subsystems and components, and that, in government programs at least, presumably are assured of financial support. Hence they have a high probability of materializing, and the program therefore is a useful forecast.

4. PROPAGANDA

This is a persuasive forecast, intended to convince someone that some event will materialize. It may be used to condition recipients to accept actions that would be necessary if it did materialize. Much of the union and some of the government agency agitation over automation and unemployment has been (perhaps unconsciously) the propaganda type of forecast. Propaganda has a distasteful connotation, but should not necessarily be discredited. It can be useful in dealing with social ills such as water and air pollution or to accelerate interest in desirable goals.

5. PARROTRY

Parrotry is citing or repeating the claims of others, either consciously or unconsciously as a valid forecast. Parrotry has been responsible for some very poor management judgments in the field of military weaponry, in automation of factories and in data processing, to name a few areas of management errors. No doubt many current fuel cell, laser, and computer development programs are the result of management's acceptance of parrotry as a valid technological forecast.

6. DYNAMIC MODELING

This is a specification of future time and state according to models of complex relationships. If it were possible to construct appropriate models of interaction of technologies, economics, social conditions, physical facilities, material resources, numbers and quality of technical personnel, and even political effort, one might be able to simulate possible and probable outcomes and their timing. This is the industrial dynamics concept inspired by Dr. Jay Forrester some ten years ago.

Another form of dynamic prediction might be called "gaming" through scenarios. It too is a "model," but it deals, perhaps, with more items and things less amenable to quantification. This form of anticipation has been employed by the military to predict responses, to determine the probable impact of possible capabilities, and thus to identify needs. If the identification were acted upon, it would lead to a "program" to achieve those needs. Hence the scenario result becomes a form of prediction of technical needs or capabilities (although not necessarily of precise technical devices or configurations). From this prediction of many scenarios we can determine or estimate the relative usefulness of various technical capabilities and devices for the more likely future conditions. This estimate becomes the basis for choosing R&D programs. This theory underlies the approaches described by Rea (pages 208–222), Linstone (pages 223–241), and Rubin (pages 242–262).

7. NEED INTERACTION

A less elaborate but somewhat similar "model of technological change" has been developed by the Battelle Memorial Institute and applied to several industrial situations (see pages 183–207). It consists of identifying current scientific and technical developments, and social and economic needs, then considering how the gaps might be matched or bridged. Thus the model leads to a program which, in turn, would become a prediction of technical accomplishment.

The approach used by the Army (pages 385–411) is still another variation of forecasting by interaction between needs and possibilities. The Army concept determines possible technical capabilities within a given time frame (in the "opinion of experts") and presents these to the managers who are concerned with needs. As the result of dialogues between managers and technical forecasters, specifications and schedules are laid down for the new devices that are wanted. A research and development program then leads to the materialization of the new technology.

From this brief review of forecasting concepts it should be apparent why it is absolutely vital for the manager to understand the philosophy and methodology of the forecast he is using; its relevance, assumptions and probability implications for his purpose. He must be sure to understand the role of the forecaster, which, in *programs, propaganda, dynamic modeling, need interaction* and *prophecy* approaches, may severely structure or limit the forecast.

Obviously, any type of forecast must be used with caution, and certain procedures should be mandatory:

1. A forecast should not be a one-time event, but should be continually revised as time brings technical, economic and social horizons closer.

2. A policy of detecting errors and making incremental corrections should be followed in order to improve the understanding of relationships.

3. There should be a continual search for key factors that change or are sensitive.

4. The organization's own pattern of experiences should be considered and applied. This means that the firm needs data files on its own technological-economic history. Unhappily very few firms maintain such files; and they have only folklore to use as a guide to plan future technical progress.

Since company files generally are poor sources of technological history, can the accumulated studies of recent innovations help us use technological forecasts? Project HINDSIGHT (pages 35–53) is the most ambitious such study to date, but it was limited (1) to defense devices, and (2) largely to the research portion of the innovation process. Research on recent technological innovations now underway suggests that there may be some patterns in technological progress. Here are some "propositions" —most definitely *not* principles—for managers which may be useful in considering action in response to a technological forecast.[7]

Proposition 1—A forecast of technological capability is not equivalent to a forecast of economic significance. While this statement seems obvious enough, neglect of it is the cause of many mistakes, large losses, and management grief. For a technological advance, even after it is a physical reality, has little economic impact until it is recognized, accepted, adopted by society and converted into a device which can be produced in substantial quantity and then widely used. There is an occasional exception to this principle, as when the use of just two atomic bombs dramatized to the world that old concepts of national military security were doomed; or when the launching of Sputnik caused the United States to respond with tremendous technical, financial, educational, and organizational changes almost overnight. But these are exceptions. Therefore, even though a technological forecast is substantially correct, the manager needs to understand that there is a *process of technological innovation*. This process (see Figure 1) is composed of different types of activities (or phases). Some of these phases may take place in different locations, and require different skills and types of resources; they also may involve different motivations. Each phase takes time, and there is much overlapping of the components of the innovation. Space will not permit detailed explanation, but the manager can see that useful questions are raised about the forecast of a new technology.

First, it is necessary to assess the innovation and to determine the approximate position of its components in this process. Is theory lacking? What are the time and cost implications? Is the product ready for commercial introduction, or is additional development needed? These types of questions should be explored, since answers will help to determine whether it is economically feasible and technically likely that the technology will be reduced to practice.

Second, although a technical *capability* may be correctly forecast, its

[7] These propositions derive from course materials and recent research at the Harvard Business School.

Phases	Description and Significance
1. Suggestion	Identification of phenomena or a need causes search for principles (scientific or engineering).
2. Development of Theory or Design Concept	Through analytical thought (and/or empirical trial) a theoretical concept emerges.
3. Experimental Verification	Experiments on laboratory scale verify that the phenomena respond approximately in accord with theory or design concept.
4. Experimental Application	Demonstration that the phenomena can be applied to perform a useful purpose. (Appropriate mostly to innovations springing from scientific discoveries, not from need.)
5. Field Trial	Full-scale trial of the concept under operating conditions.
6. Commercial Introduction	First operational use of the concept as a part of normal procedure and equipment (not as a development trial).
7. Widespread Adoption	Concept adopted by a substantial number of users.
8. Proliferation of Applications	Basic theoretical concept is adapted to a number of other purposes and fields. (Technology transfer.)

Figure 1. Phases of the Process of Technological Innovation.

diffusion is another matter. To bring innovations into widespread use takes time—and time often measured in decades, not years.

The pioneering work of Mansfield (see Preface) showed that, for some twenty innovations, the time from first adoption by a major firm to adoption by half the leading firms was as long as 12 years, with an average of 7.8 years. My own studies show a similar pattern. As a rough rule of thumb, a *radical* technological advance in a *producible* form, supported by reasonable production facilities, seems to take upwards of 7 years (and more often 10 years) for the number of adoptions and the usage of the device to have a major impact on society. One might cite as an exception Xerox's 914 office copying machine, introduced in 1960, which in two or three years attained a market beyond anyone's expectations, the only limitation being available production facilities. However, Xerox originally introduced their office copying machine Model A in 1950, and this did not meet with success because of cumbersome operating requirements. Before it could be widely used, the innovation had to be reduced to a marketable form. Thus the ten-year-plus hypothesis is substantiated even in this case.

Proposition 2—Radical new technological capabilities and also technological-economic parameters usually seem to evolve in exponential manner. Progress will seem to be on a relatively straight line for a long time; then exponential growth occurs (usually because of some technological breakthrough). Finally, the curve again approaches a straight-line limit. In using extrapolations, particularly over large time spans, the manager should consider which part of the curve is then applicable to the technology. If technological progress appears to be very slow, the technologist may be able to help the manager to identify the inhibiting factors. By monitoring technical progress in these factors, the firm may be able to react in an effective and timely manner.

The manager should be especially sensitive to the beginnings of accelerating progress. Things that seem to encourage this exponential growth include the acquisition and diffusion of knowledge on ways to overcome former technical bottlenecks; the psychological stimulus of proof positive in the technical achievements of others; the act of continual refinement once a bottleneck is broken; and the spur of competition, whether on technical, economic, intellectual, or social grounds. The achievement of nuclear weapons by numerous nations is a case in point, as is recent rapid progress in dry copying machines for office use.

Proposition 3—Progress in any one technical line eventually approaches a technical limit. These limits rarely signal the end of further capability. Instead, they are signals that a new technology must be employed to maintain the progress. (The envelope curves of Ayres (pages 77–94) illustrate this point.) This concept may be of utmost value to the firm. If its product capability appears to be limited by a basic attribute of its present technology, a firm should not assume that progress will cease. On the contrary, management must now become extremely alert to other approaches that will enable product capability to be extended. If a special need for more capability arises, other technologies surely will come into being to provide it. Gilfillan's doctrine of equivalent invention, which his historical studies have so clearly shown, is the result of society's many efforts to fill a given need. In other words, when a product approaches a limit of performance, it is likely to be high time to get a new product rather than to assume that technical progress has ceased.

Proposition 4—Although a greater technological capability may be correctly forecast, the advance will not necessarily have economic value. Consider air transportation—Boston to Paris:

Year	Device	Flight Time (Hours)	Hours Saved over Previous Mode	Economic Value of Improvement to the Traveler
Post-War II	Propeller plane	12	108 *	Very great
1960	Jet Plane	7	5	Very great
1971(?)	Mach 2 plane	3	4	Substantial(?)
1972(?)	Mach 3 plane	2	1	Small(?)

* Passenger steamship.

Perhaps passengers will still be willing to pay for Mach 3 performance for reasons of prestige, excitement, and novelty, but the economic value of the time savings will have declined. As another example, many firms will gladly pay to have their special freight shipments leave east coast airports at 6 P.M. one evening and be available in Los Angeles at 7 A.M. the next morning. How much more is it worth to them to have their shipment arrive at, say, 4 A.M.? In general, this particular speed gain has little economic value.

But note the value of signaling this economic limit. It often occurs because procedures and devices that interface with the new technology prevent users from benefiting from the gain. Opportunity then may lie in applying new technology and/or organization to remove these limiting factors. We are facing this type of problem in air freight today. The C5-A jet freighter, with its capacity of more than 100 tons, will not realize its full potential until new methods and organization for marshaling cargo—loading, unloading and dispatching—are developed. And what traveler has not fumed over the inconsistency of an hour's flight between cities 400 miles apart only to spend another hour collecting baggage and crawling fifteen miles from airport to city center? Additional air speed has little value on short trips until these two bottlenecks are broken.

Society explicitly or intuitively recognizes this kind of limiting factor and therefore tries to find other approaches and solutions. This the manager should consider when he appraises a technological forecast.

Proposition 5—One line of technical progress may accelerate enormously by the impingement of a technological advance in another field. The electronic computer could not have developed and spread as it did if the transistor and other solid-state components had not come along in 1950. This happy marriage accelerated technical capability, durability, space reduction, and economic performance; and hence the rate of adoption and application possibilities of computers. As an unhappy example, the size reduction of the H-bomb relative to the atom bomb gave the ICBM a great impetus, since prior weight and size limitations were thus removed. The converse of this proposition also may be true. In its most significant form it can be expressed as follows:

Proposition 6—Refinement of an existing technology may invalidate the incentive for pursuing a new technology. For example, from 1955 to 1965 blast furnace technology improved output between 300 and 400 per cent. As a result, new processes for direct reduction of iron ore were not pushed as vigorously as had been anticipated. Progress in moving coal by pipeline was slowed or ended in the early 1960's when the railroads introduced the unit train, which destroyed the economic value of the one major coal pipeline then in use.

Proposition 7—Technical progress responds to organization concepts and management skill. The parallel and multiple approach development program of the Manhattan Project is a prime example of the effect of organization on the rate of progress. The development of PERT and related programming efforts speeded the materialization of the Polaris missile system. No doubt the timing of technical achievements in space will be governed in substantial part by the effectiveness of U.S. and Russian space program organization. And, if articles in *Fortune* are reasonably accurate, the debacle of General Dynamic's Convair 880 program and Control Data's 6000 computer system can be traced to faulty organization. According to *Forbes* magazine, General Electric's troubles with computer progress also lay, not in technology, but in organization and management.

Proposition 8—Technological progress is sometimes abruptly accelerated by a gifted individual. It is strange but true that in this world of multimillion and multibillion dollar expenditures for technology, progress with radical technology sometimes stems from a single brilliant or inspired person. The day of the heroic technical leader is by no means over. Admiral Rickover, Werner Von Braun, Sikorsky, Edison, Kettering, and many lesser known persons have demonstrated that the driving leadership, vision, or determination of a single manager, scientist or engineer may greatly alter the materialization of new technology. This is quite at odds with the position of some economists and politicians, who assume that the application of mass resources and effective organization alone control the amount and timing of technical advance and that only a great corporation can advance technological progress. We can find instances in the most recent times where an individual, by his own vision or energy, has brought about major technical progress. One case is xerography, which now generates close to a billion dollars in sales yearly. This new technology arose solely through the technical imagination of one man, Chester Carlson (twenty-nine years old, arthritic, and broke at that!), who saw a need and was determined to satisfy it. Similarly, it was Edwin Land who single-handedly conceived and developed polaroid photography; and Ginsberg, whose skill brought audio-visual tape recording to life at Ampex in a few years, while RCA had fruitlessly poured many times the man-years into a similar effort without success.

These examples are not intended to deny the need for the organization and resources that had to be brought to bear to bring the technology into reality. They only emphasize that the existence of xerography and polaroid film was not the inevitable result of technical activity and economic resources. Individuals determined both the *existence* and the *timing* of these two inventions. And although other men probably would have eventually guided the atomic submarine and the laser to completion, it was Rickover and Townes who determined the *timing*.

Proposition 9—Technology is responsive to social pressures, which often materialize as political decisions that affect progress. War, of course, has been the main example of political action that has brought technical advances, but there are other historic examples (notably in the U.S. Department of Agriculture) in which technical progress has been significantly accelerated by political action.

Today, we have striking evidence that social pressures are forcing political decisions that will affect technological progress in peacetime. The examples are numerous: nuclear power plants, automobile safety, water desalting, high-speed trains, mass transportation, polio vaccine, urban renewal, and the electric automobile. Therefore, the validity of a technical forecast will depend, in part, upon astuteness in relating social and political pressures to technological effort.

Proposition 10—The diffusion (adoption) and financial success of technological innovation will be significantly affected by the mode of financing its ownership and use. Again the computer provides a major example. How fast would the computer have spread if IBM had insisted on selling rather than leasing? Clearly, the size of the investment and the risk would have prevented (and still would prevent) many firms from adopting computers. Suppose Bell had decided to sell telephones to subscribers and simply provide service? What would our telephone equipment look like today? Progress in dial phoning would have been delayed many years at the very least. The great financial gain in Xerox's copying machines came substantially from the decision *to sell usage;* i.e., to charge for the number of copies made. This usage exceeded anyone's expectations, and so Xerox's returns have been far greater than leasing or outright sale would have produced.

LESSONS FROM PAST FORECASTS

Since so very few systematic technical forecasts (as distinct from prophecy or speculation) have been attempted by industry, and fewer still have been published, it is difficult to learn from past practice. However, review of a few forecasting attempts is suggestive. (I shall omit the "prophecy" writings covered by Dr. Gilfillan on pages 3–34.)

In 1937, under Secretary of Interior Ickes, the U.S. Federal Government considered the technology of the future in a government publication entitled *Technological Trends and National Policy.* The book is most interesting reading, and the anticipation of technological progress in individual industries demonstrates our woefully inadequate understanding of the interaction of technology, economics, sociology, and politics. The agriculture experts dwelt largely on the malevolent impact of the Rust cotton picker, which was expected to destroy employment on Southern farms in a few years. The aviation specialist could only foresee the introduction of the diesel aircraft engine and the expansion of private flying (neither of which occurred to the extent suggested). There was not a hint of the jet engine, the helicopter, or rocket power, although all were under development at that very time. The electric power people did a little better, although they did miss atomic power plants (for which one can hardly blame them).

Obviously, the experts of that day simply had little rationale for their predictions. Many of them apparently had little contact with the current development activities and even less with current science. One conclusion can be drawn with some confidence: The record suggests that any one individual probably does *not* have complete knowledge of current technical activity, even in his own field.

A very useful technological-economic study is the Paley Report, resulting from President Truman's 1950 order to project the natural resource needs of the United States to 1975. We are indebted to the Battelle Memorial Institute for their reappraisal, in 1956, of their own contribution to the 1950 study. Battelle examined the correctness of the iron, steel and lead industry forecasts, and found these causes of error in material requirements and sources:

1. The 1950 study assumed the demands of a population of 193 million by 1975. However, the population of the United States reached 170 million in 1956, and (in 1956) was expected to be 200 to 220 million by 1975.

2. The use of taconite grew much more than predicted, partly in response to Minnesota's new tax law on taconite reserves.

3. Venezuela and Canada had become more important sources of iron ore than had been assumed.

4. The predictions on steel scrap consumption were in error, owing to very complex techno-economic relationships that underlie the availability and use of scrap.

5. Lead requirements were badly off because the analysis failed to allow for: (a) the advance in automobile battery life, which had grown from 12–18 months in 1950 to 24–36 months by 1956; (b) the effect of plastic battery cable coverings in reducing lead requirements; and (c) the loss of lead's position as an industrial chemical.

But even more instructive are the 1956 reviewer's own oversights on further progress. In 1956 he was specifically and emphatically wrong on processes. He pointed out (in 1956) that the new steel processes forecast in 1950 had not and would not materialize. Yet at that very moment continuous casting was becoming a significant development in Europe; and, as of now, it is beginning to spread into the U.S. steel industry facilities. The basic oxygen converter had been widely proven in Europe, had been adopted by one firm in the United States (McLouth Steel), and within ten years was to substantially replace the open hearth for all new construction.

These and similar experiences should convince the manager that technological progress (and hence a technological forecast) is (1) extremely sensitive to economic, social, and political interactions, and (2) highly vulnerable to interaction with other technology. Faced with the realization of what a complex phenomenon they are dealing with, the manager and forecaster may be tempted to throw up their hands and withdraw. This response is neither necessary nor desirable.

There is an inevitability to technological progress which demands concern; and the opportunities that abound in new technology should encourage our attempts at anticipation.

MANAGEMENT USES OF TECHNOLOGICAL FORECASTS

Technological forecasts have three broad areas of use to management:

1. To assist in the development of products, facilities, and markets, by guiding supporting research and development for the firm's current activities;
2. As an aid to long-range planning, including the study of the future environment, identification of opportunities and threats through technological progress, the setting of long-range research goals and budgets, and establishment of new product needs;
3. As an aid to communications between technical departments, managers of divisions and functions, top management, and corporate planning staffs.

Examples of such applications now follow.

Current Product Development Applications

By examining trends in significant parameters of his product, the manager can obtain guidelines for product planning. He can consider whether proposed performance characteristics of new models agree with the ap-

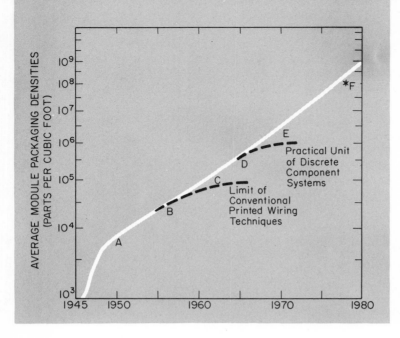

Figure 2. Packaging Densities of Electronic Components That May Be Achieved Through Microelectronic Thin-Film Circuitry. (From H. V. Noble, "Microelectronic Progress," *Ordnance*, May–June, 1965), Copyright, 1965. Reprinted by permission.

parent rate of progress in the field. If the proposed characteristics seem to be substantially behind the trend, he should consider whether they are adequate and appropriate. If the proposed characteristics are significantly ahead of the projected trend, he should consider whether the projection is indeed attainable. Is the customer able to use the gain he intends to offer? Are there limitations elsewhere in the customer's environment that will prevent him from benefiting from the new superior performance? If the firm attains this distinct edge, how can it capitalize on it most effectively? Does it suggest a new advertising theme? Does it open up new markets and new applications? Or would it be the wiser part of product strategy to program smaller increments of improvement, and keep product performance more closely related to the average? All these questions are implied, for the electronics component manufacturer and his customer, in the forecast made by Dr. H. V. Noble of Wright-Patterson Air Force Base (see Figure 2).

Choosing between product development programs is another use of technological forecasts. A neglected opportunity to benefit from such forecast applications can be inferred from Schlaifer's study of aircraft engine development:

> While it is true that even $100,000 put into each of all the various unorthodox engines proposed between the wars would have been a serious drain on the total funds available for all development, the

number of innovations which could show real promise even on paper was not so great. There was, in fact, a great difference between the turbojet and all the other unorthodox engines proposed between the wars, and this difference could have been seen even at the time. The turbojet promised enormous improvement in airplane performance on the basis of assumptions which were reasonable, even if they were not certain. All the other engines mentioned above, on the contrary, promised at the most very limited gains, and in most cases experience had already shown that the practical obstacles to the attainment of these limited gains were very great.

The real trouble with the various unorthodox engines on which public funds were spent with no result in the United States between the wars was that even granting that they were perfectly practical technically, they did not *promise enough superiority over existing engines to make it worth while to spend enough money to make them work*. As a result only small amounts were spent, and these amounts were a total loss.[8]

Technological forecasts can be applied to processes, with some extremely useful results. The director of research of a glass company plotted the time series of tons of glass produced by his firm per square foot of furnace per year. The projection of the trend showed that if that progress continued, the firm's capital expenditure plans for expansion were excessive. A technical check was made to see if it was realistic to assume that the trend could be maintained. The answer was affirmative, and the expansion funds were saved for other uses. A similar study of the speed of bottle-molding machines suggested the same thing: if technological progress could be continued at the present rate, expansion of facilities could be greatly reduced.

Long-Range Planning and Corporate Strategy Assistance

Beyond the immediate product, technical forecasts can help management to identify new and long-range technical requirements, which hold within themselves great opportunity and threat. As an easily grasped example, let us imagine a U.S. airplane engine manufacturer studying the speed of aircraft. Assume that it is 1940, and he has plotted the speed of the aircraft as shown by the solid line in Figure 3. In discussions with technical people, the manager will learn that propeller-driven craft are limited to something short of the speed of sound—under 700 miles per hour. The technologists could help him to identify the research and development work that needed to be done to squeeze the last bit of per-

---

[8] Robert Schlaifer, *The Development of Aircraft Engines and Fuels* (Boston: Harvard Business School, 1950). Italics added for emphasis.

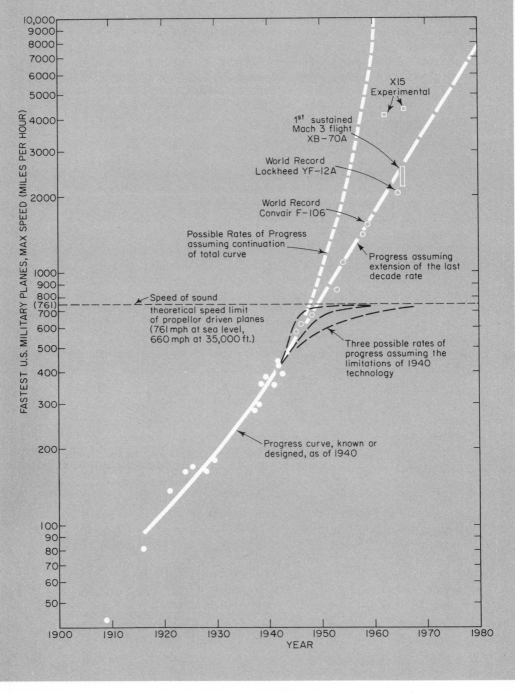

Figure 3. Speed Trend of U.S. Military Aircraft to 1940, Showing Possible Projections of That Time and Actual Experience by 1966.

formance out of the propeller-driven plane. He could thus lay out programs for its accomplishment within an appropriate time and cost framework.

Now suppose that he takes another attitude something like this: "Is it possible that this trend will somehow continue? If aircraft speed does continue to progress in this manner, we will be going about 650 mph by 1950, and 1,400 mph by 1960!" Since these data plotted are for operational aircraft, which probably means that the power technology was available a couple of years before the plane flew, the graph suggests that somewhere around 1946–48 there will have to be a new power plant capable of making an airplane break the sound barrier. What will it be? Is there anything to support this apparent technological anomaly?

Assuming he made a careful search throughout the world, the probable answer would very quickly appear. While he might have trouble getting the facts from Germany in view of international tensions, it should be possible to verify that a young flight officer in the Royal Air Force, Frank Whittle, had formed an engine company called Power Jets, Ltd., and that the British Thomson-Houston Company had designed an experimental engine for Whittle which had run in April, 1937! Although the engine was not too successful, the British government had provided financial support in 1938. He could also discover that in June, 1939, Dr. Pye, Director of Scientific Research, became so impressed with the performance of the engine that he agreed to cover all future work by Power Jets, Ltd.; and that the Gloucester Aircraft Company was even now (1940) designing and building an airframe for the new engine.

A further search of engineering work and patents in foreign countries would disclose that there had been many attempts to produce an efficient gas turbine in the early 1900's. In 1929 A. A. Griffith, a scientist in the British Royal Aircraft Establishment, had built a single-stage compressor turbine capable of driving a propeller with a fairly high degree of efficiency.

If he could gain access to German activity, he would also find that a twenty-four-year-old German student, Hans Von Ohain, had patented a centrifugal type turbojet in 1934, and that the Junkers Airplane Company began research on gas turbines in early 1936. An official on the research staff of the German Air Ministry, Helmut Schelp, had been encouraging high officials from 1937 onward to support turbojet research as well as work on rockets, pulse-jets, and ram-jets! Von Ohain had worked with an aircraft manufacturer, Heinkel, and had demonstrated a jet model plane in 1936. The Bramo Engine Company had completed designs for an axial flow turbojet engine in 1939. Possibly, he might be able to learn that the German Air Ministry's Air Frame Development Group had then engaged the Messerschmitts to design an airframe for a jet fighter (ultimately the ME 262).

If management concern over that trend line provoked them enough to put, say, just one imaginative man on a three-month study they would have found that the concept of a jet engine was at least twenty years old; and that governments in two countries, under the direction of devoted and competent technical personnel, were very seriously pursuing its development. The jet engine was not just theory in 1940, but was well into its development phase. Now management could decide whether to pursue this line of progress, to associate with the foreign inventors and developers, or to sit on the sidelines a bit longer until the likelihood of success became more clear. But the firm would not be caught flatfooted, as, in fact, the U.S. airplane engine industry was in 1944–45.

Had management added one more elementary question: What is the political situation going to do to the airplane power plant progress? they would have had an even stronger reason to assume progress. They would have had to conclude: The 1940 war is bound to accelerate aircraft engine performance, and there is a fair probability that the trend line will be shifted upward even more than past progress indicates.

Let us consider the role of the aircraft manufacturer looking at the same projection in 1940. If airplane speed progresses in approximately this manner, what is suggested? Within twenty to twenty-five years planes should be moving close to several thousand miles an hour! Even if this is only an experimental effort, it means that someone is going to have to design an airframe capable of moving at these speeds. What are the aerodynamics of such speeds and what research should the firm be doing on supersonic air-flow? The 1940 construction for the 300–400 mph airplane surely is not adequate for the 2,000 mph plane. What materials will stand the temperatures and forces involved? How will such materials be worked and shaped?

The study of this trend line further identifies a host of related problems which are bound to become opportunities if the speed materializes. If an airplane is going to move 2,000 mph, or even 1,000 mph, how does a pilot navigate? There is hardly time for shooting the sun! And what about fire control in military craft? The human being simply will not be able to see and respond fast enough to direct guns or bombs at such speeds. This leads to an even more immediate research question: Up to what speeds is human fire control practical? A little investigation of this problem would show that fire control will be a more serious problem, demanding new technical solutions for the speeds that apparently are just a few years away.[9]

Another type of assistance to strategic business planning is exemplified

[9] In 1959, Dr. Ramo of TRW, Inc., advised me that it was this very projection of the effect of aircraft speeds on fire control needs that led to the formation of the Ramo-Wooldridge Corporation, ultimately Space Technology Laboratories.

in considering the electronic content of the fighter plane. In World War II, about 12 per cent of fighter plane cost was electronics; by the time of the Korean conflict this had risen to over 45 per cent. In the F-104 and 105 planes, electronic content has been cited as approaching 70 per cent. Trends like these suggest not only new development and manufacturing needs but even questions of business strategy. If the airplane is going to become substantially an assembly of electronics, should the aircraft firm become a manufacturer of electronic devices? If the firm does not go into electronics systems work, what kind of subcontracting arrangements will be most appropriate? Does the firm have technical and purchasing staffs that are competent to deal with the electronic suppliers? It takes no great managerial insight to identify the pertinent questions (although it may very well take a genius to answer some of them).

Notice what the forecast has done. It (a) identified the growing importance of a technical-economic trend; and (b) forced the firm to face up to the implications for the structure, scope, and staffing and equipping of its business. Precision of date and degree in the forecast is quite secondary to the business policy implications revealed or inferred through the exercise.

Another strategic planning application is shown by using aircraft as a historical analogy to forecast attributes of electrical power for spacecraft in the years ahead. From data such as that shown in Figures 4, 5, and 6, V. P. Kovacik concludes:

> Using the growth of aircraft electrical power as a guide, one can conclude that manned aircraft will require 150 to 200 KW when the technology for the spacecraft matures.
>
> The evolution of electrical power of fighter aircraft has taken 40 years; transport aircraft, 43 years; and bombers, 29 years. If one as-

Figure 4. Evolution of Electric Power in Aircraft.

Vehicle	1st Major Use of Electrical Power	Power Increase 100 Times	To Maturity	Installed Capacity, kva Early	1960's	Ratio of Power in 1960's to Early Power	Annual Average Electrical Capacity Increase
Fighter Aircraft	1926	19	40	0.225	120	530	1330%
Transport Aircraft	1928	19	43	0.450	300	670	1550%
Bombers	1935	11	29	1.2	360	300	1070%
Manned Spacecraft	1962	8	—	0.5	4.2	8.4	210%
Unmanned Spacecraft	1959	10	—	0.005	0.772	155	3100%

Equipment	Start of Government R&D Support	First Major Application Year	First Major Application Vehicle	Elapsed Time, Years
Aircraft Generator	1921	1926	Fighter Aircraft	5
Photovoltaic Space Power	1955	1959	Explorer VI	5
Nuclear Dynamic Space Power	1956	1970 (Est.)	Military Comsat?	15 Est.
Isotope Thermoelectric Space Power	1958	1961	Transit IV	4
Fuel Cells	1959	1964	Gemini	6
Solar Dynamic Space Power	1959	1972 (Est.)	Large Space Station?	14 Est.

Figure 5. Time from R&D Support to Application.

sumes the continually increasing rate of technological development, spacecraft evolution may reach maturity in 20 years, i.e., in 1982.

. . . It seems reasonable to assume that specific spacecraft which will be used extensively will experience a 100 to 200 per cent increase in electrical power requirements during their useful life.[10]

The forecaster then extrapolates the electrical capacity requirement and other relationships. By identifying the scope of power requirements and the approximate timing of use, he provides guidance on power capacities, fuel supplies, and related support that will be needed in spacecraft.

Technological forecasting can identify opportunities and threats, leading to better product goals and strategies. Figure 7A illustrates Sikorsky's progress with lifting capability using conventional helicopter technology. Figure 7B shows how the Russian capability has grown. (Did they pick up the trend discontinuity in Sikorsky's S-56?) At any rate, their helicopter progress seems to take off from that point. Sikorsky's own lift development program was pushed by the firm, using its own resources, beginning about 1958. The S-60 crane helicopter (not shown) became the S-64A Sky Crane (just in time for Viet Nam). As Figure 7C shows, a very substantial gap still exists vis-à-vis the "competitor." The triangular mark shows where the "normal growth" helicopter will take the firm. Sikorsky believes DoD should close this gap by a vigorous R&D program on helicopter lift.[11]

[10] V. P. Kovacik, "Growth of Electric Power Needs for Aircraft and Spacecraft," Third Biennial Aerospace Power Systems Conference, American Institute of Aeronautics and Astronautics, September, 1964.

[11] Data from DoD presentation made by Sikorsky Division, United Aircraft (unclassified) in 1966.

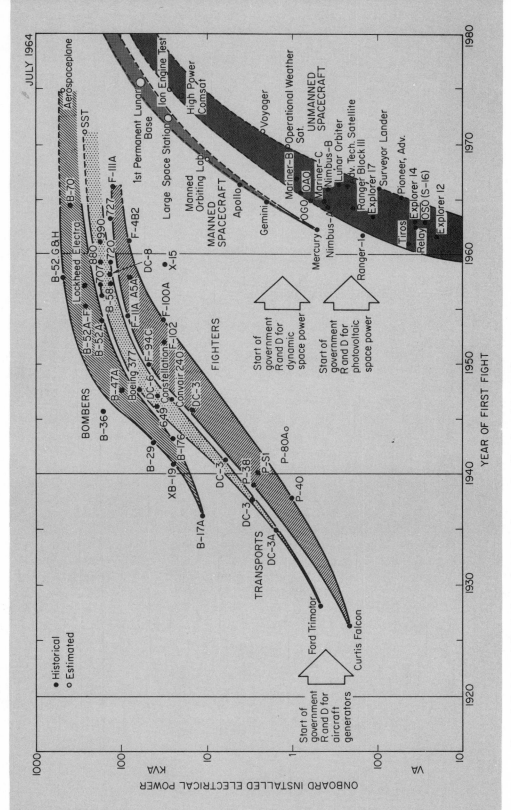

Figure 6. Evolution of Electric Power System Requirements for Aircraft and Spacecraft.

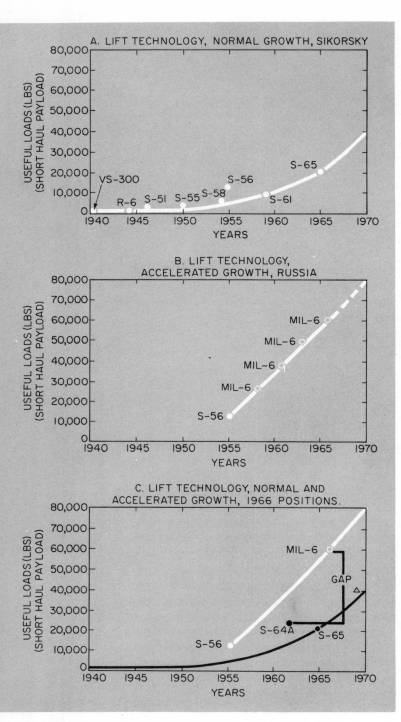

Figure 7. Helicopter Lift Comparisons.

Forecasts as a means of communications between technologists and top management, between divisions, and between different fields of technology are a third major area of use. For excellent examples in the government, the reader should consider the Army approach on pages 385–411 and for the corporation, the TRW experience described on pages 412–425.

Throughout all the chapters in this book, the reader will find other variations and possibilities of management uses. However, the basic importance to management lies in recognizing the value of systematically examining the technological future.

Technological Forecasting for the Canadian Pulp and Paper Industry

LINCOLN R. THIESMEYER

Forecasts of the future of an industry that focus primarily on market and economic trends can be misleading. The growth of the Canadian pulp and paper industry has been accompanied by many technological innovations. It is the author's thesis that projections that overlook such technological developments tend to underestimate future prospects. The examples presented also highlight the need to establish policies to guide technical developmental activities.

Dr. Thiesmeyer is President of the Pulp and Paper Research Institute of Canada. He has been involved with technological forecasting for the Canadian pulp and paper industry for more than fifteen years, and has recently completed a projection of the industry to the year 2067.

Many types of forecasting are based primarily on the projection of trends of such parameters as population size, GNP, standards of living, and the like. Generally, these turn out to be conservative because the forecasters did not and could not take the impact of science and technology into account. These factors have invariably steepened the trend lines.

Growth trends in the pulp and paper industry are generally considered to be influenced most by growth in world population; increasing demand for book and writing papers due to increasing rates of literacy; and rising standards of living which bring increased demands for sanitary papers, packaging materials, and construction papers. Using these and similar parameters, the Food and Agriculture Organization of the United Nations

(UNFAO) predicted a doubling of the world pulp and paper industry by 1975 and a subsequent doubling by the year 2000. However, it has neglected the impact of new technology, which, from extrapolation of past history, should steepen the growth curves and shorten the time it takes the industry to attain such gigantic proportions.

THE IMPACT OF SCIENCE AND TECHNOLOGY ON RAW MATERIALS

Harvesting of the industry's raw materials has, for generations, been a labor-intensive activity. As a result of spiraling wages, which more than doubled the costs of this phase of operations over the past twenty-five years, the need for greater productivity to meet the spectacular increase in the demand for products, and growing shortages of labor, it became evident, some years ago, that principles of science and technology would have to be applied to the forests and that lumbering activities would have to be mechanized. The power saw is not new. It was invented many years ago and developed over a long period of time, largely through cut-and-try methods. It remained too heavy and unwieldy to win ready acceptance until lighter construction materials became available. This happened about twenty years ago, and today the chain saw cuts about 99 per cent of the wood that is harvested in Canada.

The speed with which such an innovation is accepted depends on the size of its capital costs; the degree of increase in productivity it can make possible; the savings in time, money, and effort it introduces; the resistance of operators to change; the time interval during which its initial costs are repaid, and other factors. It is axiomatic that relatively small improvements in methods, processes, and equipments will be accepted quickly and spread rapidly, particularly in an industry like pulp and paper which has a long-established tradition of openness and free exchange of technological information. Hence, a forecaster must take these factors into account in attempting to put a time schedule on technological improvements.

THE IMPACT OF SCIENCE AND TECHNOLOGY ON CONVERSION TO PULP

In its manufacturing operations, the pulp and paper industry is decidedly capital-intensive and is becoming increasingly so. Simultaneously, the return on invested capital has been going down, not as a result of increased costs of materials, labor or taxes, but because the industry has followed a tradition of mimicry. For centuries, pulp and paper were made by hand. Mechanization was introduced during the Industrial Revolution, but there has been no *major* change in the methods of manufacture for more than a century. Increases in production have been accomplished by increasing the size and speed of paper machines and of pulping and bleaching plants. A new mill completed today is essentially the same as one built ten years ago except that it is generally bigger. Thus, the tradition of mimicry has been accompanied by the "Gargantua Complex."

Fifteen years ago, the Pulp and Paper Research Institute of Canada concluded that small improvements in conventional practices or equipment or process would have only small effects on productivity and profitability. A change in the decreasing return on capital could only come about through the introduction of revolutionary new technology aimed primarily at reducing capital costs. Hence, a detailed examination of the industry's operations, from the forest to end-products, was begun.

Woodlands operations involve a great deal of handling and rehandling of individual pieces of wood; however, mechanization tends to make woodlands operations more capital-intensive. As a solution, the idea was conceived to convert the wood to chip form in the forest and send it in a water suspension, through pipelines, to the mills. The technical feasibility of this idea was tested and proved in pilot-scale studies, and design parameters are now available for the building of a first commercial prototype chip pipeline.

Unfortunately, in Canada there are very few places where the wood is close to the mill. The capital risk for a line of fifteen to thirty miles would be considerable. Consequently, the first commercial prototype has not yet come into existence. But someday, somewhere in the world, the economics of this potential innovation will be proved out and then it will spread. One of the difficulties of introducing new technology to an old and conservative industry is that nobody wants to be the first to gamble, although all would like to be close seconds!

If and when it becomes evident that there will be commercial chip pipelines, the next step will be the simultaneous processing of the wood to pulp during transport. There are no technical barriers to doing this. The appropriate chemicals can be introduced at the right places and there will be time for their diffusion throughout the wood substance. Residence time for treatment can be provided by increasing the pipe diameter or by turning it into a tower. Bleaching can be accomplished in another tower, and bleached and washed kraft pulp can be extruded from the end of the line into the stock chests, ready for the paper machine. Hence, it can be foreseen that someday the chemical pulpmill will resemble a petroleum refinery, with interconnected tanks and towers, and the whole sequence from the forest to processing into pulp will be carried out in one continuous flow.

From the time it was introduced in the 1860's until shortly after World War II, chemical pulping had been carried out on a batch basis. Shortly after the war, a shift to continuous processing began and this has been spreading so rapidly that recently built mills and those now being designed use nothing but continuous digesters. However, these pieces of equipment are getting bigger and bigger—a trend which is the reverse of what it should be if capital costs are to be brought down.

Chemical pulping takes place by steeping chips in an excess of acid or alkali. This is performed in large pressure vessels, at elevated temperatures. The lignin, which is the second major component of the wood (cellulose being the first), becomes soluble in these aqueous solutions and can be flushed away in subsequent washing operations. Any continuous process which is run through a series of machines can be made more efficient if the stages are telescoped. (If the series of interconnected tanks and towers were attached to the end of a chip pipeline described above, essentially all the stages from chip production to pulp extrusion would be combined into a single, long, somewhat complex container.)

The trend to ever larger digesters can only be reversed if the cycle of time for the chemical pulping treatment can be shortened. Then, just as much pulp could be produced in any interval of time with smaller, less costly equipment. Moreover, it would be possible to maintain better control and to provide better instrumentation for eventual computer control. An additional benefit would come from the greater uniformity of treatment in the smaller equipment. An investigation of these considerations revealed that the time for the production of kraft pulp could be brought down from three and one-half hours to less than one hour. The first commercial prototype is now in operation in a mill in Ontario.

THE IMPACT OF SCIENCE AND TECHNOLOGY ON PAPER MAKING

Paper is formed commercially by depositing a dilute water suspension of pulp onto a fast-moving wire and permitting the water to drain by gravity and to be drawn away in suction boxes placed beneath the wire. Some time ago, in England, it was reasoned that, if drainage could be made to occur in two directions simultaneously, the higher drainage rate would permit faster operation of the machines and the two-sidedness of a paper sheet would disappear. A second wire was placed above the forming mat of fiber, and suction boxes were provided above, as well as below, in a very successful experiment. There are now several commercial variations of this operation in North America.

There would be no point in speeding up the forming of paper if the only way that paper could be dried would be by adding conventional steam-heated rolls to the end of the drying section of the machine and lengthening the building. As a result, work has begun on several new methods for removing water from a wet sheet at drying rates which are ten to fifteen times those of conventional commercial practice. Inherent in this development are also substantial reductions in capital cost, savings in operating cost, and improved quality through more uniform treatment. Hence, it would appear that the paper machine of the immediate future may not need to be more than fifty feet in total length, in contrast to present machines which are longer than a football field and cost many millions of dollars because so much whirling metal and so many supporting structures, bearings, etc., must be included.

SUMMARY

Two significant points stand out in the above examples. First is the fact that many of the technological changes were developed and introduced in response to a specific objective—the desire to reduce capital investments and thereby improve rates of return. This provided a guideline which directed the attentions and efforts of the innovators. The second point is the need to include probable or possible technological change in forecasts of the future. Simple extrapolation of demographic and economic trends is insufficient, as this neglects the effects which technology will have on costs (and, therefore, on prices and demands). It also tends to ignore the effects of new product developments.

The Application of Strategic Forecasting to the Coal Industry

CHARLES M. MOTTLEY

Strategic forecasting begins by identifying needs and then works back to identify the nature and amount of effort required to meet such needs. The application of this methodology is illustrated by an example drawn from a recent study of the future of the bituminous coal industry in the United States.

Mr. Mottley is Operations Research Scientist with the Bureau of Mines, U.S. Department of Interior. His experience with forecasting is very broad and includes pioneering studies for the Department of Defense, conducted in the early 1950's, as well as industrial consultation in this field.

Planning is a process that visualizes future situations, makes estimates of capabilities, and diagnoses future needs. Strategic forecasting is the specialized branch of the planning activity that is concerned with anticipating events and shaping appropriate courses of action. It is especially concerned with research and engineering functions. These are areas in which projects must be initiated early so that an organization can be in the best position to respond effectively to future changes and contingencies.

The long lead times inherent in modern management situations place a premium on competent strategic planning. Management must be able to "see" what needs to be discovered, engineered, and produced, what timetable should be established, and what corrections should be made as the action proceeds.

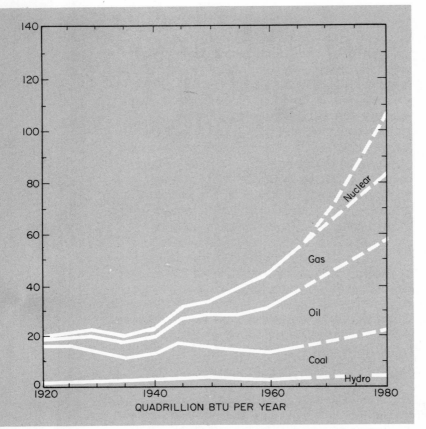

Source: *A. B. Cambel, et al., Energy, R&D and National Progress.*

Figure 1. U.S. Energy Consumption.

The role of strategic planning can best be illustrated with reference to a specific example—the supply of energy as of 1980. Forecasts indicate that the total energy supply will be adequate to meet demand.[1] However, it is difficult to project the competitive "mix" of different energy-producing materials and forces which will be employed. This example focuses on one of these sources—bituminous coal.

Coal's share of the total energy production in the United States slipped from about 70 per cent in 1900 to 23 per cent in 1965 (see the solid lines in Figure 1). It lost the transportation market to oil and now faces the prospect of losing its *growth share* of the electric utility market to nuclear

[1] A. B. Cambel, et al., *Energy, R&D, and National Progress,* Interdepartmental Study, September, 1966.

power and eventually becoming obsolete. Besides this competitive threat, coal now must conform to stringent air pollution regulations aimed at reducing the amount of sulfur oxides emitted into the atmosphere. In the time frame under consideration, natural gas and domestic oil reserves are expected to decrease. These points illustrate some of the uncertainties with which the strategic planner must deal.

For the purpose of illustration, it is here assumed that it is in the public interest, for socioeconomic reasons, to maintain the existence of a viable coal industry. The first step in strategic forecasting is to construct a model of the future (1980). In this case, a series of future conditional energy balances is required.

The techniques of the traditional econometric forecast methodology are used to project the trends of the major components of energy consumption by source and form; e.g., hydroelectric power, coal, oil, gas, and nuclear energy (see the dotted lines in Figure 1). The effects of several contingent factors, such as different rates of economic and population growth, are introduced while making these projections.

The purpose of this procedure is not to "predict" in the usual sense,

Figure 2. Coal Demand, 1965–80.

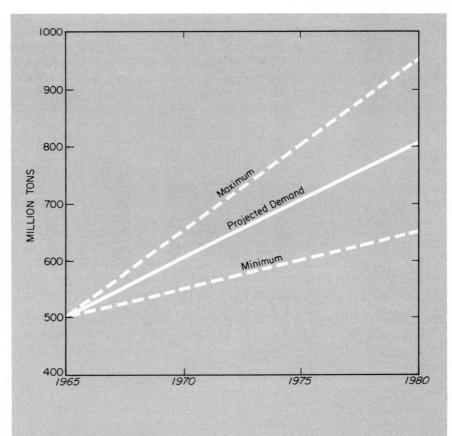

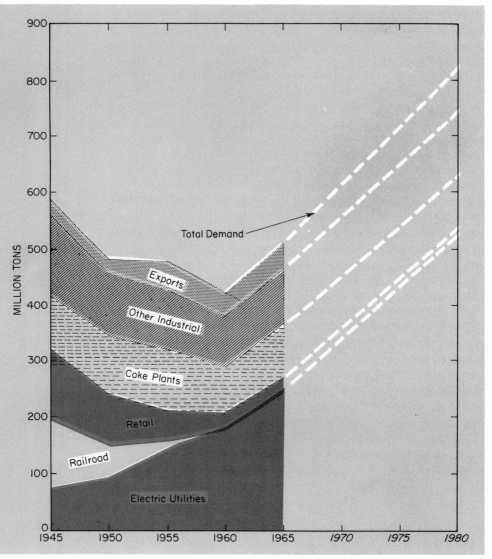

Source: Prepared by Division of Bituminous Coal, July 20, 1966.

Figure 3. Bituminous Coal Demand by Consumer.

	Installed Nuclear Generating Capacity (megawatts)	Coal Fuel 12,000 Btu/lb. (million tons)
1965	1,000	245
1980 (projected) [1]	40,000	640
	80,000	540
	120,000	440

[1] Oil and gas consumption held constant.

Figure 4. Sensitivity of Coal Consumption in the Electric Utility Sector to the Growth of Nuclear Generating Capacity.

but to discover contingent boundary conditions. For example, a model used by the Bureau of Mines [2] indicated that the consumption of coal in 1980, projected at 807 million tons, might be as high as 950 million tons or as low at 650 million tons. This compares with 1965 consumption of 500 million tons. (See Figures 2 and 3.) The swing in the estimates of future consumption depends on such things as whether or not a successful nuclear breeder reactor becomes operational, whether nuclear power can compete economically with smaller, coal-fired electric utility plants (see Figure 4), and whether coal can be transformed economically to more convenient forms. The best strategy to meet the upper boundary of 950 million tons would satisfy the increased demand not only by expanding coal mining operations, but also through increased mine mechanization and the application of evolutionary technology which would increase the productivity per man. (Figures 5 through 7 present projections of productivity and labor requirements.) In the case of the lower boundary, 650 million tons, the slower growth rate might be cushioned by expanding export markets and by improved technology which would reduce the cost of production and keep coal in a cost-pace-setting position, leading the other forms of energy. In addition, new technology may permit the transformation of coal to more convenient liquid and gaseous forms which might permit the coal industry to make inroads in the automotive fuel and piped fuel (e.g., natural gas) markets. This assumes that the air pollution problems will be solved by advances in technology.

Each of these expressed contingent needs provides a stimulus for generating new ideas to overcome the technical barriers (see Figure 8). Then the necessary research resources can be programmed to achieve the de-

[2] Warren E. Morrison, *Simulation of the 1980 Energy Model,* a working paper, Division of Economic Analysis, U.S.B.M., March, 1967.

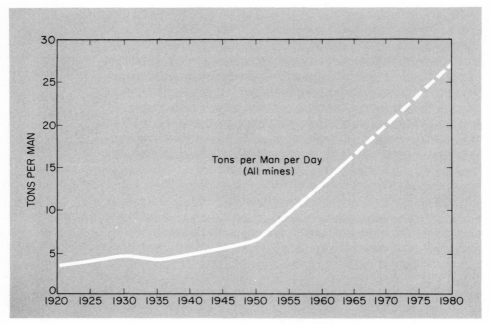

Source: Prepared by Division of Bituminous Coal, July 20, 1966.

Figure 5. Trends in Output per Man at Bituminous Coal and Lignite Mines in the U.S.

Figure 6. Potential Production for 1980 with 138,000 Employees.

Source: Prepared by Division of Bituminous Coal, July 20, 1966.

Figure 7. Employment Requirements to Produce 807 Million Tons of Coal in 1980.

Source: Prepared by Division of Bituminous Coal, July 20, 1966.

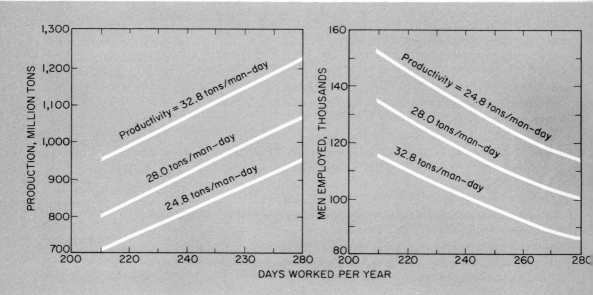

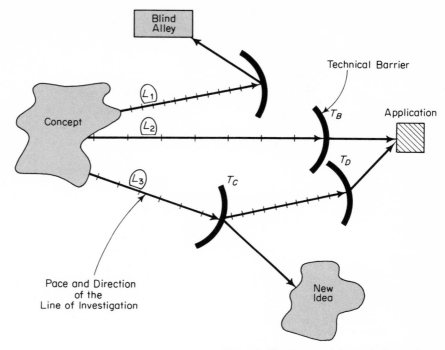

Figure 8. The Process of Strategic Forecasting.

sired technical events. Thus, the approach of the strategic forecaster is to examine future potential situations and diagnose the needs as the basis for deciding what courses of action must be initiated.

This approach differs considerably from that of the predictors and forecasters who often assume the more passive role of interested observers, watching "nature taking its course." The strategic planner, by contrast, takes an active part in the managerial process. The passive approach [3] takes policy as a given, whereas the strategic forecaster helps management reach agreement as to desired objectives and the preferred ways and means of achieving those objectives. In other words, he helps shape policy by developing appropriate courses of action and making technical events come to pass in the future.

[3] Irving Siegel's definitions are cited, in greatly modified form, on p. 345 of this book.

ORGANIZING THE TECHNOLOGICAL FORECASTING EFFORT

PART FIVE

The purpose of this section is to suggest how institutions can establish and disseminate the forecasting program and predictions.

The large government agency—in this case the U.S. Army—employs a forecasting-planning interchange in a continuous process and on levels ranging from laboratory scientist to top management. It is a process of give-and-take: the statement of possibilities, the expression of desired capabilities, and their modification against time, cost, and usefulness appraisals.

TRW, Inc., is perhaps the first corporation to apply the Delphi technique. Their Vice-President of Research explains how they evolved their first corporate level technological forecasts. The forecast as a means of communication between technologist and manager is one major theme suggested here. Apparently, the forecast has a specificity that both intrigues and demands top management attention, and is understandable to the non-technical manager.

The section—and the book—closes with the ideas of Dr. Erich Jantsch, who sums up his reaction based on his world-wide survey of technological forecasting. He sees a future in which technological forecasting and technological planning for the firm are merged into the long-range planning activity.

Developing and Using the U. S. Army Long Range Technological Forecast

JOHN R. BIRD
HALVOR T. DARRACOTT

The U.S. Army uses technological forecasting as a statement of possibilities, not predictions. One of the important features of the forecasting process is a deliberately constructed framework to insure the interchange of ideas between the technologists making the forecasts and the users who will be applying them to the development of specific hardware and systems. Analogies between the Army system and problems of industrial enterprises are highlighted to help industrialists create appropriate procedures for their own firms.

Mr. Bird was an originator of the Army Long Range Technological Forecast. Until his retirement, he was Chief of the Long Range Technological Forecast Branch of the U.S. Army. Mr. Darracott succeeded Mr. Bird as compiler and editor of the Army Forecast and is presently General Physical Scientist, Technological Forecast Branch, Science and Technology Division, U.S. Army Materiel Command.

During the mid-1950's, many people who were intimately concerned with research and development in the Army became painfully aware that planning methods were inadequate. In an age of increasingly complex and sophisticated weapons, newly developed systems often cost more than anticipated. The time elapsing between recognition of a technical capability and development of a system was unacceptably long. It was found that these difficulties were primarily due to two causes.

The first was incomplete technical planning prior to undertaking the actual development. Component capabilities necessary for the proper functioning of the system were sometimes beyond the existing state of the art and required new approaches and the development of new subsystems. The new component characteristics required redesign of other functionally interrelated components, and cumulative changes in subsystem characteristics sometimes reduced the performance of the total system from that originally envisioned. Even if the system lived up to all expectations, the unforeseen need for research and component development extended the time and increased the cost far beyond that which was planned and budgeted.

A second difficulty was the excessive time encountered in deciding on the most desirable characteristics for a new system. Delay from this cause increased the likelihood that system development would be undertaken without full knowledge of component capabilities, since the establishment of the objectives of system development was changed or postponed until it was too late for thorough and detailed planning and research.

Early technical forecasts attempted to predict future systems which would be feasible and needed. These did a fair job of forecasting possible new technical capabilities, but the technologists could not adequately project the other ingredients of an integrated planning process. For example, the demands of Army operations in the future world environment were not adequately interpreted. The forecasts, therefore, lacked the imagination which could have come from a clearer view of future demands. The Army's attempts to reverse the procedure, by asking operational planners to place demands on technology without a clear idea of the technical potential, often resulted in demands which either were beyond the potential of technology in the time period or were merely requirements for improvements in existing types of equipment.

It was necessary, therefore, to analyze and identify the fundamental elements which could form the foundation for an integrated planning process in which the ingredients would stimulate and augment, rather than constrain, each other. Two of the basic ingredients, the forecast of technology and the establishment of objectives for future operational capabilities, had to be derived simultaneously, with each providing imaginative stimuli to the other. These two had to be developed in terms of the basic objectives of the Army for fulfilling its responsibilities in the future world environment. The Army system which finally evolved incorporates a continuous dialogue between the operational and technological planners throughout the planning cycle, beginning with long-range forecasts and plans aimed twenty years in the future, continuing with the refinement until detailed descriptions of tactically desirable equipment can be agreed upon, and ending when the feasibility of such equipment is proven, prior to the undertaking of expensive system development.

This chapter examines the Army system which has evolved during the past ten or more years. The system is only now reaching full implementation, and the next few years should conclusively prove its values and disclose its shortcomings. The complex process by which the research and development plans are evolved from the forecast and objectives is not described. Instead, the focus is on the relationship of the technological forecast to each step of the planning process, the nature of the documents which are prepared, and the way they are compiled.

It has been said that small deeds done are better than great deeds planned. This chapter describes methods of changing forecasts so that they reflect even the small deeds of research and development.

BACKGROUND

The continual and rapid growth of scientific and technical knowledge has necessitated the development of increasingly sophisticated planning techniques, both in industry and in government. Just as industry must look ahead to plan its operations in order to exploit future markets and insure profits, the Army must also plan the best use of the billions of dollars Congress allocates, to ensure that the most efficient fighting machine is available for the country's defense. Some form of prognostication of the potential which growing knowledge can provide is essential to any planning process. This projection may be developed as a separate and distinct technical forecast, or it may be melded with the rest of the planning process. It may even be done subconsciously by the planner, but it is always a necessary planning ingredient. In the Army, the technological forecast is a separate and vital part of the planning process; however, it is not a plan in itself. It is not necessarily a prediction of what is expected to happen. Rather, it is a prediction of capabilities that could be developed if desired.

Until recently, most technological forecasts were a series of studies, each primarily devoted to one specific topic. Perhaps the best examples of these were the forecasts made prior to World War II by the National Research Council. The Council predicted many scientific advances but missed such things as atomic energy, radar, jet propulsion and antibiotics. Other studies were Project Lexington (made for the Air Force in 1948), which examined a number of scientific advances and resulted in the Mariner Class of merchant vessels and the atomic depth charge; Project Charles, which contributed to the establishment of the Lincoln Laboratory at the Massachusetts Institute of Technology; the Lamp Lighter Report, which resulted in the establishment of the DEW line; and the Von Karman report, which forecast the capabilities of the NATO countries and which is being revised today to reflect current technological advances in selected scientific fields.

DEVELOPMENT OF THE FORECAST

Prior to the reorganization of the Army in 1962, each Technical Service (the Signal Corps, the Ordnance Corps, etc.) had its own long-range technical forecast which it usually updated every five years. In 1955, the Army's Office of Research and Development called for a one-time "Technical Capabilities Forecast" from each of the Technical Services. There was little or no coordination and much duplication.

In 1957, the Ordnance Corps compiled an unofficial document entitled "Technical Capabilities Forecast FY 59–70." This paper outlined a number of ideas for weapons and military devices which Ordnance scientists believed to be feasible. It was distributed widely throughout the Army and its various agencies and Service schools. Comments, suggestions, ideas for new devices, and answers to problems which required technical solutions were solicited. Responses were compiled in a document entitled "Vast and Half-Vast Ideas" (Figure 1), and this was circulated among the research establishments of Ordnance in the belief that the spreading of ideas among scientists, engineers, and users would be mutually educational and would foster the generation of more ideas.

In 1960, the Army's Chief of Research and Development directed each Technical Service to submit a long-range technological forecast pertaining to areas associated with the Service's technical missions and competence. The directive was intended to strengthen both operational planning and planning for research and development.

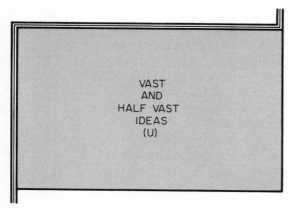

VAST
AND
HALF VAST
IDEAS
(U)

Figure 1. An Ancestor of the Army's Long Range Technological Forecast.

The forecasts for 1960 and 1961 were eight-volume editions, and again there was much overlap and duplication. Closely related Services tended to rely heavily on each other and in one instance a contractor pirated text and illustrations from one Service's forecast for inclusion in another's.

With the 1962 amalgamation of most of the Technical Services into the Army Materiel Command, the individual Service forecasts were combined into a single document presented in the format previously used by Ordnance. The task was performed by a small group in the Headquarters of the Army Materiel Command, with editorial assistance from another small group under contract from the University of Pittsburgh. The information contained in the previous years' separate forecasts was updated and expanded where necessary, with material solicited from experts in commands, laboratories, and agencies of the newly formed Army Materiel Command. In addition, a contractor, Battelle Memorial Institute, was given the job of preparing a forecast covering those areas of Army interest which lay outside the responsibility of the Army Materiel Command. The 1962 forecast appeared in two parts.

In 1963, the Army Materiel Command, under the staff supervision of the Office of the Chief of Research and Development, was assigned the task of preparing and publishing the Army's "Long Range Technological Forecast." The most recent revision, the Fourth Edition (May, 1967), is being distributed. Thus, the Army's "Long Range Technological Forecast" has gradually evolved from specific studies and end-item prognostications to its present focus on technological capabilities and systems concepts.

CONCEPT OF UTILIZATION

This subtle change came about through a gradual understanding of the needs of the planning process and the role of the forecast in this process. Early Army forecasts usually focused on a specific hardware item of increased capability and predicted the date it would become feasible. Although a major purpose of such forecasts was to assist operational planning, the concepts of the technologists often failed to blend with the ideas of the tactical planners. Furthermore, the composite of the individual items of forecasted materiel failed to provide for an integrated fighting system.

The Army also was confronted by the growing realization that, historically, the development of new tactics greatly lagged behind, and usually was forced by, technological innovations. Tactics applied at the beginning of each war were usually developed during the previous one, and change often occurred only after painful confrontation with the results of technological changes. Within the Army, therefore, a concerted effort was initiated to enable operational planning to anticipate the scientific and technical potentials and their implications for defense and warfare. This effort culminated in 1962 with the establishment of the U.S. Army Combat Development Command. This command was charged with the function of operational planning and the responsibility for developing the military characteristics of materiel needed to implement envisioned tactics. As previously mentioned, the U.S. Army Materiel Command was responsible for identifying the scientific and technical potentials and developing them into new and better materiel.

Even though these two great commands operate under the unifying planning direction of the Army General Staff, the system is unavoidably confronted by the age-old question, "which comes first, the chicken or the egg?"—the recognition of a need which can be fulfilled through technology or the recognition of a technical capability which can fulfill a still unrecognized need. When a military user tries to describe what he wants to do, he must have a good idea of the technical potential for accomplishing the job. Otherwise, he may put insolvable demands on technology or overlook technological advances which could allow the development of new operational concepts. This is one vital function of the forecast: to inform the operational planner of technical potentials. However, it is neither possible nor useful to predict all the capabilities which could be derived from current and foreseen growth of scientific and technical knowledge. Ideally, predictions should be made only for potentially useful capabilities. Here the forecaster finds himself in the predicament of selecting concepts to fulfill needs which are not yet stated.

ARMY FAMILY OF PLANS

One solution to these problems lies in continuous discussion and exchange of ideas between the operational planners and the people who are cognizant of the technical potential. The express purpose of this interchange is the development of imaginative operational capability objectives which are within the present potential of science and technology. The Army is currently revising its organization and procedures to further this process, which is conceptually illustrated in Figure 2. Within the constraints and demands of the future world environment and the Army's responsibilities therein, potentially solvable objectives for required Army Operational Capabilities are derived. The technological forecast and the operational studies inspire, augment, and feed upon each other. The objectives form the basis for planning avenues of research which can lead to development of the needed technical capabilities, while the forecast describes the possible avenues of technical approach. When one or more

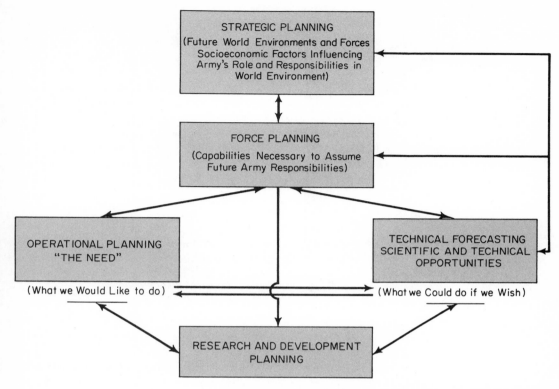

Figure 2. Conceptual Schematic of Army's Development of Objective Capabilities.

avenues have proved feasible, a requirement for definitive materiel can be specified and resources to develop it can be programmed. The technological forecast feeds back into the estimate of the world environment, since the technical future will be a part of the environment.

Figure 3 illustrates the actual relationship of the technological forecast to the Army's family of plans. The forecast is an important input to the Basic Army Strategic Estimate, which looks at the world-wide situation twenty years ahead, the position and probable policies of the United States in this situation, and the responsibilities of the Army in implementing these policies. Considered in establishing the estimate are such factors as intelligence estimates of the social, economic, and political climate; basic national policies and objectives; research capabilities; and the results of current operational planning studies and evaluations. The estimate is developed in consonance with the Joint Chiefs of Staff. The Army Strategic Plan is the Army's broad strategic plan of operation within the

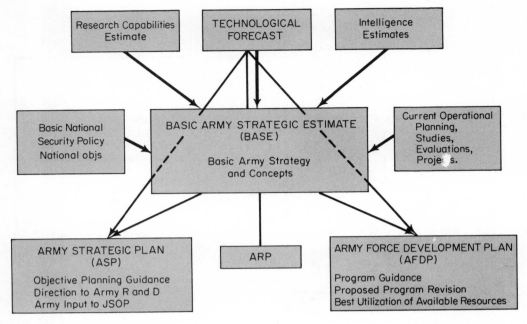

Figure 3. The Army's Family of Plans.

environment and in the direction described in the Basic Army Strategic Estimate. It is an input to, and is in harmony with, the Joint Strategic Operation Plan and the Joint Research and Development Objectives Document. The Army Strategic Plan provides guidance for operational planning, and direction to the Army's research and development activities. The Army Force Development Plan describes, in considerable detail, the forces necessary to implement the Army Strategic Plan. It provides guidance for the utilization of available resources through the Army's financial program.

The forecast continues to play a vital role in the process of refining and developing the guidelines set forth in the Army's family of plans into actual requirements. These requirements describe, in detail, individual pieces of equipment which are not only producible, but which, when combined, will provide the Army with the most efficient fighting capability.

ARMY CAPABILITY OBJECTIVES

Figure 4 outlines the relationship of the technological forecast to the more detailed planning process within the Army. The operational and tactical planning community is represented on the right, while the research

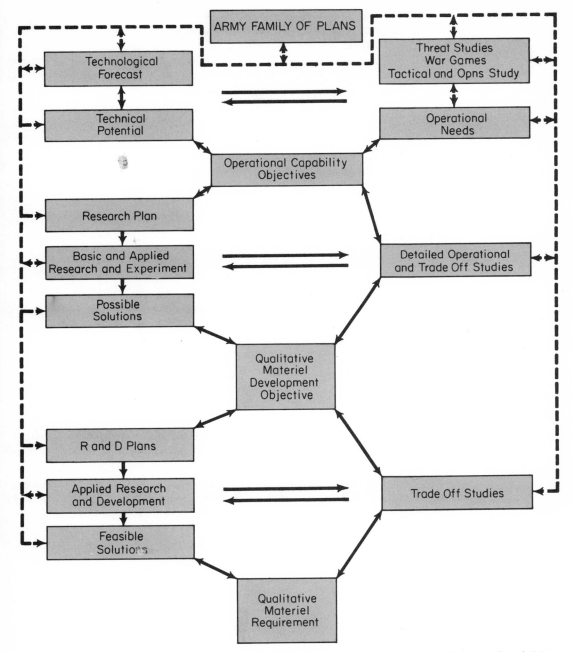

Figure 4. Iteration and Interaction Between Operational and Scientific Planners.

and development organization functions are shown on the left. In implementing the Army's family of plans, the first stage is the blending of needs, derived from threat studies, war games, and tactical and operational studies, with the forecasted technical potential, in order to describe an operational need which may be solvable through science and technology. This results in an Operational Capability Objective which quantitatively describes what is to be done on the battlefield, not the equipment which will be used.

Plans are made to exploit possible avenues—and combinations of avenues—of technical approach (which are hopefully reflected in the technological forecast) through programs of research and experiment which attempt to identify limitations and advantages. "Potentially feasible" approaches are compared and reconciled with concurrent studies of the operational advantages and disadvantages of the "possible" solutions. The result is a Qualitative Materiel Development Objective—an objective for the development of a piece of equipment with stated capabilities.

Specific research and development plans, known as Qualitative Materiel Development Objective plans, may then be prepared to ensure that the parameters of all useful avenues of technical approach are identified through applied research and that the best blend of component characteristics is chosen to provide an optimum system to fulfill the objective. The best "feasible solutions" are compared against operationally oriented studies of possible trade-offs, to develop a Qualitative Materiel Requirement for a desirable and describable piece of materiel which can actually be developed. An essential ingredient at all stages in this process is a continuing exchange of ideas between the operational and the research and development planners, as shown by the broad arrows in Figure 4.

A vital tool throughout the process is the technological forecast, which describes new scientific knowledge and the technical capabilities which can be derived therefrom. It provides illustrative examples of materiel which could be devised using such capabilities. As shown by the dotted lines in Figure 4, the forecast is useful to strategic planners, operational planners, and research and development planners alike. Also shown is the feedback from the planners to the forecast.

ORGANIZATION OF FORECAST

The organization of the technological forecast document is shown in Figure 5. Volume One—"Scientific Opportunities"—discusses the opportunities and limitations presented by new knowledge in fundamental disciplines. Since the volume essentially describes what we are learning from

Volume One—Scientific Opportunities

    Discusses opportunities and limitations presented by new knowledge of the fundamental disciplines

    Prepared for research planning

Volume Two—Technological Capabilities

    Discusses components and techniques to support advanced concepts

    Prepared for R&D and staff planners to translate into systems capabilities

Volume Three—Advanced Systems Concepts

    Describes concepts based on advances in science and technology

    Prepared to provide examples of systems for operational planners of CDC and DA Staff

Figure 5. Organization of the Long Range Technological Forecast.

science, it is one base for the prognostications of technical capabilities which are presented in Volume Two. This information is of value primarily to research planners.

An example of the sort of curve which might appear in Volume One is Figure 6, which shows past and projected improvements in the accuracy

Figure 6. The Improvement of Frequency Standards.

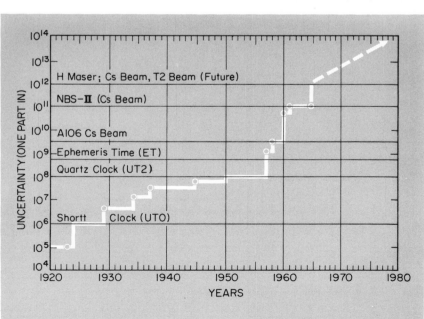

of frequency standards. For many years, time was measured in terms of the rotation of the earth, and a second of time was defined as 1/86,400th of a mean solar day. Then quartz oscillators were used as "clocks," with consequent improvements in stability. In 1956, Ephemeris time was established, but it had a drawback: an interval of time could not be measured by direct comparison with the interval of time defining the second, since a lengthy series of astronomic measurements requiring several years was needed to obtain data for comparison. It was not until the advent of the MASER (Molecular Amplification by Stimulated Emission of Radiation) that a device was available which was stable enough to allow comparisons with a high degree of accuracy. Later, Cesium beam atomic "clocks" permitted frequency measurements with an accuracy of one part in ten billion (1 in 10^{10}). Figure 6 shows that even more accurate time and frequency standards based on the hydrogen or thallium atom transitions may be established in the future.

Volume Two—"Technological Capabilities"—discusses components and techniques which can be derived from new and existing knowledge to support advanced concepts. This volume is useful to research and development, operational and staff planners. It translates available knowledge into systems capabilities. As a typical example, Figure 7 shows the Electronic Command's projection of the development of integrated, miniaturized, low-noise, solid state amplifiers during the decade from 1970 to 1980. The figure shows three frequencies—one gigaHertz (gHz), ten gHz, and one hundred gHz.[1] The dotted lines represent a decrease in the noise generated in the amplifier and thereby indicate purer signal amplifications. The solid lines represent the gain in usable band-width as a function of the square root of the power gain.

As the lower portion of the frequency spectrum (used for communications today) becomes more crowded, available frequencies are found only in the higher portions, or microwave sections. In order to use these higher communications frequencies, a more stable means of control of electronic equipment is required. During World War II, quartz crystals were used to stabilize oscillator frequencies, but it was almost impossible to insure that the right crystals would be at the right places at the right time. Also, until microelectronic circuits were developed, the very high frequencies could not be used, since microwave components were very small and hard to fabricate. The development of integrated electronic circuits has become

---

[1] A "Hertz" represents cycles per second, and "giga" means 1 billion. A point of reference is a human voice range most of which is contained in a band-width of 3,000 Hz (cycles per second). Note that 100gHz will not be available until 1970 according to the prediction.

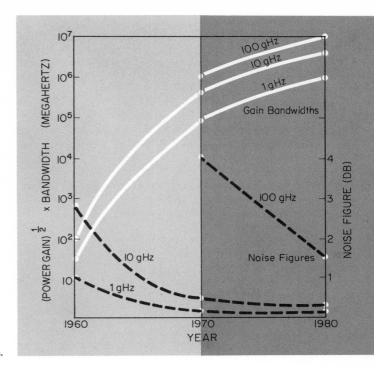

Figure 7. Solid State Amplifier Advances.

another steppingstone on which the increase in high frequency use has been built.

Parametric amplifiers, which use an alternating current "pump" frequency to raise the power of an input signal, are examples of solid state amplifiers. These amplifiers will provide lower system noise than transistors or tunnel diodes; however, the latter may have other advantages such as operability over a greater band-width. The tendency of the curves to level off derives from the limitation of present materials.

Volume Three—"Advanced Systems Concepts"—presents illustrative concepts based on advances in science and technology. It provides examples of systems for operational planners of the Combat Developments Command and the Department of the Army staff. As an example, Figure 8 shows an artist's concept of a portion of a tactical satellite network of the post-1980 era. This will be supported by a number of medium and high orbital stations which will provide network coordination, channel organization, and emergency communications.

Thus, projected developments and advances in frequency control and measurement techniques which were needed for precise control of ultra-

Figure 8. Artist's Concept—Satellite Tactical Communication System.

high frequencies, and step-by-step developments in solid state components, enabled the production of miniaturaized solid state amplifiers with bandwidth flexibility and low-noise figures which will result in the fielding of compact satellite-based tactical communications systems.

HOW DATA ARE COLLECTED

Sources of input for the forecast are shown in Figure 9. General information comes from the world scientific community, including universities, nonprofit research organizations, the laboratories of industry, Department of Defense agencies, the Department of the Army, and the Army Materiel

WORLD SCIENTIFIC COMMUNITY DEPARTMENT OF DEFENSE AGENCIES DEPARTMENT OF THE ARMY/ARMY MATERIEL COMMAND AGENCIES		
Special Request	Scheduled Contributors	
U. S. Air Force	Office of the Surgeon General (OSG)	AVCOM
U. S. Navy		ELCOM
	Office of the Chief of Engineers (OCE)	
U. S. Army Reserve		MECOM
Federal Agencies	Army Security Agency (ASA)	MICOM
(FAA, etc.)		MUCOM
	Army Research Office (ARO)	TACOM
		TECOM
		WECOM
		Separate Laboratories

Figure 9. General Input Sources to the Long Range Technological Forecast.

Command agencies. The best seer is the distinguished scientist who chooses to predict in his own field. Sometimes judicious prodding is needed to get predictions, but the nation's scientific and technical people are (and must continue to be) the Army's eyes and ears, its window on the world's technology. It takes a knowledgeable person to follow up a lead, collar the appropriate scientist, either in his office, laboratory or through correspondence, and put the information into its proper perspective. Like a good reporter a technological forecaster must have a good "nose for news"— an innate curiosity that pays dividends in reporting the facts for the forecast.

The Army Reserve Units, the Navy, the Air Force, and federal agencies like the Advanced Projects Research Agency, the Federal Aviation Agency, the National Aeronautics and Space Agency, and the National Bureau of Standards are often solicited, by special request, for opinions and contributions. Scheduled contributors include not only the commands and laboratories of the Army Materiel Command, but the Surgeon General, the Office of the Chief of Engineers, the Army Security Agency, and the Army Research Office. There are, within the Army Materiel Command, twenty-four organizational entities, laboratories, commands and agencies engaged in research and development. Within this group there are 56 discrete laboratories or elements performing research and develop-

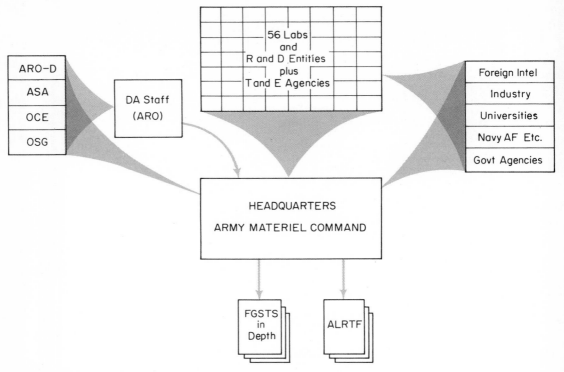

Figure 10. Organization for Forecasting.

ment activities. Each contains a group or an individual charged with the forecasting functions. Figure 10 shows how these organizations contribute to the forecast.

In addition to the technological forecast, forecasts-in-depth are compiled by the Army Materiel Command. These probe more deeply into particular subjects which are not covered in detail in the technological forecast. Forecasts-in-depth contain a survey of the state of the art for a particular topic, a forecast, and suggested research opportunities to obtain the desired goals established by the forecast. The very compilation of a forecast-in-depth helps insure the validity of the materiel which is covered in more condensed form in the Army Technological Forecast.

FORECAST INPUT

The entire technological forecast is completely revised and updated every two years. The three volumes are completely reviewed each year,

CHAPTER	DATE DUE													
	Apr	May	June	July	Aug	Sept	Oct	Nov	Dec	Jan	Feb	Mar	Apr	May
Materials Technology						O								
Power Technology	O													X
Communications, Electronics and Information Processing			X											O
Weapons Technology									X					

LEGEND: O Major Revision
X Review

Figure 11. Schedule of Input for Revision of Volume Two, Army Long Range Technological Forecast.

and about half of the material is usually found to be up-to-date. This material is simply revalidated and then scheduled for a revision within the next six months. The schedule is given in Figure 11. As an example, Power Technology is shown scheduled for a major revision in April and for a review the following May. Figure 12 shows the primary responsibili-

Figure 12. Agency Responsibility by Sections (inputs).

Chapter	Electronics Command	Missile Command	Tank-Auto Command	Munitions Command	Weapons Command
Materials technology	1, 3, 5	1, 5	1, 3, 5, 6	1–6	1, 3,5
Power technology	2	2	1, 2	1	—
Communications, electronics and information processing	1–7	4	—	—	4, 7
Weapons technology	2, 8, 9, 10	1, 2, 8	—	2–10	3, 4, 5, 7, 10

ties of the Army Materiel Command agencies for the various chapter sections within the forecast. Using the chapter on Power Technology as an example, the Electronics, Tank-Automotive and the Missile Commands are responsible for Section 2; Tank-Automotive and Munitions Commands are responsible for Section 1. In addition, all the research and scientific personnel are encouraged to contribute in areas coinciding with their knowledge and interests (not necessarily their responsibilities). The material that is received from these and other indicated sources is compiled by a small group in the Technological Forecasting Branch of the Science and Technology Division of the Army Materiel Command Headquarters. Here, two full-time physical scientists add any other data which have been collected since the last revision and send all of the information to the University of Pittsburgh's four-man scientific group, which is located in the Washington area. Working under the guidance of the Army Materiel Command Headquarters forecasters, these scientists add material which they have compiled from university and other sources and assemble it into a "review manuscript," paying particular attention to clarity and grammar. This manuscript is then reviewed for completeness, possible errors, or additions, by the staff sections of the Development Directorate of the Army Materiel Command Headquarters and the Army Office of the Chief of Research and Development. After this review process, the manuscript is prepared on mats which are furnished to the Adjutant General for final printing and distribution.

COMMAND LEVEL FORECASTING

Generally, the technical forecaster in each Army Materiel Command agency is at the heart of his installation's entire planning and administration function for research and development. Ideally, he is not a narrow specialist, since such a person is never fully qualified to evaluate the variety of problems that come before him. He is a true "interdisciplinarian," capable of mastering the essential discoveries, not only in his own field, but in those allied to it. He has a natural ability to feel at home in many branches of science. Generally, he is able to infuse his co-workers with his enthusiasm and instill in them the desire to think in broad terms.

The forecasting group assembles the forecast inputs, and although this material is generally in satisfactory form when it is received in the Army Materiel Command Headquarters, there are times when it appears to be lacking in detail, concept, or prognostication. In such cases, one of the Headquarter's staff members and a member of the University of Pittsburgh team will visit the specialist in the laboratory and try to evoke imaginative and meaningful concepts from the scientist's forecast.

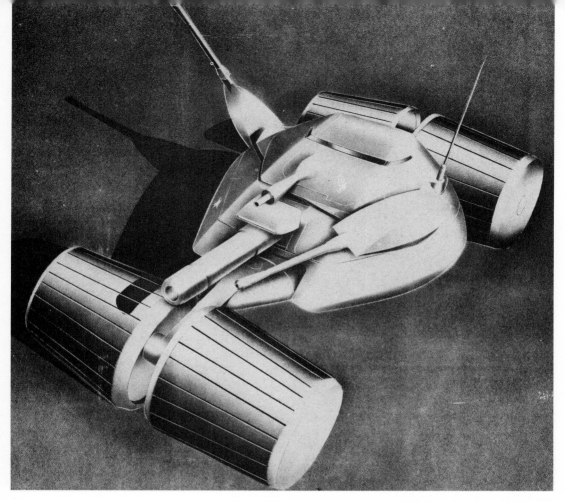

Figure 13. Concept Submitted by a Field Agency—Main Battle Tank.

Figure 13 shows an example of some of the concepts which field agencies have submitted. The picture shows a radically new design of a main battle tank. The roller-type wheels can be extended from the sides, and the machine also can inch its way along like a caterpillar.

The Army uses several interrelated methodologies to compile the Long Range Technological Forecast. It relies heavily on the "genius technique," whereby the opinions of outstanding individuals are solicited, compared, and reconciled by conference if necessary. This technique involves the asking of critical questions such as, "Why won't the current trends continue?" or "What technical, economic, or other factors will influence the curve?"

An extension of this technique is the use of study groups or symposia to delve deeply into specific technical areas. A task force is formed. Its members are people from all pertinent disciplines associated with a particular technical field, including representatives from the using organizations. Once this group has met and discussed the broad facets of the subject, their resultant analyses of the technical areas are broken into significant parts for more detailed study by a panel of experts who are versed in that particular scientific discipline. These panels formulate forecasts in each significant area. The original group is reconstituted periodically to discuss these particular areas. The final results are integrated into the Army's Long Range Technological Forecast to provide advanced concepts and systems capabilities in the broad area. Rapport between the panels is needed at all times, and a small group of roving experts channels the efforts of the panels so that they do not stray from the broad technical area being worked on.

In addition, the Army is learning to identify clues which indicate impending gains. These are discovered by analyzing major, long-term trend curves and comparing them with the curves of techniques which comprise the current trends. If a major long-term trend is upward, for example, while the trend of the current technique is flattening or is asymptotic to a theoretical limit, a new technique which will replace the current one is sought. The Army is also learning to ask the question: "Why not?" As an example, upon the discovery of the microwave-based MASER, Dr. Charles Townes predicted a similar application based on the frequency of light. He could see no fundamental scientific reason preventing such a development—even though the means of making a LASER were not apparent at the time.

POTENTIAL INTO CONCEPTS

These methods have been quite successful in detecting new and important scientific knowledge and in forecasting technical capabilities; however, they have been somewhat deficient in two major areas. The first of these is the translation of the foreseen technical potential into concepts of materiel capabilities which are truly meaningful to the operational planners. A key to overcoming this deficiency lies in the continual exchange of ideas between the technical and operational sides of the house. An example of such a method of operation is the current approach to developing Operational Capabilities Objectives—the first stage in the requirements definition process discussed earlier (Figure 4). This is a new document in the Army System and is defined as follows:

> Department of the Army approved description of an operational capability the achievement of which is desirable primarily in the long-

range time frame (10 to 20 years). It is responsive to envisioned future operational concepts, within constraints of probable technological capabilities. It provides a meaningful goal to planners of doctrine, organization, tactics, and development, and provides guidance for research and, together with the Qualitative Materiel Development Objective, for exploratory development. Operational Capability Objectives, when viewed together, represent the total capability Objectives for the Army in the field in the long-range time frame.

In order to determine the initial Operational Capability Objectives, a group of Operational planners from the Combat Developments Command, which determines the tactics and strategies to be used on tomorrow's battlefields, and a group of scientific and technical planners from the Army Materiel Command, which plans the development of the equipment the Army will use in the future, have been meeting together. They have formulated drafts of the new objectives and are now in the process of obtaining agreement within the respective commands, prior to submitting the drafts to the Chief of Staff for final approval. When approved, these objectives will become goals for both the operational and the scientific planners. The very act of developing these objectives through a joint effort inspires new, practical, imaginative, quantified technical concepts for increasing the capabilities of the future Army. These concepts will be reflected in the Army's Long Range Technological Forecast, and also will be the basis for advanced planning of the research and development necessary for the fulfillment of objectives.

The Army Chief of Staff has approved the establishment (probably to take place within the next twelve months) of two new organizations. Tentatively, these have been designated as the Army Materiel Concepts Agency and the Institute for Land Combat. They will be staffed by the Army Materiel Command and the Combat Development Command respectively, will be physically located with the Intelligence Threat Study Group, and will provide the needed integrated input for planners.

The second deficiency is a frequent failure to clearly, concisely and meaningfully translate the potential into charts and tables which are of significant value to research and development planners. However, the situation is improving. Instead of charting only the trends expected from orderly programs of research and development, two curves will be published. The first will show the curve expected from normal industrial and current government-financed growth. The second curve will show the maximum gain achievable if the Army decided on a "crash" program and employed all the resources that the nation's manpower and facilities could economically provide.

Examples of the "envelope curves" developed by the Army Materials

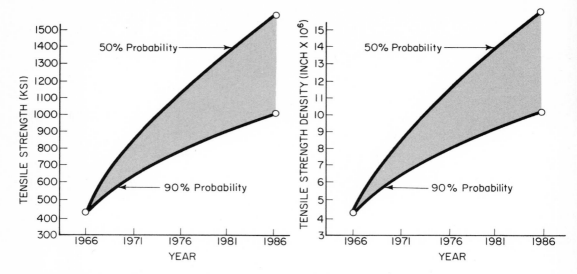

Figure 14. Hypothetical Curves Illustrating Use of Confidence Levels for Presentation of Data.

Research Agency [2] are displayed in Figure 14. The left-hand curve shows the tensile strength of metallic whiskers such as boron fibers, while the right projects the gains in the ratio of tensile strength to density which are anticipated during the next twenty years. The probability curves represent the most optimistic and the most pessimistic views of the scientists in these fields, as derived from interviews which focused on the future of metallic filaments. The prognostications were not based solely on the growth of technology which would result from presently applied resources, but included an estimation of the resources which would be devoted to the field in the future.

SOME PITFALLS

Requests to include funding prognostications in the forecasts are often received: How much will it cost to achieve a forecasted gain? This trap has been studiously avoided. Costs depend on many factors: other plans which will utilize available scientific and technical manpower; pertinent work which will be done by industry at no cost to the government, such

[2] Redesignated July 1, 1967: The Army Materials and Mechanics Research Center.

as research on steel; the amount of work which will be funded by other branches of the government, such as research in atomic energy or titanium; and similar questions which should be decided by economic and political rather than technological forecasts. The answers lie in the total planning process of which the forecast is only a vital integrated contribution.

WHAT USERS THINK

How good are the forecasts made by the Army? They are very good! However, perfectionists are never satisfied, even though realists know that the ultimate system will never be attained, since perfection is unattainable. However, the ability to predict future events can be evaluated only when the forecast period becomes history. In 1961, a materials forecast, compiled by the Army Materials Research Agency, predicted an adhesive that would retain certain room temperature characteristics at high temperatures (see Figure 15). Personnel at Picatinny Arsenal required such an adhesive for projects on which they were then working, and asked that a developmental effort be focused on the adhesive. Industry was skeptical, but technological improvements and the development of polyimide adhesives gave the arsenal the needed material in 1965, just as predicted. In 1959, a forecast made by the same agency predicted the rise in yield strengths of metals, as shown in Figure 16. Figure 17 plots the increases against time. Steel has come along in accordance with the prediction, as has titanium. Magnesium has slowed down, apparently because of more emphasis on other metals, and has not yet come up to expectations;

Figure 15. Summary of Estimated High Temperature Capabilities of Adhesives for Metals.

Status	Short Time Service, 0.1 hour	Long Time Service, 1000 hours
Current capability [1]	1100°F	500°F
1965 capability [1]	1500°F	700°F
1970 capability [2]	1700°F	1200°F
1975 capability [3]	2500°F	2000°F
1980 capability [3]	3000°F	2500°F

Source: 10 December 1961 forecast by Ordnance Materials Research Office.

[1] Organic type adhesives. Bond strengths at elevated temperatures are estimated to be 30–35% of the original room temperature values.
[2] Initially developed inorganic type adhesives.
[3] Inorganic type adhesives such as ceramics.

Metal	1945	1950	1955	1960	1965	1970	1975
Steel	150	165	180	225	275	335	415
Titanium	60	100	150	175	200	220	240
Magnesium	25	30	35	45	60	75	100
Aluminum	70	70	70	75	80	90	105

Source: September 1959 forecast by Ordnance Materials Research Office.

Figure 16. Forecasted Yield Strengths (Predicted yield strength $\times$ 1000 psi).

however, advances now in the laboratories may bring it into line with the curve within the next few years. Aluminum, after a slow start, has increased about as fast as predicted. Currently predicted values for 1970 and 1975 differ somewhat from the original forecast, but to date the curves made eight years ago have proved to be accurate, and those extending up to 1975, sixteen years from the date of the forecast, still look pretty good.

In 1960, the Signal Corps predicted that cryogenic pre-tuners would be available for development by 1966, and they were. In the mid-1950's, they also predicted that the Faraday rotational effect would be utilized in constructing ferrite circulators for radar systems, and such circulators are now in widespread use. In 1962, it was predicted that fuel cells would be in the field within the next ten years (1972); it appears that this goal will be achieved by 1968, since a 60-watt Hydrazine fuel cell for a man-packed radar is now in the engineering development stage.

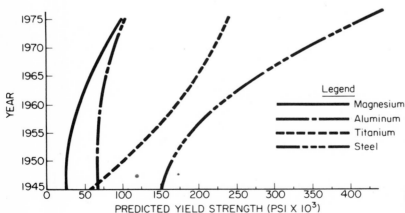

Figure 17. Plot of Predicted Yield Strengths.

Not all has been as anticipated. About 1956 or 1957 it was also predicted that by 1968 to 1970 fuel cells would be used for Army automotive propulsion. They surely will not be.

Users' opinions vary concerning how well the forecast fits their needs. Some of the staff planners who have not had intensive technical training do not use Volumes One and Two. The planners say they cannot understand these volumes and that the material should be eliminated. However, some of the research planners are offended because the contents are not more technically detailed. Even within the various groups, including the operational planners, there are wide divergences of opinion. Each group would like the forecast to be tied more closely to its sphere of work so that pertinent technical parts could be transformed easily into expanded or encapsulated documents. Special expansions or contractions of the technical contents of the forecast are often requested for special studies being conducted by the Combat Developments Command or Department of the Army staff. In general, the forecast has been well received, and a recent survey shows that the users are generally satisfied. The exceptions to user satisfaction which were previously mentioned will be corrected.

CONCLUSION

In summary, the Army's Long Range Technological Forecast has grown from a series of independent studies and prognostications to an integrated document which has taken its rightful place in the Army's family of inputs to its hard-core plans. The forecast is not designed as a projection of the future as it will be, but rather as a prognostication of the future opportunities and limitations of science and technology for use in both operational and research and development planning.

No one hard and fast system of methodology is employed in the forecast's compilation, nor can one be foreseen at this time. Goals are (1) to cultivate knowledgeable forecasters ("interdisciplinarians") who will guide the gathering of input materials from scientists and who will, themselves, become "seers," able to predict the advances and goals of the scientific and technological world; and (2) to educate these forecasters in the use of new and more sophisticated forecasting techniques. Only then can the very important interchange shown in Figure 18 take place, where ideas flow back and forth between the scientists, on the one hand, and planners and operational people on the other. Unfortunately, the document is not releasable to industry since many companies have provided some of their deepest proprietary secrets and the Army hopes to continue to obtain the advice and opinions of industry on an even greater scale.

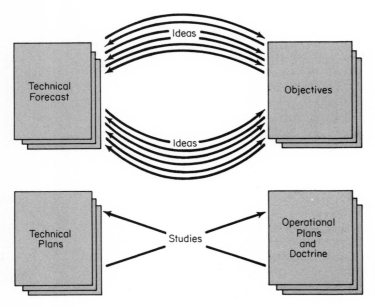

NATIONAL AND JOINT SERVICE
OBJECTIVES, STUDIES AND PLANS

ARMY OBJECTIVES, STUDIES AND PLANS

INTELLIGENCE

Technical Forecast

Ideas

Objectives

Ideas

Technical Plans

Studies

Operational Plans and Doctrine

Figure 18. Ideal Interchange of Scientists and Planners for Integrated Plans.

PARALLELS WITH INDUSTRY

The analogy between the problems of the Army and those of industry should be apparent, and some of the lessons learned in developing the Army's research and development planning system should be useful to industrial management. The basic ingredients—a set of broad, long-range objectives and a forecast of the possibly useful technological potential, each developed separately and neither one constraining the other's imaginative development, but instead continuously providing inspirational guidance to the other—appear equally applicable to planning a company's future products. The continuous interchange of ideas between people cognizant of the potential of technology and people capable of estimating future marketability, both working within the constraints of, and inspired by, broad company objectives, can provide a basis for company planning. Just as the Army tries to look ahead as far as twenty years in developing its objectives and forecast, so a company should look far enough into the future to allow time for the development of its future products and their markets.

But where is the starting point? How can technological forecasting be factored into planning? What does a manager do first?

There is within each industry, whether large or small, a group that is charged with the overall responsibility for guiding the operations of the organization and establishing a master plan for the next five to ten years. In a corporation, one such group might be a corporate planning council composed of group vice-presidents, the vice-president for marketing, vice-president and chief scientist, and the executive vice-president, who acts as the council's chairman. A working group can be selected from the company's divisions and given the necessary general guidelines, including time spans, for their effort—a Master Plan.

Three basic documents or forecasts need to be generated as inputs to this plan:

An environmental survey—this will be a projection of the environment within which the industry and company will operate.

A sociological survey—this will consider sociological developments that are an important part of the forces which influence the role of government, the consumption of products, the labor supply, and possible departures from traditional extrapolations.

A technological survey—this will consider the scientific advances in the company's technical field and the areas allied to that field.

Once these three basic documents are generated, a Master Plan draft can be readied for the guidance group to review and assess in the light of the company's major objectives. After revisions have been made and the manpower has been added, the final Master Plan can be readied for implementation.

A critical ingredient is personnel, especially the technological survey group. Working under the chief scientist should be one or more individuals who are well grounded, not only in the technical area within which the company is involved, but also in technical fields allied to that of the company. In projecting technical developments, the knowledge of the people in the Research, Engineering, and Marketing divisions should be utilized. The forecast also should include a survey of the needs of the company's customers; a survey of the work being done in private and public technical research institutions; and a projection of the needs of the ultimate users.

Final compilation of the technological survey or forecast could be done by any or several of the techniques discussed in this volume. The forecast should be presented in the format most suitable to the uses of the company's planning group.

Technology, the Chicken— Corporate Goals, the Egg

HARPER Q. NORTH
DONALD L. PYKE

The experiences of TRW demonstrate how a relatively unsophisticated application of technological forecasting can be useful as a means of communication among division technologists, division executives, and corporate managers. TRW has applied a modified Delphi approach to collect, from its large and diverse staff, new ideas for products and product areas. This procedure integrates corporate goals and objectives with technologically feasible capabilities.

Dr. North is Vice-President for Research and Development at TRW. He began his career as a physicist with General Electric, spent seventeen years in the semiconductor industry and the last five years in coordinating research and development in a diversified corporation.

Mr. Pyke, Assistant to Dr. North holds an M.S. degree in Mechanical Engineering from Purdue. His current TRW assignment of five years was preceded by seven years of experience with The Ramo-Wooldridge and Systems Development Corporations and eight years of teaching at Dartmouth and Purdue.

Business schools and workshop sessions of management organizations often imply that far too few corporations have clear corporate goals. Business consultants also stress the need for such goals and contend that they are required by directors of research and development before R&D programs can be planned. TRW management believes that this is only a half-true, "chicken and egg" situation. How can business-trained corporate executives state goals and plot a clear, long-term course without knowing what is going to be marketable many years hence? For this they depend upon analysts from their marketing departments. But if their product lines are dynamic and highly sophisticated technically, even the marketing analysts are lost without technical advisers, and such advisers come from the R&D department. A "chicken and egg" cycle is then complete. The R&D department must advise Marketing, which, in turn, advises the corporate executives who, through corporate goals, lay the course that tells R&D what to develop. Therefore, the Research and Development department must somehow divine what will be technically feasible in years ahead and work out with Marketing what will be both wanted and achievable. With sufficient insight, management can then set objectives, goals, and long-term plans in the best Harvard fashion, and R&D can get its programs approved.

All of this is somewhat oversimplified, but it serves to make the point that, in respect to today's products, technology usually plays a vital role. The course may be a "sporty" one, but the company directed solely by "business" objectives and, on a day-to-day basis, by the "seat of the pants" decisions of a good "manager" is on its way out.

In terms of corporate planning, this concept can be illustrated by referring to an exercise conducted at TRW by the authors. The basic approach was patterned after a study conducted by Dr. Olaf Helmer of the RAND Corporation and Mr. T. J. Gordon, of Douglas Aircraft. A condensation of their report appeared in the April, 1965, issue of *News Front* magazine.

Two particular features of their approach attracted TRW's attention. The first was the Delphi technique, which utilizes many experts but retains the virtues of a committee approach while eliminating many of its disadvantages, such as the "bandwagon effect" and the natural defensiveness of an expert who has adopted a publicly stated position. The second was the fact that Helmer and Gordon encouraged their experts to make quantum jumps forward to anticipate the needs and wants of future generations instead of using the commonly accepted technique of projecting today's position and extending current trends. This approach seemed necessary for a meaningful look beyond three to five years. The TRW approach modified that of Helmer and Gordon considerably, resulting in a disadvantage from the standpoint of results but allowing the creation of a "first draft" in a relatively short period of time.

TRW is a decentralized corporation, composed of four highly autonomous groups. These groups concentrate upon automotive products, electronic components, systems (largely for space and defense, but increasingly oriented toward civil systems), and aircraft equipment. In the beginning of the study, each of the group vice-presidents was asked to nominate five of his most creative, but down-to-earth, technologists, who, in turn, were asked to donate some of their spare time to "the experiment."

During a short initial meeting with each of the four groups of experts, these ground rules were established. Each man was asked to list—independently—those technical events which he felt might take place between 1966 (the year of the study) and 1985 and which would have a substantial impact upon current or potential product lines of his group. Emphasis was to be placed upon events which might appropriately be called "breakthroughs" as opposed to those which were simply logical extensions of well-established trends. The panelists were asked to estimate the dates at which they felt there was a 50 per cent probability of occurrence for each of the events. Free consultation with any member of the TRW family was permitted. Thus the contributors also served as channels through which the thoughts of a larger group were transmitted.

Because the environment of the future would have a major impact upon the directions in which technology would progress, each panel member was supplied with data on the future which was readily available. This included a McGraw-Hill economic forecast; the results of the Helmer/Gordon study, a *Time* magazine essay on the future, and a *U.S. News and World Report* article blueprinting "the future United States." Beyond this, each person was advised to make his own assumptions concerning the future environment—excluding only all-out nuclear war.

Predicting technical accomplishments twenty years into a future which depends upon many unknown variables appears futile until one realizes the truth in the statement that, limited only by natural laws, man can accomplish almost anything he can conceive. The time required, the cost of each endeavor, and the availability of competent men are the restraining factors. In today's economy, cost seems of secondary importance if a project is worthwhile; the task of probing the future thus becomes one of predicting what the world will need and what and how much time will be required to do each job. With respect to need and want, R&D people are invading the realm of the market research people, but this is a necessity in today's environment.

Approximately one month was allotted to the first phase of the study, after which the individual participants' lists of predicted technological achievements were collected. Event descriptions were edited, combined, and grouped, in a document, according to related technologies. A first draft was returned to each panelist, along with a request that he edit freely in areas of his expertise—defining events more precisely, deleting, adding, or otherwise modifying descriptions, and indicating his own estimated date of occurrence in cases of disagreement. At this point, a shortcoming on the abbreviated Delphi method was recognized. Too many panelists found it easier to agree with the predicted dates than to take time from their

Technologies
  1. Electronics
  2. Electro-Optics
  3. Materials (including coatings, fuels, propellants, and lubricants)
  4. Mechanics & Hydraulics

Subsystems
  1. Prime Movers (including motors and attitude control)
  2. Power: sources, conversion, and conditioning
  3. Information Processing
  4. Instrumentation & Controls

Systems
  1. Transportation
  2. Defense
  3. Aerospace (including weapons)
  4. Ocean
  5. Personal and Medical
  6. Urban and International
  7. Materials processing & handling plus automation

Figure 1. Classification of Events.

busy schedules to disagree with the estimates of others. In any event, the comments of each panelist were incorporated into a recompiled, re-edited, 50-page booklet entitled "A Probe of TRW's Future/The Next 20 Years." It listed 401 events. The nature of this proprietary document can be conveyed by describing its contents and presenting examples of predicted events.

Figure 1 lists the fifteen areas into which events were categorized. These relate to technologies, subsystems, and systems of interest to TRW. Events were listed only once, and where an impact might be felt in more than one area, that one was chosen in which the impact upon the company seemed to be the greatest.

Figure 2 lists six events that would have a significant impact upon the Automotive Group. The lines show the spread of estimates made by all panelists. The dots show median dates. Where there is no spread, artificial concurrence due to laziness can probably be assumed.

Selected events that will have an impact upon the Electronics Group are shown in Figure 3. Figure 4 highlights selected events that would have a substantial impact upon the Equipment Group. (This group produces equipment for aircraft and is experienced in precision metalworking.) Figure 5 lists similar events for the Systems Group. (This group began with ballistic missile systems. It is now concerned principally with spacecraft systems, and more recently with civil systems.)

TRW gained considerable benefit from the exercise, even at this point. At the very least, the exercise caused twenty-seven imaginative engineers

'65   '70   '75   '80   '85 Beyond

1. Microelectronic Techniques Will Be Widely Used
   in Automotive Applications Such as Voltage
   Regulators, Radios, Headlight Dimmers, Climate
   Controls, etc.

2. An Ultra–Light, High–Torque, Compact, Low–
   Horsepower, Economical Hydraulic Motor for
   Automotive Accessories Will Be Available.

3. Gas Turbines Will Be Widely Used in Trucks,
   Off–Highway, And Other Heavy–Duty Equipment
   –i.e., Applications Requiring in Excess of 500 H.P.

4. High Field Magnetic Bearing for Power
   Equipment Will Result In Greatly Increased
   Reliability. They Will Be Available for Engines
   and Motors, Especially for High Rotating
   Speed Applications.

5. New Personal and Mass Transportation
   Vehicles Powered by Battery–Electric Systems
   Will Be in Common Use.

6. A Hydrocarbon/Air Fuel Cell Will Be;

   A. Available Commercially
   B. Introduced in Automobiles
   C. Widely Used for Mobile Power

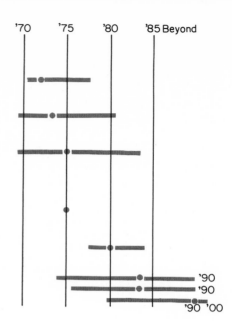

Figure 2. Events Affecting Automotive Group.

Figure 3. Events Affecting Electronics Group.

ELECTRONICS

'65   '70   '75   '80   '85 Beyond

1. Solid State Devices Will Have Been Developed
   for Power Generation at S–Band* (Continuous Wave)

   A. 10 Watts
   B. 100 Watts
   C. 1000 Watts
   D. 10,000 Watts

2. Thin Film Integrated Circuits Which Contain
   Active Elements Will Be

   A. Introduced for Military and Industrial
      Applications
   B. Introduced for Consumer Applications
   C. Used Widely for Industrial Applications
   D. Used Widely for Consumer Applications

3. A Solid State Active Filter (Other Than Piezo)
   Which Passes a Discrete Band of Frequencies
   Will Be in Practical Use.

4. Further Improvement (Speed, Reliability, Cost,
   etc.) in Circuits May Be Expected Through
   "Molecular Electronics" Employing Distributed
   Elements.

5. All TV Circuitry Will Be Microelectronic.

6. Integrated Circuits for Most (70%) Applications
   Will Be Designed By Computers.

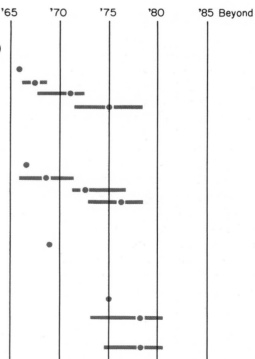

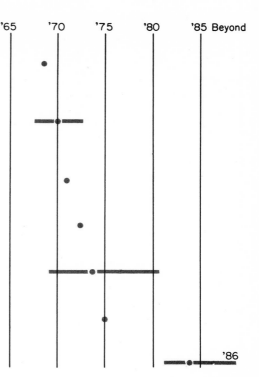

1. The Sizes of Precision Castings and Precision Forgings Will Continue to Increase and Will Be Very Large Compared to Today's Product.

2. There Will Be Substantial Use of Composite Materials Employing "Whisker" Technology in Gas Turbines and Jet Engine Airflow.

3. "Red Hot" Dies Will Be Used To Make Forgings That Are Large, Thin-Walled, and Free From Conventional Flash and Parting Lines.

4. A Frictionless Turbine with Rotor Suspended in The Working Fluid Will Have Been Developed.

5. Coated Refractories Will Replace Cooled Turbines in Aircraft Gas Turbine Engines.

6. The Foot Soldier Will Be Completely Equipped with Throwaway Weapons.

7. The First Controlled Thermonuclear (Fusion) Power Plant Will Be Demonstrated.

Figure 4. Events Affecting Equipment Group.

Figure 5. Events Affecting Systems Group.

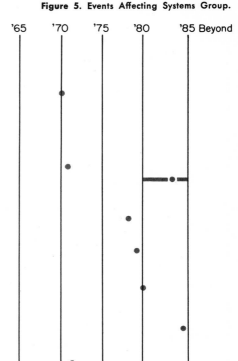

1. Photographic Techniques Utilizing Pulsed Light Sources with Gated Cameras Will Be Used in (A) Photographing Objects Obscured by A Screen of Scattering Layers, and (B) Observation from the Surface of Personnel and Equipment Working Under Water.

2. Large-Thrust, Air-Augmented Manned Recoverable Booster Rockets (Aerospace Planes) Will Be Introduced According to the Following Schedule.

    A. Development Will Have Begun
    B. Development Will Have Been Completed

3. The First (Unmanned) Space Flight of a Large-Thrust Nuclear Fission-Powered Rocket Will Be Launched.

4. A Capability Will Exist for Interception and Inspection of Enemy Earth Satellites by Manned Interceptors.

5. The First Mars Manned Fly-Around Will Take Place.

6. A Solid State Accelerometer Having a Very Wide Dynamic Range (Perhaps 10^{12}) and a "Perfect" Solid State Gyro Will Be Available.

7. Weapons Utilizing Laser Technology Will Be in Use.

and scientists—and additional technical people with whom they talked—to extend their imaginations beyond the specific demanding tasks of the moment. The results caused planners throughout TRW to consider certain events which they might not have thought about otherwise. They may have disagreed with panelists in regard to events or dates of occurrence, but at the least, they were forced to reconsider their plans if their views of the future were at variance with those of the panelists. Future product line planners and market research people, who must often dig for information, can use all of the inputs which they can get, and TRW's "Probe of the Future" is one more source of information.

If the exercise is conducted at regular intervals, the prophecies should continue to improve in accuracy. If the near-term predictions materialize, confidence will increase, and if longer-term predicted breakthroughs indicate attractive products for TRW, the company can help the predictions to come true, thereby assuring leadership in the new fields.

In July of 1966, excerpts from the document were presented to TRW management at its annual Vermont Conference (reported in the October, 1966, issue of *Fortune* magazine). Few questions were asked or comments made, but ten copies of "Probe of the Future" which were left on a nearby table disappeared immediately. By September, requests from within TRW had reached 150 copies. From a reprinting, twenty-three more disappeared.

In response to requests from the company's Public Relations office, a "sanitized" version of the "Probe" was prepared, deleting those items which seemed to be likely prospects for product development by TRW. Subsequently, requests for interviews were received from several technical publications and even from security analysts. The "sanitized" version is now out of print. A second version is being prepared, but it will be highly proprietary in nature, and releases to the public will be confined to descriptions of the methods.

TRW has also been working with "logic networks" which show the intermediate milestones which must be passed en route from today's state of the art to predicted events. The logic network can best be illustrated by reference to a specific prediction: that three-dimensional color movies utilizing holographic techniques will be feasible by 1972. A word about holography facilitates an understanding of the example.

Figure 6 shows the schematic layout of equipment used to obtain a hologram of a small tank filled with sea water and the microorganisms, or plankton, it contained. For one ten-millionth of a second, the tank was illuminated by the collimated coherent light from a ruby laser. A pattern formed by the interference of light scattered from the organisms with that transmitted directly reached the plate at the rear of the tank. This photographic plate, therefore, contained all of the information from all

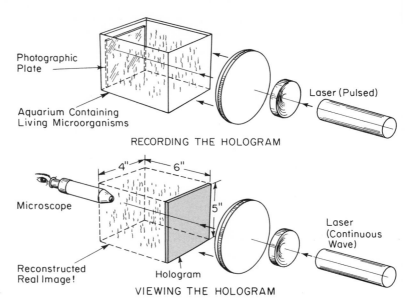

Photographic Plate

Aquarium Containing Living Microorganisms

RECORDING THE HOLOGRAM

Laser (Pulsed)

Microscope

4"

6"

5"

Reconstructed Real Image!

Hologram

VIEWING THE HOLOGRAM

Laser (Continuous Wave)

Figure 6. Making a Hologram.

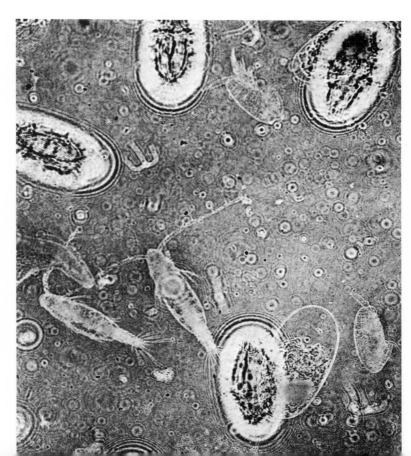

Figure 7. Magnified View of One Plane of Tank.

objects in the tank. After the plate had been developed and dried, it was placed in collimated coherent light from an Argon laser. The real image of the tank and its entire contents then appeared in space. This could be viewed at leisure with the microscope shown. Figure 7 shows one plane of the tank as seen for a particular focusing of the microscope. Each organism is seen as it was in its exact state at the time of the very short (hundred nanosecond) exposure.

The giant step from this simple setup to three-dimensional holographic color movies can now be visualized, but the route is far from clear. Figure 8 shows a very simplified version of one such possible route. The diagram is an experiment in technological planning and no more. It has been called a "logic network," rather than a PERT chart, because of the lack of a time scale, except for the estimated year of completion, 1972 (which now looks a bit close). Another difference between this and a PERT chart is the comparative looseness in milestone definitions.

The upper half of the chart is concerned with the development of lasers and technologies related to pulsing, recording media, and achieving intensity and coherence, while the top of the lower half traces developments in production techniques. The lower quarter is concerned with the development of projection techniques and the requirements associated with exhibiting the movies.

The next step, shown in Figure 9, was to expand the network in an attempt to identify some of the logical "spin-offs" which might be expected as corollary developments. Although TRW cannot visualize itself funding all of the R&D projects which would be necessary to accomplish the end item, it may well be interested in the corollary developments, if there is some assurance that one day, one or more companies will be producing three-dimensional movies. Some of the examples shown in the rectangles result from the achievement of the desired intensity and coherence of lasers. Some major possibilities are:

1. Information processing and pattern recognition technology will be enhanced, laser machining techniques improved, and synthesis of microcircuits may become commonplace.

2. The development of appropriate pulsing techniques should open a number of new possibilities in radar, telemetry, communications, and perhaps stroboscopic applications.

3. Development of appropriate recording media will undoubtedly be followed by improvements in information storage capability, filter and light technology, and high-speed photography.

4. To achieve TV reception in the home, it is necessary to transmit 2.5×10^{12} bits of information per second, or develop alternate

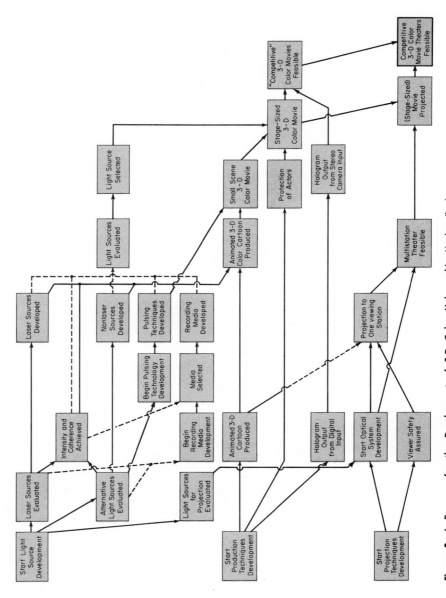

Figure 8. A Program for the Development of 3-D Color Holographic Movies (Logic Network).

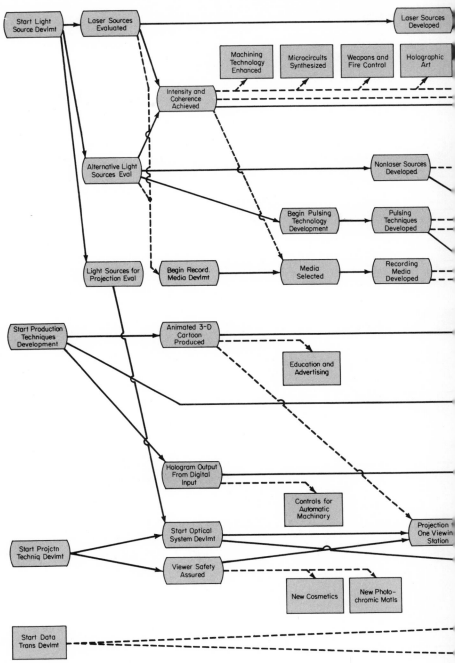

Figure 9. A Program for the Development of 3-D Color Holographic Movies with Some Probable Corollary Developments Indicated (Logic Network).

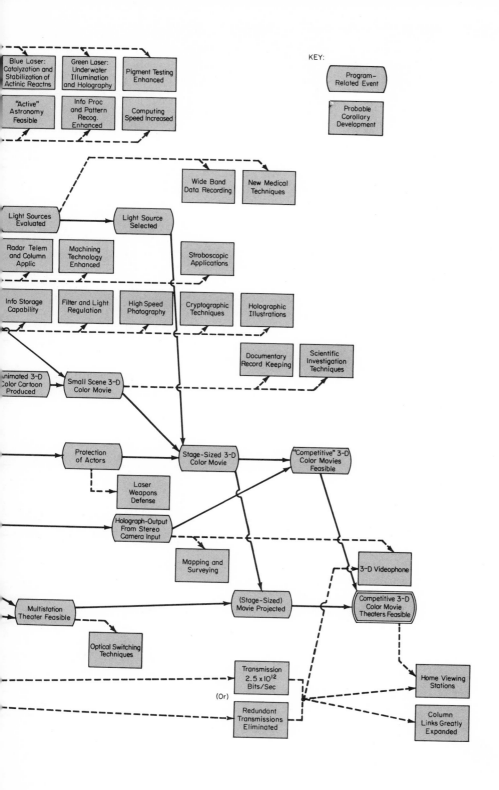

KEY:

Program-Related Event

Probable Corollary Development

Blue Laser: Catalyzation and Stabilization of Actinic Reactns

"Active" Astronomy Feasible

Green Laser: Underwater Illumination and Holography

Info Proc and Pattern Recog. Enhanced

Pigment Testing Enhanced

Computing Speed Increased

Wide Band Data Recording

New Medical Techniques

Light Sources Evaluated

Light Source Selected

Radar Telem and Column Applic

Machining Technology Enhanced

Stroboscopic Applications

Info Storage Capability

Filter and Light Regulation

High Speed Photography

Cryptographic Techniques

Holographic Illustrations

Documentary Record Keeping

Scientific Investigation Techniques

Animated 3-D Color Cartoon Produced

Small Scene 3-D Color Movie

Protection of Actors

Stage-Sized 3-D Color Movie

"Competitive" 3-D Color Movies Feasible

Laser Weapons Defense

Holograph-Output From Stereo Camera Input

3-D Videophone

Competitive 3-D Color Movie Theaters Feasible

Mapping and Surveying

Multistation Theater Feasible

(Stage-Sized) Movie Projected

Optical Switching Techniques

Transmission 2.5 x 10^{12} Bits/Sec

Home Viewing Stations

(Or)

Redundant Transmissions Eliminated

Column Links Greatly Expanded

techniques to eliminate the need for transmitting redundant information. If this occurs, the capacity of communication links will be greatly expanded, and 3-D video phone applications will accompany the three-dimensional color holographic home movies.

If expanded logic networks such as this one were to be drawn for several events in the same or adjacent technical fields, it is likely that the corollary developments which would be achieved en route to the events would tend to appear in clusters. These would present fruitful areas for TRW to explore as possible promising market areas, based on the premise that, if at least a few of the predicted final events occur, TRW may serve as a supplier to the companies which achieve them, and TRW can focus its research and development efforts upon earlier and more easily achieved objectives. The company now refers to these expanded logic networks as "SOON charts." The acronym stands for "Sequence Of Opportunities & Negatives," the negatives referring to obsolescence which may occur in existing product lines as a result of the events and their corollaries.

TRW management feels that it has barely scratched the surface in realizing the potential of the Delphi technique as a tool in technological planning, hence in market planning and in aiding the formulation of company plans and long-range corporate objectives. The sophistication of the process will increase with each reiteration. The mistake of furnishing dates to the panelists and asking for their corrections or concurrence will be corrected in the second phase of the exercise. Only the predicted events will be furnished, and the panelists will be asked for unbiased predictions on dates of occurrence. Three other items worthy of revision are:

1. An improved definition of the anticipated economic, sociological, and political environment should be agreed upon ahead of time by the panelists.
2. The first "Probe" contains a few contradictory dates. In a second edition, more attention will be given to relations between predictions.
3. The entire document can be focused more toward events which would have maximum impact upon TRW's product areas.

TRW plans to appoint one senior technical man from each of its four major groups to serve as "captain" of the team of panelists within his area. The captains will meet with the Vice-President of Research and Development and his assistant prior to the exercise, to establish the best possible revised ground rules. Deliberations and decisions of this smaller group should contribute greatly to the value of the final product. It is anticipated that this group of captains will later determine what items in the final product are worthy of analysis via logic networks. They will supervise the construction of the networks when products involved would have impact upon their groups. Attractive, "homeless" events, not fitting into the groups, or involving two or more groups, can be analyzed by the corporate R&D office.

Although the process is time-consuming, on a continuing basis it should prove to be an important guide to long-range corporate plans now in existence. Properly handled in the "chicken and egg" process, it should lay the "golden egg" which will hatch into real contributions to long-range business plans and objectives.

Integrating Forecasting and Planning Through a Function-oriented Approach

ERICH JANTSCH

In recent years, companies have begun to adopt new attitudes toward the future. No longer do they regard it as fixed and inevitable; instead, the future can be influenced and changed. This chapter examines the transition which is taking place as companies move from product-oriented to function-oriented thinking. It focuses on the integration of technological forecasting with long-range planning, and the implications for organization structure and operations.

Dr. Jantsch has been serving as a consultant to the Directorate for Scientific Affairs of the O.E.C.D. since 1962, and is presently on leave from Brown Boveri Company. He has recently completed a world-wide study of technological forecasting, the results of which are published in his book, *Technological Forecasting in Perspective* (O.E.C.D., Paris 1967).

THE CASE FOR STRATEGIC THINKING IN INDUSTRY

Traditionally, forecasting has been regarded as distinct from planning. It can even be practiced with the conscious or unconscious purpose of evading planning, if a deterministic view of the future is taken. "Planning will force action," as a high European government official sadly remarked to the author, whereas purely exploratory forecasting is sometimes accepted as depicting the inevitable future—one's own future included—so that there is little left to influence or change through planning.

Human achievement has never sprung from such a defeatist view. The ancient Greek tragedy—the strongest expression man has given to his notion of historical forces that are beyond his power of control—emphasizes that, of his own free will, man has to accept the verdict of history and that his fate will be fulfilled only if he aligns his own forces with those of the gods. This subtle communication of man with history, which looks like a basic paradox only in its superficial aspects, has underlain the dynamic development of Western civilization from the time of the Greeks to the present. On the verge of a more thorough and rapid transformation of society than the world has ever seen—the transformation by "social technology"—man is again called upon to take decisions of his own free will, to make this breathtaking turn of history actually happen.

In spite of the dramatic technological successes of the first half of this century, a surprisingly passive attitude toward technological development has dominated until recently—an attitude which was content with primarily exploratory (opportunity-oriented) forecasting. This is exemplified by comments concerning television which were made in 1936 (only one year before regular television broadcasting started), by two of the most courageous pioneers of technological forecasting in America. The metallurgist C. C. Furnas, in a collection of remarkable technological forecasts,[1] wrote:

> I am waiting for my television but I cannot live forever. When I think that the first radio impulse transmission was accomplished by Joseph Henry in 1840 and the first radio broadcast was not until 1920, I feel a little discouraged about the arrival of this television business while my eyes still function. No one has dared even to think of television in natural colours as yet.

And S. Colum Gilfillan, who had pioneered technological forecasting in the United States since 1907, asked at the same time: "Will the public accept TV and pay for it?"[2]

Even after the successful demonstration of "crash programs" such as those which led to the development of nuclear energy and radar in World War II—the result of primarily normative (mission-oriented) thinking—the impact on industry was not felt immediately. A "Forum on the Future of Industrial Research,"[3] held in New York in 1944, with an impressive

---

[1] C. C. Furnas, *The Next Hundred Years—The Unfinished Business of Science* (Baltimore, Md.: Williams & Wilkins, 1936).

[2] S. Colum Gilfillan, "The Prediction of Inventions," in U.S. National Resources Committee, *Technological Trends and National Policy* (Washington, D.C., 1937).

[3] Standard Oil Development Company, *The Future of Industrial Research*, New York, 1945.

array of some of the most distinguished names from U.S. government, industry, and universities, arrived at a consensus favoring a concept based on such notions as: no planning of research; encouragement of cooperative research; and only small science-based industry which would not "plan," but would "try out" new products. This concept for the future, which essentially expressed a desire to return to prewar habits, changed drastically only when the incentives were again stimulated by the Cold War. Europe has not yet fully caught up with this switch.

A new attitude toward the future is developing today. Based on increased confidence, gained and already "tested" in military technological development, it now penetrates from philosophical levels to applications in "social technology," and it is about to impinge on the economic area and transform industrial thinking. Olaf Helmer, in his plan for an "Institute for the Future," [4] best describes this new attitude towards the future:

> The fatalistic view that it is unforeseeable and inevitable is being abandoned. It is being recognized that there are a multitude of possible futures and that appropriate intervention can make a difference in their probabilities. This raises the exploration of the future, and the search for ways to influence its direction, to activities of great social responsibility. This responsibility is not just an academic one, and to discharge it more than perfunctorily we must cease to be mere spectators in our own ongoing history, and participate with determination in molding the future. It will take wisdom, courage, and sensitivity to human values, to shape a better world.

Technological forecasting will contribute to a multi-disciplinary, integrated analysis along these lines, and the main difficulty of making such thinking fruitful will have to be faced: the conscious or unconscious tendency to select future goals along lines of thought that are valid only for the present. Technological forecasting makes it possible to break out of the extended present—the "logical future"—and to penetrate into a "willed future" (Renè Dubos). It not only links with technological forward planning today, but is well on its way to becoming an integral part of future planning in the broadest sense and one of the principal tools for "futures-creative" thinking.[5]

The main features of modern technological forecasting, which has been finding wide application in industry since about 1960, differ radically from the older notions that went with speculative and, generally, purely

[4] Olaf Helmer et al., *Prospectus for an Institute for the Future*, Santa Monica, Calif., 1966.

[5] The term "futures-creative" thinking has been proposed by Hasan Ozbekhan. In Europe, Bertrand de Jouvenel's "futuribles" (meaning "possible futures") has become the widely recognized label for such thinking.

exploratory forecasting. The present emphasis can be summarized in four points: [6]

1. Technological forecasting is a probabilistic assessment, on a relatively high confidence level, of future technology transfer—not a straight prediction.

2. Technological forecasting concentrates on the evaluation of alternatives and the formulation of strategies to arrive there. This, for medium-range purposes, means weighing tactical alternatives for attaining a fairly clear objective. For long-range forecasts, it means relying heavily on fundamental principles, potentials, and limitations—the preparation of the big strategic options for the future.

3. Consideration of future technology transfer is set in a broad economic, political, and social context. Emphasis is placed on effects (for example, technological capabilities such as speed, temperature resistance, strength, etc.) and on impacts, not on the actual description of a technical realization (a machine or apparatus, etc.).

4. Technological forecasting essentially takes a nondeterministic view, combining exploratory (opportunity-oriented) and normative mission-oriented) thinking.[7]

Technological forecasting, gradually taking shape along these lines to become a valuable management tool, has already entered a relationship of intimate interaction with planning. In most companies today, it is still considered a separate activity and is applied in discrete time-intervals to focus and spur planning. The two can be expected to marry completely in the 1970's when industrial thinking will be more deeply affected by the basic new orientations that are already becoming visible:

1. The shift of emphasis from short- and medium-range tactical to long-range strategic thinking; and

2. The trend toward large-systems thinking, going beyond the industrial and economic systems to include more and more of the future social system.

[6] A comprehensive survey of technological forecasting, as it is practiced today in America and in Europe, may be found in E. Jantsch, *Technological Forecasting in Perspective* (O.E.C.D., Paris, 1967).

[7] The terms "exploratory" and "normative" forecasting were suggested to the author by Dennis Gabor, who, in his book *Inventing the Future* (London: Secker & Warburg, 1963), made a strong case for normative forecasting.

These important implications were grasped as far back as ten years ago by Jay W. Forrester in his visionary "Industrial Dynamics" concept, which is perhaps only now starting to bear real fruit:

> Historically, military necessity has often led not only to new devices like aircraft and digital computers but also to new organizational forms and to a new understanding of social forces. These developments have then been adapted to civilian usage. . . . As the pace of warfare has quickened, there has of necessity been a shift of emphasis from the tactical decision (moment-by-moment direction of the battle) to strategic planning (preparing for possible eventualities, establishing policy, and determining in advance how tactical decisions *will* be made). . . . Likewise in business: as the pace of technological change quickens, corporate management, even at the lower levels, must focus more and more on the *strategic* problems of running the business and less and less on the everyday operating problems. In the system development for the military, it has been amply demonstrated that carefully selected formal rules can lead to tactical decisions that excel those made by human judgment under the pressure of time and with insufficient experience and practice. Furthermore, it has been found that men are just as adaptable to the more abstract strategic planning as they are to tactical decision making, once their outlook has been lifted to the broader and longer range picture.[8]

With corporate managements of some of the innovation-minded American companies (such as the Xerox Corporation) already devoting more than half of their time to a future ten or more years distant, the truth of this statement is finding dramatic proof today.

THREE STEPS OF INDUSTRIAL DYNAMICS

Long-range strategic and large-systems thinking has already transformed the organizational schemes in U.S. military and civilian governmental environments. The *Planning-Programming-Budgeting System* (PPBS), in use in the Department of Defense since 1961, and introduced into the civilian branches of the government in October, 1965, is, on the outside, a medium-range planning scheme with five- to six-year time-depth. However, it encourages, and even enforces, long-range strategic thinking beyond the formal planning scope, by virtue of the following particular features: the upgrad-

---

[8] Jay W. Forrester, "Industrial Dynamics—A Major Breakthrough for Decision Makers," *Harvard Business Review*, Vol. 36 No. 4 (July–August, 1958), 37–66. The concept, which aims at finding a useful basis for model-building, was subsequently expanded in Jay W. Forrester, *Industrial Dynamics* (Cambridge, Mass.: The M.I.T. Press, 1961).

ing of medium-range forecasting and planning to a continuous activity which shapes thinking and decision making in the entire government area and directs government agencies to functions relevant to national objectives and broad social goals; a systems-oriented approach which is quite new in government, including the evaluation of alternatives; and the use of advanced techniques such as systems analysis, operations research, cost/effectiveness studies, and model-building.

With fully operational PPBS, which is still a vision that is only gradually materializing in the civilian U.S. government, research and development forecasting and planning (i.e., the "technological innovation structure" of the government) will be similar to that of a decentralized company, stressing decentralized initiative and centralized balancing. The departments and agencies will develop their "businesses" along the lines of the decentralized operating divisions of a company and will compete for funding in accordance with their contribution to "corporate objectives." The Executive Office of the President can be compared, in this framework, to corporate-level staff groups. (Such a "business model" of government would be utterly resented in most of the European countries today.)

The most important aspect of this system is the abolition of the traditional service structure in the military and the instrumental structure in civilian government, and their replacement by a functional framework for forecasting and planning. Weapon systems development is, in the "corporate" picture, no longer considered in the framework of the armed services—Army, Navy, and Air Force—but, instead, is seen in functional program categories such as: "Strategic Retaliatory Forces," "Continental Air and Missile Defense Forces," "Civil Defense," "Airlift and Sealift," etc.[9] In the civilian branches, the instrumental framework, e.g., the spending of the largest part of the money allocated to the Public Health Program through the National Institutes of Health, can be expected to be replaced by functional categories such as "Control and Prevention of Diseases," "Treatment and Restoration," etc.

Where does *industry* stand in this search for new organizational forms to incorporate strategic and large-systems thinking? Today, a number of underlying factors are undergoing subtle but thorough changes, and tend to form characteristic patterns. The following rough classification may be understood as a progressive sequence of patterns related to industrial dynamics (see Figure 1). Certain industrial sectors (in their broad layout, not in their organizational structure) have always been in line with func-

---

[9] Since the administrative structure is still based on the old service scheme, one may call this a "matrix management," where an innovation emphasis structure is superimposed on the administrative structure. In 1967, the Canadian armed forces abolished their service structure altogether, even for administrative purposes.

Dynamic Concept	1. "Drifting with the Main-stream"	2. "Leading the Main-stream"	3. "Shaping the Future"
Principal incentive	Hedging against threat; maintenance of average position	Maintenance of leading position (entrepreneurship, restricted to departmentalized thinking)	Challenge (entrepreneurship, development of competence, etc.)
Emphasis in future-orientation	Short-range tactics (up to 5 years)	Medium-range tactics (5 to 10 years)	Long-range strategy (10 years and beyond)
Principal optimization criterion	Low-risk profit	Maximum profit	Corporate objectives tying in with national and social goals
Typical organizational structure	Horizontal (mainly centralized initiative and control)	Vertical (decentralized initiative in distinct product lines, centralized control)	Function-oriented innovation emphasis structure, penetrating throughout the entire company and encouraging entrepreneurship at all levels; "matrix management" or basic split between "Present" and "Future" at high levels
Forecasting emphasis	Mainly exploratory	Strong normative component gives spur and guidance to product-line planning	Evaluation of strategic large-systems options in feedback cycle with planning
Planning emphasis	Mainly indicative, if at all	Pushing distinct product lines	Flexible, in functional framework, encouraging "competition between alternatives"
Typical organization of forecasting and planning	Forecasting in a corporate-level staff group or committee	Decentralized forecasting and planning in product lines, confronted with each other in discrete time intervals, at top mainly financial control	Integrated, continuous forecasting and planning at all levels, coordinated at the top
Estimated year of "management innovation" (considerable impact)	Traditional	U. S.:1953/54 Europe: 1963/64	U. S.: 1965/66 Europe: 1967/68 ?
Estimated present share in big industry with a high rate of technological innovation	U. S.: Few Europe: 30 to 50 per cent	U. S.: ~90 per cent Europe: 50 to 70 per cent	U. S.: ~10 per cent Europe: Few (e.g. big oil companies)

Figure 1. The Progressive Trend in Industrial Dynamics.

tion-oriented thinking; e.g., from the beginning, all the big electrotechnical groups, both in Europe and America, have recognized their power engineering function to be an integrated power-generation–power-distribution–power-utilization function (combining vastly different product lines in thermal and electrical machinery and apparatus). The functions that tie in with the product-line class "electronics" have been less clearly defined. Only a few of the big electrotechnical groups, for example, have entered the data processing field.

Figure 2 illustrates three typical forecasting attitudes toward a simple technological capability such as speed, strength, etc. Step 1—"Drifting with the main-stream"—is characteristic of what may be called the "bandwagon"

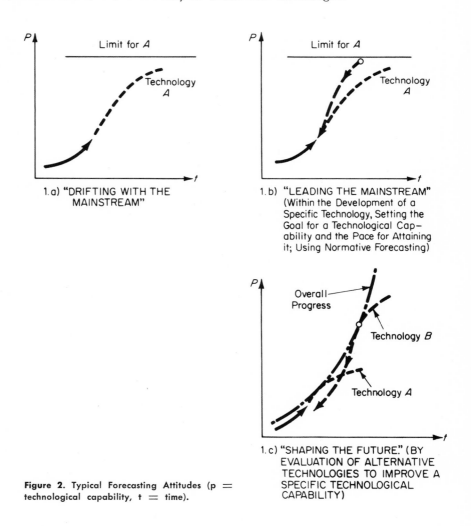

1.a) "DRIFTING WITH THE MAINSTREAM"

1.b) "LEADING THE MAINSTREAM" (Within the Development of a Specific Technology, Setting the Goal for a Technological Capability and the Pace for Attaining it; Using Normative Forecasting)

1.c) "SHAPING THE FUTURE." (BY EVALUATION OF ALTERNATIVE TECHNOLOGIES TO IMPROVE A SPECIFIC TECHNOLOGICAL CAPABILITY)

Figure 2. Typical Forecasting Attitudes (p = technological capability, t = time).

attitude. It can provide a comfortable basis for existence, but will inevitably lead to frustration of the type the bigger European countries are now labeling the "technological gap." Also, more sophisticated analysis will probably reveal that the reputation and strategic position of a company are becoming increasingly dependent on the innovation it has to offer, not on the high quality of its conventional output. Whereas in conventional power plant building, the turbogenerator manufacturer played the key role and usually subcontracted the boiler, etc., the client for a nuclear power plant now turns to the manufacturer of the nuclear "boiler" first, with the turbogenerator assigned relatively secondary importance. As a consequence, all the big electrotechnical groups—none of which had been active in the boiler field—have entered, or are trying to enter, nuclear reactor development. It may be expected that the step-1-attitude will have even more difficulty competing with a future step-3-environment than with the predominating step-2-attitude.

Today, most companies fit into the pattern corresponding to step 2— "Leading the main-stream"—which has dominated the American industrial scene for the past decade, and is now winning over Europe.[10] Here, normative thinking already goes far beyond the clear-cut problem of defining requirements for a specific mission (more a task for planning), and participates in formulating the missions themselves. This approach is representative of the current notion of "free enterprise." However, it is basically restricted by the piecemeal approach it offers. Its inadequacies can be demonstrated today in many ways and at all levels. Consider the following examples:

1. Subsidies and "government guarantees" for continued coal mining are common in a period when coal is rapidly losing ground in the interfuel competition (mainly with nuclear energy). Whereas the United States has managed to solve this problem for the time being, European countries, especially the Federal Republic of Germany, still give in, more or less helplessly, to product-oriented thinking.

2. The utilization of fossil hydrocarbons for combustion purposes is still expanding, although it is now becoming clear that the natural reserves could and should be used as valuable raw material for high-order products, such as food and textiles.

Product-oriented thinking prevails, not only in the manufacturing but

---

[10] Of course, not everybody who tries will become a leader; it is the attitude, not the result, which is discussed here.

also in the service sectors. A remarkable technological forecast,[11] published in 1930, foresaw transatlantic jet air transport and expected ship owners to rush in and diversify in time. As we now know, the ship owners missed this chance of recognizing the function "intercontinental transport" (at different speeds and by different means), and are now left with the sole possibility of diversifying into the pleasure-cruising sector.

An A. D. Little study of the introduction of semiconductors [12] dramatically revealed how some of the most renowned and most powerful electrotechnical groups lost much momentum in the decisive early development and marketing phases because they placed the transistor, whose performance is, at first glance, comparable to that of an electronic valve, in their vertically structured valve divisions, where the new device was fought as "the enemy" in an environment geared to product-oriented thinking.[13] The advantages of self-motivation which are created by giving a man a clear-cut tactical problem to solve—"Everybody loves his baby"—are now increasingly offset by the disadvantages due to a lack of strategic thinking. Product-oriented thinking is an obstacle to swift technological innovation.

Between step 2 and step 3 ("Shaping the Future"), there are a large variety of partial and transitory solutions which are coming more and more to the foreground in American industry. In a company, this process of change often starts with the addition of a scientific or technical evaluation group (or Chief Scientist) to the corporate-level staff groups that deal with "corporate long-range planning" (in this context, frequently aiming mainly at five-year budget plans). This provides the possibility of looking at a potential development which would fall in between the vertical product lines, or to persuade one of the vertical "empires" to adopt this area, or to set up new product lines, if necessary. Insofar as such diversification is not just induced by the "greener grass on the neighbor's lawn," it may be understood to some extent as a first move toward function-oriented thinking. Examples may be found in forward and backward integration of product lines: e.g., building up industrial chains from raw materials to end-products, such as the expansion of the big oil companies in the direction of agricultural chemistry and petrochemistry, and

---

[11] Earl of Birkenhead, *The World in 2030 A.D.* (London: Harcourt, 1930.) The author was not a scientist or engineer.

[12] A. D. Little, *Patterns and Problems of Technical Innovation in American Industry*, Part IV: *The Semiconductor Industry*, Report PB 181573 to National Science Foundation, Washington, D.C., 1963.

[13] Today, function-oriented thinking would deal with semiconductors in the different functional areas such as communications (aiming at microminiaturization, high frequencies, etc.); power transmission (aiming at high voltages for d.c. transmission, etc.); and power utilization (specific heat capacity/electrical conductivity characteristics, etc.). The real goals and alternatives tend to become blurred in a unified "semiconductor" development program.

now further into textiles and foodstuffs, or the food-processing industry integrating backwards to farming. Other types of "functional" diversification are exemplified by the move of almost all important aerospace companies into electronics.[14] Technological developments, pushed to their extremes, often exhibit an inherent tendency to enforce integration, such as the "growing together" of the electronic components and systems sectors in the age of microminiaturization, or of the airframe and propulsion unit sectors for hypersonic planes (Mach 5 to 7, and beyond).

The fact that a considerable position of European industry has not yet implemented the shift from step 1 to step 2—from horizontal to vertical structure, in organizational terms—points to the possibility of "leap-frogging" from step 1 straight to step 3. On the outside, a function-oriented structure does look like a compromise between horizontal and vertical organization, although there is a basic difference in attitude and in the degree of penetration of the company. At least one important industrial group in Europe can be expected to attempt such "leap-frogging" in 1967 or 1968.

Figure 3 presents a rough idea of the principal categories in which thinking differs for step 2 and step 3. The more function-oriented thinking becomes, the more it will tend to incorporate all areas in which technology makes a contribution to the particular function. Only high-level functions, ultimately tying in with social and national goals, permit flexible control over the alternatives and true leadership.

The Engineers' Joint Council stated this very clearly a few years ago in their attempt to look at the future:

> The fragmentation of most industries has led to concentration on materials and services with little relationship to the technical and socio-economic systems within which these materials and devices must function. Only those industries that have large, integrated responsibilities, and that have been organized in the past few decades in co-operation with the public interest have developed effective systems that provide service to the general population.[15]

The EJC report cites the communications field, power distribution, and fuel distribution among the positive examples.

---

[14] The present trend of aerospace companies, both in America and Europe, to diversify into the area of deep submergibles may be prompted primarily by the availability of special skill in these companies, but may develop into a bold functional concept circumscribed by "exploration—space and deep sea," or even "conquest of environments hostile to man—air, space, deep sea."

[15] Engineers' Joint Council, *The Nation's Engineering Research Needs, 1965–85,* Subcommittee Reports of the Engineering Research Committee, EJC, New York, 1962.

Product-oriented Categories		Function-oriented Categories	
Category	Example	Category	Example
		Social function	Communication, education, health, etc.
Industrial sector	Computer industry	Technological function	Information technology
Product line	Computer series	Functional capability	Data processing
Product (system)	Specific computer model	Technological capability	Speed, storage capacity, etc.
Components	Integrated circuitry	Basic technology	Microminiaturization, cryogenic memories, etc.

Figure 3. A Typical Hierarchy of Categories.

The computer industry, for example (and even its market leader), has failed, so far, to express its corporate objectives clearly in terms of high-level functions. "Data processing" ties in with function-oriented thinking but represents only the lower level of a functional capability.[16]

As the higher-order products assume the lead in product-oriented industry, the higher-order functions eventually will become increasingly dominant. Without any change in the attitude of the computer industry, the "data processing" industry is inevitably becoming the subcontractor to "communications," "education," "health," and other industries which are leading the innovation process. For maximum profit, this might not be considered a bad policy for quite some time to come; but maximum profit is not a challenging goal for professional people, as the "minority leaders" of the top 10 per cent of U.S. industry (such as Bell Laboratories and the Xerox Corporation) testify. "The corporate leader who does not try to conduct his company so as to instill pride in his people is doomed these days." [17]

It should be emphasized that the managerial capabilities of steps 2 and 3 generally include those of the lower steps; e.g., a company focusing

[16] This problem is now under consideration by IBM, for example.
[17] Joseph C. Wilson, *The Conscience of Business*, Westminster College, Fulton, Miss., 1965.

on the "challenge" incentive will not neglect "hedging against threats," and will be able to incorporate much of the momentum inherent in "product-oriented" thinking. The progression from step 1 to step 3 might best be taken as a widening of scope and horizon in overall management attitudes.

FUNCTION-ORIENTED "INNOVATION EMPHASIS" IN INDUSTRY

As far back as 1935, S. Colum Gilfillan [18] observed that social inventions tend to arrive in clusters which are grouped around functions. This bears testimony to the power of social motivation which is inherent in technological innovation. The aim in industry should be to establish function-oriented thinking at the level of comprehensive control over the interactions of technology transfer. According to Harvey Brooks,[19] technology transfer is a complex interaction between vertical transfer (from a scientific principle to a technical realization, etc.) and horizontal transfer (diffusion of existing knowledge, application and service engineering, interdisciplinary fructification, consideration of "communalities," etc.).

The integration of technological forecasting and planning is inherent in this concept, not only because forecasting participates actively in the selection of goals and missions (as is already seen in product-oriented thinking), but also because the solutions offered by planning along alternative paths into the future interact, in a feedback cycle, with the evaluation of the alternatives which are anticipated through forecasting. While forecasting provides guidance for planning, its probability and desirability statements are, in turn, modified by the possible courses of action which are worked out by planning. In addition, technological developments contribute, at the same time, to various functions (e.g., information technology to communication, education, transportation, etc.) and may change the picture considerably.

The difference (vis-à-vis product-oriented thinking) which can result may be demonstrated by a hypothetical example concerning the oil industry (see Figures 4A and 4B). If it regards itself as "oil industry" proper, i.e., concentrating on the resource oil and its derived products, a diversification policy characteristic of the development of big oil companies over the past twenty to forty years, up to the current research projects in

---

[18] S. Colum Gilfillan, *The Sociology of Invention* (Chicago, Ill.: Follett Publishing Company, 1935).

[19] Harvey Brooks, "National Science Policy and Technology Transfer," Conference on Technology Transfer and Innovation, May 15–17, 1966, Washington, D.C.

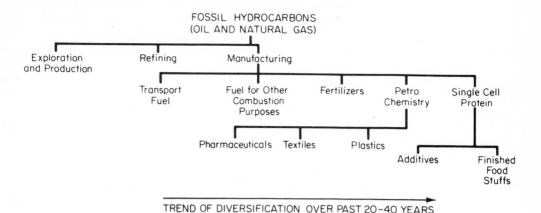

4A–Product-Oriented Thinking Exploits Alternatives Offered by the Products, Oil and Natural Gas. Diversification Moves in Direction of Higher-Order End Products

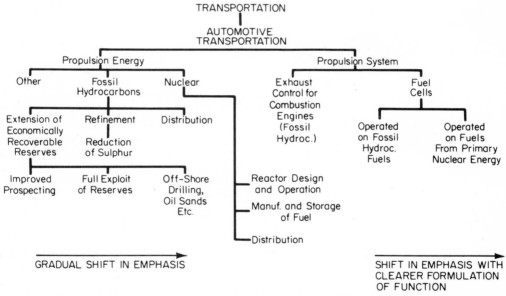

4B – Function-Oriented Thinking Moves Toward the Preparation of a Strategy Based on Primary Nuclear Energy, Tying in with the Long-Range Development of Resources Patterns, and the Social Goal of Reducing Air Pollution. The Original Interest in Propulsion Energy is Extended to Include Propulsion Systems. New Functions May Crystalize Around New Skills. At Least One Big Oil Company, with Particular Skill in Off-Shore Drilling, Contemplates Diversification Into Mineral Collection on the Sea-Bottom, and Off-Shore Gold Mining.

Figure 4. Impact of Product-Oriented and Function-Oriented Thinking on Innovation (Big Oil Companies).

the production of Single Cell Protein on a fossil hydrocarbon substrate, is the logical result (Figure 4A). If, however, a company feels responsible for the social function "transportation" (or, for simplicity of the example, "automotive transportation"), it will (1) prepare for the switch to other primary energy sources; (2) evaluate the alternatives along with their significance to social goals (including the reduction of air pollution in urban areas and conservation of fossil hydrocarbons for more important uses than combustion), and probably familiarize itself with the idea of running systems of giant base-load nuclear reactors to convert primary nuclear energy to electricity for batteries or forms of fuel that are suitable for use in fuel-cells; and (3) possibly find an incentive even to participate actively in the development of the future propulsion systems.

Present thinking in big oil companies still favors the product-oriented approach, but already introduces some action, at a still lower level of effort, that may be interpreted as the initiation of a gradual shift to more prominent function-oriented thinking. It may be noted, in this context, that the big oil companies were among those industries in the "social technology" area which first recognized the incentive to join social research and forecasting to their technological and marketing forecasting.

Two or more functions may finally be adopted by the same company (e.g. "transportation," "food," etc.). The orientation toward functions—and the trend to fill functions more and more completely—may also favor mergers between different branches. The Esso/Nestlé partnership, to develop Single Cell Protein from petroleum, is an example of this trend. It represents a functional chain that is fully integrated, from oil exploration and drilling to the manufacture and marketing of finished foodstuffs.

Large-systems thinking, which can be established at high functional levels, is illustrated by the example shown in Figure 5. A somewhat ex-

Figure 5. Alternative Technological Options for the Health Function.

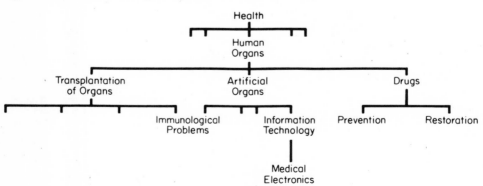

treme case has been chosen here to demonstrate the obvious limitations of function-oriented thinking. If, for example, heart diseases might be cured alternatively by transplanting heart valves (e.g., from young calves), by introducing an artificial heart (possibly a complex miniaturized electro-mechanical system), or by finding suitable drugs, one company could not hope to cope equally well with—and choose freely from—all of these. For a national health program, on the other hand, these options represent genuine alternatives which must be evaluated before research priorities are established.

Clearly, thinking in broad functions will be restricted somewhat where the alternatives demand too great a variety of skills. However, in the framework of high-level functions, companies have already expanded their interests into areas which nobody would have expected only a short time ago. Companies which are gradually aligning their thinking to an overall "communications" function are acquiring publishing houses or youth periodicals (RCA and Xerox), or are even planning to enter city building (General Electric—"the city as a communication network")—and ITT has acquired a big rent-a-car system. Companies which recognize an "education" function for themselves perform research in new educational systems (e.g., Xerox Corporation, Raytheon, and the start in function-oriented thinking in the computer industry). Airlines, taking their "tourism-abroad function" more seriously, acquire or build hotel chains (Pan American, TWA, etc.).

Another restrictive factor, which may lead to a compromise in the establishment of function-oriented thinking, can be seen in a possibly large difference in the innovation rates that apply to individual branches of the same company. In the chemical industry, for example, the large "base-load" share of traditional basic chemicals is changing very slowly, whereas the full drive for innovation is in progress in some of the end-product branches. A number of companies apply technological forecasting and conscious forward planning principally to the military part of their businesses, and that is where they contribute to rapid innovation.

Finding the *organizational framework* for industrial function-oriented thinking is a complex problem which depends much more on subtleties, such as self-motivation at all levels and the effective abolition of hierarchic and other communication barriers, than on a formal scheme. An example is the American electronics company which, at the time it established a formal function-oriented forecasting and planning scheme, adopted a policy of having as many "general managers" (people at all hierarchic levels who have full access to all facts, plans, and objectives of their company) as possible. Before that decision was made, there were eight "general managers"—just the president and the vice-presidents. Five years afterwards, there were 150, and a goal for 1,000 "general managers" had been established! The predominant attitude in industry, however, is still far from the attitude exemplified here, which calls for a certain greatness on the part of the top management people. In general, European industry is far behind American industry in encouraging entrepreneurship at the level of the "bench-people."

The following structural concepts may be distinguished in companies which are well on their way to function-oriented forecasting and planning:

1. A complex "matrix management" which is, perhaps, characteristic of the transitory stage when a company switches from product- to function-oriented thinking. The general pattern in large companies favors, on the administrative side, a product- (or program-) oriented structure for the operating divisions, and a discipline-oriented structure for the research division or the corporate level research laboratory. An ever-changing function-oriented structure is superimposed to deal with interdisciplinary functions and projects, implemented by temporary project groups and project managers. The product/function matrix for management basically represents a flexible "task force" approach which is imposed on a rigid administrative structure. The decision-making structure of North American Aviation's Los Angeles Division, for example, attempts to combine, for *independent* (i.e., noncontractual) research and development, powerful systems development management with guidance through the recognition of long-range technological options. It does this by exploiting a system/technology matrix in three areas: "systems-oriented planning," "technology-oriented planning" and "systems-oriented technology planning." The first two categories (which are more typical of function-oriented thinking) account for 93 per cent of the total effort, and the last category (more in line with product-oriented thinking) accounts for only 7 per cent.

2. An "innovation emphasis structure," resembling a relevance tree (and in this respect tying in with an important class of techniques applied to normative technological forecasting) which is superimposed over the administrative structure (see Figure 6). An example of this is SCORE (Select Concrete Objectives for Research Emphasis), implemented at the North American Aviation's Autonetics Division to relate objectives, five to fifteen years in the future, to strategies and tactics, and to define key points. A similar scheme has been used for several years in an American electronics company, where approximately 75 per cent of the activities in the corporate-level research laboratories, and approximately 80 to 90 per cent of divisional research and development, now contribute

Figure 6. Industrial "Innovation Emphasis Structure."

to specific tactical programs. The predominantly exploratory remainder, which is left outside this normative scheme, is nevertheless committed within a framework of long-range technological objectives, and is "pushed" into strategies and action programs once the relevance of this research to corporate objectives has become clear. A more formal system to link exploratory research directly to corporate objectives (bypassing the specific tactics and strategies levels) is being introduced now. The U.S. government's Planning-Programming-Budgeting System also represents such an "innovation emphasis structure" in the form of a relevance tree.

3. The tendency to strengthen an "innovation emphasis structure" (which can hardly become a rigid hierarchic concept because it needs to remain utterly flexible and stress intracompany strategies, as well as new potentials, against a more stable administrative background) which may ultimately lead to a high-level split between the "Present" and the "Future" (see Figure 7). Such a scheme would not work without a chief executive officer who de-

Figure 7. The Ultimate Consequence of Function-Oriented Strategic Thinking (from an American electronics company).

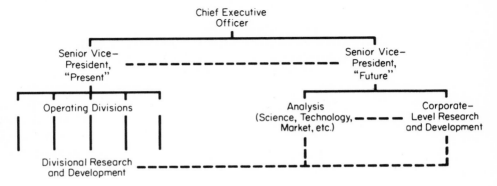

votes much of his time to the future and keeps a balance between his two commanding generals, one of which has the troops at his direct order, and the other the general staff. Also, financial control and investment policies are strongly influenced by corporate long-range objectives. The scheme means much less than the spirit in which it is implemented.

4. The "Systems Engineering" concept, already introduced in 1950 by American Telephone and Telegraph and its research branch, Bell Telephone Laboratories, which subdivides research and development work into basic research, development (with an exploratory and an applied subdivision), and systems engineering (where approximately one-fourth of the graduate staff is located). The systems engineering section is composed of mature scientists and engineers who have formerly done benchwork and now mainly perform evaluation work (60 per cent of their time is spent on writing). They prepare complete proposals, look at all major technological areas, set up inventories of technological options and alternative solutions to problems, develop criteria for effectiveness, evaluate specialists' estimates, and advise on the allocation of research funds. How "function-conscious" Bell Telephone Laboratories is may be illustrated by the following statement of its President:

To make the right choice, and then adhere to it, may not be as easy as it sounds. For example, one may have to decide rather frequently whether entrance into a new field is, in fact, compatible with the long-term objectives of the organization. We have occasionally, in the past, had the even more wrenching experience of withdrawing from promising areas in which we were already well established because they threatened to lead us too far away from our primary objective of providing even better communication service. However, such mission definition is necessary if the organization is to develop the "enduring themes" and flow of technology which I have described. In the long run, it is the best means of giving the organization continuing purposes and vitality.[20]

5. A "think group" to advise top management on long-range objectives and potentialities. The outstanding example here is General Electric's TEMPO Center for Advanced Studies. (The immediate observation to be made in this context is the fact that it is used by its own company at only 20 per cent of its capacity.)

[20] James B. Fisk, quoted in A. D. Little, *Management Factors Affecting Research and Exploratory Development,* Report for DDRE, Cambridge, Mass., 1965.

Future forms of organization will depend mainly on their suitability to cope with problem areas which are assuming increasing importance today; interdisciplinary developments; the gradual shift of emphasis from vertical to horizontal technology transfer (i.e., emphasis on applications, "software," and services); and the accent on "communalities" between development lines. In any case, organizations can be expected to be designed so that they permit more and more intimate linking with high-level national and social goals. Areas of "social technology," such as transportation, urbanization, food production, and others which are only now becoming the subject of long-range strategic thinking and large-systems analysis on a national and international level, will present the foremost industrial tasks of tomorrow.

FORECASTING TECHNIQUES FOR FUNCTION-ORIENTED STRATEGIC THINKING

The most important and most difficult task will be to formulate high-level functions and to choose the future overall "system" at which to aim. In the words of Norbert Wiener, "know-what" has become a more important quality than "know-how."[21] And this is no longer left to the discretion of industry alone.

The second important task will be to develop technological forecasting so it becomes an effective "coupling device" between the research, development, and engineering phases that lead to technological innovation: discovery, creation, substantiation, development, advanced engineering, and application and service engineering.[22] Effective coupling can be achieved only in the presence of a strong normative component. Of special importance is the coupling between the early phases, or—to use more traditional, though vague categories—in the areas of fundamental and applied research, and their interface. The ultimate aim is to translate high-level functions into research priorities on a fundamental level. In a few of the most advanced-thinking companies (again exemplified by the Xerox Corporation) technological forecasting has already begun an intimate dialogue with fundamental research, and has both changed the nature and increased the volume of the latter.

Exploratory forecasting *alone* will become less valuable, the more effective strategic thinking—and the guidance of action it provides—becomes. The direction and pace of technological movement will depend increas-

[21] Norbert Wiener, *The Human Use of Human Beings* (Boston, Mass.: Houghton Mifflin Company, 1950).
[22] Adapted from a scheme used by the Stanford Research Institute.

ingly on interaction within large systems, and on human decisions. The proper time frame for such strategic thinking will probably be about fifty years, although the picture of the future will continuously change as deeper insight is attained and high-level functions are adjusted accordingly.

Four important current trends in the development of technological forecasting techniques tie in with the gradual switch toward function-oriented, integrated forecasting and planning:

1. The search for techniques to improve *intuitive thinking,* as exemplified by the "Delphi" model.[23] Intuitive thinking will become most important in the formulation of goals, the recognition and discussion of social values, and the specification of functions.

2. The search for *"integrated" techniques* which combine the forecasting of technological development with the determination of the impact of such developments on the market, on economic or industrial sectors, on the nation, or on society in general. Straight cost/benefit analysis, which is widely used in product-oriented industry to maximize strictly monetary profit on a return on investment basis, is already inadequate and is being replaced or supplemented more and more by simple formulas or operations research concepts which try to include at least some strategic aspects. The success of the cost/effectiveness approach, in combination with systems analysis for the purposes of military planning, may stimulate attempts to develop an equivalent in the economic area. Already, adaptations to social areas have been attempted in the new strategic framework of the U.S. government (as outlined above), and by study groups such as Resources for the Future. The development of numerical and nonnumerical relevance tree techniques (e.g., Honeywell's PATTERN), multidimensional decision matrices (e.g., the "National Space Program Total System Development Matrix," designed by W. E. Walter for the Space and Information Division of North American Aviation), and other normative forecasting techniques already mark considerable progress in this area and bear testimony to the growing incentive for industry to link its objectives to supreme national and social goals.[24]

3. The adaptation of *systems analysis techniques* to forecasting, as pioneered by the California "think groups." The following prob-

[23] See Olaf Helmer's contribution to this book.

[24] The techniques mentioned here, together with approximately 100 other versions or elements of techniques related to forecasting, are discussed in Jantsch, *Technological Forecasting in Perspective.*

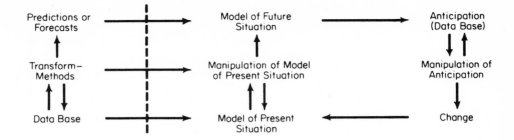

Predictions or Forecasts	Model of Future Situation	Anticipation (Data Base)
Transform–Methods	Manipulation of Model of Present Situation	Manipulation of Anticipation
Data Base	Model of Present Situation	Change

SPACE OF ACTUAL TECHNOLOGY TRANSFER

TOTALITY OF PATTERNS EMERGING FROM ACTUAL OR FORECAST DEVELOPMENTS

ALTERNATE "POSSIBLE" FUTURES

Figure 8. The Basic Layout of a Feedback Scheme as Proposed by Hasan Ozbekhan in "The Idea of a 'Look-Out' Institution," Systems Development Corporation, Santa Monica, March, 1965. The left-hand column represents the space of actual technology transfer; the middle column, the totality of patterns emerging from actual or forecast developments; and the right-hand column, alternative "possible futures." Transform-methods include the methods of technological forecasting.

lem areas will become of particular importance: the degree of freedom of choice and how to preserve a high degree for the generations to come; [25] development patterns which elucidate communalities, are sensitive to internal and external factors, and stress the probabilistic formulation of influencing factors and trends; the impact of specific technologies on large systems, and their contribution to pre-set objectives; and a dynamic framework for human motivation and social values.

4. The search for *feedback schemes* (see Figure 8) which will permit the application of forecasting techniques to the procedures of "futures-creative" thinking (i.e., the anticipation and evaluation of alternative "possible futures" and the corresponding reorientation of today's action in a feedback cycle). The valid functions will become visible only in such a process. The main difficulty may lie, not in defining the most desirable direction of movement, but in optimizing the transition to a new direction—in mathematical terms, changing the curvature of the systems tra-

---

[25] Prof. Dennis Gabor, in a lecture before The RAND Corporation on Feb. 8, 1967, attempted a first mathematical formulation of this problem on the basis of the "systems space" concept.

jectory.[26] Forecasting and planning, in such schemes, are interdependent. Specific courses of action as outlined by planning, for example, may influence forecasting considerably, and vice versa.

The ultimate form of forecasting techniques will permit their incorporation in future comprehensive management information systems. Having mastered the "lower" steps of straight information processing and the use of mathematical and statistical methods for decision making, information technology is now aiming at the simulation (by means of extended use of computers, etc.) of higher-order, long-range strategic thinking, particularly in the framework of feedback schemes.

CONCLUSION

Industry is gradually adapting from medium-range tactical to long-range strategic thinking, which, at the same time, marks a shift from product-oriented to function-oriented thinking and considerably extends "visibility" into the future. Technological forecasting and planning, parallel to this development, tend to become fully integrated—with forecasting aimed at anticipating and evaluating alternative strategic options in a large-systems framework, and planning focused on shaping the course of action accordingly. Both are interlinked in a feedback cycle. The foremost question will be "know-what," not "know-how."

Function-oriented thinking can best be implemented by means of a flexible "innovation emphasis structure," which, in present attempts, has usually been superimposed over a more rigid administrative structure. The formulation of special forecasting techniques to tie in with this development will concentrate on techniques to improve intuitive thinking, "integrated" techniques (development and its impact), systems analysis, and feedback schemes.

[26] As an example, agricultural productivity would have to be increased by every possible means up to the end of the century while, at the same time, the world prepares for the change to predominantly nonagricultural food production.

APPENDICES

Technological Forecasting Bibliography

(Partially Annotated)

Prepared by MARVIN J. CETRON

Abt Associates, Inc., "Survey of the State of the Art: Social, Political, and Economic Models and Simulations," report prepared for the National Commission on Technology, Automation, and Economic Progress; published in *Applying Technology to Unmet Needs,* Appendix, Vol. V, *Technology and the American Economy.* Washington, D.C.: Government Printing Office, February, 1966.

Aerospace Industries Association, *Aerospace Technical Forecast—1962–1972.* Washington, D.C., 1962.

Air Force (U.S.) publications:

Technology for Tomorrow, 5th ed., 1962–63, Aeronautical Systems Division, AFSC, Wright-Patterson AFB, Ohio; 62ASOP-300, December, 1962. (SECRET)

> "Technology for Tomorrow" is a preparation of motivational concepts, outlining the approach to an optimum plan. It is a guide to the organization and selective application of resources and capabilities for an aggressive support of the long-range Air Force technical mission. Thus it represents a step in the planning process. The contents and organization of the document reflect, in themselves, the fact that a cohesive detailed plan exists collectively in the minds of the engineers, scientists, and management personnel who have contributed to its formulation.

Operation FORECAST, 14 vols., SCGF-46-7 Forecast Special Project Office, HQ, AFSC, Andrews AFB, Maryland, January, 1964. (SECRET)

Project FORECAST, Organization and Mission Planning Group Report dated April 13, 1963.

> Discusses organization and planned operation of the 1963 study, *Project FORECAST,* conducted by the Air Force. Explains duties of the individuals and panels and how it was expected the panels would interact. Project Forecast Panel Reports:
>
> a. Navigation and Guidance (AD 354-060)
> b. Electronic Countermeasures and Counter-Countermeasures (AD 354-062)

c. Intelligence and Reconnaissance (AD 354-063)
   d. Communications, Volumes I and II (AD 354-058, AD 354-059)
   e. Weapons (AD 354-057)
   f. Power Generation (AD 354-053)
   g. Flight Dynamics (AD 354-051)

A Systems Development Planning Structure, an interim report by Abt Associates, Inc., 14 Concord Lane, Cambridge, Mass., to HQ, Air Force Systems Command (SCLS), Andrews Air Force Base, Washington, D.C., November 18, 1965.

> In the development of systems, this computerized technique is intended to provide the decision maker with an estimate of the implications of placing special emphasis on particular policies. It describes possible situations related to each policy. The technique is designed to assist with the assignment of a consistent set of relative values to any number of objectives by eliciting "Yes" or "No" responses from the decision maker to questions about preferences for various combinations of objectives.

An Approach to Research and Development Effectiveness, a paper presented by A. B. Nutt, Air Force Flight Dynamics Laboratory, Wright-Patterson Air Force Base, Dayton, Ohio, to 17th NAECON Conference Proceedings, May 12, 1965.

> This paper describes the rationale and use of RDE (Research and Development Effectiveness)—a computerized planning program developed in-house and designed to utilize analytical techniques in the management of R&D resources in the Air Force Flight Dynamics Laboratory, RTD, AFSC.

AFSC Technological War Plan, prepared by Deputy Chief of Staff, Plans, AFSC, Washington, D.C., Basic Plan No. TWP Basic SCL-65-3, dated March, 1965. (SECRET)

> This report is the AFSC Command Plan for the conduct of R&D activity in support of their assigned responsibility. The TWP consists of a basic plan and five supporting annexes. The purpose of each is briefly stated as follows:
>
> The "Basic Plan" integrates the content of the annexes and provides the transition of planning effort into programs and budgets.
>
> Annex A, "Environment," discusses the broad setting within which the technological threat and military policy goals are evolved.
>
> Annex B, "Threat," describes the expected evolution of aggressor systems and technology.
>
> Annex C, "Systems," projects and describes concepts and capabilities which may evolve into the systems of the future AF force structure.
>
> Annex D, "Technology," describes technology for deriving system capabilities, and projects efforts to strengthen the Command's technological base.
>
> Annex E, "Resources," projects mission man-years, technical facilities and RDT&E funds necessary to develop, test and evaluate both technology and systems.

Technical Objectives Documents, Research and Technology Division, AFSC, 36 Technical Area Reports, November, 1965. (Unclassified)

> These documents are prepared to provide means of communicating with science and industry, and to describe the Air Force's objectives in each of 36 different technical areas. As in any selective grouping in science and technology, it is difficult to draw sharp boundaries between areas, and thus overlapping does occur.

RTD Technological War Plan/Long Range Plan, Research and Technology Division, AFSC, Washington, D.C., Report No. RTL 64, April 25, 1964 and changes. (SECRET)

This Plan describes the future course of action that the Research and Technology Division will take in managing the Air Force Exploratory and Advanced Development Programs. It is prepared by the people most familiar with these programs—the working scientists and engineers in the Air Force Laboratories. It is an attainable Plan. It describes how RTD will allocate those resources which it may realistically expect to have available over the next decade.

The Plan is oriented toward achieving the level of technology required to attain the future Air Force capabilities identified by *Project FORECAST*. It also recognizes that a major objective of this Division is the building and maintaining, in our laboratories, of a strong in-house technical capability.

Changes will undoubtedly alter various parts of this Plan. Breakthroughs will occur and unsuccessful efforts will be terminated. On the whole, however, the Plan represents a coordinated picture of where RTD is going over the next decade, as we now see it.

Army (U.S.) publications:

Long Range Technological Forecast, 3d ed. Prepared by the Office of the Chief of Research and Development, Department of the Army, 3 vols., April, 1965. (SECRET)

>The Army *Long Range Technological Forecast* (*LRTF*) is designed to be of value in both technical and operational planning. It covers a period of twenty years.

>The Forecast describes knowledge, capabilities, and examples of material which science and technology can be expected to produce if supported by orderly programs of research and development. It represents one element of a current and comprehensive plan for long-range technical planning. The document is published in 3 volumes, entitled: "Scientific Opportunities," "Technological Capabilities," and "Advanced Systems Concepts."

Forecast in Depth—Information Processing Systems for the Field Army, H. T. Darracott, Technical Forecasting and Objectives Branch, Research and Development Directorate, U.S. Army Materiel Command, Washington, D.C. (UNCLASSIFIED)

>Comprehensive study of the peripheral equipments in an automatic information processing system. Part of its purpose was to provide a tool to aid in the design of such equipment for tactical data processing systems.

The Army Research Plan, Industry Edition, Office of the Chief of Research and Development, Department of the Army, No. ARP-65, dated March 1, 1965. (CONFIDENTIAL)

>The Army Research Plan (ARP) is an extension of the Army Research and Development Long Range Plan. Its purpose is to afford guidance to those commanders and agencies responsible for the detailed formulation of the Army's research programs by assigning relative levels of recognition to scientific and technological areas of interest to the Army.

Combat Development Objectives Guide, Combat Development Command, Department of the Army, dated August 15, 1964. (SECRET)

>The purpose of the *Combat Development Objectives Guide* is to provide guidance for the development of future operational concepts, organizations, and materiel. It states general combat development objectives and consolidates the studies, and lists field experiments and approved qualitative materiel requirements which are pointed toward the attainment of those objectives.

The Army Study System, Director Special Studies, Department of the Army, Office of the Chief of Staff, Washington, D.C., 3 vols., dated May 18, 1964. (Official use only)

> Examines current (1964) Army major study activities and evaluates effectiveness of the studies as inputs to planning, programming, budgeting, and other needs. The three volumes are: Basic Study (Vol. I); Study Documentation and Information Retrieval (Vol. II); and Bibliography of Current Major Army Studies, 1962 to date (1964) (Vol. III).

The Army Master Study Program 1967, Army Study Advisory Committee, Chief of Staff, Department of the Army, dated December 27, 1966. (CONFIDENTIAL)

> The Army Master Study Program, 1965, is designed to provide:
>
> 1. A formal, approved list of those major studies being pursued under the sponsorship of the Army Staff Agencies, HQ., Department of the Army, which are considered to be of prime importance to overall Army planning, force development and programming.
> 2. A mechanism for the use of the Army Staff to determine gaps or unbalanced emphasis within the overall study effort and thus enable studies to provide more effective support to the orderly development of the well-balanced, multipurpose Army of the future.
> 3. An orientation of the Army's study processes toward the unifying concepts, missions and guidance for the Army of the future which are enunciated in the document "Assessment of the Army, 1964."
> 4. A useful compendium of major Army study efforts for the information of the Office of the Secretary of Defense and other interested government agencies.

Ayres, Robert U., *On Technological Forecasting,* report HI-484-DP. Hudson Institute, Harmon-on-Hudson, N.Y., January 17, 1966. (Restricted)

———, *Technology and the Prospects for World Food Production,* report HI-640-DP (Rev. 2). Hudson Institute, Harmon-on-Hudson, N.Y., April 19, 1966. 71 pp.

Baade, Fritz, *The Race to the Year 2000.* New York: Doubleday & Company, Inc., 1962. 246 pp.

Bagby, F. L., et al., *A Feasibility Study of Techniques for Measuring and Predicting the State-of-the-Art.* Battelle Memorial Institute, Columbus, Ohio., July, 1959. DDC Report (AD 233-350)

> Discusses the results of a feasibility study on techniques for measuring and predicting the state of the art. The method used relied heavily on case histories in systems development. The study was conducted for the Air Force.

Bell, Daniel, "Twelve Modes of Prediction," in *Penguin Survey of the Social Sciences,* ed. J. Gould. Baltimore, Md.: Penguin Books, 1965.

Bicker, Robert E., *The Changing Relationship Between the Air Force and the Aerospace Industry,* Memorandum RM-4101-PR. The RAND Corporation, Santa Monica, Calif., July, 1964. 79 pp.

Bisplinghoff, R. L., *New Technology, Its Selection and Development.* Office of Advanced Research and Technology, National Aeronautics and Space Administration, Washington, D.C., February, 1965.

Blackett, P. M. S., "Tizard and the Science of War," *Nature,* March, 1960.

Bliven, Bruce, *Preview For Tomorrow: The Unfinished Business of Science.* New York: Alfred A. Knopf, 1953. 345 pp.

Bright, James R., "Opportunity and Threat in Technological Change," *Harvard Business Review,* November–December, 1963.

Bright, James R., ed., *Research, Development, and Technological Innovation.* Homewood, Ill.: Richard D. Irwin, Inc., 1964. 783 pp.

————, *Technological Planning on the Corporate Level*. Division of Research, Harvard Business School, Boston, Mass., 1961.

Brown, Bernice, and Olaf Helmer, *Improving the Reliability of Estimates Obtained from a Consensus of Experts,* report P-2986. The RAND Corporation, Santa Monica, Calif., 1964.

Brown, Harrison, *The Challenge of Man's Future: An Inquiry Concerning the Condition of Man during the Years that Lie Ahead*. New York: The Viking Press, 1954. 290 pp.

Brown, J. H., and E. S. Cheaney, *Report on a Study of Future Research Activity and Pertinent Forecasting Techniques for Battelle's Trends in Research Study*. Battelle Memorial Institute, Columbus, Ohio, 1965. 51 pp.

Brozen, Yale, "Determination of the Direction of Technological Change," *American Economic Review*, Vol. 43 (May, 1953), 288–302.

Bruce, Robert D., *The Dimensions of Change*. Paper presented at the First National Joint Meeting, Operations Research Society of America and The Institute of Management Sciences, San Francisco, Calif., November 9, 1961.

Calder, Richie, *After the Seventh Day: The World Man Created*. New York: Simon and Schuster, Inc., 1961. 448 pp.

Cetron, M. J., "Forecasting Technology" *International Science & Technology,* September, 1967. 83–92.

Cetron, M. J., "Quantitative Utility Estimates for Science and Technology (QUEST)," *IEEE Transactions on Engineering Management,* Vol. EM-14, No. 1 (March, 1967), 51–62.

Cetron, M. J., et al., *A Proposal for a Navy Technological Forecast,* Parts I and II 2 vols. Headquarters, Naval Materiel Command, Washington, D.C., May 1, 1966. (AD 659-199) and (AD 659-200)

> *Part I, Summary Report,* presents in concise form the results of a six month study carried out by the Navy Technological Forecasting Study Group. The document recommends a Navy technological forecast and describes the nature and utility of such an effort in addition to the procedure for accomplishing it.
>
> *Part II, Back-up Report,* presents much detail supporting material, sample forecasts, methodologies and a classification scheme. The backup report will aid those responsible for actually generating technological forecasts.

Cetron, M. J., Joseph Martino and Lewis Roepcke, "The Selection of R&D Program Content—Survey of Quantitative Methods," *IEEE Transactions on Engineering Management,* Vol. EM-14, No. 1 (March, 1967), 4–12.

Cheaney, E. S., *Technical Forecasting as a Basis for Planning*. ASME paper 66-MD-67, presented at the Design Engineering Conference, Chicago, Ill., May 9–12, 1966.

Conant, James B., *Science and Common Sense*. New Haven: Yale University Press, 1952; Yale Paperbound (tenth printing) July, 1964. 344 pp.

Dalkey, N., and Olaf Helmer, "An Experimental Application of the Delphi Method to the Use of Experts," *Management Science,* 9 (April, 1963), 458–67.

Darwin, Charles Galton, *The Next Million Years*. London: Rupert Hart-Davis, 1952. 210 pp.

De Solla Price, D. J., "The Acceleration of Science—Crisis in Our Technological Civilization," *Product Engineering,* 32 (March 6, 1961), 56–59.

————, "A Calculus of Science," *International Science and Technology,* No. 15, March, 1963.

————, *Little Science, Big Science*. New York: Columbia University Press, 1963; Columbia Paperback Edition, 1965. 118 pp.

Dockx, S., and P. Bernays, eds., *Information and Prediction in Science*. New York: Academic Press, 1965. 272 pp.

Domar, E. D., "On the Measurement of Technological Change," *Economic Journal,* 71 (December, 1961), 709–29.

Doyle, L. B., *How to Plot a Breakthrough*. System Development Corporation, Santa Monica, Calif., December, 1963. (AD 427-161)

Ellul, Jacques, *The Technological Society*. New York: Alfred A. Knopf, Inc., 1964. 449 pp.

Emme, Eugene M., *A History of Space Flight*. New York: Holt, Rinehart & Winston, Inc., 1965.

Ewell, L. N., "Uncle Sam Gazes into His Crystal Ball," *Armed Forces Chemical Journal,* Vol. VI (January, 1953), 9–15.

Fedor, Walter S., Senior Editor, "Commodity Forecasting by Computer Time Sharing," *C&EN Feature,* September 12, 1966.

Forrester, Jay, *Industrial Dynamics*. Cambridge, Mass.: The M.I.T. Press, 1961.

Furnas, C. C., *The Next Hundred Years—The Unfinished Business of Science*. Baltimore, Md.: Williams & Wilkins, 1936.

"The Future," *New York Times Magazine* Section 6, Part 2, April 19, 1964, pp. 86–118.

"The Future as Suggested by the Development of the Past 75 Years," *Scientific American,* October, 1920.

Gabor, Dennis, *Inventing the Future*. London: Secker & Warburg, 1963; Pelican Book A 663, Penguin Books, Harmondsworth, Middlesex, 1964. 199 pp.

Garrison, W. L., and D. F. Marble, *A Prolegomenon to the Forecasting of Transportation Development*. Northwestern University, Evanston, Ill., August, 1965. (AD 621-514)

Gilfillan, S. Colum, "The Prediction of Inventions," in U.S. National Resources Committee, *Technological Trends and National Policy*, Part One, Section II, pp. 15–23. Government Printing Office, June, 1937.

————, *The Sociology of Invention*. Chicago, Ill.: Follett Publishing Company, 1935.

————, "The Prediction of Technical Change," *The Review of Economics and Statistics,* Vol. XXXIV (November, 1952), 368–385.

Gilman, William, *Science: USA*. New York: The Viking Press, 1965.

Gordon, T. J., and O. Helmer, *Report on a Long-Range Forecasting Study,* report P-2982. The RAND Corporation, Santa Monica, Calif., September, 1964. (UNCLASSIFIED)

> Describes an experimental trend-predicting exercise covering a period extending as far as fifty years into the future. The experiment used a sequence of questionnaires to elicit prediction from individual experts in six broad areas: scientific breakthroughs; population growth; automation; space progress; probability and prevention of war; and future weapon systems.

Gordon, Theodore J., *The Future*. New York: St. Martin's Press, 1965. 185 pp.

Granger, Charles H., "The Hierarchy of Objectives," *Harvard Business Review,* May–June, 1964, pp. 63–74.

Greenberger, Martin, ed., *Computers and the World of the Future*. Cambridge, Mass.: The M.I.T. Press, 1962.

Griliches, Zvi, "Hybrid Corn: An Exploration in the Economics of Technological Change," *Econometrica* (Journal of the Econometric Society), Vol. 25, No. 4 (October, 1957), 501–22.

Haase, R. H., and W. H. T. Holden, *Performances of Land Transportation Ve-*

hicles, Memorandum RM-3966-RC. The RAND Corporation, Santa Monica, Calif., January, 1964, p. 138.

Helmer, Olaf, *Social Technology,* report P-3063. The RAND Corporation, Santa Monica, Calif., February, 1965. (AD 460-520)

Helmer, O., and N. Rescher, *On the Epistemology of the Inexact Sciences,* report R-353. The RAND Corporation, Santa Monica, Calif., February, 1960. (AD 236-439)

Hertz, D. B., "The Management of Innovation," *Management Review,* April, 1965, pp. 49–52.

Hetrick, J. C., and G. E. Kimball, "A Model for the Discovery and Application of Knowledge," in *Basic Research in the Navy,* Vol. II. U.S. Department of Commerce, Washington, D.C., 1959, pp. 5–29.

Hitch, Charles J., *Decision-Making for Defense.* Berkeley and Los Angeles: University of California Press, 1965.

Holton, Gerard, ed., "Science and Culture—A Study of Cohesive and Disjunctive Forces," *The Daedalus Library,* Vol. 4. Boston, Mass.: Houghton Mifflin Company, 1965.

Isenson, Raymond S., "Technological Forecasting in Perspective," *Management Science,* October, 1966.

Industrial Research, "Exploring the Sea, etc.," series of articles in *Industrial Research,* March, 1966, pp. 7–114.

Institute of Radio Engineers, "Communications and Electronics—2012 A.D.," *Proceedings of the IRE,* Vol. 50, No. 5, The Institute of Radio Engineers, Inc. (IEEE—The Institute of Electrical and Electronics Engineers), New York.

Jantsch, Erich, *Technological Forecasting in Perspective,* Organization for Economic Cooperation and Development, Paris, France, April, 1967.
> Undoubtedly the most comprehensive international survey of the field of Technological Forecasting.

Jestice, A. L., "Project PATTERN-Planning Assistance Through Technical Evaluation of Relevance Numbers." Paper presented to Operations Research Society of America, October 7-8-9, 1964. Pamphlet Minn.-Honeywell, Inc., Washington, D.C. (n.d.)
> Discusses a method of evaluating and determining how to structure a research and development program, utilizing Honeywell's relevance tree approach.

Jewkes, John, David Sawers and Richard Stillerman, *The Sources of Invention.* London: Macmillan & Co., Ltd., 1958.

deJouvenel, B., *Futuribles,* report P-3045. The RAND Corporation, Santa Monica, Calif., January, 1965. (AD 610-217)

———, *The Art of Conjecture,* trans. Nikita Lang. New York: Basic Books, Inc., Publishers, 1967.

Lenz, R. C., Jr., *Technological Forecasting,* 2d ed., Aeronautical Systems Division, AFSC, ASD-TDR-62-414, Wright-Patterson AFB, Ohio, June, 1962. (AD 408-085)
> Presents several methods of forecasting rates of technological advance. The methods include forecasting by extrapolation of existing rates; by analogies to biological growth processes; by precursive events; by derivation from primary trends; by interpretation of trend characteristics; and by dynamic simulation of the process of technological improvement. The investigation included a search of the literature for references to principles of technological progress and for methods which have been used for predictive purposes.

Lessing, Lawrence, "Where the Industries of the Seventies Will Come From," *Fortune,* January, 1967, p. 96.

Arthur D. Little, Inc., *Patterns and Problems of Technical Innovation in American Industry,* report to National Science Foundation, Boston, Mass., September, 1963. (available OTS, Washington, D.C., PB-181573)

Litton Systems, Inc., *U. S. Defense Posture—Overview 1964–1974,* Guidance and Control Systems Division, Publication No. 3373, OPR64-1, June, 1964.

> Provides an overview of the economic, political and military context of the defense market over the next ten years. The major environmental conditions that will shape the domestic and international economic and political climate which will prevail during this time period are evaluated in light of their impact on the defense market.

Linstone, H. A., *Mirage 75—Military Requirements Analysis Generation 1970–75,* Report No. LAC/592371. Lockheed Aircraft Corporation, Burbank, Calif., January, 1965. (SECRET)

> This report is the Lockheed corporate planning study on military requirements. It projects the environment to 1970–75 and forecasts systems and technology to meet the projected environment. A similar study, "Mirage 80," has just been published.

> *Long-Range Forecasting and Planning*—A symposium held at the U.S. Air Force Academy, Colorado, comprising the following articles: Marvin J. Cetron, "Background and Utility of Technological Forecasting"; Thomas I. Monahan, "Current Approach to Forecasting Methodology"; James E. Hacke, Jr. "A Methodological Preface to Technological Forecasting"; Howard A. Wells, "Weapon System Planner's Guide"; Robert H. Rea, "A Comprehensive System of Long-Range Planning"; H. T. Darracott, "The U.S. Army Long-Range Technological Forecast—Its Past, Present and Future"; E. S. Cheaney, Technological Forecasting by Simulation of Design"; Donald Yeager, "Planning and Organizing a Technological Forecast"; Ralph C. Lenz, Jr. "Technological Forecasting"; J. E. McGrolrick, "Planning Launch Vehicles for Space Science and Application"; T. J. Rubin, "Environmental Information Systems: New Aids for Decision Making"; Clearing house, U.S. Dept. of Commerce, Springfield, Va.

Lovewell, P. J., and R. D. Bruce, Stanford Research Institute, "How We Predict Technological Change," *New Scientist,* No. 274, February 15, 1962.

McGraw-Hill, *Research and Development in American Industry,* Department of Economics. New York: McGraw-Hill Publications, May 6, 1966.

McLuhan, Marshall, *Understanding Media: The Extensions of Man.* New York: McGraw-Hill Paperbacks, McGraw-Hill (third printing), 1966. 364 pp.

Magee, John F., "Decision Trees for Decision-Making," *Harvard Business Review,* Vol. 42 (July–August, 1964), 126–38.

Mansfield, Edwin, and Carlton Hensley, "The Logistic Process: Tables of the Stochastic Epidemic Curve and Applications," *The Journal of the Royal Statistical Society,* 1960, pp. 332–37; Reprint No. 60, Graduate School of Industrial Administration, Carnegie Institute of Technology, Pittsburgh, Pa., 1960.

Mesthene, Emmanuel G., "On Understanding Change: The Harvard University Program on Technology and Society," *Technology and Culture,* Spring, 1965, pp. 222–35.

Mumford, L. S., "Loneliness of the Long Range Forecaster," *Chemical Industry,* 1788–96 (November 9, 1963).

Myers, Sumner, *Industrial Innovations—Their Characteristics and Their Scientific and Technical Information Bases,* a special report to the National Science

Foundation. National Planning Association, Washington, D.C., April, 1966. 24 pp.

Navy (U.S.) publications:

Navy Long Range Strategic Study (NLRSS)-73, prepared by Strategic Plans Division (Op-60), Chief of Naval Operations, May 9, 1965. (SECRET)

Navy Mid-Range Objectives Through 1975 Under Limited Funding Assumptions (MRO-75), prepared by Long Range Objectives Group (Op-93), Chief of Naval Operations, June 1, 1964. (SECRET)

Bureau of Naval Weapons Research and Development Planning Guide, Plans Division, RDT&E, BuWeps, July 1, 1963. (SECRET)

Bureau of Ships Long Range Plan for Research and Development (LRP-62), Volume IA (CONFIDENTIAL), Volume IB (SECRET), Volume IC (CONFIDENTIAL); Department of the Navy, Washington, D.C., August, 1962.

Index of Navy Development Requirements, DCNO (D), Encl (1) to CNO 0201P70, January, 1965. (CONFIDENTIAL)

> Contains: (a) A list of Planning Objectives, General Operational Requirements, Tentative Specific Operational Requirements, Specific Operational Requirements and Advanced Development Objectives (Part I) for use in verifying that requirements files are current; (b) An index of Operational Requirements and Development Characteristics (Part II), which will be phased out as they are replaced by updated GOR's and SOR's.

Department of the Navy RDT&E Management Guide, vols. I and II, NAVEXOS P-2457, July, 1964.

> Published in two volumes: "Vol I—Organization and Procedures" and "Vol II—Appendixes." Prepared to aid both newcomers and practicing "journeymen."

Rationales for Goals in Part I—The Undersea Target of Goals for Technology in Exploratory Development. Draft report, Chief of Naval Development (MAT 311), August 31, 1965. (SECRET)

> Gives rationales used in deriving the Goals for Technology in Exploratory Development.

Goals for Technology in Exploratory Development—The Undersea Target, Preliminary report published by the Chief of Naval Development (MAT 311), August 31, 1965. (SECRET)

> Purpose is to assist in formulating the Exploratory Development Program of the Navy. The goals included herein are based on various formal long-term statements of need expressed by the Chief of Naval Operations and the Commandant of the Marine Corps. This document is intended for in-house use by personnel concerned with planning and programming the Exploratory Development Program at all levels of the technical community.

Goals for Technology in Exploratory Development—The Air Target, Preliminary report published by the Chief of Naval Development (MAT 311), November 17, 1965. (SECRET)

> Purpose is to assist in formulating the Exploratory Development Program of the Navy. The goals included herein are based on various formal long-term statements of need expressed by the Chief of Naval Operations and the Commandant of the Marine Corps. This document is intended for in-house use by personnel concerned with planning and programming the Exploratory Development Program at all levels of the technical community.

"Advanced Developments and Advanced Development Candidates for Tactical Missiles and Weapons," *PROJECT SMEADO '67* Missile Development Office (RM), Bureau of Naval Weapons, RM-67-1A, June, 1965. (SECRET)

Main body, Sections 1 through 9, consists of brief summaries of FY 67 plans for Advanced Developments and Advanced Development Candidates in the Tactical Missiles and Weapons Area. These summaries are abstracts of forty individual current planning documents, prepared under PROJECT SMEADO. Taken together, the forty summaries constitute a SMEADO '67 Catalog for Missile Development Office (RM) operations. Plans for the Missile Flight Evaluation Systems Area are not included.

Navy Program Factors, Office of Chief of Naval Operations, OPNAV 90P-02, revised May, 1965. (CONFIDENTIAL)

"Navy Program Factors" supplements the Navy Programming Manual (OPNAV 90P-1). It is comprised of Program Factor Description Sheets and Program Factor Data Sheets grouped by the major resource areas of ships and aircraft. The program factors will be used in the Navy planning and programming analytical procedure (Cost Model) for estimating the resource implications (materiel, personnel, dollars) of various force levels and varying levels of support of these forces.

"Project SEABED," *Advanced Sea-Based Deterrence Summer Study 1964,* Naval Ordnance Laboratory, Silver Spring, Md., July, 1964. (SECRET)

Four-volume report giving the results of the summer study held in Monterey, California, by the Special Projects Office. The four volumes are as follows:

Volume I—Summary
Volume II—Contemporary Analysis of Sea-Based Deterrence
Volume III—Weapons Systems for Sea-Based Deterrence
Volume IV—Advanced Undersea Technology

Pellini, W. S., *Status and Projections of Developments in Hull Structural Materials for Deep Ocean Vehicles and Fixed Bottom Installations,* Naval Research Laboratory, NRL Report 6167, Washington, D.C., November 4, 1964.

Projects state of the art in materials for deep ocean operation. Used at PROJECT SEABED in defining the potentials for deep-ocean vehicles and installations in the 1980's and the R&D necessary to make these potentials a reality.

Nelson, Richard A., *The Link Between Sciences and Invention: The Case of the Transistor.* The RAND Corporation, P-1854-RC, December 15, 1957. (AD 222, 163)

Neumann, John von, "Can We Survive Technology," *Fortune,* June, 1955.

Ozbekhan, Hasan, *The Idea of a "Look-Out" Institution,* System Development Corporation, Santa Monica, Calif., March, 1965. 20 pp.

———, *Technology and Man's Future,* report SP-2494. System Development Corporation, Santa Monica, Calif., May 27, 1966. 41 pp.

Page, Robert Morris, "The Origin of Radar," *Science Study Series.* Garden City, N.Y.: Anchor Books, Doubleday & Co., 1962. 198 pp.

Pardee, F. S., *State of the Art Project and Long Range Planning of Applied Research.* The RAND Corporation, Santa Monica, Calif., 1965. (AD 618-516)

Peterson, M. S., "The Trouble with Technological Forecasting," *Science,* 144, May 15, 1964, pp. 795–96.

Prehoda, Robert W., *The Future and Technological Forecasting.* Pre-publication manuscript, expected to be published in the United States in 1968.

Quade, E. S., ed., *Analysis for Military Decisions.* The RAND Corporation, R-387-PR, November, 1964.

Quinn, James Brian, "Technological Forecasting," *Harvard Business Review,* March–April, 1967.

Report on Technological Forecasting, interservice ad hoc study group sponsored by the Army Materiel Command, the Navy Materiel Command, and the Air Force Systems Command, 30 June 1967. Available from the Department of Defense Documentation Center, Cameron Station, Alexandria Va. This Report Assesses the State of the art and synthesizes available information.

Ridenour, Louis N., "Physical Science and the Future," in Lyman Bryson, ed., *Facing the Future's Risks—Studies Toward Predicting the Unforeseen,* New York: Harper & Brothers, 1953, pp. 60–89.

Rogers, Everett M., *Diffusion of Innovations,* New York: The Free Press, 1962. 367 pp.

Samson Science Corporation, *Microelectronics—Revolutionary Impact of New Technology,* Samson Report No. 2, available from Samson Science Corporation, 270 Park Avenue, New York, N.Y., 1965. 34 pp.

———, *Satellite Communications—Comsat and the Industry,* Samson Report No. 1, Samson Science Corporation, 270 Park Avenue, New York, N.Y., December, 1964. 84 pp.

Sarnoff, David, "By the End of the Twentieth Century," *Fortune Magazine,* May, 1964, pp. 116–19.

Schaeffer, K. H., J. B. Fink, M. Rappaport, L. Wainstein, and C. J. Erickson, *The Knowledgeable Analyst: An Approach to Structuring Man-Machine Systems.* Project IMU 3546, Stanford Research Institute, Menlo Park, Calif., 1963. (AD 297-432)

Schon, D., et al., *The Role of the Federal Government in Technological Forecasting,* Interagency Task Group on Technological Forecasting in Federal Government, January, 1966.

A report to the President's Committee on Manpower and to the National Commission on Technology, Automation and Economic Progress. Specifically, the investigation focused on:
1. Action points in government at which technological forecasting might be useful, if available;
2. Criteria for information at these points;
3. Current technological forecasting activities and methodologies and their adequacy to federal requirements.

Scientific American, a symposium comprising the following articles: J. Bronowski, "The Creative Process"; Paul R. Halmos, "Innovation in Mathematics"; Freeman J. Dyson, "Innovation in Physics"; George Wald, "Innovation in Biology"; John R. Pierce, "Innovation in Technology"; John C. Eccles, "The Physiology of Imagination"; Frank Barron, "The Psychology of Imagination"; Warren Weaver, "The Encouragement of Science"; *Scientific American,* September, 1958.

Science Journal, a special issue of forecasting the future: Robert Jungk, "The Future of Future Research"; Erich Jantsch, "Forecasting the Future"; Olaf Helmer, "Science"; Ali Bulent Cambel, "Energy"; Hasan Ozbekhan, "Automation"; John R. Pierce, "Communication"; Robert C. Seamans Jr., "Space"; Gabriel Bouladon, "Transportation"; Robert V. Ayres, "Food"; William L. Swager, "Materials"; Roger Revelle, "Population"; Herman Kahn, "World Futures" (October, 1967) Vol. 3, No. 10 (London, England).

Semkov, B. F., "Soviet Scientists Discuss Methodology and Planning of Scientific Research," translation from Voprosy (Problems of Philosophy) (Vopr. Filosofii), No. 7, TT-65-30027, Joint Publ. Research Service, OTS U.S. Department of Commerce, Washington, D.C., 1964.

Siegel, Irving H., "Technological Change and Long-Run Forecasting," *The Jour-*

nal of Business of the University of Chicago, Vol. XXVI, No. 3 (July, 1953), 141–56.

Sigford, J. V., and R. H. Parvin, "Project PATTERN: A Methodology for Determining Relevance in Complex Decision-Making," *IEEE Transactions on Engineering Management,* Vol. EM-12, No. 1 (March, 1965), pp. 9–13.

Silberman, C. E., "Is Technology Taking Over?" Philosophies of J. Ellul and M. McLuhan, *Fortune,* 73 (February, 1966), pp. 112–15.

Smith, Bruce L., *The Concept of Scientific Choice: A Brief Review of Literature,* report P-3156. The RAND Corporation, June, 1965. 54 pp. (AD 616, 977)

Stanford Research Institute, *The World of 1975* (composite of following SRI Reports: 232, 233, 234, 235, 236). (n.d.)

> Composite of reports on forecasts by SRI Long Range Planning Service in predicting the world of 1975. It includes the following subjects:
> 1. The International Prospect
> 2. Economic Trends
> 3. Governmental and Political Trends
> 4. Science and Technology
> 5. Social and Cultural Framework

Stockfish, J. A., ed., *Planning and Forecasting in the Defense Industries,* (papers presented at a UCLA seminar on 4–5 May 1960). Belmont, Calif.: Wadsworth Publishing Company, 1962.

Stromer, P. R., *Long-Range Planning and Technological Forecasting: An Annotated Bibliography,* SRB-63-12. Lockheed Missiles and Space Co., Sunnyvale, Calif., November, 1963. (AD 441-618)

———, *Long-Range Planning and Technological Forecasting: An Annotated Bibliography, Supplement I,* SRB-65-1. Lockheed Missiles and Space Co., Sunnyvale, Calif., February, 1965. (AD 457-949)

Swager, William L., *Industrial Implications of Technological Forecasting.* Paper presented to the Fourth Symposium of the Engineer-Economy Division of the American Society for Engineering Education in Chicago, Ill., June 19, 1965. Battelle Memorial Institute.

———, "Technological Forecasting for Practical Planning," *Petroleum Management,* July, 1966.

Sweezy, Eldon E., *Technological Forecasting—Principles and Techniques.* Paper presented at the 4th Symposium of the Engineering Economy Division, The American Society for Engineering Education, Chicago, Ill., June 19, 1965.

Syracuse University Research Corporation (Project 1985), *The United States and the World in the 1985 Era,* DDC Report AD 613-527 (Annex, AD 613-528), March, 1964.

> Prepared in response to a request by the Marine Corps to predict what certain aspects of the world will be like in 1985. In the language of the Marine Corps, "This study will examine projected national objectives and policies, and international and domestic military, economic, and technological factors affecting the United States in the 1985 era."

Syracuse University Research Corporation, *Science and Technology in the 1985 Era* (Project 1985), DDC Report AD 613-525 (Appendix AD 613-526), May, 1964.

> Covers the technological aspects of the projection. Forecasts technology as related to the Marine Corps of the next two decades.

Teilhard de Chardin, Pierre, *The Future of Man.* London: Collins, 1964.

Thirring, Hans, *Energy for Man: From Windmills to Nuclear Power.* New York: Harper and Row, Publishers, 1958. 409 pp.

Thomson, Sir George, *The Foreseeable Future*. London: Cambridge University Press, 1955. 166 pp.

Ubbelohde, A. R., *Man and Energy*. New York: George Braziller, Inc., 1955. 247 pp.

U.S. Department of Labor, *Measurement of Technological Change,* by Solomon Fabricant, Seminar on Manpower Policy and Program, No. 4, October, 1964. 32 pp.

U.S. National Academy of Sciences, National Research Council, *Chemistry: Opportunities and Needs,* publication 1292. Academy of Sciences, National Research Council, Washington, D.C., 1965.

———, *Physics: Survey and Outlook: Reports on the Subfields of Physics*. National Research Council, Washington, D.C., 1966.

———, *Theoretical Chemistry—A Current Review,* Publication 1292-D. National Research Council, Washington, D.C., 1966. 44 pp.

U.S. National Bureau of Economic Research, *The Rate and Direction of Inventive Activity—Economic and Social Factors*. A Conference of Universities. Princeton, N.J.: Princeton University Press, 1962.

U.S. National Commission on Technology, Automation, and Economic Progress, report, Vol. I, *Technology and American Economy*. Washington, D.C., February, 1966. 115 pp.

U.S. National Resources Committee, *Technological Trends and National Policy— Including the Social Implications of New Inventions,* a report of the subcommittee on Technology. U.S. Government Printing Office, Washington, D.C., June, 1937.

United Nations, *A Select Bibliography on Industrial Research, from 1944 to June 1964,* reference paper 1, prepared for the Interregional Seminar on Industrial Research and Development Institutes in Developing Countries, November 30– December 12, 1964, Beirut, Lebanon: Centre for Industrial Development, Department of Economic and Social Affairs, United Nations, New York, 1964. 37 pp.

Vassiliev, M., and S. Gouschev, eds., *Life in The Twenty-First Century,* translated from Russian, first published in Russia 1959, Penguin Special, Penguin Books, Harmondsworth, Middlesex, 1961. 222 pp.

Wagle, B., "Some Statistical Aids in Forecasting," internal report Esso Petroleum Co., Ltd., London; introduction published under the title "A Review of Two Statistical Aids in Forecasting," *The Statistician,* Vol. 15, No. 2 (1965).

Warner, Aaron W., and Dean Morse, eds., *Technological Innovation and Society*. New York: Columbia University Press, 1966.

——— and Alfred S. Eichner, eds., *The Impact of Science on Technology*. New York: Columbia University Press, 1965.

Ways, Max, "The Road to 1977," *Fortune,* January, 1967, p. 93.

Wolstenholme, Gordon, ed., *Man and His Future*. A Ciba Foundation Volume. Boston, Mass.: Little Brown and Company, 1963. 410 pp.

Wohlstetter, A., "Technology, Prediction and Disorder" *Bulletin of the Atomic Scientists,* October, 1964, pp. 11–15.

Zwicky, Fritz, *Morphology of Propulsive Power,* Monographs on Morphological Research No. 1, Society for Morphological Research, Pasadena, Calif.; Available from the Bookstore of the California Institute of Technology, Pasadena, Calif., 1962. 382 pp.

Bibliography of Appraisal Techniques for Research, Development, and Technological Planning

Prepared by MARVIN J. CETRON

Ackoff, Russell L., *Scientific Method: Optimizing Applied Research Decisions.* New York: John Wiley & Sons, Inc., 1962.

——, ed., *Progress in Operations Research,* Vol. I. New York: John Wiley & Sons, Inc., 1961.

——, "Specialized Versus Generalized Models in Research Budgeting." Paper presented at the Second Conference on Research Program Effectiveness, Washington, D.C., July 27–29, 1965.

——, E. Leonard Arnoff, and C. West Churchman, *Introduction to Operations Research.* New York: John Wiley & Sons, Inc., 1957.

Adams, J. G., R. O. Nellums, and R. E. Howard, "Engineering Evaluation—Tool for Research Management," *Industrial and Engineering Chemistry,* XLIX (May, 1957), 40A.

Albertini J., *The QMDO Planning Process as It Relates to the U.S. Army Materiel Command.* Cornell Aeronautical Lab. Report No. VQ-2044-H-1 on USAMC Contract DA-49-185 AMC-237(X), August 31, 1965.

——, *The LRTP Planning Process as It Relates to the U.S. Army Materiel Command.* Cornell Aeronautical Lab. Report No. VQ-2044-H-2 on USAMC Contract DA-49-186 AMC-237(X), October 30, 1965.

——, *LRTP Mathematical Model Brochure.* Cornell Aeronautical Lab. Report No. VQ-2044-H-3 on USAMC Contract DA-49-186 AMC-237(X), October 30, 1965.

Amey, L. R., "The Allocation and Utilization of Resources," *Operations Research Quarterly* June, 1964.

Andersen, Sigud L., "Venture Analysis, A Flexible Planning Tool," *Chemical Engineering Progress* March, 1961, pp. 80–83.

——, "A 2 × 2 Risk Decision Problem," *Chemical Engineering Progress,* May, 1961, pp. 70–72.

Anderson, Carl A., "Notes on the Evaluation of Research Planning." Paper presented at the Research Program Effectiveness Conference, Washington, D.C., July 21–23, 1964.

Andrew, G. H. L., "Assessing Priorities for Technical Effort," *Operational Research Quarterly,* Vol. 5 (September, 1954), 67–80.

Ansoff, H. I., "Evaluation of Applied Research in a Business Firm," in *Technological Planning on the Corporate Level,* J. R. Bright, ed., Proceedings of the Conference at Harvard Business School, Harvard University, Cambridge, Mass., 1962, pp. 209–24.

Anthony, Robert N., and John S. Day, *Management Controls in Industrial Research Organizations.* Cambridge, Mass.: Harvard University Press, 1952.

Asher, D. T., "A Linear Programming Model for the Allocation of R&D Efforts," *IRE Transactions on Engineering Management,* EM-9, No. 4 (December, 1962), 154–57.

———, and S. Disman, "Operations Research in R&D," *Chemical Engineering Progress,* Vol. 59:1 (January, 1963), 41–45.

Aumann, R. J., and J. B. Kruskal, "Assigning Quantitative Values to Qualitative Factors in the Naval Electronics Program," *Naval Research Logistics Quarterly,* March, 1959, p. 15.

Bakanas, V., *An Analytical Method to Aid in the Choice of Long Range Study Tasks.* Cornell Aeronautical Lab. Report No. VQ-1887-H-1. AMC contract DA 49-186 AMC-97(X), May 19, 1964.

Baker, N. R., and W. H. Pound, "R&D Project Selection: Where We Stand," *IEEE Transactions on Engineering Management,* Vol. E-11, No. 4 (December, 1964).

Barmby, John G., "The Applicability of PERT as a Management Tool," *IRE Transactions on Engineering Management,* Vol. EM-9, No. 3 (September, 1962).

Battersby, A., *Network Analysis for Planning and Scheduling.* New York: St. Martins Press, 1964.

Baumgartner, John Stanley, *Project Management.* Homewood, Ill.: Richard D. Irwin, Inc., 1963.

Beckwith, R. E., "A Cost Control Extension of the PERT System," *IRE Transactions on Engineering Management,* Vol. EM-9, No. 4 (December, 1962).

Belt, John Robert, "Military Applied R&D Project Evaluation," U.S. Navy Marine Engineering Laboratory, Annapolis, Md., June, 1966. (Unpublished thesis)

Bensley, Dean E., "Planning and Controlling a Research and Development Program: A Case Study." Master's thesis, Massachusetts Institute of Technology, Cambridge, 1955.

Berman, E. R., "Research Allocation in a PERT Network Under Continuous Activity Time-Cost Functions," *Management Science,* Vol. 10, No. 4 (1964).

———, *Theoretical Structure of a Methodology for R&D Resource Allocation* (draft). Research Analysis Corp., May 26, 1965.

Berstein, Alex, and Ithiel de Sola Pool, "Development and Testing of an Evaluation Model for Research Organization Substructures." Paper presented at the Research Program Effectiveness Conference, Washington, D.C., July 21–23, 1964.

Blinoff, V., and C. Pacifico, *Chemical Processing,* Vol. 20 (November, 1957), 34–35.

Blood, Jerome W., ed., *The Management of Scientific Talent.* New York: The American Management Association, Inc., 1963.

Blum, Steven, *Time, Cost, and Risk Analysis in Project Planning.* U.S. Army Frankford Arsenal Report, August 22, 1963.

Bock, R. H., and W. K. Holstein, *Production Planning and Control.* Columbus: Charles E. Merrill Books, Inc., 1963.

Bonini, Charles P., Robert K. Jaedicke, and Harvey M. Wagner, *Management Controls: New Directions in Basic Research.* New York: McGraw-Hill Book Company, 1964.

Boothe, Norton, et al., *From Concept to Commercialization, A Study of the R&D Budget Allocation Process.* Stanford University Sloan Program, The Graduate School of Business, Stanford, Calif., 1962.

Brandenburg, R. G., *A Descriptive Analysis of Project Selection: A Summary Report.* Pennsylvania: Carnegie Institute of Technology, July, 1964.

———, *Toward a Multi-Space Information Conversion Model of the Research and Development Process.* Carnegie Institute of Technology Management Sciences Research Report No. 48, August, 1965.

Bright, James R., ed., *Technological Planning on the Corporate Level.* Proceedings of the Conference at Harvard Business School, Harvard University, Cambridge, Mass., 1962.

Busacker, Robert G., and Thomas L. Saaty, *Finite Graphs and Networks: An Introduction With Applications.* New York: McGraw-Hill Book Company, 1965.

Bush, George P., *Bibliography on Research Administration, Annotated.* Washington, D.C.: The University Press, 1964.

Carroll, Phil., *Profit Control—How to Plug Profit Leaks.* New York: McGraw-Hill Book Company, 1962.

Caulfield, Patrick, and Robert Freshman, *Technology Evaluation Workbook,* HQ Research and Technology Division, AFSC, Bolling AFB, Washington, D.C., January, 1967.

Cetron, Marvin J., "Programmed Functional Indices for Laboratory Evaluation, 'PROFILE.'" Paper presented at the 16th Military Operations Research Symposium (MORS), Seattle, Wash., October 10–14, 1965.

———, "Quantitative Utility Estimates for Science & Technology 'Quest.'" Paper presented at the 18th MORS, Fort Bragg, N.C., October 19–21, 1966.

———, and Freshman, Robert, "Some Results of 'PROFILE.'" Paper presented at the 17th MORS, Monterey, Calif., May 21–25, 1966.

Charnes, A., "Conditional Chance-Constrained Approaches to Organizational Control." Paper presented at the Research Program Effectiveness Conference, Washington, D.C., July 21–23, 1964.

———, and Stedry, A. C., "Optimal Real-Time Control of Research Funding." Paper presented at the Second Conference on Research Program Effectiveness, Washington, D.C., July 27–29, 1965.

Churchman, C. West, *Prediction and Optimal Control.* Englewood Cliffs, N.J.: Prentice-Hall, Inc., 1960.

———, C. Kruytbosch, and Philburn Ratoosh, "The Role of the Research Administrator." Paper presented at the Second Conference on Research Program Effectiveness, Washington, D.C., July 27–29, 1965.

Clark, Wallace, *The Gantt Chart.* London: Sir Isaac Pitman & Sons, Ltd., 1938.

Clarke, Roderick W., "Activity Costing—Key to Progress in Critical Path Analysis," *IRE Transactions on Engineering Management,* Vol. EM-9, No. 3 (September, 1962), 132.

Combs, Cecil E., "Decision Theory and Engineering Management," *IRE Transactions on Engineering Management,* Vol. EM-9, No. 4 (December, 1962).

Cook, Earle F., "A Better Yardstick for Project Evaluation," *Armed Forces Management,* April, 1958, pp. 20–23.

Cramer, Robert H., and Barnard E. Smith, "Decision Models for the Selection of Research Projects," *The Engineering Economist,* IX, No. 2 (January–February, 1964), 1–20.

Crisp, R. D., "Product Planning for Future Projects," *Duns's Review and Modern Industry,* March, 1958.

Dantzig, George B., *Linear Programming and Extensions.* Princeton, N.J.: Princeton University Press, 1963.

Daubin, Scott C., "The Allocation of Development Funds: An Analytic Approach," *Naval Research Logistics Quarterly,* III (September, 1958), 263–76.

Davidson, Harold F., "Surveys as Tools for Acquisition of Research Management Information." Paper presented at the Research Program Effectiveness Conference, Washington, D.C., July 21–23, 1964.

Davis, Keith, "The Role of Project Management in Scientific Manufacturing," *IRE Transactions on Engineering Management,* Vol. EM-9, No. 3 (September, 1962), 109.

Dean, Burton V., ed., *Operations Research in Research and Development,* Proceedings of a conference at Case Institute of Technology. New York: John Wiley & Sons, Inc., 1963.

———, *Scoring and Profitability Models for Evaluating and Selecting Engineering Projects.* Case Institute of Technology, Operations Research Group, 1964.

———, "Allocation of Technical Resources in a Firm." Paper presented at the Research Program Effectiveness Conference, Washington, D.C., July 21–23, 1964.

———, "Stochastic Networks in Research Planning." Paper presented at the Second Conference on Research Program Effectiveness, Washington, D.C., July 27–29, 1965.

———, and Glogowski, *On the Planning of Research.* ONR-AMC Project NOOR 1141(19), July, 1965.

———, and Hauser, L. E., *Advanced Material Systems Planning.* Case Institute of Technology, Operations Research Group Tech. Memo. No. 65, ONR-AMC Project NOOR-1141 (19), September 15, 1966.

———, and Sengupta, S., "On a Method for Determining Corporate Research Development Budgets," *Management Sciences, Models, and Techniques,* Vol. II, C. West Churchman and Michel Verhulst, eds. New York: Pergamon Press, 1960.

Dean, Joel, *Managerial Economics.* Englewood Cliffs, N.J.: Prentice-Hall, Inc., 1951, pp. 249–610.

———, "Measuring the Productivity of Capital," *Harvard Business Review,* January–February, 1954.

de L'Estoile, H. D. LeCerf and G. Gastaut "One Method for the Selection of the Research and Development Program," 25 September 1967; French Ministère Des Armées, Centre de Prospective et D'evaluations, 10, Rue Saint Dominique-F5-Paris (7) France.

DeVries, Marvin G., *A Dynamic Model for Product Strategy Selection,* Industrial Development Research Program Institute of Science and Technology. Ann Arbor: The University of Michigan, 1963.

———, "The Dynamic Effects of Planning Horizons on the Selection of Optimal Product Strategies," *Management Science,* X, No. 3 (April, 1964), 524–44.

Disman, S., "Selecting R&D Projects for Profit," *Chemical Engineering,* Vol. 69 (December, 1962), 87–90.

Dooley, Arch R., "Interpretations of PERT," *Harvard Business Review,* XLII (March–April, 1964), 160–71.

Drucker, Peter F., "Twelve Fables of Research Management," *Harvard Business Review,* January–February, 1963.

———, *Managing for Results.* New York: Harper & Row, Publishers, 1964, pp. 25–50.

Easton, David, *A Systems Analysis of Political Life.* New York: John Wiley & Sons, Inc., 1965.

Eisner, Hoard, "Generalized Network Approach to the Planning and Scheduling of a Research Program," *Operations Research,* X (1962), 115–25.

―――, "The Application of Information Theory to the Planning of Research." Paper presented at the TIMS American International Meeting, September 12–13, 1963.

Elmaghraby, Salah E., "An Algebra for the Analysis of Generalized Activity Networks," *Management Sciences,* X, No. 3 (April, 1964), 494–514.

Emlet, H. E., *Methodological Approach to Planning and Programming Air Force Operational Requirements, Research and Development (MAPORD).* Analytic Services Report 65-4, October, 1965.

Esch, Maurice E., "Planning Assistance Through Technical Evaluation of Relevance Numbers, PATTERN." Paper presented at the 17th National Aerospace Electronics Conference, Dayton, Ohio, May 10–12, 1965.

Ewing, David W., ed., *Long-Range Planning of Management.* New York: Harper & Row, Publishers, 1958.

Flood, Merrill W., "Research Project Evaluation," *Coordination, Control, and Financing of Industrial Research,* Albert R. Rubenstein, ed. New York: (Columbia University); King's Crown Press, 1955.

Fong, L. B. C., "A Visual Method of Program Balance and Evaluation," *IRE Transactions on Engineering Management,* Vol. EM-8 (September, 1961), pp. 160–63.

Ford, L. R., Jr., and D. R. Fulkerson, *Flows in Networks.* Princeton, N.J.: Princeton University Press, 1962.

Freeman, Raoul J., "An Operational Analysis of Industrial Research." Ph.D. dissertation, Department of Economics, Massachusetts Institute of Technology, Cambridge, Mass., 1957.

―――, "A Stochastic Model for Determining the Size and Allocation of the Research Budget," *IRE Transactions on Engineering Management,* Vol. EM-7, No. 1 (March, 1960), 2–7.

―――, "Quantitative Methods in R&D Management," *California Management Review,* XI, No. 4 (Summer, 1960), 36–44.

―――, "A Generalized Network Approach to Project Activity Sequencing," *IRE Transactions on Engineering Management,* Vol. EM-7, No. 3 (September, 1960), 103–7.

―――, "A Survey of the Current Status of Accounting in the Control of R&D," *IRE Transactions on Engineering Management,* Vol. EM-9, No. 4 (December, 1962), 179–81.

Fry, B. L., "SCANS—System Description and Comparison with PERT," *IRE Transactions on Engineering Management,* Vol. EM-9, No. 3 (September, 1962), 122.

Galbraith, John Kenneth, *The Affluent Society.* New York: Mentor Books, 1958.

Gargiulo, G. R., et al., "Developing Systematic Procedures for Directing Research Programs," *IRE Transactions on Engineering Management,* Vol. EM-8, No. 1 (March, 1961), 24–29.

―――, "Research on a Research Department: An Analysis of Economic Decisions on Projects," *IRE Transactions on Engineering Management,* Vol. EM-7, No. 4 (December, 1960), 166–72.

Gloskey, C. R., "An Analysis of Economic Decisions and Research Programming in a Chemical Manufacturing Corporation," Massachusetts Institute of Technology, Cambridge, Mass., 1959.

Goldberg, L. C., "Dimensions in the Evaluation of Technical Ideas in an Industrial Research Laboratory." M.S. thesis, Northwestern University, Evanston, Ill., 1963.

Guy, K., *Laboratory Organization and Administration.* London: Macmillan & Co., Ltd.; also New York: St. Martin's Press, 1962.

Hackney, J. W., "How to Appraise Capital Investments," *Chemical Engineering,* May 15, 1961, 146–67.

Hahn, W. A., and H. D. Pickering, "Program Planning in a Science-Based Service Organization." Paper presented at the Second Conference on Research Program Effectiveness, Washington, D.C., July 27–29, 1965.

Hanser, B. J., *Practical PERT Including Critical Path Method,* Washington: America House, 1964.

Harrel, C. G., "Selecting Projects for Research," in *Research in Industry: Its Organization and Management,* C. C. Furnas, ed. New York: Van Nostrand, 1948, Chap. 7, pp. 104–44.

Heckert, J. E., and J. B. Willson, *Business Budgeting and Control.* New York: The Ronald Press Company, 1955.

Henke, Russ, *Effective Research & Development for the Smaller Company.* Houston: Gulf Publishing Company, 1963.

Hertz, David B., *The Theory and Practice of Industrial Research.* New York: McGraw-Hill Book Company, 1950.

————, and A. H. Rubenstein, *Costs, Budgeting and Economics of Industrial Research,* Proceedings of the First Annual Conference of Industrial Research. New York: Columbia University Press, 1951.

————, and A. H. Rubenstein, eds., *Research Operations in Industry,* Proceedings of the Third Annual Conference on Industrial Research. New York: Columbia University Press, 1953. (See especially J. A. Stewart, p. 55, and E. Hartstone, p. 153.)

————, and Phillip G. Carlson, "Selection, Evaluation, and Control of Research and Development Projects," in *Operations Research in Research and Development,* B. V. Dean, ed. New York: John Wiley & Sons, Inc., 1963, pp. 170–88.

Hess, Sidney W., "On Research and Development Budgeting and Project Selection." Ph.D. dissertation, Case Institute of Technology, Cleveland, Ohio, 1960.

————, "A Dynamic Programming Approach to R&D Budgeting and Project Selection," *IRE Transactions on Engineering Management,* Vol. EM-9, No. 4 (December, 1962), 170–78.

Heyel, Carl, ed., *Handbook of Industrial Research Management.* New York: Reinhold Publishing Corporation, 1959.

Hickey, Albert E., Jr., "The Systems Approach: Can Engineers Use the Scientific Method?" *IRE Transactions on Engineering Management,* Vol. EM-7, No. 2 (June, 1960), 72.

Hildenbrand, W., "Application of Graph Theory to Stochastic Scheduling." Paper presented at the Second Conference on Research Program Effectiveness, Washington, D.C., July 27–29, 1965.

Hill, F. I., and L. A. Roepcke, "An Analytical Method to Aid in the Choice of Long Range Study Tasks." Paper presented at the 1964 U.S. Army Operations Research Symposium at Rock Island Arsenal, May 25–27, 1964.

Hill, Lawrence S., "Toward an Improved Basis of Estimating and Controlling R&D Tasks." Paper presented at the 10th National Meeting of the American Association of Cost Engineers, Philadelpia, Pa., June, 1966.

Hitchcock, L. B., "Selection and Evaluation of R&D Projects," *Research Management,* Vol. 6 (May, 1963), 231–44.

Hodge, M. H., Jr., et al., *Basic Research as a Corporate Function,* The Graduate School of Business, Stanford University Sloan Program, Stanford University, Calif., 1961.

Honig, John G., "An Evaluation of Research and Development Problems." Paper presented at the Research Program Effectiveness Conference, Washington, D.C., July 21–23, 1964.

Horowitz, Ira, "The Economics of Industrial Research." Ph.D. dissertation, Massachusetts Institute of Technology, Cambridge, Mass., 1959.

Janofsky, L., and S. Sobleman, "Balancing Equations to Project Feasibility Studies." Paper presented to Operations Research Society of America, Detroit, October 10, 1960.

————, and Helen S. Milton, "A Proposed Cost-of-Research Index," *IRE Transactions on Engineering Management,* Vol. EM-8, No. 4 (December, 1961), 172–76.

Johnson, E. A., and H. S. Milton, "A Proposed Cost-of-Research Index," *IRE Transactions on Engineering Management,* Vol. EM-8 (December, 1961), pp. 172–76.

Johnson, Richard A., Fremont E. Kast, and James E. Rosenzweig, *The Theory and Management of Systems.* New York: McGraw-Hill Book Company, 1963.

Karger, D. C., and R. G. Murkick, *Managing Engineering and Research.* New York: The Industrial Press, 1963, pp. 193–253.

Kelley, James E., Jr., and Morgan R. Walker, "Critical-Path Planning and Scheduling," Proceedings of the Eastern Joint Computer Conference, 1959.

————, "Critical Path Planning and Scheduling. Mathematical Basis," *Operations Research,* IX (1961), 296–320.

Kiefer, D. M., "Winds of Change in Industrial Chemical Research," *Chemical Engineering News,* Vol. 42 (March, 1964), 88–109.

Klein, B., "The Decision-Making Problem in Development," in *The Rate and Direction of Inventive Activity.* Princeton, N.J.: Princeton University Press, 1962, pp. 477–508.

————, and W. Meckling, "Applications of Operations Research to Development Decisions," *Operations Research,* May–June, 1958, pp. 352–63.

Kliever, W. R., and R. Z. Bancroft, "Choosing and Evaluating Research Projects," *Production Engineering,* June, 1953.

Koontz, Harold, *Toward a Unified Theory of Management.* New York: McGraw-Hill Book Company, 1963.

Landi, D. M., *A Model of Investment Planning for Research and Development.* Evanston: Northwestern University, 1964.

Leermakers, J. A., "The Selection and Screening of Projects," in *Getting the Most from Product Research and Development.* New York: American Management Association, 1955, pp. 81–94.

Levy, F. K., G. L. Thompson, and J. E. Wiest, "Multiship, Multishop, Workload-Smoothing Program," *Naval Research Logistics Quarterly,* XI (March, 1962).

Lipetz, Ben-Ami, *Measurement of Effectiveness of Science Research.* Carlisle, Mass.: Intermedia, Inc., 1965.

Lytle, A. A., "The Yardsticks for Research Success," *Production Engineering,* Vol. 30 (October, 1959), 34–37.

McMaster, Samuel B., "Study of Project Selection Techniques in an R&D Organization." Unpublished Master's thesis, Northwestern University, Evanston, Ill., 1964.

McMillian, Claude, and Richard F. Ganzalez, *Systems Analysis: A Computer Approach to Decision Models.* Homewood, Ill. Richard D. Irwin, Inc., 1965.

Magee, John F., "How to Use Decision Trees in Capital Investment," *Harvard Business Review,* September–October, 1964, pp. 79–96.

Manning, P. D., "Long-range Planning of Product Research," *R&D Development Series #4.* New York: American Management Association, 1957.

Marples, D. L., "The Decisions of Engineering Design," *IRE Transactions on Engineering Management,* Vol. EM-8 (June, 1961), 55–71.

Marschak, T. A., "Strategy and Organization in a System Development Project," in *The Rate and Direction of Inventive Activity.* Princeton, N.J.: Princeton University Press, 1962, pp. 509–48.

——, "Models, Rules of Thumb, and Development Decisions," in *Operations Research in Research and Development,* B. V. Dean, ed. New York: John Wiley & Sons, Inc., 1963, pp. 247–63.

Marquis, Donald G., "Organization and Management of R&D." Paper presented at the Research Program Effectiveness Conference, Washington, D.C., July 21–23, 1964.

Marshall, A. W., and W. H. Meckling, "Predictability of the Costs, Time and Success of Development," in *The Rate and Direction of Inventive Activity.* Princeton, N.J.: Princeton University Press, 1962, pp. 461–75.

Mees, C. E. K., and J. A. Leermakers, *The Organization of Industrial Scientific Research,* 2nd ed. New York: McGraw-Hill, 1950, especially Chap. 11.

Martino, Joseph, Patrick Caulfield, Marvin Cetron, Harold Davidson, Harold Liebowitz, and Lewis Roepcke, "A Method for Balanced Allocation of Resources Among R&D Projects." AF Office of Scientific Research Technical Report, February, 1967.

Massey, Robert J., "A New Publication: Department of the Navy RDT&E Management Guide." Paper presented at the Research Program Effectiveness Conference, Washington, D.C., July 21–23, 1964.

Mellon, W. Giles, *"An Approach to a General Theory of Priorities: An Outline of Problems and Methods,"* Princeton University Econometric Research Program, Memorandum No. 42. Princeton, N.J.: Princeton University Press, 1962.

Miller, D. W., and M. K. Starr, *Executive Decisions and Operations Research.* Englewood Cliffs, N.J.: Prentice-Hall, Inc., 1960.

Miller, Robert W., *Schedule, Cost and Profit Control with PERT.* New York: McGraw-Hill Book Company, 1963.

Miller, T. T., *Projecting the Profitability of New Products,* Special Report #20. New York: American Management Association, 1957, pp. 20–33.

Morgenstern, O., R. W. Shephard, and H. G. Grabowski, "Adaptation of Graph Theory and an Input-Output Model to Research Description and Evaluation." Paper presented at the Second Conference on Research Program Effectiveness, Washington, D.C., July 27–29, 1965.

Moshman, Jack, Jacob Johnson, and Madalyn Larson, "RAMPS—A Technique for Resource Allocation and Multi-Project Scheduling," *Proceedings of the Spring Joint Computer Conference,* 1963. Baltimore, Md.: Spartan Books, Inc., 1963, pp. 17–27.

Mottley, C. M., and R. D. Newton, "The Selection of Projects for Industrial Research," *Operations Research,* Vol. 7 (November–December, 1959), pp. 740–51.

National Science Foundation, *Science and Engineering in American Industry,* Final Report on 1953–1954 Survey. Washington, D.C., October, 1956.

Norden, P. V., "Curve Fitting for a Model of Applied Research and Development Scheduling," *IBM Journal of Research and Development,* Vol. II, No. 3 (July, 1958), 232–48.

——, "The Study Committee for Research, Development and Engineering

(SCARDE), A Progress Report and an Invitation to Participate," *IRE Transactions on Engineering Management,* Vol. EM-8 (March, 1961), 3–10.

————, "Some Properties of R&D Project Recovery Limits." Paper presented at the Second Conference on Research Program Effectiveness, Washington, D.C., July 27–29, 1965.

Norton, J. H., "The Role of Subjective Probability in Evaluating New Product Ventures," *Chemical Engineering Progress Symposium,* Ser. #42, Vol. 59 (1963), 49–54.

Nutt, Ambrose B., "An Approach to Research and Development Effectiveness," *IEEE Transactions on Engineering Management,* September, 1965, pp. 103–12.

Nyland, H. V., and G. R. Towle, "How We Evaluate Return from Research," *National Association of Cost Accountants Bulletin,* May, 1956.

Olsen, F., "The Control of Research Funds," in *Coordination, Control and Financing of Industrial Research,* A. H. Rubenstein, ed. New York: King Crown Press, Columbia University, 1955, pp. 99–108.

Pacifico, C., "Is It Worth the Risk?" *Chemical Engineering Progress,* Vol. 60 (May, 1964), pp. 19–21.

Pappas, G. F., and D. D. MacLaren, "An Approach to Research Planning," *Chemical Engineering Progress,* Vol. 57 (May, 1961), pp. 65–69.

Pound, William H., "Research Project Selection: Testing a Model in the Field," *IEEE Transactions on Engineering Management,* Vol. EM-12, No. 3 (September, 1964), 16–22.

Quinn, James Bryan, *Yardsticks for Industrial Research: The Evaluation of Research and Development Output.* New York: The Ronald Press Company, 1959.

————, and James A. Mueller, "Transferring Research Results to Operations," *Harvard Business Review,* XLI (January–February, 1963).

————, *A Systems Development Planning Structure,* ABT Associates, Inc., November 18, 1965.

————, *An Automated Scenario Generator,* ABT Associates, Inc., January, 1966.

Raiffa, Howard, and Robert Schlaifer, *Applied Statistical Decision Theory.* Boston: Division of Research, Harvard Business School, 1957.

Roberts, C. S., "Product Selection—Witchcraft or Wisdom," *IRE Transactions on Engineering Management,* Vol. EM-6 (September, 1959), pp. 68–71.

Roberts, E. B., *The Dynamics of Research and Development,* New York: Harper & Row, Publishers, 1964.

————, "Facts and Folklore in Research and Development Management," *Industrial Management Review,* MIT. (Spring, 1967), 5–18.

Roman, Daniel D., "The PERT System: An Appraisal of Program Evaluation Review Technique," *Journal of the Academy of Management,* Vol. V, No. 1 (April, 1962).

————, "Organization for Control," *Journal of the Academy of Management* (Proceedings of the Annual Meeting, Pittsburgh, December 27–28, 1962).

————, "Project Management Recognizes R&D Performance," *Journal of the Academy of Management,* VII (March, 1964), 7–20.

————, and Jacob N. Johnson, "On the Allocation of Common Physical Resources to Multiple Development Tasks." Paper presented at the 18th Military Operations Research Society, Fort Bragg, N.C., October 19–21, 1966.

Roseboom, J. H., C. E. Clark, and W. Fazer, "Application of a Technique for Research and Development Program Evaluation," *Operations Research,* VII (September–October, 1959), 651–53.

Rosen, E. M., and W. E. Saunder, "A Method for Allocating R&D Expenditures,"

IEEE Transactions on Engineering Management, Vol. EM-12, No. 3 (September, 1965), 87–92.

Rubenstein, Albert H., ed., *Coordination, Control, and Financing of Industrial Research.* New York: King's Crown Press, Columbia University, 1955.

———, "Evaluation of the Possibilities of Research Effort in a New Field of Technology," *Sweden,* Vol. 6 (1955), 239–51.

———, "Setting Criteria for R&D," *Harvard Business Review,* January–February, 1957, pp. 95–104.

———, and I. Horowitz, "Project Selection in New Technical Fields," *Proceedings of the National Electronics Conference,* Vol. 15, 1959.

———, "Studies of Project Selection Behavior in Industry," in *Operations Research in Research and Development,* B. V. Dean, ed. New York: Wiley & Sons, Inc., 1963, pp. 189–205.

———, and C. W. Maberstroh, eds., *Some Theories of Organization.* Homewood, Ill.: Richard D. Irwin, Inc., 1960.

———, "Some Common Concepts and Tentative Findings from a Ten-Project Program of Research on R&D Management." Paper presented at the Second Conference on Research Program Effectiveness, Washington, D.C., July 27–29, 1965.

Saaty, Thomas L., *Mathematical Methods of Operations Research.* New York: McGraw-Hill Book Company, 1959.

Sacco, W. J., *On the Choice of Long Range Study Tasks.* Ballistic Research Laboratories Memo Report No. 1693, August, 1965.

Savage, J. J., *The Foundations of Statistics.* New York: John Wiley & Sons, Inc., 1954.

Scherer, F. M., "Time-Cost Tradeoffs in Uncertain Empirical Research Projects," Paper in *Naval Research Logistics Quarterly,* ONR, Vol. 13, No. 1 (March, 1966).

Schweyer, Herbert E., "Graphs Can Reveal Project Feasibility," *Chemical Engineering,* September 18, 1961, pp. 175–78.

Seiler, Robert E., *Improving the Effectiveness of Research and Development.* New York: McGraw-Hill Book Company, 1965.

Shaller, H. I., *An Exploratory Study in Research Planning Methodology,* ONR Tech. Report ACR/NAR-27, Department of the Navy, Washington, D.C., September, 1963.

Shank, R. J., "Planning to Meet Goals," *Optimum Use of Engineering Talent,* AMA Report No. 58 Cambridge, Mass.: Riverside Press, 1961.

Sher, I. H., and E. Garfield, "New Tools for Improving and Evaluating the Effectiveness of Research." Paper presented at the Second Conference on Research Program Effectiveness, Washington, D.C., July 27–29, 1963.

Silk, Leonard S., *The Research Revolution.* New York: McGraw-Hill Book Company, 1960.

Simon, H. A., *The New Science of Management Decisions.* New York: Harper & Row, Publishers, 1960.

———, "An Optimal Method for Selection of Product Development Projects." Paper presented at the 15th National Meeting, Operations Research Society of America, May, 1959.

Sobin, Bernard, and Arthur Proschan, "Search and Evaluation Methods in Research and Exploratory Development." Paper presented at the Second Conference on Research Program Effectiveness, Washington, D.C., July 27–29, 1965.

———, *Proposal Generation and Evaluation Methods in Research and Exploratory Development.* Research Analysis Corp. Paper RAC-P-11, November, 1965.

Sobelman, S. A., *Modern Dynamic Approach to Product Development,* Picatinny Arsenal, Dover, N.J., December, 1958.

———, *An Optimal Method for Selection of Product Development Projects,* presented at the 15th National Meeting of the Operations Research Society of America, Washington, D.C., May, 1959.

Special Projects Office, *PERT Summary Report I.* Bureau of Naval Weapons, Department of the Navy, Washington, D. C., 1959.

Spencer, M. H., and L. Siegelman, *Managerial Economics.* Homewood, Ill.: Richard D. Irwin, Inc., 1964, pp. 461–567.

Stanley, A. O., and K. K. White, *Organizing the R&D Function,* AMA Research Study No. 72. New York: American Management Association, 1965.

Steiner, George A., *Managerial Long-Range Planning,* New York: McGraw-Hill Book Company, 1963.

Stilian, C. N., et al., *PERT—A New Management Planning and Control Technique.* New York: American Management Association, 1962.

Stoessl, L., "Linear Programming Techniques Applied to Research Planning." Master's thesis, U. S. Naval Post-graduate School, 1964.

Stoodley, F. H., *A Study of Methods Which Could Improve the Relevance of Naval Applied Research and Exploratory Development.* Office Naval Research Report, June 1, 1966.

Sullivan, Charles I., "CPI Management Looks at R&D Project Evaluation," *Industrial and Engineering Chemistry,* Vol. 53 (September, 1961), 42A–46A.

Synnot, T. W., "Project RDE, A Framework for the Comprehension and Analysis of Research and Development Effectiveness," TM 63-22 Air Force Flight Dynamics Laboratory, Dayton, Ohio, October, 1963.

Taylor, Frederick Winslow, *Scientific Management.* New York: Harper & Row, Publishers, 1947.

Theil, H., "On the Optimal Management of Research: A Mathematical Approach." Paper presented at the Conference of the International Federation of Operations Research Societies, Oslo, Norway, July, 1963.

Thompson, R. E., "PERT—Tool for R&D Project Decision-Making," *IRE Transactions on Engineering Management,* September, 1962, 116–21.

University of California, *A System Engineering Approach to Corporate Long-Range Planning,* Department of Engineering, Report EEP-62-1. Berkeley: University of California, June, 1962.

Wachold, G. R., "An Investigation of the Technical Effectiveness of a Government Research and Development Test and Evaluation Organization." Navy Missile Center, Pt. Mugu, Calif., July, 1965. (Unpublished thesis)

Walters, J. E., *Research Management: Principles and Practice.* Washington, D.C.: Spartan Books, 1965.

Wasson, Chester R., *The Economics of Managerial Decision.* New York: Appleton-Century-Crofts, 1965, pp. 147–218.

Wells, Howard A., "Systems Planners Guide." Paper presented at the 18th Military Operations Research Society, Fort Bragg, N.C., October 19–21, 1966.

———, "The Allocation of Research and Development Resources," Wright-Patterson Air Development Center, August, 1958. (AD 155-784)

Yovits, M. C., et al., "Research Program Effectiveness." New York: Gordon and Breach, 1966.

INDEX

Basic Army Strategic Estimate, 391–392, *(fig.)* 392
Battelle Memorial Institute, 184, 188, 351, 358, 389
Batteries, for electric automobiles, 90–93, *(figs.)* 91, 92
Baxter, William, 18, 27
Bellamy, Edward, 17
Bennis, Warren, 58
Biological analogies to technological development, 61, *(fig.)* 62
Birkenhead, Earl of, 435*n.*
Bliven, Bruce, 26
Boyd, T. A., 346*n.*
Bramo Engine Company, 363
Brave New World (Huxley), 17
Bright, James R., 8*n.*, 25*n.*
Brooks, Harvey, 438
Brown, Bernice, 141
Brown, Harold, 36
Bryson, H. C., 25
Buck, 179

C

California "think groups," 446–447
Cambel, A. B., 376*n.*
Campbell, Robert M., 135*n.*
Canadian pulp and paper industry, technological forecasting for, 370–374
Cantril, H., 27
Capability objectives, U. S. Army, 392–394
Cargo aircraft development, 72–74, *(fig.)* 73
Carlson, Chester, 356
Causality and chances, 6–8, 29
Cavanaugh, R. M., 265*n.*
Cetron, 349
Chances and causality, 6–8, 29
Chemical pulping, 373
Chorlton, F. O. L., 25
Chubb, L. W., 24
Churchman, C. W., 201, 207
Churchman-Ackoff approximate Measure of Value procedure, 211
Clarke, I. F., 26
Coal industry, and strategic forecasting, 375–381, *(figs.)* 377, 378, 379, 380
Command level forecasting, 402–404
Commercial chip pipelines, 372
Commercial environment, context for analysis, 331
Commercial profitability, transition from technical feasibility to, 331–339
Common measure of value, 220, *(fig.)* 220
Communication technology, 249

Competitors, in technological environment, 212–214
Computer-controlled feedback, in Delphi technique, 140–141
Computers:
and corporate objectives, 437
applications in information environment, 249–251, *(fig.)* 250
progress of, 79–80
use in determining product utility, 313
Computer trends, *(fig.)* 79
Concept attainability, 204–206, *(fig.)* 205
Concept scoring matrix, *(fig.)* 203
Conceptual research, 201–202
Condorcet, M. J. de Caritat, Marquis de, 14, 15, 16, 28, 29, *(fig.)* 30
Connecting research, 267
Consensus, in forecasting, 146–147
Constrained variables, *(fig.)* 81
Constraint equations, 222
Constraints, 81
on vehicular speed, *(fig.)* 82
Corporate communications, and technological forecasting, 369
Corporate goals and technology, 412–425
Corporate strategy and long-range planning, 361–369
Correlation, prediction by, 5*n.*
Correlation analysis, technological forecasting by, 149
Cost comparisons, in MIRAGE study approach, *(fig.)* 30
Crookes, *(fig.)* 230
Cross, H. C., 109*n.*
Cross correlations, in Delphi technique, 135–139
Crude oil, stocks of, *(figs.)* 102
Current product development applications, 359–361
Curve fitting, *(fig.)* 218
in technological forecasting, 147
Customers' demands, in technological environment, 210–212, *(fig.)* 213
Cycles, 5

D

Daedalus, or Science and the Future (Haldane), 24
Dalkey, Norman, 116, 134
D'Argenson, René Louis de Voyer de Paulmy, Marquis, 14
Da Vinci, Leonardo, 198
Decision-making process:
appraisal systems in, 172–178